Teaching Civic Engagement

AMERICAN ACADEMY
of RELIGION

TEACHING RELIGIOUS STUDIES

SERIES EDITOR
Karen Y. Jackson-Weaver, Princeton University

A Publication Series of
The American Academy of Religion
and
Oxford University Press

TEACHING LÉVI-STRAUSS
Edited by Hans H. Penner

TEACHING ISLAM
Edited by Brannon M. Wheeler

TEACHING FREUD
Edited by Diane Jonte-Pace

TEACHING DURKHEIM
Edited by Terry F. Godlove, Jr.

TEACHING AFRICAN AMERICAN
RELIGIONS
Edited by Carolyn M. Jones and Theodore
Louis Trost

TEACHING RELIGION AND HEALING
Edited by Linda L. Barnes and Inés
Talamantez

TEACHING NEW RELIGIOUS
MOVEMENTS
Edited by David G. Bromley

TEACHING RITUAL
Edited by Catherine Bell

TEACHING CONFUCIANISM
Edited by Jeffrey L. Richey

TEACHING THE DAODE JING
Edited by Gary Delaney DeAngelis
and Warren G. Frisina

TEACHING RELIGION AND FILM
Edited by Gregory J. Watkins

TEACHING DEATH AND DYING
Edited by Christopher M. Moreman

TEACHING UNDERGRADUATE
RESEARCH IN RELIGIOUS
STUDIES
Edited by Bernadette McNary-Zak
and Rebecca Todd Peters

TEACHING JUNG
Edited by Kelly Bulkeley and Clodagh
Weldon

TEACHING MYSTICISM
Edited by William B. Parsons

TEACHING RELIGION AND
VIOLENCE
Edited by Brian K. Pennington

TEACHING THE *I CHING*
(BOOK OF CHANGES)
Geoffrey Redmond and Tze-ki Hon

TEACHING CIVIC ENGAGEMENT
Edited by Forrest Clingerman
and Reid B. Locklin

AAR
AMERICAN ACADEMY
of RELIGION

Teaching Civic Engagement

Edited by

FORREST CLINGERMAN

and

REID B. LOCKLIN

OXFORD
UNIVERSITY PRESS

OXFORD

UNIVERSITY PRESS

Oxford University Press is a department of the University of Oxford.
It furthers the University's objective of excellence in research, scholarship,
and education by publishing worldwide.

Oxford is a registered trade mark of Oxford University Press
in the UK and in certain other countries

Published in the United States of America by Oxford University Press
198 Madison Avenue, New York, NY 10016, United States of America

Library of Congress Cataloging-in-Publication Data
Teaching civic engagement / edited by Forrest Clingerman and Reid B. Locklin.
p.   cm.
Includes bibliographical references and index.
ISBN 978–0–19–025050–8 (cloth : alk. paper); 978–0–19–069299–5 (paper : alk. paper)
1. Service learning—Study and teaching. 2. Social justice—Study and teaching.
3. Religious education—Social aspects.
I. Clingerman, Forrest. II. Locklin, Reid B.
LC220.5.T38 2016
361.3'7—dc23
2015016792

Typeset in Scala Pro

Contents

SECTION III: *What Are the Theoretical Issues and Challenges
in Teaching Civic Engagement in Religious Studies and Theology?*

Acknowledgments

THIS BOOK IS the result of several years of collaboration, which began when most of the contributors met each other in Crawsfordville, Indiana, at the Wabash Center for Teaching and Learning in Theology and Religion. For many of the chapter authors—and certainly for the editors—the Wabash Center served as a formative place for reflection on teaching. A debt of gratitude is owed to the Wabash Center staff, especially Tom Pearson, Paul Myhre, Rita Arthur, Patricia Overpeck, and the Center Director, Dena Pence. We learned a great deal from the workshop coordinators Carolyn Medine, Tina Pippen, Joe Favazza, and Charlie Hallisey. We also owe a great deal to our fellow workshop participants Jeff Brackett, Clark Chilson, Melanie Harris, and Helen Rhee.

This project has also benefited from the work of several others who have been instrumental in a variety of ways, including Caitriona Brennan, Verna Ehret, Ella Johnson, Kevin O'Brien, and Jenna Sunkenberg. We offer special thanks to Kathleen Baril of the Heterick Memorial Library at Ohio Northern University for her help on the bibliography of this book. We also wish to thank Karen Jackson-Weaver of Princeton University and Cynthia Read of Oxford University Press, who worked with us as editors to get these ideas into print.

Contributors

Swasti Bhattacharyya—is Professor of Philosophy and Religion at Buena Vista University. She earned her A.S. in nursing and B.A. in religion from Loma Linda University; an M.A. from Fuller Theological Seminary; another M.A. in Judaism and Christianity in Antiquity from the University of Virginia; and a Ph.D. in Religion and Social Ethics from the University of Southern California. She has been on the Committee on Teaching and Learning of the American Academy of Religion and is a board member for the Peace and Justice Studies Association. She is the author of *Magical Progeny, Modern Technology* (SUNY, 2006), along with other articles and presentations on ethics, religion, and pedagogy. Her current project is exploring the living legacy of Vinoba Bhave (disciple, friend, confidant, and spiritual successor to Mahatma Gandhi).

Forrest Clingerman—is Associate Professor of Philosophy and Religion at Ohio Northern University. His scholarship investigates the intersection between theology, philosophical hermeneutics, and environmental thought. He is co-editor of *Interpreting Nature: The Emerging Field of Environmental Hermeneutics* (Fordham University Press, 2013) and *Placing Nature on the Borders of Religion, Philosophy, and Ethics* (Ashgate, 2011). He is also author of a number of articles and essays on environmental thought and the idea of place. His recent scholarship has focused on climate change, geoengineering, and religion.

Elizabeth W. Corrie—is Associate Professor in the Practice of Youth Education and Peacebuilding and Director of the Youth Theological Initiative at Candler School of Theology, Emory University, in Atlanta, Georgia. She received her B.A. in Religion from the College of William & Mary in 1993, her M.Div. from Candler School of Theology in 1996, and her Ph.D. in Historical Studies from the Graduate Division of Religion at Emory University. Her research interests include practical theology and youth ministry, transformative pedagogy, theories of nonviolence, and conflict transformation.

Marianne Delaporte—is Professor and Chair of the philosophy and religious studies department at Notre Dame de Namur University in Belmont, California. She received her Ph.D. at Princeton Seminary in Medieval Church history with a dissertation on the abbot Hilduin of St. Denis and his vita of Saint Denis, the headless holy man. She is the co-author of "Hell as a Residual Category" in *Companion to Sociology of Religion* (Blackwell Publishers, 2001), as well as of many other published articles. Her current research focuses on the connection between motherhood and spirituality. She began her work on this subject by concentrating on the fourteenth century and Birgitta of Sweden's mystical experiences. Since then she has focused her attention on the LaLeche League and The Farm commune in Tennessee.

Karen Derris—is Professor of Religious Studies and the Virginia C. Hunsaker Distinguished Teaching Chair of the College of Arts and Sciences at the University of Redlands in Redlands, California. Her research and publications primarily consider the intersections of literature, ethics, and history in Buddhist traditions. She is co-editor with Damcho Diana Finnegan of a book by His Holiness the 17th Karmapa, *The Heart Is Noble: Changing the World from the Inside Out* (Shambala, 2012) that developed from an international studies course she led in Dharamsala, India, where her students spent three weeks in conversation with the Karmapa.

Rebekka King—is an Assistant Professor of Religious Studies in the Department of Philosophy at Middle Tennessee State University. She is a cultural anthropologist and teaches courses on Christianity, ethnographic practices, and method and theories in the study of religion.

Reid B. Locklin—holds a joint appointment in Christianity and Culture at Saint Michael's College and the Department for the Study of Religion, University of Toronto. A graduate of Boston University and Boston College, he is the author of *Spiritual But Not Religious?* (Liturgical Press, 2005), *Liturgy of Liberation* (Peeters, 2011), and other works in comparative theology, Hindu-Christian studies, and spirituality.

Carolyn M. Jones Medine—is Professor in the Department of Religion and the Institute for African American Studies at the University of Georgia. She is the General Sandy Beaver Teaching Professor for 2014–2017. Dr. Medine writes about African American religion and literature, particularly that of Southern black women and on theoretical issues. Her most recent work, co-written with John Randolph LeBlanc, is *Ancient and Modern Religion and Politics: Negotiating Transitive Spaces and Hybrid Identities* (Palgrave Macmillan 2012). In 2013 she received the American Academy of Religion's Award for Excellence in Teaching.

Thomas Pearson—is the Associate Director of the Wabash Center for Teaching and Learning in Theology and Religion in Crawfordsville, Indiana. He has published on cross-cultural religious conversion in the central highlands of Southeast Asia during the Vietnam War.

Tina Pippin—is the Wallace M. Alston Chair of Bible and Religion at Agnes Scott College, a liberal arts college for wymyn, in Decatur, Georgia. As an activist educator she teaches in the areas of biblical studies, ethics and social justice, gender and wymyn's studies, and human rights. Publications include *Death and Desire: The Rhetoric of Gender in the Apocalypse of John* (Westminster/John Knox, 1992) and *Apocalyptic Bodies: The Biblical End of the World in Text and Image* (Routledge, 1999). She was also a member of the collaborative writing group The Bible and Culture Collective (*The Postmodern Bible*, Yale University Press, 1995) and a co-editor (with David Jobling and Ron Schleifer) of *The Postmodern Bible Reader* (Blackwell, Spring 2001). She is the editor, with Cheryl Kirk-Duggan, of *Mother Goose, Mother Jones, Mommie Dearest: Biblical Mothers and Their Children* (Semeia Studies, 2010). For the past fifteen years Professor Pippin has been involved, along with students at Agnes Scott, in a mentoring relationship with "at-promise" young women and teen moms at Decatur High School. As part of her involvement in the Agnes Scott Living Wage Campaign, Tina facilitates and teaches in the ESOL program for college staff. In 2000, she was the first recipient of the American Academy of Religion's Award for Excellence in Teaching.

Ellen Posman—is Associate Professor of Religion at Baldwin Wallace University in Berea, Ohio. She holds degrees in religious studies from Stanford University, Harvard University, and the University of California, Santa Barbara. Her expertise lies in the area of comparative religion, with specializations in Buddhism and Judaism.

Nicholas Rademacher—is Associate Professor of Religious Studies and Coordinator of the Social Justice Minor at Cabrini College in Radnor, Pennsylvania. Community collaboration and interfaith dialogue are central to his teaching and scholarship. Dr. Rademacher has long been involved in the practice and scholarship of teaching and learning. He is co-founder and faculty fellow in the Voices of Justice Living and Learning Community, and he has published collaboratively and individually in the area of community-based learning. More broadly, his scholarship focuses on the intersection of faith and justice, with special attention on the lived tradition of Catholic social thought and practice across the twentieth century.

Erin Runions—is Associate Professor at Pomona College (in Claremont, California) in Religious Studies and Gender Studies, and Chair of the Department of

Religious Studies. She is a specialist in the Hebrew Bible, which she reads from the perspective of cultural studies and gender and sexuality studies. Her most recent book is *The Babylon Complex: Theopolitical Fantasies of War, Sex, and Sovereignty* (Fordham University Press, 2014). She has also been involved in social justice movements for many years. She currently helps facilitate a writing workshop inside a women's prison in Chino, California.

Melissa C. Stewart—is Professor of Religion at Adrian College, where she teaches courses in Judaism, Christianity, Islam, ethics, and women's studies. She holds a Ph.D. from Vanderbilt University. She is the director of Adrian College's Center for Effective Teaching in Adrian, Michigan, and she most recently published "Mary, the Mother of God: Ecumenical Bridge or Barrier?" in *Theology Today* (January 2011).

Hans Wiersma—is Associate Professor of Religion at Augsburg College in Minneapolis, Minnesota. He is a fellow at Augsburg's Center for Teaching and Learning (2011–2014). He was awarded a Wabash Center for Teaching and Learning fellowship (2006–2007) and has written for the journal *Teaching Theology & Religion*. He has contributed to the development and content of a wide range of books and learning resources, including *The Lutheran Handbook* (2005), *Crazy Talk: A Not-So-Stuffy Dictionary of Theological Terms* (2008), *Crazy Book: A Not-So-Stuffy Dictionary of Biblical Terms* (2009), *The Westminster Handbook to Theologies of the Reformation* (2010), and the digital edition of *Introduction to The History of Christianity: First Century to Present Day* (2014).

Philip Wingeier-Rayo—is Associate Professor of Mission, Evangelism, and Methodist Studies at Austin Theological Seminary in Austin, Texas. Previously he was Professor of Religion at Pfeiffer University in North Carolina, where he taught for eleven years. He has also served as adjunct professor at Garrett-Evangelical Theological Seminary and Wesley Theological Seminary, and has lived and taught at seminaries in Cuba and Mexico. He has published numerous articles and two books: *Cuba Methodism: The Untold Story of Survival and Revival*, 2nd edition (Atlanta, GA: Dolphins and Orchids, 2006) and *Where Are the Poor? An Ethnographic Study of a Base Christian Community and a Pentecostal Church in Mexico* (Pickwick Publications, 2011).

Introduction

A MODEL FOR TEACHING CIVIC ENGAGEMENT, IN THE RELIGION CLASSROOM AND BEYOND

Forrest Clingerman and Reid B. Locklin

SHORTLY AFTER THE 2014 U.S. midterm elections, Drew Stelljes posted a *Huffington Post* blog entitled, "US Colleges and Universities Earn a Poor Grade for Civic Engagement."[1] In his blog, Stelljes notes the high levels of discouragement and distrust in the post-election landscape, along with an apparent decline in the core civic virtues of civility, reasoned deliberation, and a commitment to the common good. Though universities have in many cases invested in centers dedicated to addressing this concern, he argues, they tend to focus on facilitating student volunteer opportunities rather than the harder, riskier work of fostering these particular virtues, so necessary for democratic citizenship. He concludes:

> The history of higher education in the first part of the 21st century is partially written and for the most part, it does not read well for civic engagement. It is largely deplete of the democratic virtues our nation is so desperate to recapture. Imagine if a college was so bold as to remain wholly dedicated to its civic mission—to really prepare students to be dedicated civic leaders, equipped with skill set to engage in thoughtful dialogue across differences, with compromise the shared goal and solutions the standard. How could higher education be most thoughtful about getting closer to this aim for the benefit of the next generation of engaged citizens and public servants?[2]

Stelljes' criticism might be regarded as at least slightly self-serving: He is, after all, Director of the Office of Community Engagement at the College of William and Mary—presumably among those centers whose scarce funding he deplores. Nevertheless, he joins a chorus that has been sounding at least since the publication of Robert D. Putnam's 1995 article "Bowling Alone" and subsequent book of the same name.[3] In these works, Putnam and his collaborators noted a sharp decline in "social capital" in the late twentieth century, as North Americans withdrew from active community connections at all levels, from the family dinner table to the political party convention. This and other alarms from a range of social theorists led to what is frequently termed the "civic engagement movement" in higher education, as organizations like Campus Compact, the Association of American Colleges and Universities, and those many centers of community engagement celebrated and criticized by Stelljes set out to renew the civic mission of the university.[4] Reflecting on such trends in his encyclopedic manifesto *Multiversities, Ideas, and Democracy*, the Canadian economist George Fallis differentiated two aspects of a robust democratic mission for the contemporary "multiversity": (1) a "social contract for research" that fosters innovation and supports intellectuals willing and able to contribute their expertise to questions of public interest; and (2) a broad, liberal arts curriculum that cultivates "civic wisdom" on the part of the undergraduate students that represent the university's largest and most consequential constituency.[5]

What significance do such a movement and mission have for religious studies and theology? At one level, civic engagement and religion reveal a natural connection: As Putnam and William E. Campbell argue in their 2010 work *American Grace*, religious *belonging* of almost any variety reveals a strong, positive correlation with most aspects of civic engagement, including volunteerism, political activism, and contributions to both religious and secular social initiatives.[6] The study of religious studies and theology would thus seem, by virtue of its subject matter, to imply some level of engagement with issues of social and political concern. Insofar as such study may presume or encourage any religious belonging on the part of its teachers or students, it may also implicate them more directly in the connections that, according to Putnam and Campbell, nourish a robust, healthy civic sphere.

But such a presumption is, at best, highly problematic for teachers of religious studies and even theology. The contemporary study of religion in North America and Europe is often built on a distinction between religious belonging, on the one hand, and the critical analysis of religious practices, institutions, and intellectual traditions, on the other. Though many scholars might stop short of raising this distinction to the level of a sine qua non or ideological absolute, most accept it to one degree or another in practice. This has been important for the definition of the field of religious studies in the last few decades, as seen in how scholars challenge traditional Western theological concepts of "religion" in favor of new modes of study. Therefore, we can perhaps narrow the questions at the heart of this volume: What is the civic relevance of the academic *study* of religion, considered on its own terms and in its increased diversity? What unique contributions does religious studies offer the public sphere, especially when seen as separate from the work of religious communities who concentrate on religious belonging? How might the disciplines dedicated to such study offer a distinctive shape and response to the civic mission of the contemporary university?

These became the guiding questions of a faculty workshop on Pedagogies for Civic Engagement, conducted under the auspices of the Wabash Center for Teaching and Learning in Theology and Religion in 2008–2009 and directed by Clark Chilson, Forrest Clingerman, Reid Locklin, and Erin Runions. The workshop brought together nineteen faculty members from the United States and Canada, from a diverse range of disciplines in religious studies and theology, to develop a shared framework and particular classroom strategies to foster and assess our students' capacity for effective civic engagement. The present volume consists of selected insights generated in the course of this workshop, supplemented by further research and reflection on the part of workshop participants—along with several additional essays, solicited by the editors as the book began to take its present shape.

The workshop itself is described in some detail in chapter 3, so we will not discuss it in detail here. Instead, we wish to highlight the distinctive, heuristic framework for assessing civic engagement as it emerged from the workshop conversations. That is, as the group reviewed relevant literature and reflected on our own teaching, participants together identified four core capacities central to civic engagement and, thus, to the project of teaching for such engagement in the religion classroom. These are:

1. the capacity to engage in sustained, complex modes of deliberation and discussion;
2. the capacity to understand the dynamics of social location and diverse social frameworks, including the imbrication of such frameworks in networks of power and privilege;
3. the capacity not merely to foster empathetic connections across boundaries of social, economic, and/or religious difference but to identify such connections as a source of moral obligation; and
4. the capacity to act, motivated by careful deliberation, a consciousness of social location, and empathetic connections across boundaries of difference.

These four capacities of intellectual complexity, social framing or location, empathetic accountability, and motivated action obviously include the development of particular skill sets, but they are better understood as dynamic, recursive, and mutually reinforcing habits of thought, disposition, and practice. They can, moreover, be very briefly captured in the short formula Complexity-Location-Empathy-Action, or CLEA. From this point forward, we refer to this as the CLEA model.

The CLEA model provides the foundation for the chapters of this book, as well as a lens through which to understand the coherence of the diverse perspectives presented by these authors. Elaborating this model is the task of the first section of this book. In the first two chapters, Reid B. Locklin and Ellen Posman offer an introduction and rationale for the CLEA model of teaching for civic engagement, as it may relate to the teaching of religious studies and theology. Chapter 1 makes a case for the model itself by drawing insights from the civic engagement movement together with selected theorists of cognitive development and liberatory education. On the one hand, Locklin and Posman note, advocates of liberal education tend to emphasize the civic importance of education, but they frequently do so entirely in terms of an intellectual complexity oriented toward participation in democratic processes, public discourse, and the adjudication of constitutional rights. Liberatory educators, on the other hand, critique any artificial separation of academic methods of deliberation and discourse from the political context(s) in which such methods are necessarily implicated. They call both for a deeper understanding of civic participation in terms of social justice, activism, and solidarity and for a deeper practice of critical thinking that includes the negotiation of power in the classroom and in the wider world. The CLEA model is proposed in this chapter as a way to widen the understanding of civic engagement beyond its equation with critical thinking and deliberative discourse, and, following liberatory theorists such as Paulo Freire and bell hooks, to suggest how practices of social framing, empathy, and even direct action may deepen rather than detract from traditional emphases on intellectual complexity as a primary civic virtue.

Posman extends this discussion in chapter 2 by applying the CLEA model to the wide variety of disciplines, contexts, and practices that constitute the "religion classroom"—including, in this case, primarily undergraduate classrooms in religious studies and theology. The religion classroom does not offer a unique context for the cultivation of intellectual complexity, the navigation of social difference, empathetic accountability, or motivated action. Such capacities can be cultivated across a liberal arts curriculum. Religion, however, does offer distinct challenges and opportunities. Chief among these is the intrinsic, ambiguous attraction of its subject matter, insofar as religious traditions represent volatile sources of meaning, value, motivation, passion, and concern for many persons in our societies, including many if not most students. But religion also stands out for its interdisciplinary character and diverse methods of instruction, many of which conduce well to one or more of the objectives comprehended by the CLEA model. Myth and ritual, cultural studies, political analysis, literature and film, community-based learning, moral philosophy—all of these and more find a natural home in the religion classroom, and all of them have deep implications for fostering these core civic capacities. The final section of the chapter addresses the question of assessment, exploring methods to evaluate such capacities as empathetic accountability or participation in direct, motivated action through structured reflection as well as the virtue of articulating civic goals that may be encouraged "sub rosa," around the edges of a course, rather than becoming an object of direct assessment.

The first two chapters deal with the question of civic engagement and the CLEA model almost entirely in the abstract. The seven chapters that follow turn instead to specific classroom strategies as both exempla and opportunities for self-reflection, and thereby form the second section of this book. In chapter 3, Melissa Stewart offers an overview and analysis of the various projects under-taken by members of the workshop group during our two-year grant project. In so doing, she explores the possible correlation between particular kinds of class assignments—reflective writing, textual and media analysis, field trips, community-based projects, and other forms of experiential learning—with par-ticular capacities of the CLEA model. It might seem that core capacities of com-plexity and social location should correlate more closely to in-class exercises, while empathetic accountability and motivated action require experience outside the classroom; yet, in practice, the instructor cannot assume any such neat cor-relations. This has consequences not only for the teaching of civic engagement but also for how we imagine the religion classroom itself. "Due to the interrela-tionships among the skills needed to teach civic engagement," Stewart concludes, "the binary definitions of 'in' and 'out' of the classroom break down."[7] The key, then, is to teach with multiple methods, attentive to the ways that they may over-lap and inform one another in unexpected and potentially fruitful ways.

One way of approaching this task is to think not in terms of one-to-one corre-spondence but in terms of central and peripheral objectives: identifying one core capacity as the starting point and central lens while also attending to its integral relations with other such capacities. Thus, the following three chapters might each be characterized as exploring empathy, relationship, and imagination as a distinctive, and clarifying, points of entry for the civic project. In chapter 4, Marianne Delaporte examines the interpersonal patterns of hospitality, reciproc-ity, and relationship in local, community-based learning activities. In chapter 5, Rebekka King extends her view more widely to include students' imaginative con-ceptions of a whole urban environment—in this case, the city of Toronto—and the ways that such conceptions may be fruitfully de-familiarized from the perspective of those who live on the margins of power. In chapter 6, Hans Wiersma reaches still further afield, exploring the potential and perils of the virtual "global village" constructed as new media sources provide students with immediate, experiential access to the Vatican, temple complexes in Angkor Wat, or a protest in Cairo's Tahrir Square—all without leaving the comfort of the university classroom.

For our present purposes, it is important to note how Delaporte's, King's, and Wiersma's respective appeals to imagination and empathy are crafted to open space for cultivating other core capacities. King, for example, describes her "Religion in the City" course as an exercise in theoretic imagination, informed by the *Epic of Gilgamesh*, the fiction of Michael Ondaatje, postcolonial theory, and a guided tour of "homeless Toronto." Yet, in and through such an expansion of their imagined environment, students learn to re-frame and re-locate themselves and their positions of power within this environment. Both King and Delaporte also note occasions in which students go on to take political action, deeply informed by their experiences in class. Wiersma, for his part, draws a straight line from the imaginative engagement of new media to motivated action: Not only does training in media equip student activists with new tools, but teaching with such media can also be construed as the self-conscious construction of—in the idiom of Marshall McLuhan—a "counter-environment," an act of subversive resistance to a "media-infused cultural environment that misunderstands and misrepresents a variety of religious/spiritual subjects."[8] And all three chapters emphasize the heuristic value of their respective imaginative projects to strengthen intellectual habits and practices of critical reflection, analysis, and evaluation. For King, the integration of field work and personal engagement with traditional sources functions to complicate easy binaries of teacher and learner and thus to reconfigure learning itself as a complex, ongoing "reflexive process."

The following two chapters shift the central focus from empathy to action, describing community-based learning as a privileged locus for taking up the civic project in the religion classroom. As noted at the start of this introduction, many assume classroom civic engagement projects consist of volunteerism; in turn, community-based learning is often the "face" of civic engagement on campuses. But these two chapters challenge the too-easy reduction of civic engagement and community-based learning, instead contextualizing action in a broader model of civic engagement. In chapter 7, Philip Wingeier-Rayo offers an introduction to community-based learning at both local and international levels as both a practice of civic engagement and an opportunity for critical self-reflection. In chapter 8, Nicholas Rademacher details a partnership between Cabrini College and two community partners forged over multiple years in relation to courses in social justice and Catholic Social Teaching. For Wingeier-Rayo, a service trip to Cuba becomes an occasion for students not only to discover the economic impact of the U.S. embargo but also to explore the effects of a trade deal like NAFTA in their own, North Carolina backyard. In his teaching, service opens into authentic civic engagement when students widen their view beyond the construction of a school, church, or community center to systemic, political analysis. Rademacher—similar to Delaporte—focuses instead on reciprocity and hospitality, bringing students to a homeless shelter and intentional community and bringing members of those communities to the classroom to foster interfaith dialogue and solidarity. In both cases, the pedagogical strategies presume that civic engagement involves habit formation as much as discursive knowledge of political processes and systems of power; hence, immersion in such action—even in the limited space of an international service trip or a fifteen-week semester—can provide an effective entrée into the civic project.

In the chapter that concludes this section of the volume, Elizabeth W. Corrie effects a startling reversal, commending the cultivation of good practices of civic engagement not by action but by deliberate, strategic *in*-action: what she calls the Ascetic Withdrawal Project. Positioning consumer culture and preoccupations with the "private self" as a primary threat to the civic commons, Corrie leads her students in a fasting exercise. On the one hand, she notes, the countercultural significance of voluntary withdrawal from fast food, cable news, or impulse shopping, in and of itself, is well-attested by the surprised and sometimes hostile reactions students receive from families and friends. On the other, the broader civic potential of the project emerges most fully when this six-week practice is combined with research into a related social issue and subsequent application in a final project. Corrie's exercise—offered in a seminary context and oriented toward youth ministry leaders—also helpfully blurs the line between the study of religion and religious belonging, with which we began this introduction. Though the Ascetic Withdrawal Project clearly incorporates a number of capacities of the CLEA model, the language Corrie prefers is theological, including the tropes of sin, repentance, justification, and a strong connection to the Christian liturgical season of Lent. Whereas Rademacher asks students to identify their diverse, personal expressions of "faith" in generic terms borrowed from James W. Fowler and King leads students to identify their own, distinctive experience of the city of Toronto as preparation for their shared study, Corrie presumes a specific religious formation on the part of her students. Yet, all three strategies suggest that teaching for civic engagement ideally takes its start from students' own experience, formation, and values as an intrinsic aspect of the classroom and the civic sphere itself.

In the third section of the volume, contributors raise their view from specific classroom strategies and the particular capacities of the CLEA model to address several more general, theoretical questions that arise when civic engagement and civic goals are specifically identified as learning objectives in the religion classroom. Most important, perhaps, is our understanding of the "civic" itself. Taking up this question in chapter 10, Carolyn M. Jones Medine briefly traces the recent history of the civic engagement movement, contrasting the citizenship model in the influential U.S. high school textbook *Magruder's American Government* with the more decentralized, organic "cellular model" proposed by the anthropologist Arjun Appadurai. Appadurai's work suggests that voting patterns and political participation may not offer a full picture of our students' engagement: perhaps, Medine suggests, current generations of undergraduate and graduate students are not "disengaged" but "differently engaged."[9] In light of this analysis, Medine proposes a special role for teaching civic engagement in the religious studies classroom, one that focuses less on those practices of citizenship engagement fostered in political science or history departments and more on the cultivation of trust, genuine encounter, and the "interpretive capacity" to de-exoticize the cultural, racialized, and religious other and to engage a globalized community in the telling and receiving of our shared stories.

The complex, contested notion of global citizenship invoked in passing by Medine moves to the center of inquiry in the following chapter, by Karen Derris and Erin Runions. In chapter 11, Derris and Runions interrogate the notion of mobility by drawing on three experiences: a three-week, intensive conversation with a significant Tibetan Buddhist leader, the 17th Karmapa, in India; a collaborative writing workshop in a local women's prison; and religious and political mobilization around the firing of seventeen undocumented, immigrant workers on the campus of Pomona College. Drawing on Foucault, Derris and Runions suggest "biopolitics" as a framework to interrogate and analyze the freedom of mobility as embedded in wider, systemic structures of power. The religious studies classroom offers a distinctively fruitful site for such interrogation not only because students are often asked to travel literally or imaginatively to temples and churches outside their ordinary experience, but also because of the particular topoi of study in the discipline, including the relation of ontologies and ethics, cultural criticism, intercultural competence, and attentiveness to the myriad ways that ideals become embedded in structures of power. These tools offer the possibility of a necessary self-critique and a re-positioning of the rhetoric of global citizenship as only one form of engagement with the freedom of mobility and global community—and one that is, like religious traditions themselves, deeply implicated in patterns of power and domination.

If Derris and Runions suggest that an apparently neutral phenomenon may emerge in the religious studies classroom as part and product of contested political processes, the argument of chapter 12, by Swasti Bhattacharyya and Forrest Clingerman, explores the potential of making explicitly political processes part of the religious studies curriculum. Bhattacharyya and Clingerman propose that there is—or should be—a place for political advocacy in the religion classroom, but only insofar as it takes the form of "advocacy of process," rather than advocacy for a particular party or political cause. This argument depends in part on broad definitions of its key terms, such that "politics" encompasses any activity that contributes to the shared, public life of a community, and "advocacy" implicates students in the relatively straightforward project of "taking a side in a debate and arguing for it."[10] For Bhattacharyya and Clingerman, the theology or religious studies instructor serves both as advocate for a particular, reasoned approach to political processes and as a facilitator for students to try on such advocacy in the contrived but still political environment of the classroom. This can take many forms—the authors describe exercises in guerilla theater and letters to elected officials—but necessarily implicates such instructors in concerns about indoctrination, classroom incivility, and assessment. An appropriate response to such concerns, Bhattacharyya and Clingerman contend, is to become more self-conscious, careful, and reasoned in one's advocacy for informed political involvement, rather than to send politics into an artificial and ultimately self-deceptive exile from the college or university classroom.

Though the chapters in this final section of the volume take up various meta-issues related to teaching for civic engagement, rather than specific classroom strategies, their proposals can nevertheless be seen as bringing out one or another element of the CLEA model proposed in this volume. Medine proposes an understanding of the civic sphere more firmly rooted in empathy and imagination than political processes; Derris and Runions' analysis of mobility carries clear implications for students' emerging understandings of their own social locations and dynamics of privilege; Clingerman and Bhattacharyya advocate for the integration of political action into classroom instruction; and all of them relate such practices to the foundational practice of knowledge-production and critical thought. In general—following the majority of our contributors—they also situate these practices in a putatively generic "religious studies" or "religion" classroom. In one of two summative chapters of the volume, Thomas Pearson asks what difference, if any, one can discern between the distinctive approaches of theology and religious studies, respectively, in the civic project. Reviewing the preceding essays, Pearson differentiates multiple orders of normativity, from first-order (students encounter and analyze normative judgments in their sources) to fourth-order (students are encouraged or obliged to assume a normative judgment prescribed in the class) and eventually even fifth-order (learning directly from an authoritative religious other in the context of a course).

Some degree of normativity, Pearson notes, is implied in any pedagogy of civic engagement, and this, in turn, would seem to make it more amenable to the theology than to the religious studies classroom. Yet, empirically, he locates the highest levels of normativity in both the more theological contributions of Corrie and Delaporte and the materialist and neo-Marxist analyses of Derris and Runions. He places most of the other contributors, regardless of discipline, somewhere between first- and fourth-order normativity, encouraging students to form some type of normative commitment without necessarily prescribing the content of such commitments for them. But this, he concludes, may ultimately be an unsafe position: given the suspicion of both theology and religious studies in the contemporary academy, perhaps scholars in our disciplines are well advised to defer the civic project to other, more well-established disciplines. When we have all become more comfortable with normativity in the academic project, in multiple disciplines, then the distinctive commitments that characterize religion classrooms of various types will no longer leave us vulnerable to critique.

The contributors to this volume endeavor to explore how the student experience in the religion classroom—be it in an undergraduate or seminary setting—might help foster the intellectual complexity, sensitivity to social location, empathetic accountability, and motivated action necessary for effective civic engagement. It must be noted, however, that if such initiatives succeed only in preparing such students for their own engagement in the public sphere, the university may well have fallen short of its civic purpose. In a 2010 piece entitled, "Still Bowling Alone?" Thomas H. Sander and Robert D. Putnam updated Putnam's earlier analysis and noted that, though there was an upsurge of civic engagement following 9/11 on the part of high school seniors from middle-class backgrounds, less advantaged populations withdrew still further.[11] Notwithstanding the general disaffection noted by Stelljes, with which we began this introduction, college students and recent graduates nevertheless show significantly higher levels of engagement than their generational peers.[12] To concentrate only on this population's capacity for engagement risks further entrenchment of their privilege, relative to other, more marginalized members of our societies.

Tina Pippin takes up this and related questions in her concluding chapter, entitled "Dreams of Democracy." Surveying a range of civic engagement initiatives in higher education, from the foundational work of John Dewey to the Imagining America initiative, founded in 1999, Pippin asks whether an authentic pedagogy of civic engagement implies a systemic change in the structure of the university, its funding sources, and the professional and activist roles of its professoriate. Echoing Paulo Freire's refusal to allow his dialogical method to be reduced to a teaching technique rather than a strategy for social change, Pippin calls for a practice of civic engagement that places universities, their hierarchies of staff and faculty, and the communities they ideally serve together as co-participants in the construction of a shared, reciprocal "knowledge of living experience."[13] Though she introduces her chapter with reference to the CLEA model proposed in this volume, her argument also implies a critique. Insofar as instructors in the religion classroom aim to foster particular civic capacities on the parts of our students, we may be overlooking the need to transform the face of higher education itself.

Taking Pippin's critique to heart, however, we still find a hopeful alternative to Stelljes' dire diagnosis. Throughout this volume, there is a desire to illustrate how those of us who "profess" religious studies have a responsibility to contribute to civil society in meaningful ways. Indeed, collectively these chapters show that it is imperative to connect higher education with a vibrant society. This impulse toward civil responsibility in religious studies and theology classrooms returns us to the question of belonging and commitment. The contributing authors seek to show new ways of engaging civil society, belying the stereotype that college educators live in the ivory tower and promote the idiosyncratic and arcane. Teachers and students may or may not belong to the particular religious traditions we study. Nevertheless, we all belong to civil society—in the midst of its complexity, from their own locatedness, empowered by personal, empathetic connections, and sustained by informed action. Perhaps it is time that we began teaching like it.

Notes

1. Drew Stelljes, "US Colleges and Universities Earn a Poor Grade for Civic Engagement," *Huff Post Education*, November 10, 2014, accessed December 5, 2014, http://www.huffingtonpost.com/drew-stelljes/us-civic-engagement_b_6,127,608.html.

2. Ibid.

3. Robert D. Putnam, "Bowling Alone: America's Declining Social Capital," *Journal of Democracy* 6 (January 1995): 65–78; Robert D. Putnam, *Bowling Alone: The Collapse and Revival of American Community* (New York: Simon and Schuster, 2000).

4. See Barbara Jacoby, "Civic Engagement in Today's Higher Education: An Overview," in *Civic Engagement in Higher Education: Concepts and Practices*, by Barbara Jacoby and Associates (San Francisco: Jossey-Bass, 2009), 5–30; and, with a more critical perspective on the movement, Ben Berger, *Attention Deficit Democracy* (Princeton and Oxford: Princeton University Press, 2011), 24–51.

5. George Fallis, *Multiversities, Ideas, and Democracy* (Toronto, Buffalo and London: University of Toronto Press, 2007), 355–76, 381–87. See also George Fallis, *Rethinking Higher Education: Participation, Research and Differentiation* (Montreal and Kingston: McGill-Queen's University Press, 2013), esp. 144–51; and George Fallis, "Reclaiming the Civic University," *Academic Matters* (June 2014): 3–6.

6. Robert D. Putnam and David E. Campbell, with the assistance of Shaylyn Romney Garrett, *American Grace: How Religion Divides and Unites Us* (New York: Simon & Schuster, 2010), 443–92. The notable exception to these civic virtues is tolerance for the public expression and advocacy of opposing views, where persons affiliated with either progressive or conservative religious traditions reveal themselves as less committed to freedom of expression than their more secular peers.

7. Melissa Stewart, this volume, 59.

8. Hans Wiersma, this volume, 90.

9. Carolyn Medine, this volume, 169.

10. Bhattacharyya and Clingerman, this volume, 209.

11. Thomas H. Sander and Robert D. Putnam, "Still Bowling Alone? The Post-9/11 Split," *Journal of Democracy* 21.1 (2010): 9–16. See also Berger, *Attention Deficit Democracy*, 166–70.

12. Mark Hugo Lopez and Abby Kiesa, "What We Know about Civic Engagement among College Students," in Jacoby et al., *Civic Engagement in Higher Education*, 31–48.

13. Pippin, this volume, 257.

Teaching Civic Engagement

What Are the Dimensions of Teaching Civic Engagement in the Religious Studies or Theology Classroom?

I

Discourse, Democracy, and the Many Faces of Civic Engagement

FOUR GUIDING OBJECTIVES FOR THE UNIVERSITY
CLASSROOM

Reid B. Locklin with Ellen Posman

IN HER BOOK *The Clash Within,* the University of Chicago law professor and philosopher Martha Nussbaum documents a tragic collapse of civic and political culture: the 2002 anti-Muslim religious pogrom in the Indian state of Gujarat.[1] Following an incident in Godhra, in which a train filled with Hindu pilgrims burst into flames after a confrontation with local Muslims, highly politicized members of the Hindu majority destroyed businesses, dispossessed Muslim families from their homes, and put approximately two thousand Indian citizens to death. Muslim women paid a particularly high price in the violence, as they were often systematically raped and tortured, and children ripped from their wombs, before being killed.

Many details of the Gujarat pogroms remain in dispute to this day, and Nussbaum readily concedes that the causes were complex, reaching back from the rise of the Hindu nationalist Bharatiya Janata Party government in the 1990s to the politics of Partition at Indian Independence (1947) and, beyond that, to the identity politics of the British colonial government. But one of the primary problems, in her analysis, lay in the particular character of the Indian educational system, particularly its emphasis upon rote methods and technical expertise. Drawing inspiration from Visva-Bharati, the experimental university pioneered by Rabindranath Tagore (1861–1941), Nussbaum champions independent inquiry and self-critical reflection as the first, foundational plank of a broadly liberal curriculum that empowers its students to test political claims, to value evidence and argument, to recognize the common humanity of all persons across boundaries of national, ethnic, or religious difference, and to enter imaginatively into other experiences and other lives.[2] Such intellectual and imaginative capacities, she claims, represent a sine qua non for democracy in pluralistic societies like India and the United States. Indeed, in a more recent critique of American public education, Nussbaum has generalized this insight as a basic axiom: "cultivated capacities for critical thinking and reflection are crucial in keeping democracies alive and awake."[3]

Nussbaum is not alone in highlighting critical reasoning and free inquiry as the primary civic capacities fostered by a university education. So too the former president of Cornell University, Frank H. T. Rhodes, identifies "the cherished values of the university" as "integrity, excellence, community, openness, respect, civility, freedom, responsibility, impartiality and tolerance, all exercised within an autonomous community of learning." "[W]ithout respect for these values," he argues, "there can be no university worthy of the name. Without them, there can be no true democracy."[4]

In this chapter, we attempt to examine and to critique such claims, which tend to equate teaching for civic engagement with a fairly traditional view of the university, the liberal arts, and the value of critical thinking. Key to our argument is an observation that the "civic" in civic engagement does not represent a stable, but a malleable, interpretive category. Insofar as participation in democratic society is constructed primarily in terms of deliberative discourse, academic skills of weighing evidence, advancing arguments, and fostering more elaborate modes of reasoning, along with such core values as civility, autonomy, and openness to rival points of view, naturally take a central position. But civic engagement in its fullest sense also implicates teacher and student in questions of motivation, relationship, and value—above all, a cultivated valuing for the civic sphere. And this, in turn, recommends a wider range of academic objectives for those scholar-teachers who wish to teach for civic engagement in the religion—or any liberal arts—classroom. Far from detracting from a more traditional focus on critical thinking, we suggest, such a broader range of academic objectives corresponds to a broader and deeper understanding of such critical thinking itself.

Our argument proceeds in four stages. In the first section of this chapter, we attempt briefly to delimit what educators may typically intend by such terms as "free, reasoned inquiry" or "critical thinking and reflection," for the most part following the theories of intellectual development advanced by William Perry, Jack Mezirow, and the *Women's Ways of Knowing (WWK)* collaborative. After this, we offer an initial, heuristic definition of civic engagement and trace its close relationship with intellectual complexity. We then widen the inquiry to include the more political approaches of bell hooks, Paulo Freire, and other critical theorists who, while granting and indeed insisting upon the value of intellectual complexity, also valorize principles of conscientization, inclusivity, and embodied praxis. Considering both sets of theories together, in the final section of the chapter, we suggest that teaching for civic engagement requires reflection on not one but at least four heuristic capacities: (1) intellectual complexity; (2) critical awareness of social location and diverse frames of reference; (3) empathetic accountability; and (4) motivated action. This fourfold model of teaching civic engagement will serve to frame and in some cases to shape the chapters that follow (we refer to this as the CLEA model). Though it may be unreasonable to expect that any individual assignment could realistically aim for all of these objectives in any particular classroom setting, instructors do well to reflect on them as different aspects or dimensions of a single, integrated approach to student development, attentive to the complex, multifaceted reality of civic participation itself.

In this chapter, we speak of civic engagement and higher education entirely in the abstract; in the chapter that follows, we both extend and narrow our view to address the distinctive shape such teaching takes in the religion classroom.

Intellectual Complexity and Critical Thinking: Setting Some Limits

There are very few academics in the humanities and social sciences who do not value critical thinking as a central academic objective in their courses. Individual definitions of this term, however, can and often do vary widely.[5] In her 2008 survey of introductory college and university religion courses, for example, Barbara E. Walvoord characterizes critical thinking both in terms of the habits and dispositions of the "ideal critical thinker" and in terms of specific, assessable skills of interpretation, comparison, analysis, and evaluation.[6] In the religious studies classroom, she suggests, critical thinking consists of specific "intellectual tasks," including:

- analysis of the cultural, historical, economic, sociological, political, ideological, linguistic, literary, symbolic, and other aspects of religious beliefs, texts, and practices;
- use of evidence and reason to reach conclusions and to formulate and critique arguments;
- use of multiple perspectives to understand an issue; and
- the achievement of interpretive distance from [students'] own autobiographies and communities.

Accompanying these tasks, moreover, are specific "attitudes, dispositions and habits of mind" such as a willingness to challenge personal beliefs and assumptions, recognition of the value of positions other than one's own, a complex, dynamic view of truth-claims and the ongoing development of persons and traditions, rejection of stereotypes, and intellectual autonomy.[7] To the extent that teachers specify such intellectual skills or personal dispositions in their course objectives, or students report them in their evaluations, such courses can be described as fostering "critical thinking."

From one point of view, then, critical thinking may be reduced to particular tasks and habits of mind that can be identified, modeled, and assessed. Yet, from another, more developmental perspective, such tasks and habits themselves can also be situated within broader patterns of psycho-social maturation. Thus, the educational theorist William G. Perry, Jr., advanced a complex scheme of progressive development that turns on two major transitions. First, students ideally shift from the dualist, authority-based patterns of thought, characteristic of adolescence, to what Perry terms "Multiplicity," in which "everyone has a right to his own opinion; none can be called wrong." Again ideally, this development leads to a subsequent, no less significant shift from pure Multiplicity to a more context-sensitive, disciplined "Relativism" which includes, at its furthest extent, a willingness to form self-reflective, provisional commitments.[8] More recently, Jack Mezirow has advocated a broader, recursive "transformation theory" that tracks intellectual development in a particular field of inquiry from its origin in a "disorienting dilemma," through a process of critical examination, experimentation, and imaginative "reframing," and finally to its culmination in a new, "more dependable frame of reference . . . that is more inclusive, differentiating, permeable (open to other viewpoints), critically reflective of assumptions, emotionally capable of change, and integrative of experience."[9] Both theories emphasize students' developing capacities for negotiating intellectual conflicts and making reasonable, revisable judgments.

Both Perry and Mezirow locate the development of such capacities in what Mezirow calls "reflective discourse," namely, "that specialized use of dialogue devoted to searching for a common understanding and assessment of the justification of an interpretation or belief. This involves assessing reasons advanced by weighing the supporting evidence and arguments and by examining alternative perspectives."[10] Emphasis falls squarely on the methods, modes, and discursive processes by which differences can be adjudicated, provisional judgments affirmed, and alternative perspectives acknowledged. Critical thinking is, from this perspective, both cultivated and assessed by means of deliberative discourse.

In concrete practice, of course, students will arrive in the classroom at various levels of readiness for this kind of reflective, dialectical discourse. Even more pressingly, as argued by members of the *WWK* collaborative, upholding such specialized discourse as a uniform ideal may also risk masking power inequalities among students and ignoring the distinctive experience and learning styles of female students in particular.[11] In their landmark study *Women's Ways of Knowing*, the collaborative drew on interviews with 130 adult women to offer an alternative sequence of five cognitive positions, beginning with the experience of being "Silenced" and culminating in a position of critical, self-consciously "Constructed Knowledge." These positions loosely cohere with Perry's scheme while also challenging many of his fundamental, arguably masculinist assumptions. Notably, the collaborative advanced the more passive but no less dichotomous mode of "Received Knowledge" in place of Perry's "Dualist" position, as well as a position of "Subjective Knowledge," rooted in personal experience and attention to one's "inner voice," in place of a more generalized "Multiplicity."[12] In these cases and many others, recognition of both the strong correspondence to Perry's scheme and distinctive differences from it is intended to help teachers meet the needs of a wider range of students without abandoning the desire "to challenge and stimulate them to develop more elaborate approaches to the construction of knowledge."[13]

Absolutely central to this task, moreover, is the development of what the collaborative nicely clarifies as "Procedural Knowledge," defined as the understanding that "ideas can be communicated, analyzed, developed, and tested by making good use of procedures."[14] Here, it is worth noting, the *WWK* collaborative differentiates not between Perry's "Relativism" and their "Procedural Knowing" as such, but between the kinds of procedures emphasized in each scheme: "Separate Knowing" in one case and "Connected Knowing" in the other. To illustrate the difference, they draw on Peter Elbow's distinction between the "doubting game" and the "believing game."[15] The members of the *WWK* collaborative, like Peter Elbow, readily concede that both forms of reasoning may be necessary for full cognitive development, and they assert that, though there may be gender-related tendencies, "Separate and connected knowing are not gender-specific."[16] Yet, they also observe that it is invariably the pattern of Separate Knowing that is upheld as the primary ideal of sound reason in the theories of Perry and Mezirow, as well as in the broader academy.[17]

With this corrective in mind, one can nevertheless affirm the cultivation of intellectual complexity and what the *WWK* collaborative calls "more elaborate approaches" to knowledge-creation[18] as a relatively stable ideal of university instruction. Such an ideal is not strictly reducible to particular procedures of analysis, evaluation, and synthesis; yet, it is only through practice in the use of such procedures that students come to what these theorists consider more mature, integrative, and empowering perspectives on learning itself. The strong presumption seems to be that, once achieved, such intellectual maturity may in many cases transfer from the classroom to the wider world, from the specific subject-centered inquiry of a particular academic discipline to the acquisition of knowledge and formation of commitments beyond the university or college campus. One of the goals of this chapter is to re-examine, to nuance, and to some extent to challenge this presumption.

Intellectual Complexity and Civic Engagement

Do such "more elaborate" modes of reasoning reliably transfer from the classroom to the civic sphere? Does intellectual complexity necessarily make students into better citizens of their local communities, their nations, and their global society?

Complicating our responses to these questions is the fact that there is, if anything, less consensus on comprehensive definitions for "civic engagement" or "good citizenship" than on critical thinking and intellectual complexity.[19] One of the leaders in the civic engagement movement in higher education, Barbara Jacoby, notes that definitions of such engagement usually include, from most to least frequent, "community service," "political participation," and political "activism or advocacy."[20] She cites with approval the very broad definition advanced by the Coalition for Civic Engagement and Leadership at the University of Maryland:

> Civic engagement is defined as "acting upon a heightened sense of responsibility to one's communities. This includes a wide range of activities, including developing civic sensitivity, participation in building civil society, and benefiting the common good. Civic engagement encompasses the notions of global citizenship and interdependence. Through civic engagement, individuals—as citizens of their communities, their nations, and the world—are empowered as agents of positive social change for a more democratic world."[21]

This definition of civic engagement is deliberately broad, attempting to comprehend a variety of activities under a single umbrella. A problem arises, however, due to the fact that what is actually valued as responsible participation and "positive social change" may take different shapes, depending upon prior conceptions of democratic citizenship. In part for this reason, Ben Berger has suggested that the term "civic engagement" be dropped entirely, in favor of more specific, delimitable categories of "political engagement," "social engagement," and "moral engagement." Though all three may be necessary to keep democracy, in Nussbaum's language, "awake and alive," they are properly distinguished one from the other.[22]

Richard M. Battistoni draws a different set of distinctions. Instead of differentiating "the social" from "the political," he notes five distinct yet overlapping models of "the civic" current in literature from the social sciences: "Constitutional Citizenship," focused on individual rights, voting, and political processes; "Communitarianism," focused on community values, shared responsibilities, and the common good; "Participatory Democracy," focused on active participation of all citizens in public deliberation and collective action; "Public Work," focused on collaboration among citizens on a variety of initiatives in the public sphere; and "Social Capital," focused on membership in voluntary organizations and civil society.[23] To this list Battistoni adds a number of perspectives borrowed from other disciplines, such as "Civic Professionalism," "Engaged Scholarship," "Social Justice," and "Connected Knowing" or cultivation of an "Ethic of Care."[24] In the present volume, several authors reflect on the political, social, and ethical dimensions of civic engagement, as well as a number of the perspectives highlighted by Battistoni, well illustrating just how complicated teaching for civic engagement can become.

The fluidity and variety of these definitions alerts us to the fact that, though one can hardly doubt that any model of good citizenship would exclude intellectual complexity as an academic and civic virtue, it assumes its most central role in relation to those conceptions of citizenship that place strong value on deliberation and argument, such as "Constitutional Citizenship" and "Participatory Democracy." Jack Mezirow, as just one quite striking example, speaks in the idiom of individual rights, public discourse, and participatory democratic structures when he emphasizes the civic importance of critical thinking. Transformation theory aims primarily to help adult learners "gain greater control over our lives as socially responsible, clear-thinking decision makers," and Mezirow draws a direct parallel between "reflective discourse" and what sociologist Robert Bellah calls "democratic habits of the heart."[25] He goes on:

> Transformation Theory suggests that transformative learning inherently creates understandings for participatory democracy by developing capacities of critical reflection on taken-for-granted assumptions that support contested points of view and participation in discourse that reduces fractional threats of rights and pluralism, conflict, and the use of power, and foster autonomy, self-development, and self-governance—the values that rights and freedoms presumably are designed to protect.[26]

The line from reflective discourse to responsible civic engagement is, for Mezirow, a relatively straight one, precisely because both require substantively identical skills, understandings, and dispositions. Such a contention is further substantiated by Laurent A. Parks Daloz, who uses the example of Nelson Mandela to illustrate how a "rich ecology of mentors, colleagues, adversaries, events, and critical discourse" offers resources for the formation of critical, race-transcending frames of reference and, with it, a commitment to public engagement and the common good.[27]

This also resonates well with the position of Martha Nussbaum, with whom we began this chapter. Like Mezirow, Nussbaum defines civic life and democratic participation in terms of individual citizens navigating "reasonable disagreement" among various secular and religious perspectives, informing themselves on important social issues, voting or engaging in public deliberation as elected or appointed public servants, and "making choices that have a major impact on the lives of people who differ from themselves."[28] Such participation, in turn, requires a cultivated capacity for argument, evaluation, and debate, sensitive to multiple perspectives and diverse constituencies and highly differentiated in its commitment to the interests of the local community, the nation, and the world[29]—all skills closely related to intellectual complexity, as described in the previous section.

Here it may be important, however, to recall that the full account of intellectual development articulated by Perry, Mezirow, and the *WWK* collaborative includes not merely the acquisition of cognitive skills but also the active formation and articulation of personal commitments. This is of key importance for tracing a line from such complexity to actual civic engagement. As Jacoby puts the matter, "Knowledge and skills are acknowledged to be necessary but not sufficient. Values, motivation, and commitment are also required."[30]

Values represent not merely a desired result of the kind of critical thinking that leads to civic engagement; they can, in many cases, function as the bridge from one to the other. Thus, in one widely cited 1982 article, Richard L. Morrill recommends that the critical inquiry that characterizes the best classroom instruction include explicit attention to the "sea of values" on which democracy rests: "participation, responsibility, respect for self and others, equality, freedom, justice, tolerance, and trust."[31] Inveighing against a liberal model of seeking "knowledge for its own sake" and the dichotomy between thinking, feeling, and action such a model can be read to imply, Morrill envisions an education for democratic citizenship that pushes beyond fostering knowledge of particular political structures or analysis of particular social issues to address students as whole persons, as "unified, responsible agents of their own choices and actions."[32] Importantly, such an education does not proceed by one or another form of indoctrination.[33] For Morrill, education proceeds by means of a deepened and broadened discourse, one that includes open-ended processes of analysis, self-reflection, assessment, revision, and rigorous debate and justification on topics related to these democratic values. In order for critical reflection to open into effective civic participation, in other words, it is crucially important that such reflection include a no less critical inquiry into the "primary springs of human self-evaluation, motivation, and action": our values.[34]

Liberatory Education and Civic Engagement

Richard L. Morrill's proposal raises an interesting conundrum. While he, like Mezirow and Nussbaum, acknowledges the formative role of reflective discourse in fostering both intellectual complexity and the civic participation ideally formed by it, his emphasis on values also acknowledges the limitations of discourse, as such, to stimulate public action. As noted earlier, Richard Battistoni suggests that there is not one, but multiple models of citizenship employed in the social sciences and other disciplines—and only some of these, such as "Constitutional Citizenship" and "Participatory Democracy," place strong emphasis upon procedural skills of discourse and deliberation. Others, such as "Communitarian," "Social Capital," or "Ethic of Care" models, place a much stronger emphasis on social connections and voluntary participation.[35] Still other models, such as "Social Justice," tend to refigure citizenship in terms of activism and social critique.[36] Thus, no less fervent an advocate of classroom discussion as Stephen D. Brookfield questions any facile equation between reflective discourse and personal transformation, unless critical reflection includes something like "ideology critique" in the tradition of the Frankfurt School.[37] "For something to count as an example of critical learning, critical analysis, or critical reflection," he writes, "I believe the person involved must engage in some sort of power analysis. . . . They must also try to identify assumptions they hold dear that are actually destroying their sense of well-being and serving the interests of others: that is, hegemonic assumptions."[38] Ideally, on Brookfield's reading, such critical reflection opens naturally into, and in some sense requires, transformative political action in the public sphere.[39]

Brookfield's argument here accords well with the various models of liberatory education advanced by Paulo Freire, bell hooks, and other contemporary critical theorists. Freire is perhaps best known for his critique of the "banking model" of education, focused on lecture and the delivery of course content, in favor of more participatory, broadly "liberative" dialogue focused on the posing of problems for shared reflection.[40] In this sense, his theory affirms many of the principles and practices of reflective discourse, already discussed. Yet, for Freire and his interpreters, simply focusing on discussion as a *method* of education tends to occlude the radical, political role of dialogic methods to illumine and thus to critique structures of domination and oppression in the wider society.[41] In a public conversation with Ira Shor in the mid-1980s, Freire underlined the continuity between the classroom and the wider world:

> Through your search to convince the learners, your own testimony about freedom, your certainty for the transformation of society, indirectly you must underline that the roots of the problem are far beyond the classroom in society and in the world. Precisely because of that, the context for transformation is not only the classroom but extends outside of it. The students and teachers will be undertaking a transformation that includes a context outside the classroom, if the process is a liberating one.[42]

The relation works both ways, of course. For Freire, one of the reasons that questions of politics and social equity must be addressed in the university classroom is that this classroom is an intrinsically political space, shaped by market structures and supported by power elites as a means of perpetuating a hegemonic order.[43]

Few theorists have adapted this insight of Freire more creatively and thoroughly in the North American context than the African American feminist bell hooks.[44] For hooks, a truly engaged pedagogy requires continual attention to questions of difference and power, particularly the entrenched inequities of gender, race, and social class. As the members of the *WWK* collaborative observed, conventional models of teaching and theorizing intellectual development have tended to favor masculinist patterns and assumptions. Along similar lines, hooks and other theorists have noted the myriad ways that race and class function to inhibit the democratic potential of classroom spaces.[45] With this in mind, scholars in religion and other disciplines have developed a number of methods to help instructors and students alike acknowledge their social locations, address questions of privilege, and work for social transformation.[46] For hooks herself, such a process involves both a negative process of critique—the "decolonization of our minds"—and a positive process of community building—the "practice of beloved community."[47] Because structures of sexism, racism, and class oppression are perpetuated through habitual, learned behaviors on the part of both oppressor and oppressed, so also must these structures be opposed not merely by intellectual analysis but also by an activist commitment that begins in the classroom and extends into the wider world.[48] Such an embodied, holistic pedagogy for equality, diversity, and community represents the only "democratic education" worthy of the name, because equality is the primary value that differentiates authentic democracy from oligarchy.[49]

At first blush, the more activist orientations of Freire, hooks, and other theorists may seem to diminish the value of intellectual complexity, reflective discourse, and objectivity as primary ends of university education—displaced, it may seem, by more explicitly political or ideological objectives.[50] Most critical theorists would insist that this is not the case. First of all, for Freire and hooks, liberatory education represents not a diminishment of critical thought but its fullest expression. For Freire, the quest for liberation begins and flourishes on the basis of natural curiosity, an innate, unrestricted desire to know the world and to realize its full potential as a realm of creativity.[51] For her part, bell hooks advances engaged pedagogy as a distinctive form of training in critical thinking, in "radical openness" to multiple perspectives, and in discernment, analysis, and evaluation.[52] Other theorists have noted that activist and community-based methods of teaching and learning can function to strengthen rather than weaken traditional measures of critical thought and scholarly productivity, while also broadening the scope of their inquiry.[53]

What these theorists question, perhaps, is not critical thinking as such, but the implicit separation between such thinking and political context implied when such thinking is rendered exclusively in terms of cognitive skills and intellectual procedures, as well as the pretense of neutrality in the learning process. "To make reality opaque is not neutral," writes Freire. "To make reality lucid, illuminated, is also not neutral. In order for us to do that, we have to occupy the space of the schools with liberating politics."[54] In the political space of the classroom, the liberatory teacher directly engages students in a form of civic practice oriented to critique and resistance against one or more hegemonic orders. The outcome of such an education, of course, is radically open, dependent upon the subjectivities of the students and instructor who engage together in it. Instructors cannot dictate students' politics, precisely because this would violate the very freedom that stands at the center of the educational project; instead, they aim to provide such students with concrete experiences of freedom, critique, and authentic community—embodied, habituating experiences that will, at least ideally, not only structure but also motivate their engagement in a wider, civic sphere.[55]

Teaching for Civic Engagement: Four Guiding Objectives

Thus far, we have drawn a soft contrast between two different approaches to the civic function of university education. In the first, drawing on the developmental theories of William Perry, Jack Mezirow, and the *WWK* collaborative, the primary civic capacities fostered in the university classroom find their home in critical discourse, in the weighing of evidence, and in the formation of provisional commitments, attentive to the multiplicity of perspectives on any particular question. In the second, exemplified in the critical pedagogies of Paulo Freire and bell hooks, the classroom is reconfigured as an intrinsically political space, and critical thinking is extended to include a liberative dialectic of dialogue, reflection, and embodied action. Though there is ample shared ground among these approaches, they also bring to light diverse—in some cases conflicting—conceptualizations of higher education and the civic sphere itself. If civic engagement consists primarily of participation in constitutional processes and democratic structures, then Mezirow's ideal of "reflective discourse" would seem to fit the bill. But is democracy really reducible to reasoned discourse? As Richard Morrill states succinctly, "Democratic literacy is a literacy of doing, not simply of knowing. Knowledge is a necessary but not sufficient condition of democratic responsibility."[56] For Morrill himself, as we have seen, such attention to "doing" implicates the university instructor in the analysis and clarification of values; for Freire, hooks, and other activist theorists, it necessarily involves practice in the "doing" of civic engagement itself.

In 2008 and 2009, a group of nineteen religious studies and theology faculty gathered in a series of workshops to ask the question, "What is effective civic engagement? How do we teach for civic engagement in our classrooms?"[57] Early on, we resolved to adopt an intentionally wide view on the question, with the intention of incorporating insights from both traditional and liberative perspectives on the educational project. We were not, of course, the first to make such an attempt. In the vision of the "active citizen" advanced by the Council of Europe or the "Civic Learning Spiral" developed by the Civic Engagement Working Group of the Association of American Colleges and Universities, for example, the achievement of intellectual complexity and the clarification of values and commitments represent a necessary but not sufficient objective for civic education; such personal, cognitive development must be matched by habituating practices of intercultural awareness, empathy and respect developed through lived relationships with others, and direct civic action.[58] While appreciative of such models, our group resisted settling on a single, normative vision of the ideal citizen. Instead, we set out to articulate a loose framework of core capacities, which could be adapted in a wide variety of ways and which would facilitate conversation and collaboration without presuming a settled consensus.

With this goal in mind the workshop group settled on four broad, guiding objectives for educators who wish to educate for civic engagement in the university classroom: (1) intellectual complexity; (2) frames of reference and social location; (3) empathetic accountability; and (4) motivated action.[59] For convenience, these core civic capacities may be reduced to the formula Complexity-Location-Empathy-Action, or CLEA. In our view, the objectives represented in the CLEA model are cumulative and recursive: Each builds on the other in a mutual and holistic movement, rather than in a strictly linear order. It seems unlikely that any single class, much less any single assignment, could attend equally to all four of them. We suggest that educators are likely to focus on one or two, while remaining attentive to connections with other values and to the task of civic engagement as a whole. We describe each of these guiding objectives in turn.

1. *Intellectual complexity* (C) entails the cultivation of powers of analysis, reasoning, and ever "more elaborate approaches" to knowledge-construction, as detailed by the *WWK* collaborative and other theorists treated in this chapter. Such complexity, we recognize, represents an intrinsic good in the civic sphere, conducing to critical discernment in the use of news sources, the capacity for reasoned debate, and the acknowledgment of alternative perspectives. It serves as a foundation for the three subsequent objectives; it also draws strength from them, insofar as the acknowledgment of multiple frames of reference, experiences of empathetic accountability, and reflection on motivated

action tend to complicate existing views and, thus, provide fodder for greater complexity and more elaborate cognitive procedures.

2. *Frames of reference and social location* (L) represent two sides of a similar cognitive skill in navigating multiplicity in the abstract and the concrete, the personal and the embodied. As Mezirow in particular has noted, truly critical thought entails the ability not merely to acknowledge multiple perspectives on any particular position but to move flexibly between different, sometimes conflicting clusters of assumptions that ground these perspectives. Feminist, Womanist, and other critical pedagogies of gender, race, and class deepen this cognitive awareness to include reflection on one's own social location, including the phenomenon of privilege, and clear recognition of the dynamics of difference, power, and positionality in social life and in the academy. Such awareness of and comfort with difference can function to deepen intellectual complexity and to create opportunities for empathetic accountability across boundaries of difference; it can also, particularly when acknowledgment of difference includes reflection on inequity and structures of oppression, ground motivated action in the classroom and in the wider civic sphere.

3. *Empathetic accountability* (E) comprehends both the ability to enter imaginatively into other life worlds and cultural frameworks and, ideally, the actual practice of forming relationships and cultivating an ethic of care with persons different from oneself. At one level, this objective entails an education in diversity and multiculturalism. As Nussbaum writes:

> An adequate education for living in a pluralistic democracy must be multicultural, by which I mean one that acquaints students with some fundamentals about the history and cultures of the many different groups with whom they share laws and institutions. These should include religious, ethnic, economic, social, and gender-based groups. Language learning, history, economics, and political science all play a role in facilitating this understanding—in different ways at different levels.[60]

Nussbaum presumes, and many scholar-teachers would likely affirm, that multicultural education represents a genuine encounter with difference. Yet, effective civic engagement becomes more likely when empathy moves beyond the purely notional, when students are empowered to cross boundaries of difference and form relationships with actual persons of diverse religions, languages, and ethnicities—to practice what hooks refers to, following Martin Luther King, Jr., as "beloved community."[61] Such empathy presumes a candid acknowledgment of difference and an imaginative ability to navigate multiple perspectives in constructing one's own point of view—and thus builds upon the previous two objectives.[62] At the same time, experiences of relationship and community across boundaries of difference can serve as the impulse to recognize the realities of social location, to confront privilege, and to construct more complex capacities for reasoning and discourse. Involvement in the lives of others can also suggest possibilities for service, advocacy, and other forms of motivated action in the public sphere.[63]

4. *Motivated action* (A) is, in many ways, the desired result of all of the previous objectives, insofar as they fit under the rubric of "teaching for civic engagement." But, too often, a gap remains between notional command of political issues or intellectual acknowledgment of social privilege and taking concrete action to address them. One way to address this gap, advocated by K. Edward Spiezo, is to provide students with the "basic knowledge, requisite skills and hence the confidence to participate politically" through contact with political activists, interactions with student- and citizen-based interest groups, and community placements.[64] Other pedagogies oriented toward motivated action include service-learning, guerilla theater, documentary filmmaking, and "letter to the editor" writing assignments. Such strategies presume that effective civic engagement is not just a matter of intellect but also a consequence of habituating practice. Students learn civic engagement by engaging directly in the civic sphere; at the same time, such engagement can, particularly if matched with reflective work, also function to foster greater intellectual complexity, to deepen awareness of diverse frames of reference and positionalities, and to cultivate both imaginative and actual bonds of empathetic accountability.

We began this chapter on teaching for civic engagement with an event that could be interpreted as its failure: the 2002 Gujarat pogrom. More recently, between April 7 and May 12, 2014, the Bharatiya Janata Party of former Gujarat Chief Minister Narendra Modi won a sweeping victory in the Indian federal elections, taking 282 of 543 seats in the lower house of parliament, the Lok Sabha. On the one hand, this was a very significant achievement of civic participation, with a 66 percent voter turnout across the country—the highest in Indian electoral history.[65] The same event could also, however, be read by some critics in the Indian and international media as a kind of failure of civic intelligence, particularly in light of Modi's record in Gujarat.[66] This appears to be the view of Martha Nussbaum herself, who during the campaign period publicly criticized Modi for fear-mongering and challenged widespread appeals to Gujarat as a miracle of economic development under his leadership.[67] Yet, the very fact that Nussbaum was able to articulate such concerns in Indian venues such as *The Hindu Centre for Politics and Public Policy* highlighted another element of the event and of Indian public culture more broadly: namely, the intense coverage of the campaign by a vibrant, engaged, and highly critical national media.[68] The election, finally, highlighted many divisions in India's pluralistic society, extending well beyond Hindu and Muslim to include the complexities of caste and class and Modi's own humble origins as a street tea-seller.

Our purpose here is not to pass judgment on Indian federal elections but simply to note the sheer complexity of assessing the event as an achievement of civic engagement. Ben Berger suggests that "engagement" can be coded relatively simply as "attention" and "activity"—political attention and activity, social attention and activity, moral attention and activity.[69] In practice, such attention and activity are worked out across a complex tapestry of identities, relationships, and judgments of fact and value. Teaching for civic engagement cannot adequately address this complexity by simply fostering critical reflection and deliberative discourse in the classroom, though these are essential. Ideally, it aims to deepen such critical thinking by addressing questions of identity and motivation directly and encouraging the formation of empathy, imagination, relationships across difference, and the lived habits of thought and action conducive to effective engagement in the political and social orders. The four guiding objectives detailed under the rubric of CLEA—Complexity, Location, Empathy, and Action—represent one attempt to capture this complex tapestry for the purposes of classroom instruction, as well as for the ongoing formation of teacher and student alike.

Notes

1. Martha Craven Nussbaum, *The Clash Within: Democracy, Religious Violence, and India's Future* (Cambridge, MA: Belknap Press of Harvard University Press, 2007).
2. Ibid., 82–94, 290–96.
3. Martha Nussbaum, *Not for Profit: Why Democracy Needs the Humanities* (Princeton and Oxford: Princeton University Press, 2010), 10.
4. Frank H. T. Rhodes, "Universities and the Democratic Spirit," in *Higher Education and Democratic Culture: Citizenship, Human Rights and Civic Responsibility*, ed. Josef Huber and Ira Harkavy (Council of Europe higher education series No. 8) (Strasbourg: Council of Europe Publishing, 2007), 45.
5. The following section depends in part on the fuller discussion offered in Reid B. Locklin, "Teaching with Complicating Views: Beyond the Survey, Behind Pro and Con," *Teaching Theology and Religion* 16.3 (July 2013): 205–208.
6. Barbara E. Walvoord, *Teaching and Learning in College Introductory Religion Courses* (Malden, MA: Blackwell Publishing, 2008), 19–20.
7. Ibid., 34–35.
8. William G. Perry, Jr., "Cognitive and Ethical Growth: The Making of Meaning," in *The Modern American College: Responding to the New Realities of Diverse*

Students and a Changing Society, by Arthur W. Chickering et al. (San Francisco: Jossey-Bass, 1981), 78–80, 94–96.

9. Jack Mezirow, "Learning to Think Like an Adult: Core Concepts of Transformation Theory," in *Learning as Transformation: Critical Perspectives on a Theory in Progress,* by Jack Mezirow and Associates (San Francisco: Jossey-Bass, 2000), esp. 19–20. See also his earlier work, *Transformative Dimensions of Adult Learning* (San Francisco: Jossey-Bass, 1991).

10. Mezirow, "Learning to Think Like an Adult," 10–11.

11. See Mary Field Belenky, Blythe McVicker Clinchy, Nancy Rule Goldberger, and Jill Mattuck Tarule, *Women's Ways of Knowing: The Development of Self, Voice, and Mind,* 2nd ed. (New York: Basic Books, 1997), and, with specific reference to Mezirow's theory of transformative learning, Mary Field Belenky and Ann V. Stanton, "Inequality, Development, and Connected Knowing," in *Learning as Transformation,* by Jack Mezirow and Associates, 71–102.

12. Belenky et al., *Women's Ways of Knowing,* 43–45, 62–68.

13. Belenky and Stanton, " Inequality, Development, and Connected Knowing," 93.

14. Ibid., 86.

15. See especially Peter Elbow, "The Doubting Game and the Believing Game—An Analysis of the Intellectual Enterprise," in *Writing Without Teachers* (London, Oxford, and New York: Oxford University Press, 1973), 147–91, as well as the further elaboration and discussion of these ideas in Wayne C. Booth, "Blind Skepticism Versus a Rhetoric of Assent," *College English* 67.4 (March 2005): 378–88; Peter Elbow, "Bringing the Rhetoric of Assent and the Believing Game Together—And Into the Classroom," *College English* 67.4 (March 2005): 388–99; and Peter Elbow, "The Believing Game," in *Nurturing the Peacemakers in Our Students: A Guide to Writing and Speaking Out about Issues of War and Peace,* ed. Chris Weber (Portsmouth, NH: Heinemann, 2006), 16–25.

16. Belenky et al., *Women's Ways of Knowing,* 102.

17. See Ibid., 103–12; Belenky and Stanton, "Inequality, Development, and Connected Knowing," 90–91.

18. Belenky and Stanton, "Inequality, Development, and Connected Knowing," 93.

19. See Steven Lawry, Daniel Laurison, and Jonathan VanAntwerpen, *Liberal Education and Civic Engagement: A Project of the Ford Foundation's Knowledge, Creativity and Freedom Program, with a New Prologue Assessing Developments in the Field Since 2006 by Steven Lawry.* The Ford Foundation, May 2009,http://www.fordfoundation.org/pdfs/library/liberal_education_and_civic_engagement.pdf, 22–31 (accessed September 8, 2012). Ben Berger traces the popularity of the term to its use in Robert Putnam et al.'s 1993 study *Making Democracy Work.* Reviewing mentions of the term in newspapers and scholarly literature, he notes an explosive rise from the 1990s, when it was scarcely ever mentioned, to 400 and 100 mentions, respectively, at the turn of the century, and then to nearly 2,000 and 400 mentions in 2009. See his *Attention Deficit Democracy:*

The Paradox of Civic Engagement (Princeton and Oxford: Princeton University Press, 2011), 30–35.

20. Barbara Jacoby, "Civic Engagement in Today's Higher Education," in *Civic Engagement in Higher Education: Concepts and Practices*, by Barbara Jacoby and Associates (San Francisco: Jossey-Bass, 2009), 8–9.

21. Ibid., 9.

22. Berger, *Attention Deficit Democracy*, 2–5.

23. Richard M. Battistoni, *Civic Engagement across the Curriculum: A Resource Book for Service-Learning Faculty in All Disciplines* (Providence, RI: Campus Compact, 2002), 13–17.

24. Ibid., 19–26.

25. Mezirow, "Thinking Like an Adult," 8, 14. This is also a claim developed persuasively by Stephen D. Brookfield and Stephen Preskill, *Discussion as a Way of Teaching: Tools and Techniques for Democratic Classrooms*, 2nd ed. (San Francisco: Jossey-Bass, 2005), esp. 263–76.

26. Mezirow, "Thinking Like an Adult," 28.

27. Laurent A. Parks Daloz, "Transformative Learning for the Common Good," in *Learning as Transformation* by Jack Mezirow and Associates (see n. 9), 103–23, quotation at 109.

28. Nussbaum, *Not for Profit* (see n. 3), 9.

29. Ibid., 25–26.

30. Jacoby, "Civic Engagement," 7.

31. Richard L. Morrill, "Educating for Democratic Values." *Liberal Education* 68.4 (1982): 368.

32. Ibid., 367.

33. In chapter 12 of the present volume, Swasti Bhattacharyya and Forrest Clingerman reflect further on how an advocacy for democratic process avoids indoctrination.

34. Morrill, "Educating for Democratic Values," 371.

35. Battistoni, *Civic Engagement* (see n. 23), 14, 16, 24–25. Peter Levine also distinguishes between two fundamental kinds of political activity: (1) political dialogue and contestation aimed at shaping public policy, and (2) what he terms "open-ended" political activity that often takes the form of direct participation. See his "Civic Renewal in America," *Philosophy and Public Policy Quarterly* 26.1–2 (Winter/Spring 2006): 2–12.

36. Battistoni, *Civic Engagement*, 22–24. See also Kathleen Skubikowski, Catherine Wright, and Roman Graf, eds., *Social Justice Education: Inviting Faculty to Transform Their Institutions* (Sterling, VA: Stylus, 2009).

37. Stephen D. Brookfield, "Transformative Learning as Ideology Critique," in *Learning as Transformation* by Jack Mezirow and Associates (see n. 9), 125–48.

38. Ibid., 126.

39. See Ibid., 143–46.

40. See especially Paulo Freire's seminal work *Pedagogy of the Oppressed*, 30th anniversary ed. (New York: Continuum, 2000), chs. 2–3.

41. Ira Shor and Paulo Freire, *A Pedagogy for Liberation: Dialogues on Transforming Education* (South Hadley, MA: Bergin & Garvey Publishers, 1987), 39–50.

42. Ibid., 33.

43. Ibid., 35–38; Ira Shor, "Educating the Educators: A Freirean Approach to the Crisis in Teacher Education," in *Freire for the Classroom: A Sourcebook for Liberatory Teaching*, ed. Ira Shor (Portsmouth, NH: Boynton/Cook Publishers, 1987), 7–32; and Henry A. Giroux, "Neoliberalism, Corporate Culture, and the Promise of Higher Education: The University as a Democratic Public Sphere," *Harvard Educational Review* 72.4 (Winter 2002): 427–63.

44. See especially her trilogy of works dedicated to engaged pedagogy: bell hooks, *Teaching to Transgress: Education as the Practice of Freedom* (New York and London: Routledge, 1994); bell hooks, *Teaching Community: A Pedagogy of Hope* (New York and London: Routledge, 2003); and bell hooks, *Teaching Critical Thinking* (New York and London: Routledge, 2010).

45. E.g., hooks, *Teaching to Transgress*, 177–89; hooks, *Teaching Community*, 25–40; hooks, *Teaching Critical Thinking*, 169–76; Aída Hurtado, "Strategic Suspensions: Feminists of Color Theorize the Production of Knowledge," in *Knowledge, Difference, and Power: Essays Inspired by Women's Ways of Knowing*, ed. Nancy Rule Goldberger, Jill Mattuck Tarule, Blythe McVicker Clinchy, and Mary Field Belenky (New York: Basic Books, 1996), 372–91; and Peggy McIntosh, "White Privilege: Unpacking the Invisible Knapsack," *Independent School* 49.2 (Winter 1990): 31–35.

46. See Jack A. Hill, Melanie Harris, and Hjamil A. Martínez-Vázquez, "Fighting the Elephant in the Room: Ethical Reflections on White Privilege and Other Systems of Advantage in the Teaching of Religion," *Teaching Theology and Religion* 12.1 (January 2009): 3–23; Katie Geneva Cannon, "Metalogues and Dialogues: Teaching the Womanist Idea," in *Katie's Canon: Womanism and the Soul of the Black Community* (New York: Continuum, 1995), 136–43; Lee Anne Bell, "Learning through Story Types about Race and Racism," in *Social Justice Education*, ed. Kathleen Skubikowski et al. (see n. 36), 26–41; Beverly Daniel Tatum, "Talking about Race, Learning about Racism: The Application of Racial Identity Development Theory in the Classroom," *Harvard Educational Review* 62.1 (Spring 1992): 1–24; and Vicki L. Reitenauer, Christine M. Cress, and Janet Bennett, "Creating Cultural Connections: Navigating Difference, Investigating Power, Unpacking Privilege," in *Learning through Serving: A Student Guidebook for Service-Learning Across the Disciplines*, ed. Christine M. Cress, Peter J. Collier, and Vicki L. Reitenauer (Sterling, VA: Stylus, 2005), 67–79.

47. hooks, *Teaching Community* 35–36.

48. Ibid., 39–40.

49. See Ibid., 41–49, and hooks, *Teaching Critical Thinking*, 13–18.

50. For an argument of this sort, see Stanley Fish, *Save the World on Your Own Time* (Oxford and New York: Oxford University Press, 2008).

51. A beautiful expression of the connection Freire draws between curiosity and political commitment can be found in a video interview from the end of his career: Paulo Freire, "Paulo Freire—An Incredible Conversation," *YouTube*, December 30, 2009, http://www.youtube.com/watch?v=aFWjnkFypFA&feature=related (accessed September 8, 2012).

52. hooks, *Teaching Critical Thinking*, 7–11.

53. See, e.g., Barry Checkoway, "Renewing the Civic Mission of the American Research University," *The Journal of Higher Education* 72.2 (Mar/April 2001): 133–37; Dan W. Butin, "The Limits of Service-Learning in Higher Education," *Review of Higher Education* 29.4 (Summer 2006): 490–93.

54. Friere and Shor, *A Pedagogy for Liberation* (see n. 41), 36–37.

55. A particularly strong statement of the inextricably located and value-laden character of civic engagement education can be found in Eric Hartman, "No Values, No Democracy: The Essential Partisanship of a Civic Engagement Movement," *Michigan Journal of Community Service* 19.2 (Spring 2013): 58–71.

56. Morrill, "Educating for Democratic Values" (see n. 31), 365.

57. This project is described in greater detail by Melissa Stewart in chapter 3 of this volume.

58. See Rolf Gollob, Peter Krapf, and Wiltrud Weidinger, eds. *Educating for Democracy: Background Materials on Democratic Citizenship and Human Rights Education for Teachers* (Strasbourg: Council of Europe Publishing, 2010), esp. 25–27; and Caryn McTighe Musil, "Educating Students for Personal and Social Responsibility: The Civic Learning Spiral," in *Civic Engagement in Higher Education* by Barbara Jacoby and Associates (see n. 20), 49–68.

59. We would like to thank Joseph Favazza for helping us articulate these four objectives in discussion with participants in a "Teaching for Civic Engagement" grant project in November 2008.

60. Nussbaum, *Not for Profit* (see n. 3), 91.

61. hooks, *Teaching Community* (see n. 44), 35–36.

62. See Nussbaum, *Not for Profit*, 72.

63. On this point, see especially Nicholas A. Bowman, "Promoting Participation in a Diverse Democracy: A Meta-Analysis of College Diversity Experiences and Civic Engagement," *Review of Educational Research* 81.1 (March 2011): 29–68.

64. K. Edward Spiezo, "Pedagogy and Political (Dis)Engagement," *Liberal Education* 88.4 (Fall 2002): 18–19. See also the full account of the Participating in Democracy Project at Cedar Crest College, for which Spiezo served as executive director, in Elizabeth Meade and Suzanne Weaver, eds., *Toolkit for Teaching in a Democratic Academy* (Allentown, PA: Cedar Crest College, 2004).

65. Bharti Jain, "Highest-Ever Voter Turnout Recorded in 2014 Polls, Government Spending Doubled since 2009," *Times of India*, May 13, 2014, http://timesofindia.indiatimes.com/news/Highest-ever-voter-turnout-recorded-in-2014-polls-govt-spending-doubled-since-2009/articleshow/35033135.cms (accessed 5 July 2014).

66. Though Modi himself was cleared in April 2012 of direct culpability in the riots and pograms by a Special Investigation Team constituted by the Supreme Court of India, many critics continued to raise questions about how his leadership may have contributed to the crisis.

67. See, e.g., N.P. Ullekh, "Narendra Modi's Campaigns Play on Fears of the Muslim Minority: Martha Nussbaum," *The Economic Times*, December 15, 2013, http://articles.economictimes.indiatimes.com/2013–12-15/news/45191832_1_tagore-national-role-martha-c-nussbaum (accessed July 5, 2014); and Martha Nussbaum, "Development Is More than Growth," *The Hindu Centre for Politics and Public Policy*, May 8, 2014, http://www.thehinducentre.com/verdict/commentary/article5985379.ece (accessed July 5, 2014).

68. Nussbaum had earlier highlighted the national press as one of the very positive forces for democracy and pluralism in India, even with respect to the Gujarat pograms. See her *Clash Within* (see n. 1), 30–31, 47–48, and passim.

69. Berger, *Attention Deficit Democracy* (see n. 19), 4–5. As noted briefly earlier, Berger distinguishes the political, the social, and the moral as a way to clarify what he regards as a highly problematic lumping of all three together as "the civic."

Sacred Sites and Staging Grounds

THE FOUR GUIDING OBJECTIVES OF CIVIC ENGAGEMENT IN THE RELIGION CLASSROOM

Ellen Posman with Reid B. Locklin

MOST READERS OF this volume will know what it is like on the first day of a religion class[1]: students are nervous. Some are nervous because they feel they are at a disadvantage, having been raised outside any particular religious commitments. These same students may in turn be nervous because they are concerned they will be preached to and encouraged to practice a religion. Others who have faith commitments are often equally nervous due to the rumors that religious studies—or even theology—classes are antagonistic to faith and challenge it; some students are cautioned by family members or faith-based organizations not to take such classes. In the case of theology or ethics courses in confessional contexts, many of these fears may be even more pronounced. Some students arrive at class with relativistic worldviews and are loath to take definite positions, whether on belief or morality, about anything; and again other students with deeply held faith commitments may be afraid of having that faith challenged. Finally, whether in a secular religious studies class or a theology course, students may be afraid to share deeply held questions or convictions out of fear of what other students may think.

All these factors pose unique challenges in terms of pedagogical choices in religion classes, but they also provide unique opportunities, not only for teaching content but also for developing such civic capacities as discursive reason, empathy, and the clarification of values. To analyze a piece of literature or a political position can certainly engender critical thinking and allow one to glimpse a different worldview. But when the view being examined is the core of one's own beliefs and values, or one that contradicts those beliefs and values, this allows for a deeper level of inquiry and engagement. Questions of value, relationship, and motivation are never far from the surface in the religion classroom, in a way that renders its approaches at least distinctive, if not unique, among liberal arts disciplines. As stated in the 2007 American Academy of Religion/Teagle White Paper

on the religion major, "If we truly wish for students to engage the tremendous variety of human understandings of life, death, suffering, love and meaning, there
is perhaps no more direct path than through the study of religion."[2]

Moreover, the content of religion classes, across its many methodological approaches, allows for relatively straightforward connections to questions of civic
engagement. Theological ethics, for example, cannot avoid the specific issues
facing our society and can find community partners with whom to work collaboratively on service projects, political activism, or other types of engagement.
Courses on Religion and Culture, World Religions, and Spirituality can also
attend to how religion and spirituality enter into public life. Courses that focus on
religious traditions other than those with which students and faculty personally
identify can bridge differences and work to develop empathy and understanding.
And courses in Sociology of Religion as well as other social scientific approaches
can investigate issues of power and challenge students to examine their own
social location and how such locations function to frame issues of religious identity and political advocacy in the civic sphere.

The previous chapter proposed a heuristic framework—abbreviated as
Complexity-Location-Empathy-Action, or CLEA—to understand the relationship
between higher education and civic engagement by emphasizing four guiding
objectives that overlap and build upon one another: (1) intellectual complexity; (2)
frames of reference and social location; (3) empathetic accountability; and (4) motivated action. Religious studies and theology are by no means the only subjects
that can develop these aspects of civic engagement; surely civic engagement can
be developed across the curriculum. However, religious studies and theology can
make a distinctive contribution to this wider project due to the content of religion
classes and the methods used in them. In this chapter, we illustrate how some of
the aspects of teaching and learning in religion can advance the civic capacities
identified in the CLEA model, attentive both to the function of these pedagogical
methods to the study of religion and their potential to enhance education for civic
engagement across the curriculum. These four capacities, which can function
to frame the teaching of civic engagement in any discipline, assume distinctive
shapes and claim distinctive relevance in religious studies and theology. We conclude the chapter with a few thoughts about the difficult question of assessment.

C: Intellectual Complexity and the Practice
of Deliberative Discourse

As discussed in chapter 1, higher education has traditionally been understood as
supporting the common good and fostering responsible citizenship through its
ability to engage students in analytical thinking in ways that prepare them for

deliberative democracy—that is, by cultivating students' capacities for intellectual complexity. Such analytical thinking can take place in any subject within a liberal arts curriculum. As the influential religion scholar Jonathan Z. Smith is fond of arguing, at the undergraduate level, *"there is nothing that must be taught, there is nothing that cannot be left out,"*[3] because the goal of a liberal arts curriculum is not to cover all the material. Rather,

> What we seek to train in college are individuals who know not only that the world is more complex than it first appears, but also that, therefore, interpretive decisions must be made, decisions of judgment which entail real consequences for which one must take responsibility, from which one may not flee by the dodge of disclaiming expertise.[4]

Yet, transformational learning may be most likely to occur when those interpretive decisions involve an investigation of one's own assumptions, values, and motivations. The more deeply held the assumptions, the more challenging and liberating the critical inquiry can become. While classes in any discipline can and often do challenge assumptions, a religion class must necessarily do so at some level—often at a deep level. Whether these assumptions revolve around an understanding of one's own religion or that of another, religion courses tend to be places where students enter thinking they know the material very well, only to find themselves struggling to understand at greater levels of depth and detail and to apply new methods that function to de-familiarize even what was previously well known.

Pedagogically, religion classrooms can utilize those developing viewpoints through discussions or assignments that require students to reflect on what they have learned, not infrequently in reference to their own beliefs and values. While faith-based institutions and private colleges can do this more overtly, there is no reason why public institutions cannot. Contrary to popular belief, as long as one does not advocate a specific religious viewpoint, nothing in the first amendment prevents college students from exploring their own beliefs and values in light of knowledge gained in the classroom. Barbara Walvoord's book, *Teaching and Learning in College Introductory Religion Courses*, notes exactly this: while most faculty stress that they are teaching critical thinking, meaning analysis of the material, students report goals of both factual knowledge and moral and spiritual development in the classroom.[5] These goals are not as far apart as they may seem. Through facilitated in-class discussions and reflective writing assignments, students can reach a higher level of intellectual complexity by analyzing assigned material as well as their own views.

As Joseph C. Hough, Jr., argues, the project of the University in its inception— discourse about the common good, a central aspect of civic engagement—is itself a theological project.[6] As students construct their own theologies or personal commitments and study the worldviews of others, questions of the common good and deliberation about how to achieve it cannot help but arise. Paula Cooey makes this case particularly clearly in her essay, "The Place of Academic Theology in the Study of Religion from the Perspective of Liberal Education." Though she is writing explicitly with reference to a theology course, her description of topics and assignments itself shows the blurry line between theology and religious studies. The description resonates with the approach of many possible courses on Comparative Religion, Religious History, Biblical Studies, or Religion and Culture:

> The course focuses on the role played by religion in the construction of human identity and the worlds of value in which humans find themselves. It explores foundational narratives of Jewish, Christian, Muslim, and Buddhist traditions as these are appropriated through ritual and practice and reflectively challenged and reconstructed in the present. The last three weeks of the semester are devoted to student presentations in oral and written form on the significance of religion in contemporary life. These projects confront issues such as: religious pluralism in a secular democracy and First Amendment freedoms; the significance of religion for contemporary US politics; religion and racism; religion and the militias; emerging religious traditions; international religious movements; and the role of religion in international conflict . . . the course requires that students think critically and constructively about religious meaning and value in ways that consider explicitly their own possible responsibilities and choices as "co-makers of culture," in relation to the culture in which they live—goals at the very heart of liberal education.[7]

Here one finds many aspects of civic engagement intertwined: The content students are researching concerns the public sphere; students are engaged in critical inquiry related to issues of the common good; and students' own beliefs and values are implicated in such a way as to draw them into further analysis.

Cooey continues:

> The content of what I teach, whether Augustine's theology and Buddhist sutras from the past, or liberation theology, feminist theory, and comparative environmentalist thought of the present, draws on and builds on religious legacies to contemporary culture. By its very nature the content forces questions of meaning and value. As students study formative writings and subsequent reflection upon them in Western or Eastern religious history, they exercise the skills definitive of critical thinking.[8]

Certainly, this involves critical inquiry, both of the material and of one's own deeply held assumptions about meaning. Attending to those issues of meaning overtly through readings, written and oral assignments, and discussion engenders the type of critical thinking necessary for a deliberative democracy.

The classroom in this case can also serve as a model of deliberative discourse in the wider public sphere. In our current polarized society, the opportunities for civil conversations about strongly held convictions are rare. Academic classrooms in general and religion classrooms in particular have a long history of managing discussions about thorny issues within a safe, structured environment where it is acceptable to ask questions and learn others' positions in a nonthreatening way. Religious issues can, in fact, be some of the most divisive of our time, and the opportunity for students to discuss those in a calm, conversational manner rather than through attacks and debates will serve our societies well as these future leaders enter the world of public discourse. Distinct pedagogical techniques used across the curriculum can aid in this process. Setting ground rules for discussion collaboratively with students and community-building exercises in which students come to know one another personally can work to build trust and provide a safe environment for difficult ethical, political, and theological conversations. Whether in religion or another discipline, the classroom is a political space, and the way it is managed can encourage attitudes and skills also applicable in the context of public advocacy and deliberation.

L: Standing Somewhere

Cooey's comments on religion and culture lead us directly to the idea of the investigation of institutional frames and social location. For, as one investigates the role of religion in culture, one cannot avoid the issue of power. Religion courses are distinctively conducive to conversations about institutional structures, hegemonic discourses, and majority/minority politics. Engaging such questions does not detract from, but further deepens, the level of intellectual complexity.

As with intellectual complexity, so also here many disciplines implicate students and learners in conversations about social location, but in the study of religion, such conversations are nearly impossible to avoid. On the one hand, any scholarly approach to religion and culture will raise questions of power dynamics related to race, gender, sexuality, age, and creed with particular urgency. On the other hand, perhaps uniquely, in the discipline of religion such questions of power arise not merely from the particular methodological approaches applied to particular religious traditions, but very often from the traditions themselves. As students examine these issues critically, it will be important for them to examine their own social locations—including their locations vis-à-vis the traditions under examination—and how these affect their own assumptions and viewpoints. While for many faculty members this is an unstated goal of religion courses, there are good reasons to bring it to the forefront and to engage these issues directly in discussion, exercises, and written assignments.

Encouraging students to name social locations and to negotiate questions of ethnic and religious difference will often meet with resistance; arguably, such resistance only underscores its vital importance for contemporary social life. In *The Engaged Sociologist*, for example, Kathleen Odell Korgen and Jonathan M. White draw attention to Nina Eliasoph's study, "Avoiding Politics: How Americans Produce Apathy in Everyday Life." They summarize this study as follows:

> Intensive participant observation of several volunteer and activist organizations led [Eliasoph] to determine that our culture teaches us that political discussions and activism are divisive, fruitless, negative exercises that should be skirted, if at all possible. . . . However "civic" the groups might have been, they did not foster a culture in which members would discuss and debate issues of political significance. The few members of the groups who did bring up political topics of conversation in a "public" setting (in the group, rather than in private conversation) or who did suggest taking political action (other than the "normal" actions on the issues that the activist groups pursued) were discouraged from doing so. It appears to be a norm in American culture to make displays of consensus rather than broach important topics over which people might disagree.[9]

In other words, even in activist organizations, people avoid discussion of "politics". . . and we all know the old adage about discussing politics or religion. They are not "polite" topics of conversation. Yet, they deal with the deep assumptions driving our public choices, as well as local, national, and global cultures. Conversations about social location, not to mention religion, can be difficult and divisive. But that is exactly why it is our responsibility to prepare students for public life by providing classrooms in which we can broach these topics even— perhaps especially—when there is no consensus. Here pedagogy, intellectual complexity, and social location all overlap.

Religion departments can take this on topically by offering courses on Religion and Gender, Sexuality, Race, Class, or Nationality, and as such can examine the institutional power structures endemic to religion and how that influences society. But these topics can be broached in any class from Theological Ethics or Comparative Ethics to Biblical (or Scriptural) Studies to community-based learning courses. Any course that entails some analysis of religion and culture, in fact, also opens the door to inquiries about social location and frames of reference. Courses involving religious history, literature, law, or ritual ideally foster open discussions about who within a particular religious tradition instituted practices and structures, and whom those practices and structures benefit.

One of the criticisms of early work in religious studies was that scholars viewed religious traditions as ahistorical, apolitical, and consensual. Too many accounts of Hinduism or Judaism, for example, have been written from the perspective of Brahmin or Orthodox male clergy, and these accounts further perpetuate ingrained hierarchies and mislead the public about the complex, pluriform character of these traditions. Thus a main task of religious studies from the mid-twentieth century on has been to unmask the power dynamics involved in religions that reveal issues of social location.[10] Moving from issues of power dynamics and social location within religious traditions to those within society is a fruitful move for the purposes of civic engagement, and exercises centering on social location can help students find out where they are privileged, who in society is disadvantaged, and how to utilize their power effectively. At a meta-level, investigating the discipline of religious studies itself and even the structures of traditional university pedagogy with students in open, honest discussion can once again influence students' awareness of power and privilege, deepen their skills of critical analysis, and motivate them to work in society to create more equal and just systems.

E: Religion, Imagination, and Empathy

A recent study at the University of Michigan found college students today to be less empathetic than students twenty to thirty years ago:

> Compared to college students of the late 1970s, the study found, college students today are less likely to agree with statements such as "I sometimes try to understand my friends better by imagining how things look from their perspective" and "I often have tender, concerned feelings for people less fortunate than me."[11]

If accepted, sociological studies such as these provide evidence of a problem regarding the development of empathy in the current generation. As social scientists ponder what may have caused this decline, educators for our part need to consider how to counteract this decline and to institute practices directed specifically to the development of empathy. This is particularly true for higher education. With a goal of fostering citizenship or civic engagement, empathy is a key quality: civic engagement, by definition, entails a sense of caring about the common good and therefore about others' needs in addition to one's own. This is yet another area in which religion courses can be particularly helpful, both in content and in pedagogy. For the discipline of religion locates itself squarely within a broader project of fostering understanding across boundaries of difference: differences of language and culture, differences of religious traditions, and differences between the emic perspectives of adherents and etic perspectives of scholarly study. Insofar as difference is constitutive of the field, so also is empathy.

The decline in college students' ability to empathize with others may be tied to a general critique of recent trends in higher education. In recent decades, critics contend, higher education has been subsumed by cultural shifts toward individualism, materialism, and corporatization. Such shifts accompany a welcome expansion of the student body, as previously excluded demographic groups enter college and university in greater numbers. In light of both trends, however, colleges are often pressured to offer more career-oriented coursework and fewer traditional liberal arts–style courses aimed at moral and civic development, once the bedrocks of higher education.

Still, civic engagement is explicitly named or at least alluded to in most college or university mission statements, and numerous initiatives have emerged intentionally to restore its place in higher education.[12] Civic engagement includes making decisions about a community in which others are different from oneself. To do so effectively, one must be able to evaluate issues in terms of one's own interests but also be able to see issues from multiple perspectives. This is the goal of a liberal education in general, and many institutions list an ability to view issues from multiple perspectives as a specific learning outcome. There is an unstated notion that this can be done cognitively, that one can memorize how others view an issue or intellectually analyze how others would view an issue. This can be the case, and scholars have differentiated between cognitive empathy (role-playing) and affective empathy (feeling how another feels).[13] But an empathy that results in concrete action would seem to involve both cognition and emotion. Beyond knowledge or analytical skills, empathy relates to attitudes we expect from university or college graduates. The American Council on Education (ACE), for example, has compiled measurable learning outcomes for knowledge, skills, and attitudes in international education.[14] While there is sometimes wariness about admitting that higher education aims at specific attitudes in addition to knowledge and skills, this has been a central mission of education, perhaps precisely because of its historical mission of preparing citizens for democratic participation. Some scholars have specifically advocated for empathy training as a central part of education for democracy.[15]

Religion classrooms can function to nurture both cognitive and affective empathy among students. To start with, comparative religion courses introduce students to various perspectives, importantly including the base assumptions and values that inform decision-making. Learning those various worldviews allows students to enter into a new perspective cognitively and imaginatively.

Cognitively, students learn the worldviews of various religions and can learn as well as analyze various positions and points of view. Ninian Smart famously refers to the method of learning world religions descriptively as "structured empathy."[16] In this phenomenological method, students learn the myths, rituals, ethics, experiential accounts, and institutional structures of various religions, getting a sense of the whole worldview.

Crossing over to a different perspective may consist primarily in a cognitive shift of frame, but it can also—intentionally or unintentionally—involve the student at an affective and imaginative level. Some scholars have tied literature to empathy education precisely because of its relationship to imagination. The ability to imagine a literary character from the character's perspective, it is claimed, can increase empathy in other contexts as well. As the educational philosopher Maxine Greene states,

> One of the reasons I have come to concentrate on imagination as a means through which we can assemble a coherent world is that imagination is what, above all, makes empathy possible. It is what enables us to cross the empty spaces between ourselves and those who we teachers have called "other" over the years. If those others are willing to give us clues, we can look in some manner through the strangers' eyes and hear through their ears. That is because, of all our cognitive capacities, imagination is the one that permits us to give credence to alternative realities.[17]

In literature, scholars point to the ability of narrative phrases such as "once upon a time" as a way to enter into a world of imagination.[18] The religious myths of creation *in illo tempore* strike a similar cord.

In specialized Religion and Literature or Religion and Film courses, a student's imagination is activated directly, and she or he is invited to enter imaginatively into other religious worlds. Here the methods of literature and, in a similar way, film can be utilized in a religious studies classroom to enhance empathic understanding. But this is not the exclusive preserve of courses devoted explicitly to literature or film. Faculty can incorporate literature or films into course material for many different courses in religious studies. Moreover, the primary texts of many religions are themselves forms of literature that ask students to imagine worldviews from different times or places. The phenomenological method of comparative religion is in this way an act of imagination that works in much the same way that literature does to enhance empathy.

Certain caveats need to be made at this point. If the goal is empathy, and the method is imagination, then textbook descriptions are not ideal ways of imagining other religious worldviews. Asking students to memorize concepts and names of ritual practices will not generate the same type of empathic understanding.

While there is worth in providing religious literacy and a general awareness of the main features of the world's religions, such pedagogies may not fully open up religious worlds imaginatively in a way that allows students to develop empathy. If textbooks are to be used, they should ideally incorporate voices from within the tradition, and, again ideally, a diverse range of such voices.[19] In her book, *Understanding Other Religious Worlds*, Judith Berling explains the ways in which pedagogy must accompany content in teaching comparative religion. She not only cautions faculty to avoid textbook- and lecture-based memorization of concepts, but she advocates a variety of methods that can be incorporated in order to open up imaginative possibilities and allow for empathic development. These include the use of primary texts, literature, film and video, site visits, and guest lecturers from members of religious communities.[20]

It is perhaps telling that Berling makes her recommendations not in the context of a secular department of religious studies but in the confessional context of the Graduate Theological Union. Theological education, from ethics to spirituality, arguably provides a particularly rich context for the development of empathy. As students delve into core religious beliefs and morals, love and compassion for others are key virtues, and the cultivation of these virtues is often an explicit aim of theological education. At the same time, as noted in the AAR/Teagle White Paper, there has been a steady shift in even confessional colleges and universities from a "seminary model" to a "comparative model" of education in religion, as they increasingly focus "on promoting student understanding of the beliefs, practices, and histories of multiple religious traditions in a comparative context."[21] Such a movement can also be discerned in Christian and Jewish seminary contexts themselves, wherein "Multifaith Education" has emerged as a desideratum for individual institutions and for such accrediting agencies as the Association of Theological Schools.[22] Insofar as a comparative model is pursued in an explicitly confessional context, there arise distinct possibilities for distortion in light of a triumphalist or missionary agendas, but also distinct opportunities to reflect explicitly on questions of faith identity and moral obligation in relation to religious difference. It also implicates students in a deeper engagement with questions of location, insofar as participants in Multifaith Education often find themselves struggling as much or more with the intrafaith diversity of their own traditions than the interfaith diversity they experience in dialogue or collaboration with religious others.[23]

Pedagogical methods in the secular religious studies classroom can also be helpful for moral and empathic development, including the cultivation of affective connections across boundaries of difference. Students have noted that their own reasons for taking religion classes in college and university are frequently less for the development of critical thinking and writing skills—that is, those objectives most often cited by faculty—and more for personal reasons, to investigate one's own spirituality and core values.[24] Many faculty accept this as an appropriate byproduct, but such faculty can also, even in a secular context, work on moral development and help students to develop compassion and empathy. Even basic but in-depth discussions of the deeper meaning of these religious virtues and the various ways such words have been interpreted can be helpful in that endeavor, again bridging critical inquiry and moral development. Learning to discuss subjects among others with deeply held yet diverse worldviews allows for the understanding of one another as classmates, and can be used as a baseline from which to show empathy toward members of any religion or community. As such, cognitive understanding opens into a deeper, affective connection: Students ideally come to imagine themselves not merely as spectators of these religious others but as joined in a relationship of shared community and co-responsibility.

As an objective oriented toward civic engagement, empathy cannot stop with imaginative connection and mutual understanding; it must, ideally, open into actual, lived accountability across boundaries of acknowledged difference. For this reason, as the economist David P. Levine has pointed out, the educator must aim not for total identification of self and other but for "a kind of identification that is consistent with, rather than destructive of, difference."[25] He writes:

> Empathy begins when we enter into the mental state of another person. This is done, however, in a way that acknowledges the other's experience is not our own but something separate and distinct from it. . . . In empathizing, we do not ask how would I feel were I in your situation; we ask how you feel in your situation. This is not, however, something we can know from introspection but rather something we can only find out.[26]

It seems self-evident that the kind of empathy described by Levine, in which one becomes accountable to another precisely as different from the self, is most likely to be achieved through the formation of actual relationships across boundaries of religious, ethnic, and gender difference.[27] Such relationship-formation can take place in classroom settings, as already noted, particularly where students identify with a range of religious traditions or none at all. But it may also implicate teacher and learner alike in the wider collaborative work of service and advocacy in a community wider than that of the classroom.

A: *The Religion Classroom as Site and Staging Ground*

Developing the skills for participation in civic life in a democracy has long been a stated goal of higher education, and traditionally that has meant cultivating the skills of critical inquiry, which we have argued here can only be enhanced by critically examining and fostering discussion of social location as well as by cultivating empathetic accountability. But teaching deliberation is not the same as fostering actual habits of civic participation. One way to address this is fairly simple, if also problematic: namely, one can assign such participation as a course requirement, so that students gain direct experience in one or more forms of political or social engagement.

What comes to mind when one hears about civic engagement in general, and political engagement in particular, is action. It brings to mind town hall meetings, community organizing, citizen letters, petitions, voting drives, and protests. Some might say that no matter how much one is aware of civic issues and cares about them, it is not civic engagement until it involves some form of public action. Religion classrooms can, of course, encourage such action in many respects. They may examine religious teachings about social responsibility and the requirement to act upon one's deepest values and convictions, in the hopes that this may arouse interest in some form of service or public advocacy. More than this, such courses may actually require motivated action as an assignment. Students can reach out to the campus community as a model for subsequent engagement in the civic sphere or can even reach out to the wider community as students. They may organize interreligious dialogues on issues in the community, educate the public on an ethical issue, write to legislators, compose op-ed pieces for newspapers, start petitions, or work alongside an organization as a way to learn more about a civic issue. However, assigning the action itself is not engagement in the fullest sense and may not be appropriate to a university context, unless one purpose is to learn—to learn about civic issues, to learn about ethics or social responsibility, to learn about the dynamics of religious diversity, or perhaps all of these. From one point of view, motivated action builds upon intellectual complexity, location, and empathetic accountability; but it can also precede these capacities and serve as a catalyst for them.

In present-day university settings, the phrase "motivated action"—and particularly action aimed at the common good—very often translates to various community-based, community-engaged, or service-learning methods. Korgen and White note the rise of community-based learning opportunities and situate that rise as part of a goal of increasing civic engagement on college campuses: "University administrative leaders also now realize the importance of teaching students how to effectively fulfill their obligations as citizens. Today, 231 state colleges and universities participate in the American Democracy Project, which focuses on providing service learning opportunities for students."[28] The *learning* is key to the notion of community-based learning; this is what distinguishes it from simple community service and what ties it to the cognitive goal of furthering understanding of civic issues and to related objectives of critical inquiry, social framing, and empathic accountability. One volume dedicated to concepts and models of community-based learning in religious studies defines it as

> a type of experiential education in which students participate in service to the community and reflect on their involvement in such a way as to gain further understanding of course content and of the discipline and its relation to social needs and an enhanced sense of civic responsibility.[29]

Critical reflection on service experience is an important aspect of this exercise, as is the requirement that the assigned service be related to course content.

How does community-based learning fit into the religious studies classroom? It would seem to be a natural fit given the long-standing emphasis on service in many religious traditions and the fact that many service opportunities available for students already take place via faith-based organizations. Fred Glennon conducted a survey of religious studies professors engaged in community-based learning and found that faculty use this pedagogical method in all types of institutions (public, private, church-related) and in all kinds of courses (biblical studies, theology, introduction to religion, world religions, ethics, ritual studies, and more).[30] For these professors, community-based learning as a pedagogy fulfills not only academic objectives of mastery of content and critical thinking but also overtly civic objectives of promoting change in student values and student perspectives on social issues, encouraging citizenship, and promoting social change.[31]

In these ways, community-based learning as a pedagogy for civic engagement for religion is efficient and valuable, as it can encompass all of the guiding objectives for teaching civic engagement that we identified in this and the previous chapter. Reflection on service, the connections to course content, and the social issues involved promote deep levels of critical inquiry and provide classes with textual and experiential material from which to engage issues and practice deliberative democracy in the classroom. Direct engagement with community partners allows for critical investigation into social location, and readings and discussions with students on the nature of service and its inherent power dynamics can be truly transformative. Community-based learning, when done with true community partners, can be a forum for exploring these power dynamics and can allow students to further discern their distinct locations as university students.

But beyond these more cognitive possibilities are possibilities for affective change. Not only can community-based learning enhance empathy by providing students with opportunities to relate to actual people of other religions and backgrounds and by further grasping the effects of social structures, but researchers have also found affective and behavioral changes in students' attitudes toward citizenship. One study found that when involved in community-based learning, students "are more likely to see themselves as connected to their community, to value service, to endorse systemic approaches to social problems, to believe that communities can solve their problems, and to have greater racial tolerance."[32] Such studies suggest greater empathy as well as habits of citizenship being formed through interactions with community partners.

However, we should not assume that community-based learning, as one ideal, represents a form of panacea, or the only way to cultivate motivated action in the religion classroom. In fact, there are those who are concerned that the recent focus on community service in institutions of higher education comes at the expense of learning more old-fashioned political activism and engagement. Douglas Jacobsen and Rhonda Hustedt Jacobsen, for example, have written that:

> Overall rates of civic involvement on the part of young adults are lower than in the past, and many young people seem to be more interested in pursuing nonpolitical forms of engagement than in political action. One report states somewhat ominously that although "young people are being trained in the habits of civic participation [they] are not learning the ropes of political activism—and it appears to be taking a toll." Other social activists charge that higher education is largely to blame, having "largely side-stepped the political dimensions of civic engagement." This led activists to frame the discussion in terms of an impending crisis of democracy.[33]

Can religious studies classrooms engage students in these more political habits of civic engagement? Certainly. In fact, some of the aforementioned community-based learning projects result in advocacy projects as part of that service. But to innovate further, we may need to think beyond essays, tests, and, yes, even community service. Earlier, we mentioned community organizing, citizen letters, voting drives, petitions, and protests as traditional modes of civic engagement. Can these be utilized as part of furthering knowledge about religion or religions? In some theology and religious studies courses, students can identify issues that matter to particular religious groups and get involved to better analyze why that religious group is concerned with the specific issue. Perhaps students can express their own commitments through such direct forms of civic participation as letters to the editor, guerilla theater, or public education. There is a wide range of possibilities, but, as with community-based learning, it is important that the connections to course content be clear, relevant, and well integrated, rather than tacking on service or activism for its own sake.

Such a task becomes considerably easier if we broaden the notion of "religion" to include civil religion both as a phenomenon in itself and in terms of how religious beliefs and values often motivate public action. This can be examined in the United States or contrasted with other societies, and an experiential foray into public life can only increase one's understandings of the implicit beliefs, values, and norms associated with it. The tools of religious studies can be applied to almost any form of political action, as students might be asked analyze a pro-life march through the perspective of ritual studies or to identify elements of community-definition in immigration debates. Participation in secular forms of civic engagement may, from this point of view, be just as fruitful for considering the nature and function of religion in society as participating in an overtly religiously based activism.

We might also consider the "civic" in its broadest sense and consider forms of engagement with all varieties of "the wider community" that might constitute contributions to public deliberation and the common good. In the world of blogs and wikis and social media, there are many ways to contribute to and influence society. Requiring students to update Wikipedia entries, to blog about social issues related to class, or to comment on online articles in intelligent, critical ways can all be ways of developing habits of civic engagement and can easily be tied to the content of many religion courses. Motivated action requires students to develop habits of engagement that can express knowledge from class, build on it, or form the basis of it, depending on how it is used. The key factor is that the action functions both as a habituating practice in its own right and as a resource for deepening the intellectual engagement that lies at the center of the university project.

A Note on Assessment

Once a value like empathetic accountability or motivated action is admitted as an objective of a university course, the question of assessment follows almost immediately thereafter.[34] Indeed, one of the reasons that intellectual complexity is often privileged in discussions of the university's public role is no doubt the fact that this capacity may seem more accessible to direct evaluation. As we have noted, many scholars in the discipline understand the academic study of religion, as distinct from religious adherence, precisely in terms of critical analysis.[35] Though the boundaries between analysis and adherence are arguably more permeable in the study and teaching of theology, in that case too critical reflection, argument, and analysis assume central, even constitutive importance.[36] As well illustrated by Barbara Walvoord's 2008 study, instructors in both disciplines possess a significant repertoire of pedagogical tools to promote these capacities, including well-worn techniques of Socratic dialogue, essay assignments that emphasize comparison and argument, weekly journals, group presentations, debates, and a variety of examination formats, as well as more innovative methods that incorporate site visits, online portfolios, interactive agenda-building exercises, and student-led discussion.[37] Such methods generally respect the boundaries of the classroom as a site of critical inquiry, and they are, on the whole, conducive to evaluation and assessment.

With regard to the other capacities we have specified, the questions become more complex. How can an instructor assess empathy? How does one grade students' participation in community service or political activism? The difficulty of assessing civic learning outcomes is widely acknowledged in the literature on community-based learning.[38] On the level of the individual student or course group, as already noted, the dilemma of assessment is addressed by evaluating students' critical reflection on service rather than the service itself. When such reflection activities precede, accompany, and conclude the course, instructors can access students' developing articulations of capacities such as empathy or critical awareness of social location and the ability to relate these capacities to course content, if not the capacities themselves.[39] At an institutional level, faculty and student affairs professionals at Indiana University–Purdue University Indianapolis have developed an integrated series of quantitative self-reports, narrative prompts and interview protocols to assess students on a "Civic-Minded Graduate Scale."[40]

One difficulty with such assessments of civic capacities is that they often rely on one or another form of self-reporting by students. And these, as demonstrated by Nicholas A. Bowman, often reveal a weak correlation to the results of more quantitative, longitudinal studies.[41] At the same time, as Bowman has also shown, such longitudinal studies appear to verify a strong correlation between such desirable civic outcomes as empathetic accountability and motivated action and certain types of learning activities in college and university, such as interpersonal diversity experiences.[42] The tension here is similar to that adduced by Barbara Walvoord as the "great divide" between students' desires for spiritual growth and professors' goals of critical inquiry in introductory religious studies and theology classes. As already noted, students in such courses not only desire but also frequently report significant development in their personal values as a result of their academic work, notwithstanding faculty intentions.[43] Following Walvoord's analysis, such development may follow from at least two factors. First of all, critical inquiry into questions of value itself promotes clarification, revision, and affirmation of students' own commitments. Beyond this, many religious studies and theology instructors articulate what Walvoord calls "sub rosa" hopes that students in their courses may come to affirm such broadly democratic values as tolerance and sympathy for perspectives other than their own. In many cases, such instructors may endeavor to create safe spaces for students to engage in explicit reflection about their own values and spiritual development.[44]

The assessment of civic engagement objectives in the religion classroom can, then, take place in several different ways and on multiple levels. Skills in social framing and values such as empathy—as well as the application of course theory to particular instances of motivated action—can become the subject of explicit reflection, evaluated according to relatively familiar rubrics of detail, complexity, and analytic depth. Alternatively, the instructor can articulate to students the desired civic outcomes of their academic work and/or provide safe spaces for conversation and reflection. Either way, the question of assessment tends to return us to various forms of intellectual complexity as the primary focus of evaluation and other values as an indirect object of inquiry, accessible primarily through the student's reflective discourse. This, we suggest, is perfectly appropriate, insofar as disciplined awareness of social location, empathetic accountability, and a willingness to engage in motivated action represent the complex foundations and true depth of critical thinking, rather than its opposite.

Conclusion

The disciplines of religious studies and theology are ideally situated at a time when there is a renewed conversation about the mission of higher education to develop good citizenship in students. While any discipline can and should focus on critical inquiry, social framing, empathic accountability, and motivated action, religion is a natural fit for these processes. Its unique contribution cannot be located in one particular methodology or locus of inquiry. Instead, in the context of civic engagement, religious studies stands out by the cumulative weight of the various activities that define study in the discipline: adjudicating competing value claims, addressing questions of power as these are embedded in histories and structures, imaginatively crossing boundaries of religious and cultural difference, and engaging directly with particular traditions and communities in the civic sphere through service, public education, and/or social media. As with the four core capacities articulated in the first chapter under the rubric of CLEA, so also here one may wonder whether it is possible for any particular class to engage all of these strategies. But it is difficult to imagine any course in contemporary theology or religious studies that could evade them altogether.

In each case, moreover, the strategies detailed briefly herein—and those described in more detail in the chapters that follow—will be even more transformative when they self-consciously advert to the distinctive subjectivities of students and teachers as the very focus of analysis. In the words of Parker Palmer:

> The orthodoxy of objectivism insists that we can know the world only by distancing ourselves from it, separating our internal lives from the external objects we want to know. Such objectivism is morally deforming because its distancing us from knowledge prevents a moral engagement with the world we study and [prevents us from] taking responsibility for it. One of the most important contributions our religious and spiritual traditions can make through dialogue on our campuses is the alternative epistemologies they offer which are more capacious, more relational, and more responsive than classic objectivism.[45]

Rather than shying away from interrogating our own assumptions, beliefs, and values, successful pedagogies in religious studies classrooms—or elsewhere—can deepen inquiry, acknowledge social locations, increase empathy, and develop habits of civic participation. These pedagogies begin in the religion classroom, but they should not end there.

Notes

1. In this chapter, we use the term "religion" when discussing issues pertaining to both the disciplines of religious studies and theology. When it is necessary to distinguish them from one another, one or the other term will be used. This should not be read to imply that there are no significant differences: A more detailed discussion of the different levels of normativity in these diverse approaches is available in Thomas Pearson's chapter 13, later in this volume.

2. American Academy of Religion/Teagle Working Group, "The Religion Major and Liberal Education—A White Paper," American Academy of Religion. https://www.aarweb.org/sites/default/files/pdfs/About/Committees/Academic Relations/Teagle_WhitePaper.pdf (accessed July 6, 2014).

3. Jonathan Z. Smith, *On Teaching Religion* (New York: Oxford University Press, 2013), 13.

4. Ibid., 14.

5. Barbara Walvoord, *Teaching and Learning in College Introductory Religion Courses* (Malden, MA: Blackwell Publishing, 2008), 20–22.

6. Joseph C. Hough, Jr. "The University and the Common Good," in *Theology and the University: Essays in Honor of John Cobb, Jr.*, ed. David Ray Griffin and Joseph C. Hough, Jr. (Albany: State University of New York Press, 1991), 121.

7. Paula Cooey, "The Place of Academic Theology in the Study of Religion from the Perspective of Liberal Education," in *Religious Studies, Theology, and the University: Conflicting Maps, Changing Terrain*, ed. Linell E. Cady and Delwin Brown (Albany: State University of New York Pess, 2002), 182.

8. Ibid.

9. Kathleen Odell Korgen and Jonathan M. White, *The Engaged Sociologist* (Thousand Oaks, CA: Pine Forge Press, 2011), 55.

10. See Judith A. Berling, *Understanding Other Religious Worlds: A Guide for Interreligious Education* (New York: Orbis Books, 2004), 42–45.

11. "Empathy: College Students Don't Have As Much As They Used To," University of Michigan News Service, May 27, 2010, http://ns.umich.edu/htdocs/releases/story.php?id=7724 (accessed March 10, 2012).

12. See, e.g., the Association of American Colleges and Universities, "Liberal Education and America's Promise (LEAP): Essential Learning Outcomes," AAC&U. http://www.aacu.org/leap/vision.cfm (accessed July 23, 2014).

13. Roslyn Arnold, *Empathic Intelligence* (Sydney, Australia: University of New South Wales Press, 2005).

14. See "ACE/FIPSE Project on Assessing International Learning," American Council on Education: Leadership and Advocacy. http://www.acenet.edu/newsroom/Pages/ACEFIPSE-Project-on-Assessing-International-Learning.aspx (accessed July 23, 2014).

15. Michael E. Morrell, *Empathy and Democracy: Feeling, Thinking, and Deliberation* (State College: Pennsylvania State University Press, 2010).

16. Ninian Smart, *Worldviews: Cross-Cultural Explorations of Human Beliefs* (New York: Pearson, 1999), 13.

17. Maxine Greene, *Releasing the Imagination: Education, the Arts, and Social Change* (San Francisco: Jossey-Bass, 1995), 3.

18. See Arnold, *Empathetic Intelligence*, 11, 40, 63–64, 82–83, and passim.

19. Berling, *Understanding Other Religious Worlds*, 97.

20. Ibid., 81–109.

21. AAR/Teagle Working Group, "Religion Major"(see n. 2), 6.

22. See especially Justus Baird, "Multifaith Education in American Theological Schools: Looking Back, Looking Ahead," *Teaching Theology and Religion* 16.4 (October 2013–10): 309–21. This themed issue of *Teaching Theology and Religion* includes essays on a number of initiatives in Multifaith Education, as well as specific proposals for the curriculum and the classroom.

23. Ibid., 315–16.

24. Walvoord refers to the difference between faculty and student expectations on this issue as "the great divide." See her *Teaching and Learning* (see n. 5), 13–55, and the further discussion hereafter.

25. Daniel P. Levine, *The Capacity for Civic Engagement: Public and Private Worlds of the Self* (New York: Palgrave Macmillan, 2011), 173.

26. Ibid., 79.

27. This intuitive conclusion receives some support from both the anecdotal experience of those working in multifaith education and longitudinal studies of diversity experiences in college and university. See, e.g., Baird, "Multifaith Education," 316, and Nicholas A. Bowman, "Promoting Participation in a Diverse Democracy: A Meta-Analysis of College Diversity Experiences and Civic Engagement," *Review of Educational Research* 81.1 (March 2011): 29–68.

28. Korgen and White, *The Engaged Sociologist*, 56–57.

29. Julie A. Hatcher and Robert G. Bringle, "Bridging the Gap Between Service and Learning," *College Teaching* 45 (1997): 153, cited in *From Cloister to Commons: Concepts and Models for Service-Learning in Religious Studies*, ed. Richard Devine, Joseph A. Favazza, and F. Michael McLain (Washington, DC: American Association for Higher Education, 2002), 1.

30. Fred Glennon, "Service-Learning and the Dilemma of Religious Studies: Descriptive or Normative?" in *Cloister to Commons*, ed. Richard Devine et al., 17.

31. Ibid., 18.

32. Dwight E. Giles, Jr., and Janet Eyler, "A Service Learning Research Agenda for the Next Five Years." *New Directions for Teaching and Learning* 73 (1998): 66, cited in Glennon, "Service-Learning," 15.

33. Douglas Jacobsen and Rhonda Hustedt Jacobsen, *No Longer Invisible: Religion in University Education* (New York: Oxford University Press, 2012), 109. See also Ben Berger, *Attention Deficit Democracy: The Paradox of Civic Engagement* (Princeton and Oxford: Princeton Unviersity Press, 2011), esp. 41–43.

34. For another perspective on the issue of assessment of motivated action, see Bhattacharyya and Clingerman, in this volume, 218–21.

35. A compact, accessible presentation of such an argument is available in *Rethinking Religion: A Concise Introduction* by Will Deming (New York and Oxford: Oxford University Press, 2005).

36. See, e.g., Ibid., 20–21, and especially Berling, *Understanding Other Religious Worlds* (see n. 10), 49–64.

37. These methods are described in the course of examining a number of case studies in Walvoord, *Teaching and Learning* (see n. 5), chapters 4, 5 and 6. Also see Barbara E. Walvoord and Virginia Johnson Anderson, *Effective Grading: A Tool for Learning and Assessment in College*, 2nd ed. (San Francisco: Jossey-Bass, 2010).

38. E.g., Dan W. Butin, "Of What Use Is It? Multiple Conceptualizations of Service Learning within Education," *Teachers College Record* 105.9 (December 2003–12): esp. 1688–1690; and R. W. Hildreth, "Theorizing Citizenship and Evaluating Public Service," *PS: Political Science and Politics* 33.3 (September 2000–09): 627–32.

39. See Janet Eyler, "Reflection: Linking Service and Learning—Linking Students and Communities," *Journal of Social Issues* 58.3 (2002): 517–34; Sarah L. Ash and Patti H. Clayton, "The Articulated Learning: An Approach to Guided Reflection and Assessment," *Innovative Higher Education* 29.2 (Winter 2004): 137–54; Sarah L. Ash, Patti H. Clayton, and Maxine P. Atkinson, "Integrating Reflection and Assessment to Capture and Improve Student Learning," *Michigan Journal of Community Service-Learning* 11.2 (Spring 2005): 49–60.

40. Kathryn S. Steinberg, Julie Hatcher, and Robert G. Bringle, "Civic-Minded Graduate: A North Star," *Michigan Journal of Service-Learning* 18.1 (Fall 2011): 19–33; and the Center for Service & Learning, "Civic-Minded Graduate," Indiana University-Perdue University Indianapolis. http://csl.iupui.edu/teaching-research/opportunities/civic-learning/graduate.shtml (accessed July 6, 2014). See also the rubric developed in the American Association of Colleges and Universities, "Civic Engagement Value Rubric," AAC&U. http://www.aacu.org/value/rubrics/pdf/All_Rubrics.pdf (accessed July 23, 2014).

41. See Nicholas A. Bowman, "Validity of College Self-Reported Gains at Diverse Institutions," *Educational Researcher* 40.1 (2011): 22–24; Nicholas A. Bowman,

"Understanding and Addressing the Challenges of Assessing College Student Growth in Student Affairs," *Research and Practice in Assessment* 8.2 (Winter 2013): 5–14.

42. Bowman, "Promoting Participation" (see n. 27), 18–22. Bowman notes, however, that the changes reported by students were again often more significant than the actual changes that could be verified through longitudinal studies.

43. Ibid., 58–63.

44. Ibid., 35–37.

45. Cited in Peter Laurence and Victor H. Kazanjian, Jr., "The Education as Transformation Project" in *Transforming Campus Life*, ed. Vachel W. Miller and Merle M. Ryan (New York: Peter Lang, 2001), 61. The quotation is drawn from the proceedings of a meeting on the topic, "Education as Transformation: Religious Pluralism, Spirituality and Higher Education," on September 27–28, 1998. See Mary Gottman, *Summary Report of the National Gathering* (Wellesley, MA: The Education as Transformation Project, 1998).

*What Practical Strategies and Questions
Emerge from Teaching Civic Engagement
in Religious Studies and Theology?*

Teaching for Civic Engagement

INSIGHTS FROM A TWO-YEAR WORKSHOP

Melissa C. Stewart

AS TEACHERS OUR hope is to develop pedagogies that will (at least in part) encourage students to be engaged citizens. The first chapters of this book, Reid Locklin and Ellen Posman focused on definitions of civic engagement and theories of what it means to be civically engaged. A model of teaching civic engagement was suggested—the CLEA model—which offers four categories of pedagogies of civic engagement: intellectual complexity (C), frames of reference and social location (L), empathic accountability (E), and motivated action (A). The second section, of which this chapter is a part, focuses on concrete classroom practice related to pedagogies for civic engagement. As the first section shows, civic engagement as assessed in a university setting requires a broadened definition. One reason for this is that the classroom may or may not be viewed as a public arena. Whichever side one falls on in this debate, most teachers could agree that the classroom is one significant place where students can learn about the *possibilities* of civic engagement once the students take their place in the public arena.

This insight was the starting point for the research project "Pedagogies for Civic Engagement in Religious Studies," funded by the Wabash Center for Teaching and Learning in Religion and Theology. Nineteen of us participated in the two-year research workshop, several of whom have contributed to this volume. The goals of this grant project were to investigate the meaning of civic engagement in the classroom and to collect ways of promoting civic engagement in religious studies and theology. As part of the project, participants developed both a teaching strategy that we thought might encourage civic engagement and an assessment tool by which to measure any increase in civic engagement, or at least civic-mindedness. I will explore seven of these strategies and their results in detail in this chapter. In our preliminary meetings, held following the 2008 American Academy of Religion meeting in Chicago, we realized right away that

"civic engagement" in relation to the classroom setting took on a different understanding from more formal definitions of civic engagement among political
scientists. We expanded our definition of "pedagogies for civic engagement" to
include four skills that might help a student on the path to becoming civically
engaged: critical inquiry, framing identities, empathetic engagement, and motivated action. Then, after we assessed our individual pedagogical exercises, we
realized there is a wide-ranging variety of assignments that will encourage one,
some, or possibly all skills outlined in the four areas of civic engagement noted
in the CLEA model.

In our assessment, our research group asked several questions of ourselves.
Is teaching the skills required for civic engagement even under the purview of
a religious studies professor? Which best practices in (or out of) the classroom
teach students to be civically minded? Is civic-*mindedness* enough or is *practice* required? Do students have to cross the boundaries of the four-walled classroom to
experience civic engagement in order to learn it? A typology of the assignments
used by the grant participants reveals four general categories: reflective writings;
critical engagement with texts, especially contemporary media; field trips; and
service and experiential learning projects. No one assignment successfully engenders a civically engaged student. Rather, different course projects promote
and possibly teach one or more of the four identified skills.

In this chapter, I look at how the more robust understanding of civic engagement in relation to university classroom education changes how we assess the
successes and failures of the grant participants' array of assignments. The reader
should keep in mind that there is not a one-to-one correlation of type of assignment to one of the four skills required for civic engagement. It will, indeed,
become apparent that seemingly unrelated pedagogies sometimes encouraged
the same skill. For example, both understanding media bias against Muslims
(in-class assignment) and an experiential learning project in a predominantly
Jewish nursing home (out-of-class assignment) may help students understand
how identities are formed, thereby reflecting back to students the importance
of their own social locations. Further, a typology and investigation of the pedagogical strategies show that any particular project often leads to overlapping
experiences of the aforementioned assessment categories or skills, because each
evaluative criterion takes its shape from the others. For example, writing an
informed and persuasive letter to one's congressperson (a clear instance of activism) requires a certain level of critical thinking. And a final related issue is
that the binary definitions of "in" and "out" the classroom break down as the
project results point to the classroom itself as a living, breathing locus of civic
engagement and point to the off-campus sites as places for critical reflection and
places from which to evaluate one's own social location and to be empathetic
with others.

Typology of Pedagogies with Sample Projects from Project Contributors

Pedagogical strategies that could encourage civic engagement range widely on the in-class versus out-of-class spectrum, for example, reflective writings and service learning, respectively. In between the ends of this spectrum, character-izations of the project contributors' pedagogies for civic engagement also include interactions with contemporary media, field trips, and service and experiential learning projects. Therefore, an incomplete typology (is there any other kind?) of pedagogies for civic engagement can be developed, which includes reflective writings; critical engagement with texts, especially contemporary media; field trips; and service and experiential learning projects. Reflective writings include personal reflections on assigned readings and media and pre- and post-writing reflections for assessment of other types of assignments such as service and ex-periential learning projects. Service and experiential learning projects serve as pedagogical strategies to increase student engagement and further augment traditional in-class assignments. By taking students outside of the classroom to learn, these projects extend the boundaries of the traditional classroom space as the place where critical reflection takes place to encompass literally a larger world.

The in-class assignments, broadly speaking, concentrated on the first two evaluative criteria of civic engagement, critical thinking and identity formation, through two types of assignments: subject-centered critical reflection and media interpretation and critique. Some professors in the grant project assigned read-ings and writings concerning other ways to be in the world, while others required analyses of contemporary media journals to understand how cultural identities are created and manipulated. Readings and subject-oriented responses to read-ings examined cross-cultural models of what it means to be religious or ethical, or ways a person could best serve society. Analyses of media assignments ranged from opening the newspaper to Google and YouTube searches to see the role reli-gion plays in civic life and detect the media's role in creating and shaping cultural assumptions about religion and society.

The out-of-class experiences, broadly speaking, emphasized empathetic en-gagement and motivated action (activism) by means of two types of experiences: field trips and experiential/service learning projects. Some professors took stu-dents on traditional field trips but still required preparative readings and subject-oriented reflective writings after the fact, and others required a more substantial involvement in a community-based service project. Service projects were clear ex-amples of motivated action. Both of these types of projects led to critical examina-tion of religion in local communities, thereby helping students cross boundaries by challenging their assumptions about the civic community itself and getting them personally involved. Most obviously in terms of the evaluative criteria we developed, these out-of-class experiences were specifically intended to increase student empathy for those from different faith backgrounds and to increase opportunities for activism.

Reflective Writings

I will summarize examples from all four forms of the pedagogies used by the grant participants: reflective writings; critical engagement with texts, especially contemporary media; field trips; and service and experiential learning projects. One of the grant participants, Clark Chilson, who teaches at University of Pittsburgh, modified an existing assignment and added pre- and post-reflective writing assessments to gauge increased understanding of civic engagement. Chilson wanted to know if a normal exercise in the critical reading of texts, specifically portions from the *Analects* of Confucius, would influence students' understanding of civic engagement. His survey course, Religion in Asia, is designed to introduce students to Hinduism, Buddhism, Confucianism, Daoism, and to a lesser degree Shinto and popular religious practices. Seventy-eight students took the class, and required readings included both primary and secondary readings. Course goals were to help students demonstrate historical knowledge of major events, people, texts, doctrines, concepts, and practices in the religious traditions of Asia, and to help students improve critical thinking skills. As Chilson states in his syllabus, "this course is intended . . . to improve your ability to summarize different points of view, analyze texts, evaluate arguments, and discover new ideas."[1] With regard to civic engagement, Chilson simply wanted students to think about their own roles in society from a Confucian perspective. His teaching strategy involved classroom activities and an essay assignment. He assigned a 1,000- to 1,100-word essay based on the following question: According to the *Analects* of Confucius, how can people best serve the society in which they live? As expressed in both the goals of the class and the grant project, Chilson's main objective in the classroom is to foster critical inquiry by teaching students to identify the complexity of different social, political, and cultural situations and to recognize other frames of reference. Chilson, as he articulated it several times during the grant workshops, argues that "this is the proper purpose of university education, and that the civic virtues such as empathetic engagement and motivated action for the good of society can and should emerge naturally from critical inquiry."[2]

To measure whether his assignments influenced the way students thought about civic engagement, Chilson asked students to answer a self-reflective question in week 1 and week 13 of the course. In week 1, students answered the question "How do you think a person can best serve society?" In week 13, students answered the question "Regardless of Confucianism, how do you think a person can best serve society?" Using grounded theory, Chilson coded the two assessments separately in order to identify changes. He coded the answers ac-cording to the types of answers and repeated words and phrases he received from students, such as "helping others," "open-minded," and "teaching." The answers changed from week 1 to week 13, but not in the ways one might expect. Surpris-ingly, there was a move away from helping others and civic engagement to more self-oriented concerns. The focus shifted to terms such as "pursue self-interests" and "self-cultivation," "use gifts," and "do what you love." The answer "open-minded" occurred most often as the best way "to serve society." By this most students meant you should not judge others; rather, you should try to understand others' perspectives. Chilson was interested in the complete lack of references to "justice" and "peace."

Another grant participant who used reflective writings to encourage civic en-gagement was Helen Rhee. Rhee teaches at Westmont College in Santa Barbara, California. In contrast to Chilson, who used reflective writings to gauge increased understanding of civic engagement from the beginning to the end of a course, Rhee used them specifically to teach a particular understanding of civic engage-ment. She chose her History of World Christianity course, which is required for religious studies majors and meets a general education requirement, to teach students to think globally and historically. The course description emphasizes the roles "surrounding cultures and socio-political contexts" play in developing Christian faith and communities. Related to teaching civic-mindedness, a key objective already embedded in this course is critical, interdisciplinary thinking. In addition, Rhee added two more objectives with specific respect to the grant project: for students (1) to demonstrate increased contextual thinking on how their beliefs, values, ideas, and practices are influenced by social class, gender, ethnicity, culture, and historical moment and how the socio-cultural, political, and religious values and perspectives of a given society shaped Christians in that culture, and (2) to recognize global inequities, injustices, and/or inter-religious issues and commit themselves to thoughtful, concrete responses growing out of their Christian faith. The first speaks directly to identity formation, and the latter to empathetic engagement. It should also be noted that the college-wide rubric used for thinking globally and historically at Westmont College rewards with highest marks those who "empathize with the people of another culture, seeing them from their own point of view without romanticizing," and "demonstrate a commitment to specific actions or changes in lifestyle on the basis of the un-derstanding" of the relationship between thinking globally and historically and Christian action. Students attended ten weekly small discussion groups for which they completed discussion responses to primary sources regarding such topics as just war, pacifism, free will and predestination, social gospel, feminism, evolu-tion, etc. Types of questions included observational, interpretive, analytical, and reflective. Students also wrote two essays, one a book review of a text addressing

one aspect of geographical area of global Christianity and issues related to contextualization, and one take-home essay focusing on how the student's understanding of identity formation had changed and how that understanding might affect
future decisions. With regard to assessment, Rhee was largely pleased with the
quality and depth of answers. Students, in varying degrees, expressed a sophisticated understanding of the complexity of issues and "concern for social justice
(local/global poverty, racial and gender discrimination, etc.) although many of
them lacked concreteness and specificity in articulating appropriate actions or
change of lifestyle or worldview."

Several grant participants assigned students to read the media at large (newspapers, social media, blogs, etc.) to find relevant articles or posts illustrating the
interrelations between religion and contemporary culture in the public arena. I
will summarize two of these. First, Philip Wingeier-Rayo, at that time a professor at Pfeiffer University, chose to focus on his Christianity and Culture course.
Similar to Rhee, mentioned earlier, Wingeier-Rayo's course objectives focused
on teaching identity formation through the exploration of power dynamics and
tensions between a new religion (such as a new Christian mission site) and pre-
existing cultures and religions. The specific assignment was to find three articles
about Christianity or another religion and its struggle with culture. Students
wrote three one-page reflections on how religion related to culture in these news
stories. There were nine students in the class. All identified as active Christians
who would like to serve the church eventually. Students initially resisted the assignment, citing their perceived difficulty of finding religion in the news. Students, due to binary thinking, also originally tended to see religion as its own
category, unrelated to culture or politics. This thinking was evidenced by students in the first assignment only looking to religion sections of newspapers for
articles or using "religion" in the search command on online news sites. In the
next assignment, Wingeier-Rayo encouraged students to look for overlapping stories in general news. By the third assignment students developed a keener sense
of the relationship between religion and culture indicated by choosing articles
with religious undertones. For example, one student wrote a one-page reflection
about Muslims in New York City pressing Mayor Michael Bloomberg to close
public schools at the end of Ramadan and the pilgrimage to Mecca. An article in
the *Wall Street Journal* described this dilemma for the New York City Council that
currently gives recess for certain Jewish and Christian holidays. This is a clear
example of the media representing the relationship between religion and politics.
The student referred to the Muslim holidays as "foreign" holidays, thereby failing
to recognize that the Muslims making the request were most likely U.S. citizens.
His analysis equated U.S. culture with Christianity, thereby missing the power
dynamics between religion and politics. In general, Wingeier-Rayo concluded
that the course objective to help students see connections between religion and

culture was met, but the objective to sensitize the students to the power of the dominant Christian religion in culture was not.

Critical Engagement with Texts

Karen Derris, from the University of Redlands, also assigned students to read articles and further assigned a media analysis journal, where they write a two-page media analysis of a news event for each of the traditions covered in a world religions course. A general goal in her course is to have students learn to critically assess the representations of religious traditions in media. For several years, Derris has been tweaking this assignment. During the first iterations of the assignment, students were only able to apply the new knowledge they gained in class to the articles they studied; that is, they could recognize and explain concepts, practices, and events presented in articles, but students could not critically assess how religious traditions were represented. Derris changed the assignment. She asked students to compare the news coverage of an event in at least two news sources (one preferably from a foreign English-language newspaper). The comparative format helped students to analyze issues of representation. Derris also dedicated an entire class session to practicing media analysis wherein she explained the purpose and approach of the assignment and then broke students up into groups to work on a set of articles about a current issue related to one of the religious traditions studied in the course. Each group reported back, and this allowed all students to see the broad range of possible topics. "By considering differences in information, explanation, description of context, tone, etc. . . . students could identify the choices that were made in how the religious news event was represented."

To gauge results, Derris had students complete a self-assessment of their relationship to the news at the beginning of the semester. Of the twenty-three students in the class, ten reported actively following the news, four of whom explicitly described civic responsibility as their motivation for doing so. The remainder of students reported not following the news because they found it either depressing or unrelated to their world. Nine out of the twenty-three could describe an article on a religious event or issue, five of whom referred to Muslim violence and four of whom recalled national policy debates or sex scandals. The majority understood the news to be shaped by contexts and agendas—although two stated that news reporting was unbiased. Students offered two general reasons why one should follow the news: to understand the power of the media to shape perceptions of the role of religion in world events; and to broaden one's own worldview. After covering Hinduism and Buddhism, Derris assessed the journals in terms of the objectives of the media journal assignments. Three common elements in the journal essays indicated that students were indeed learning to critically evaluate representations of religious traditions in news sources. First, students drew on both national and international news services. Second, they identified clear differences in choices of sources, quotes, background content to stories, and conclusions. Third, students successfully applied class knowledge of traditions to analyze information included and excluded from articles.

Field Trips

The other types of projects focused on out-of-class experiences such as field trips and service learning projects. With regard to field trips, the experience itself was actually part of the objective articulated by those who required them. Another objective, of particular importance for evaluating civic engagement, was increased student empathy for those from different faith backgrounds. Marianne Delaporte at Notre Dame de Namur University teaches a course called Modern Christianity: 1600 to the Present, which includes a group project that explores a non-mainstream Protestant denomination.[3] Her two main goals for this project aim (1) to introduce material often not found in textbooks, because they often end with Vatican II, and (2) to help students engage with the outside world by making connections between what they learn in class and what is going on in society. She made some modifications to her teaching strategy, the group project, in light of the grant's interest in assessing increased critical engagement. The groups chose from five modern denominational categories: Unitarian Universalist, AME, Church of Latter-Day Saints, Seventh-Day Adventist, Pentecostal, and "Megachurch." The nine project requirements were: read and summarize two encyclopedia articles on the denomination; write a two-page history of the group and fill out a template; write a statement of theology of the denomination; attend a service and write a four-page reflective paper; interview two members, one professional (only upper-level students did this part); a multimedia assignment; an oral presentation; a final eight- to ten-page research paper (only upper-level); and a final portfolio. Requirements to be included in the church service report were outlined in detail following "Guidelines for Research" found on the Pluralism Project website (http://pluralism.org/research/guidelines.php). Students had to give field information, make initial observations, describe the service, and then analyze the doctrinal, practical, and sociological aspects of the service. Delaporte assessed her project in fours ways: a question on the final examination; the final paper written by upper-level students; the oral presentations; and a student questionnaire. Through a question on the final examination, she asked students to place their denomination's development within the historical context of the United States that they had covered, or, in other words, to explain how their denomination had been affected by the larger world around it. Delaporte was disappointed that even though many could give the history of their denomination, few were able to link it to the greater history of the United States. Further, many continued all semester to accept denominationally created websites as uninterpreted truth. Lastly, students often presented their denomination's beliefs and policies uncritically.

The upper-level research papers were, on the other hand, more insightful. The personal interview experiences appeared to have the most influence on students. Students empathetically presented their denomination's place in the local history and in the wider world. The oral presentations produced uneven results. Presentation of denominational theologies was shallow, but descriptions of rituals were very detailed, evidencing a high level of engagement on the students' part during the services. The ability to compare these rituals to similar ones in their previous experiences (Catholic or otherwise) appeared to provide the context needed to engage the students. The student evaluations mainly appreciated the opportunity to visit an off-campus site. It is important to note that even though the "field trips" (site visits) were the focus of this example of encouraging civic engagement, specifically encouraging empathetic engagement, Delacorte still assigned extensive research, writing, and reflective writing to make the site visit successful.

Community-Based Learning Projects

Community-based learning projects were another type of out-of-class assignments employed by some of the grant participants. Reid Locklin, a professor at St. Michael's College, University of Toronto, used his course, "Interreligious Dialogue and Practice," to assess the possibility of encouraging civic engagement through religious studies courses.[4] This class is particularly appropriate because one of the objectives of the course is geared toward a civic purpose: namely, "to develop greater sensitivity to the complexity of their own social identities, stronger skills in cross-cultural and interreligious communication, and a richer sense of the important role played by diverse religious persons and institutions in Canadian society." Students undertook three-hour placements each week of the course where they met persons from religious traditions other than their own. Placements were made for the specific semester related to the grant at Baycrest, a medical and long-term care facility that serves a mainly Jewish population; at the University of Toronto Multi-Faith Center; and at the University of Toronto Anti-Racism and Cultural Diversity Office. In preparation for these placements, students studied a variety of primary sources by Jewish, Christian, and Muslim theologians and read public statements by Jewish, Christian, and Muslim leaders and organizations concerning interreligious dialogue. For Locklin the most important criterion for choosing placement sites was which sites best encouraged significant contact with persons and institutions different from students' own traditions. As Locklin states in his initial teaching strategy, "Ideally, students will become more motivated to understand the tradition(s) of their placement institution and/or the clients served by their placement institutions in order to better to fulfill their service assignment, and their academic reflection on interreligious dialogue and practice will, in turn, be informed by the *personal relationships* and the *context of care* they encounter in their placement."

Locklin expected that, in regard to encouraging civic engagement, the placements would most help increase students' empathy for religiously diverse others and framing their own social identities. To assess his class in relation to developing civically engaged students, Locklin administered a final, reflective writing assignment and a final civic engagement survey. In the final, reflective writing assignment, he asked students to review their writing from throughout the term and report their own "Most Significant Change."[5] Eight of ten students completed this task. Six of these wrote that they had developed a greater commitment to common human values such as honesty, human dignity, and integrity. Among other things, several wrote about a greater openness to difference; others discussed greater attention to interpersonal relationships, greater willingness to challenge their own and others' views, and a greater appreciation for difference itself. Several students showed dramatic attitudinal change toward the sheer fact of religious diversity. These students came to appreciate similarities and differences between traditions, and the contextualization of individual religious identities. In the final civic engagement survey the questions were specifically geared to the four areas related to civic engagement as decided in our workshop: critical inquiry, framing identities, empathetic engagement, and motivated action. As stated previously, Locklin expected students to identify framing identities and empathetic engagement as outcomes, but surprisingly students gave highest evaluation to critical thinking and motivated action on a Likert scale, whereas framing identities and empathetic engagement were rated somewhat lower. Locklin suggests that, since most students on the survey didn't list specific courses of future action in their comments, the motivated action that students valued was the service itself, and they were not clear how they might expand their own civic engagement outside of the limited contexts of their service placements. Further, I suggest that the high evaluation given by students to critical thinking indicates Locklin's attention to the importance of accompanying community-based learning projects with primary readings and reflective writings. Altogether, they help develop a civically engagement student. And, once again as we have seen in several of the other projects, there is no direct correlation between traditional assignments and the first two areas of development for civic engagement, namely, critical inquiry and framing identities, nor between out-of-class assignments and the final two categories, namely, empathetic engagement and motivated action. Instead, we find overlap and surprises.

Experiential Learning Projects

In the final project that I will summarize, Forrest Clingerman, who teaches at Ohio Northern University, assigned students to choose an ethical issue discussed in class and to write their U.S. Representative or Senator about it. The assignment requires students to use traditional class assignments such as research, reading, and logic development for the purpose of engagement in the public arena. Clingerman chose his Christian Ethics course for the grant project. The class is divided into three units. The first introduces main ethical theories. The second unit focuses on personal responsibility and moral choices, and the third on social ethics. As part of the Pedagogies for Civic Engagement project, Clingerman added two assignments to the course: a letter to a U.S. Senator or Representative and a reflection paper. These assignments further advanced the overall course objective of evaluating ethical arguments and constructing one's own ethical argument. The specific goals of the letter were to write an argument for concrete action using ethical viewpoints; to examine the role of faith in public policy; and to encourage engagement in public discourse. Students were required to advocate for a particular congressional action; to show awareness of the basic arguments and statistics related to the issue; and to note the current position taken by the politician. Clingerman also assigned a follow-up reflection paper, where students wrote 750 to 1,000 words addressing how faith might influence one's understanding of the issue. In other words, what is the relationship between faith and public policy?

Students wrote letters on numerous issues, from the support of welfare, to increased education spending, to the support of pro-life legislation. In their assessments of the experience (the reflection paper), some students recognized how critical reflection on religion and ethics informed their arguments on public policy. Some students noted the need to get involved since legislation directly affects their lives, and others added that the letter-writing experience taught them to take civic responsibility more seriously. Yet, students were cautious. They noted the difficulty of engaging in civic discourse due to the complex relationship between religion and public policy, where one sometimes feels the pressure to stay "neutral" or to "not offend." And finally, some students worried that letter-writing would have little effect anyway. Once again, we see in Clingerman's assessment of his pedagogical experiment that directed readings and reflective writing combined with an assignment in the public arena (letter to representative) work especially well in developing civic engagement.

Concluding Remarks

All typologies are flawed. The one I have used in this chapter is no exception. Yet both the strengths and weaknesses of a typology help us identify important insights. After reviewing the four categories of assignments employed by the grant participants: reflective writings; critical engagement with texts, especially contemporary media; field trips; and community-based and experiential learning projects, I conclude that no one type of assignment better inculcates civic-mindedness or engagement than another. Rather, a variety of projects will promote and possibly teach one or more of the four identified skills of the CLEA model that together create a civically engaged person. A neat package whereby in-class civic-engagement assignments correlate plainly to critical thinking and forming identities, and out-of-class civic-engagement experiences correlate plainly to empathetic engagement and motivated action, is not possible. In other words, there was no one-to-one correlation of a particular assignment to a particular skill required for civic engagement. Instead, the project leaders in their assessments discovered significant overlap. For example, even though for Delaporte the "field trips" (site visits) were the focus of her project to encourage civic engagement, Delaporte still assigned extensive research, writing, and reflective writing to make the site visit successful.

In fact, multiple strategies appear necessary! Since teaching civic engagement has at least four dimensions, and some pedagogies are more oriented toward one or two of these than other pedagogies, it is important to have a variety of pedagogical tools. And, meanwhile, since each of the four dimensions of civic engagement can be approached through different pedagogies, the teacher has a great deal of flexibility.

Further, we see how a more robust definition of civic engagement as it relates to the university classroom (as established in the first section of this volume) changes how we assess the successes and failures of the grant participants' array of assignments. Because we are not directly in the public arena, but instead are preparing students for the public arena, there are many ways to help inculcate in students civic-mindedness and eventual civic engagement. All of the assignments in some way exposed students to such skills that, added together, would lead to civic engagement. Once again, for example, most grant participants used reflective writings and textual analysis no matter whatever else they required.

The analysis also reveals that seemingly unrelated pedagogies sometimes encouraged the same skill. For example, both Rhee's and Derris's assignments (site visits and media analyses, respectively) resulted in a deeper understanding of the relationship between enculturation and identity formation. Derris's students, due to a comparative media analysis of how other religions are presented, noted the way context shapes cultural representations of religious others. While Rhee's students, through readings and reflective writings on global Christianity and issues related to contextualization, and further reflection on how their understanding of identity formation had changed and how that understanding might affect future decisions, were guided through an analysis and self-reflection on identity formation specifically.

Significantly, an investigation of several of the pedagogical strategies has shown that any particular project often leads to overlapping experiences of the aforementioned assessment categories or skills, because each evaluative criterion takes its shape from the others. Therefore, not only do different types of assignments teach overlapping skills but the reverse is also true; the four skills needed for civic engagement imply each other. They are interrelated skills. For example, as we saw in Clingerman's activism exercise, writing an informed and persuasive letter to one's congressperson requires a certain competency in critical inquiry and reading. And issues of social location further complicated the role students' personal faith played in their advocacy for public policy.

Due to the interrelationships among the skills needed to teach civic engagement, the binary definitions of "in" and "out of" the classroom break down. The project results point to the classroom itself as a living, breathing locus of civic engagement and further point to the off-campus sites as places for critical reflection and places from which to evaluate one's own social location and empathy for others. The idea of the classroom as a place where empathy for others can take place even if critical inquiry is lacking was poignantly made clear by the mixed results of Delaporte's site visit by her lower-level students. Students were not able to compare and contrast the way denominations might be uncritically reporting their own histories on websites with more critical summaries of denominational histories; yet, given their own experiences of ritual in other denominations, the students easily were able to compare these rituals to similar ones in their previous experiences. Students exhibited insights and empathetic understandings of those who are often thought strange and on the margins of Christian sects. Further, the truth that civic engagement requires a posture of lifelong learning and critical inquiry outside of the classroom is evidenced by Locklin's community-based learning project. Several of his students reported that the project had made them open to difference and more willing to challenge their own and others' views. Challenging assumptions is one of the key requirements for critical inquiry. These examples point to the inherently self-reflective nature of religious studies courses. Religious studies courses are uniquely situated to encourage students to make connections between their own religious commitments or non-commitments and their roles in society. This by-product, the self-reflective nature of religious studies courses, additionally serves to break down the binary references to "in" and "out of" the classroom.

Clearly, there is no one-size-fits-all assignment to encourage civic engagement—nor would it ever be possible. But if encouraging students to be engaged citizens is one goal of a religious studies professor, then utilizing assignments with several layered requirements, including critical engagement with texts, field trips, service and experiential learning projects, accompanied always with reflective writings, is best practice.

Notes

1. Where I quote directly from workshop participants, here and throughout the chapter, I am drawing on discussions and materials shared in the course of the workshop. All material has been used with permission.

2. Quoted in Forrest Clingerman and Reid B. Locklin, "'Pedagogies for Civic Engagement': Collaborations and Complications in Religious Studies." Paper presented at the 10th annual National Outreach Scholarship Conference, University of Georgia, Athens, Georgia, September 29, 2009.

3. See also the further discussion in Marianne Delaporte's chapter in this volume.

4. See the further discussion of this project in Reid B. Locklin, Tracy Tiemeier, and Johann M. Vento, "Teaching World Religions without Teaching 'World Religions,'" *Teaching Theology and Religion* 15 (2012): 165–70.

5. A technique modeled after Rick Davies and Jess Dart, "The 'Most Significant Change' (MSC) Technique: A Guide to Its Use" (2004), *Monitoring and Evaluation NEWS*, http://www.mande.co.uk/docs/MSCGuide.pdf (accessed March 19, 2009).

4

Giving and Receiving Hospitality during Community Engagement Courses

Marianne Delaporte

> *When you give a luncheon or a dinner, do not invite your friends or your brothers of your relatives or rich neighbors, in case they may invite you in return, and you would be repaid. But when you give a banquet, invite the poor, the crippled, the lame, and the blind.*
>
> —LUKE 14:12–13 (NRSV)

WHILE IT MIGHT be counterintuitive for those who think of community engagement in terms of charity, hospitality is more often received than given in community engagement classes, as students are sent out into the community to encounter the hospitality of others. This presents an important pedagogical point (especially in response to the CLEA model of teaching civic engagement discussed in earlier chapters of this book): In community engagement, the receiving of hospitality cannot be passive if it is to be successful. Rather, the receiving of hospitality must be thoughtful and engaged. As a professor who has recently begun being involved in community engagement courses I have found, time and again, that the most time-consuming, difficult, and possibly explosive part of the preparation for such a course is the question of hospitality. How do we prepare for an off-site experience with our students? How do we prepare the community partners to give hospitality to our students, and can we offer some form of hospitality to them in return? The importance of hospitality, of being able to both receive it and give it, has a great impact on our sense of civic engagement. By the very inclusion of the term "engagement," civic engagement implies a bond or relationship with others. Most often the state of this bond is assumed and not thought through. By thinking in terms of hospitality one brings these assumptions to light. The virtue of hospitality, therefore, makes explicit the implicit understanding that the civil sphere is one of reciprocity, relationship, and empathy, and that it is through attention to these relationships that societies thrive.

Engagement requires assent from both parties, and hospitality makes it clear that the bond created is not merely a utilitarian one but one of mutuality, as conveyed by the Greek terms *agape* or *philia*. In this chapter I give suggestions for preparing a class that will benefit both the students and the community partners. A theory of hospitality is presented, followed by a short discussion of the way in which hospitality functions both in and out of the classroom in a community engagement course.

In making these suggestions, I am linking hospitality to social justice.[1] However, while civic engagement and social justice are connected, they are not always understood as the same thing. Education in the United States has always been understood to be a place where civic engagement is taught. From teaching children the pledge of allegiance to requiring courses in political science, it has long been argued that the school is an appropriate place for preparing the young to take part in the civic lives of their communities. This limited understanding of civic engagement, however, can also lead to a broader understanding of the student as being a member of a larger social fabric than their classroom or family, and therefore to having a responsibility for and a stake in the social problems surrounding them. This realization, in turn, can lead to an emphasis on social justice in community engagement, as the morality of the society which we inhabit is questioned and the students feel a responsibility to make changes.

Often the line between civic engagement and social justice is much more of a semantic one, as social justice is seen as a "liberal" concern that has been attacked by conservative critics. One conservative think tank argues that "the university must never be used for political purposes, or as an instrument of social change or social justice as defined by particular social and political philosophies."[2] Because of such associations, some universities avoid using the term "social justice" in connection with civic engagement so as to avoid the debate that this might engender. Others argue that it is not the job of academics to practice justice with their students, insofar as it dilutes the academic enterprise.[3]

At Notre Dame de Namur University, where I work, the term "community engagement" covers internships, immersion programs, community-based learning courses, and community-based research courses. Obviously, in some departments—business departments come to mind—community engagement takes on more of the internship side of the definition, as students are required to work for a company to fulfill their general education requirement—work which may or may not benefit society as a whole. In the Humanities this can also occur, as in the example of sending students to visit religious services, a form of community-based research which I discuss later. However, even here it can be argued that the larger purpose of the engagement is social justice, as students seek to understand the diverse world around them, engage with it, and live in harmony with others. There is a distinction therefore between social justice work and community engagement. However, when community engagement involves itself in difficult questions concerning race, class, equality, and justice in general, there is the possibility of growth and openness. Critical thinking is one aspect of a university's desired learning outcomes that can greatly benefit from community engagement done in this way. As Dan Butin argues:

> Justice learning is concerned most prominently with making visible the contingency of our present situations; that we are always-in-the-making of our beliefs, practices, and structures. This is radical undecidability in that all conditions are open to contestation and reconstruction. This leaving open of conversations—for instance, about race, about equity, about justice—short-circuits any attempt at dilution for the sake of simple (and simplistic) answers.[4]

If one attempts to take community engagement to the level of justice-learning, as is my hope for my courses, then the importance of hospitality to the community engagement experience is apparent. It is hospitality which opens the students to this new world and gives rise to the possibility of social justice. The radical nature of a pure form of hospitality cannot be underestimated, and while this purity cannot be achieved at the university level, it is well worth examining what it might mean and to work toward such an ideal.

Introducing Hospitality into the Classroom

Hospitality, as faculty often tell students, is one of the basic and necessary duties of religious life. In reading the story of Sodom and Gomorrah we point out to students that the sin of Sodom was inhospitality; in telling the death of Buddha we point to Buddha's embrace of hospitality as a virtue, even to his death. Working in a Catholic university, I find myself stressing the stories of hospitality in the Bible repeatedly, as they are inevitably linked to those of social justice and peace. Preceding the story of Sodom is that of Abraham's hospitality to three strangers; together these stories tell a story about hospitality and its link to social justice (Genesis 18–19). They define hospitality from the biblical standpoint as a welcoming of God in the welcome of the stranger. In both stories the visitor is a foreigner, not a neighbor or family member, and yet the host welcomes them and treats them with respect, giving them the best of what they have. In the story of Sodom, the host goes as far as to offer up his daughters in exchange for his guests' protection.

Reading these stories closely, my students come to see the link between giving hospitality, welcoming others into our home, and social justice—questioning who are these others, the respect which they deserve, and the way in which welcome into our space gives us a responsibility toward them. The students come to define hospitality more broadly, expanding upon the idea of hospitality from being something we do to strengthen existing relationships to building relationships with strangers. We discuss the components of biblical hospitality as portrayed by Letty Russell and others: the creation of community, advocacy for the marginalized, mutual welcome, and the hidden face of the divine.[5] Hospitality in this sense is radical and dangerous: It requires a leap of faith, as we open our homes and ourselves to the foreign, the unknown; we invite the stranger in and as we say, "my home is your home," so the stranger becomes the host. The host is responsible for the guest's safety and comfort, but more than that, they must make them feel at home.

Returning to the story of Abraham, Marianne Moyaert argues that the story of the three strangers reinforces Judaism's emphasis on universality over particularity. As she points out, this story occurs soon after Abraham has been circumcised. He is recovering from an operation that deals with the particulars of his faith, yet the invitation to strangers, not to members of his tribe, becomes the central story.[6] The central message of openness to the stranger continues in Christianity, as is argued in the World Council of Churches in their 2006 document on "Religious Plurality and Christian Self-Understanding," which bases its theology on the virtue of hospitality and its transformative aspects. Just as community engagement ideally transforms its participants, so does hospitality. Both leave its members in a different, more open state. The document declares:

> Because of the changing world context, especially increased mobility and population movements, sometimes we are the "hosts" to others, and at other times we become the "guests" receiving the hospitality of others; sometimes we receive "strangers" and at other times we become the "strangers" in the midst of others. Indeed we may need to move to an understanding of hospitality as "mutual openness" that transcends the distinctions of "hosts" and "guests."

> Hospitality is not just an easy or simple way of relating to others. It is often not only an opportunity but also a risk. . . . Further, dialogue is very difficult when there are inequalities between parties, distorted power relations or hidden agendas. . . . Christians have not only learned to co-exist with people of other religious traditions, but have also been transformed by their encounters.[7]

This emphasis on the centrality of the virtue of hospitality, and its inherent danger and possibility, harkens back to Derrida's many discussions on the subject.

Immanuel Kant had argued that hospitality delimits borders because it relies on reciprocity and duty; this is the hospitality of diplomats and family members. In response to this definition Derrida argues for an ethics of infinite and unconditional hospitality that is at the very foundation of ethics and culture.[8] This ideal hospitality, which Derrida calls "the hyperbolic law" of hospitality, calls for a meeting with the stranger in which we do not try to interpret or understand the other, since such an interpretation, even one done in good faith, always does violence to the other. It is a hospitality which is unconditional and which requires us to go beyond the very understandings of home and property which allow us to be hospitable in the first place. In this understanding, ethics equals hospitality; it is not merely a subset of ethics but its foundation. While we are limited in our achievement of this ideal of hospitality by the needs and responsibilities of our institutions and individual states, we still need to strive to maintain this ideal.[9]

Guests and Hosts: Working Out the Basics

Having begun to establish the connection between a host's responsibility to their guests and social justice with a discussion of Abraham, the question then becomes: What are a guest's role and responsibility? How are these related to social justice? Here I often discuss the importance of eating together found throughout the Bible, the meaning of sharing a meal, and how rejection of such is seen as a rejection of the other's humanity. This brings Buddha's story, as extreme as it might first seem, into alliance with the story of the angels, who seemingly don't need Abraham's food or Lot's protection but accept them with grace and thanks. There is reciprocity and vulnerability involved in hospitality which can transform both the host and the guest.

One of the courses that I have taught over the years, Theologies of Liberation is a community-based learning (CBL) course. At our university all students must take one CBL course in order to graduate. These courses are meant to simultaneously help students reach the learning goals of the class and help communities change in a positive manner.[10] Theologies of Liberation is an obvious choice as a CBL course, since liberation theology is engaged and active theology. In order for the course to fulfill the CBL requirement at my institution, the community engagement must not be separate from the classroom learning. Instead, the two must be blended and work together; the CBL must be part of the pedagogical structure of the course. This can only be done if the professor works closely with the community partner and spends time both in and out of the classroom, with students making sense of their outside experience with the readings they have done in class.

Exploring the meaning of hospitality and its link to social justice at the beginning of this Theologies of Liberation course allows students to see the connection between all of their engagements with "strangers" and social justice, and to understand the reciprocity which is necessary in a partnership with an outside community organization, replacing the model of charity for one of hospitality, and a model of hierarchy for one based on mutuality. Having discussed biblical understanding of hospitality and its obligations, one can imagine an absolute hospitality in which nothing is asked of the guest and everything given. How does this differ from the carefully circumscribed hospitality which we experience daily? While this absolute hospitality may be impossible in an academic setting, it is worthwhile to push our students to imagine how far hospitality can be taken and what the implications would be for our society.

This chapter does not delve into detail as to how to choose a community partner, nor does it show how to work with your university to get the help you need communicating with partners and students throughout the semester, even though these are important topics. Choosing and developing relationships with community partners is a time-consuming task which must be done before the semester begins.[11] Here I presuppose these things and focus on ways in which hospitality occurs during the semester in community engagement, using examples both from my teaching and from that of my colleagues at Notre Dame de Namur University.

Giving Hospitality: Inviting Community Partners into the Classroom

How would you feel if someone came to your house for dinner five times but when you came to their house to drop off their child after a play-date, they left you on the doorstep and never once asked you in? This feeling of rejection is one that can be created if, as is often the case, hospitality is one-way in a community-engagement course. In the majority of cases students are the guests, the community partner is the host, and we drop off our "children" without setting foot in the home of the other or inviting them into ours. Yet we know from our daily experience that we feel more intimacy and trust for others when we are invited into their homes and they are willing to visit ours.

As noted before, students and faculty in a community-based learning course will more often receive hospitality, as they are sent out into the community to engage with others, than give that hospitality. However, for the community engagement to truly work one must model hospitality, both toward one's students and toward the community group with whom one is working. At its most basic, hospitality involves the first visit of the community partner into the classroom.

It is the teacher's role as host not only to make the community partner feel welcomed but also to foster respect for the partner among the students.

According to Derrida, as noted earlier, one of the most revolutionary or difficult parts of being a host is the interruption of one's life, the giving away of one's power. This sharing of power is often the most difficult thing for a professor to do. As teachers we are used to being the kings of our little realms: the syllabus is the rulebook and our word is law. However, by inviting our community partners in, we give up that absolute rule: we step aside and share power with someone whose needs and beliefs about education and community may be quite different from our own. This will mean giving up some of our own desires for the class, working with someone as a partner before the first day of class, and then, when class begins, sharing the stage and the locus of authority. As the hosts we must invite our community partners to have this authority and we must support them when they take it, sharing in giving grades and assignments if they so choose.

While it is common and expected to invite a representative of the community partnership into the classroom for a presentation, it is less common to extend this hospitality to the whole community one is engaged with. Being the host can come in many forms. At our university a biology professor invites a classroom of elementary school students to come to our campus for the day, where they use the labs and end the day blowing coke rockets into the air on the quads. This exercise not only teaches science but also allows the children to get a glimpse at the lives of the university students who have been coming to their classrooms regularly to teach science; it is a form of intimacy which is appreciated by children. What child does not ask to see another's bedroom when they come for a visit? By extending the visit outside of the classroom and onto the general campus, the children are brought into an intimacy with the college students which would not occur otherwise.

Dr. Don Stannard-Friel of the sociology department at Notre Dame de Namur takes his students into the Tenderloin district in San Francisco for community engagement courses. But he reverses this process once a year. College students who come from marginalized backgrounds first speak to the youth in the Tenderloin. Teenagers from the Tenderloin are then brought to the university campus, sit in on a class, visit the campus, and eat lunch at the cafeteria with the students they have already met. In this way the teenagers are introduced to the possibilities of college, and that opportunity is made tangible. The college students are also given the chance to share their lives with those who have shared theirs already, bringing about a circle of mutuality and trust.

In other cases, the community partner can best be served by giving hospitality of a more general kind. Non-profit organizations may be in need of space in which to hold meetings or fund-raisers. They may need access to the library or other resources of the university. For example, our university has hosted an art exhibit for at-risk youth in our library that has been very well attended and a basketball camp for children in our gym. An in-depth conversation, first with the university administrators and then with the community partner, can unearth a variety of ways in which hospitality can be given rather than imposed.

Hospitality involves intimacy, as noted in the preceding examples, and this intimacy and vulnerability are part of the reason academics may feel discomfort with the community engagement model. We have been trained to separate our emotions from our knowledge, to discuss social justice and ethics in the abstract rather than in how they affect our own lives. In teaching feminism and women's spirituality I have encountered this discomfort repeatedly, as the feminist maxim, "The Personal Is Political" is dissected and examined in class but then rarely put into action.[12] Once one has accepted the premise that our academic lives are not separate from our personal lives, the breach has been made and one can discuss hospitality and its implications for intimacy. This intimacy is not one-sided. It is not only learning the personal stories of the community partners—something which is expected as we peer into the lives of others—but also sharing our own stories and hearing those of our students, something that can cause much more discomfort.

Stannard-Friel told me of a case in which one of his community partners, a former drug addict, came into the classroom to discuss his drug abuse and the larger problems of drug abuse in society. After his presentations students came to him asking for help for their siblings, friends, and themselves. Teachers will also find students coming to them. While students may, from the outside, appear to be the "advantaged" persons, as opposed to the community's "dispossessed," the intimacy fostered by a community engagement project can lead to discoveries of students who have been homeless, addicted, abused, and marginalized. These discussions would not happen as frequently in a non-community engagement class, but the boundaries broken by these courses as we share food and transportation can lead to a much more intimate bond between learning and life, and we must be sure to offer hospitality to our own students as well as to our community partners.

Learning to integrate these personal experiences into the more traditionally academic goals of the course can lead to improved student learning outcomes, as we all learn better when the knowledge is meaningful. This requires assignments that show a connection not only between the community engagement and the classroom work but also between these two and the students' own lives. Good reflection exercises can make this productive for all. Welch has developed a reflection technique which ensures that students cover the cognitive, affective, and behavioral aspects of the community engagement experience. Reflections are graded on whether they cover all three of these aspects of the community engagement activity, and in addition are graded on the depth at which students show reflective awareness, ranging from "self" to "systemic/global." I have found that it is often the reflection exercises that allow students to bring together the outside activity, their own life experience, and the critical thinking being done in the classroom. If reflections are left vague, students will often fall back on "I learned how lucky I am" and will not tie the experience to the readings in any way.[13] The professor also needs to carefully word the assignments and grading so as not to appear to be grading the student's life experience.

Receiving Hospitality: Site Visits and Being a Guest

Being a guest in community engagement is as important as being a host, and this also requires preparation on the part of the professor and students. In my experience there are two very different sorts of community engagement which require differing preparation and expectations of the guest: site visits and engaging in work in the community.

In my World Religions course I require all students to make a site visit, participating in a religious ceremony outside of their own faith tradition. This is the most basic form of community engagement, as students step outside of their comfort zones and depend upon the welcome of strangers who are very much at home. This sort of engagement requires a simple preparation for hospitality. I remind students to dress appropriately, to call ahead and find out if the date they have chosen is a good one, to participate as much as they comfortably can, and to thank their hosts—yes, it can feel like being their mother, but I have found time and again that these reminders are necessary for undergraduates.

While this assignment is simple and does not have as much depth as other community engagement courses, I have consistently discovered that it succeeds in one of the primary goals of hospitality: strangers become neighbors, people we care about and seek to understand. Students are often resistant to this exercise, but most come back enthusiastic and amazed at the hospitality which they received. They begin to see themselves as part of the larger community outside the borders of the university and are able to examine the particular as well as the theoretical when it comes to world religions. While this activity is simple, it is based in the bedrock of hospitality: that of expanding our borders and knowing experientially, as well as through an embodied encounter with that love well captured by the Greek term *philia,* mutual friendship or affection. Once this foundation of hospitality has been set up, then the structure can be made more complex and more durable with repeated exercises and relationships within the community.

Preparing to receive hospitality in a more sustained community engagement environment, where one is doing volunteer work with a community partner, for instance, is much more time-consuming. In order for the community engagement exercise to be successful one must be very clear—with oneself, the community partner, and the students—as to what the goals of the experience are. This should be set up first with the community partner, and then, explicitly and with continued discussion, with the students. I have found that most often it is best not to begin the "guest" part of the community engagement course until several weeks into the semester, when the students and faculty have bonded and trust each other. We must remember that we are hosts to our students, in any classroom situation, before we can be hosts to others.

One year I was involved in a Freshman Experience class in which all freshmen were sent out to various community partners to do a day of volunteer work with their professors before the semester began. This assignment had several goals: to bond the students who had just met, to introduce them to their new community, and to have them start thinking about social justice, which is part of our school's mission. My group was assigned a family shelter, and we were given bus tokens and sent on our way. I packed twenty-five students onto a bus, which I vaguely believed to be taking us in the right direction. Problem one: Never send people off without very good directions and a carefully pre-planned route. We did make it to the shelter after a bit of confusion, only to encounter problem two—a much greater one. Our community partner had not been warned that we would be arriving with such a great number of students or that we were expecting to be there for five hours. The community partner was unprepared for both our arrival and our numbers. Gallantly, they strove to make us welcome and to include us in their activities. They found things for us to do, and our students gamely cleaned and played with the children. However, it was clear that our presence was more of an imposition than a help, as we quickly finished our assigned tasks and students wandered aimlessly, attempting conversation with sleepy mothers getting their children breakfast.

Here I have demonstrated at least two of the reasons why John Eby argues that service learning is bad: We had diverted the community agency's energy away from their primary work, as they greeted us, spent lunch time talking with us, and looked for work for us to do, and we had "diverted attention from social policy to volunteerism."[14] The experience was not tied into the course in any substantial way. Students wrote a short essay about their experience, with no background discussion. I was told to hand the essays in to the dean of students, and the whole thing disappeared into the ether. Not surprisingly, the students did frame their reflections as ones of volunteerism. With no prior discussion of hospitality, of social justice, and no connections between themselves and their teacher (it was my first day meeting them also), the experience had little meaning and felt like just one more freshman orientation hoop through which they must jump. We might have been better served with a community picnic in

Golden Gate Park, achieving the first two goals. We could then have waited until the class had developed the trust with the teacher and each other that is needed for effective community engagement, and subsequently moved on to discussions of social justice.

Rooted within a class whose goals are clear and consistent, community engagement can avoid these pitfalls. As noted earlier, a community engagement class should be one in which the community partner shares in the teaching and goal-creation of the class. The needs of both sides must be taken into account and made clear to all. Prior to the beginning of the semester the professor should sit down with the community partner, bringing in the syllabus and copies of the textbook. Together they can revise the syllabus as the partner sees fit and discuss how much the partner wishes to be involved in class work or grading. The community partner will experience the students in ways which differ from the professors and are often the best judge of the student's growth in a particular area. Hospitality which has been first offered by the university, by inviting the community partner into the classroom, will prepare the class for receiving hospitality and giving it meaning. In addition, one must not forget to give hospitality to the students or to ensure that they give it to each other. This means encouraging them to build trust in each other and taking the time to have conversations, both in the classroom and outside of it. Several successful community engagement teachers have told me that it is the conversations on the bus, or in a café after the community engagement experience, which really affected their relationships with the students and the students' development. The classroom setting is perfect for certain kinds of work, but it can also limit students' comfort in discussing their own life experience and its relationship to the larger subject being studied. Don't be afraid to take your students out of the classroom, even if it is only to lie on the grass one afternoon for a discussion.

By taking a critical approach to the exercise of hospitality which is implied in any community engagement experience, students will see the connection of hospitality to ethics and to religious foundations and be able to understand the difference between the ideal of an ethics of hospitality and the limits set on this hospitality by their institution, their country, and their own needs. Examining this separation between the ideal and the lived, and discussing how that ideal can be striven for, is part of a pedagogical practice which advances hospitality as a political and ethical need in our society while teaching critical thinking skills and allowing for a more nuanced understanding of service learning. In order to self-consciously advance hospitality as an ethical and political goal the pedagogy used must engage students on both social and personal scales, as well as asking them to think critically about the social and personal and its interactions.

Conclusion

In my Liberation Theologies course students have spent a long weekend at Dorothy's Place in Salinas. There they fed the homeless, but they also ate with them, worked with them, and slept in a room provided by the Franciscan organization. This extended hospitality to our students allowed them engage in the many aspects of hospitality which make it so central to ethics. Sharing a meal is one of the basics of hospitality: It humanizes the other, as the roles of host and guest become fluid through the passing of food and drink. The intimacy of sharing a meal is often recreated between students and teachers as they travel to their community partners' locations. It is in these moments, over a cup of coffee, that the personal is brought into the theoretical, that the boundaries of the academic break down. This form of hospitality serves one of the objectives of the CLEA model of civic engagement noted by Locklin and Posman: the objective of empathetic accountability. By stepping outside of the classroom and testing the roles of both host and guest, students negotiate multiple perspectives, acknowledging their own limitations and seeking out knowledge and connection with an other. This objective is also linked to the second objective of civic engagement, that of "frames of reference and social location" as the practice of hospitality helps students not only reflect upon their own social location but recognize the power dynamics occurring both on campus and off, and the limits which these power dynamics impose upon the possibility of radical, absolute hospitality.

Jesus notes in the Gospel of Luke that one should not expect anything in return when one is a host, and this is the absolute hospitality which Derrida describes as the basis for ethics: encounter not as a social obligation or quid pro quo but for its own sake and for love. This hospitality given is not, however, equal to charity, as it involves knowing the stranger and letting oneself be known by them while acknowledging that they are truly other and can never be fully known. Hospitality, given and received, is at the basis of religious ethics as it is at the basis of relationship. In hospitality we view the other not as a means to an end, not as an "other" but as an aspect of the divine, one which demands mutuality and vulnerability and which enriches both sides.

Notes

1. This suggests an analogy with how empathy and motivated action are related, but not the same, in the CLEA model.
2. California Association of Scholars, *A Crisis of Competence: The Corrupting Effect of Political Activism in the University of California*. National Association of Scholars, April 2012. http://www.nas.org/images/documents/A_Crisis_of_Competence.pdf (accessed June 7, 2013).

3. See Stanley Fish, *Save the World on Your Own Time* (New York: Oxford University Press, 2008).

4. Dan W. Butin, "Justice-Learning: Service-Learning as Justice-Oriented Education," *Equity and Excellence in Education* 40 (2007): 4.

5. Letty M. Russell, *Just Hospitality: God's Welcome in a World of Difference* (Louisville, KY: Westminster John Knox, 2009).

6. Marianne Moyaert, "Biblical, Ethical and Hermeneutical Reflections on Narrative Hospitality" in *Hosting the Stranger*, ed. Richard Kearney and James Taylor (New York: Continuum Publishing Group, 2011), 102.

7. World Council of Churches, 2006 Assembly, "Religious Plurality and Christian Self-Understanding." http://www.oikoumene.org/en/resources/documents/assembly/porto-alegre-2006/3-preparatory-and-background-documents/religious-plurality-and-christian-self-understanding.html.

8. M. W. Westmoreland, "Interruptions: Derrida and Hospitality," *Kritike* 2 (2008): 3.

9. Irwin Jones, *Derrida and the Writing of the Body* (Burlington VT: Ashgate Publishing Group, 2010), 157.

10. Notre Dame de Namur University, "Community Based Learning," Notre Dame de Namur University website (accessed June 7, 2013). www.ndnu.edu/academics/community-based-learning.

11. See Marshall Welch, "O.P.E.R.A.: A First Letter Mnemonic and Rubric for Conceptualizing and Implementing Service Learning," *Issues in Educational Research* 20 (2010): 76–82; and Christine M. Cress, Peter J. Collier, and Vicki L. Reitenauer, *Learning through Serving: A Student Guidebook for Service-Learning across the Disciplines* (Sterling, VA: Stylus Publishing, 2005), chapters 2 and 3.

12. See bell hooks, *Teaching to Transgress: Education as the Practice of Freedom* (New York: Routledge, 1994).

13. Marshall Welch and Regenia C. James, "An Investigation on the Impact of a Guided Reflection Technique in Service-Learning Courses to Prepare Special Educators," *Teacher Education and Special Education* 30 (2007): 278.

14. John W. Eby, "Why Service-Learning Is Bad," Villanova College website, March 1998. https://www1.villanova.edu/content/dam/villanova/artsci/servicelearning/WhyServiceLearningIsBad.pdf (accessed July 7, 2015).

5

Civic Engagement in the Heart of the City

Rebekka King

ONE OF MY objectives in teaching religion is to make familiar spaces seem unfamiliar. Within the discipline of religious studies, professors often contend with preconceived notions and assumptions on the part of students about what constitutes "authentic" religion.[1] Teaching a course about religion and civic spaces to third-year undergraduate students at the University of Toronto inherently means that students bring to the classroom a wide range of assumptions and global experiences concerning what constitutes cities and civic identities.[2] Torontonians have for many years contested claims by larger American cities and declared their city to be the most culturally diverse city in North America—a point of pride corroborated by a 2011 report by CivicAction, insofar as it identifies Toronto as the most "global" city in the world.[3] Throwing religion into the mix only complicates things, as students from what is arguably North America's most culturally diverse city contend with a myriad of understandings of religious agency, beliefs, and practices.

These issues I kept in mind as I designed the curriculum and course content for a course titled Religion and the City, which intended to look explicitly at both familiar and unfamiliar spaces. This commitment meant that the design of the course diverted from popular models whereby Religion and the City courses seek to map religious structures and activities within a municipal area.[4] Instead, this course was designed to examine the layers of religious interpretations that are produced within the city itself by different players. In doing so, I sought to follow the Canadian model of understanding society as a cultural mosaic rather than a melting pot.

In this chapter, I outline my own approach to civic engagement, which focuses on some of the theoretical and practical issues that emerged out of teaching a course on religion and urban spaces at the University of Toronto. First, I explore the potential that I see in courses that integrate teaching for civic engagement with learner-centered pedagogies. Second, I describe the course that I designed and focus on the class field trip to a local homeless shelter that served as one of the key sites of engagement and analysis. I discuss my students' interactions with urban spaces as they are defined by homelessness, as well as the ways that this field trip shaped our learning environment and their final projects for the course. In the spirit of the pedagogical methods that I promote, I conclude by drawing attention not only to the positive experiences the course generated for both the students and me, but also those issues that emerged during the course that surprised me and in some instances remain unresolved—an experience which I contend should be the aim rather than a by-product of this pedagogical exercise.

Civic Engagement or Civic Identities?

For the purposes of this chapter, I divert from familiar models of civic engagement that focus upon engagement and participation by linking their pedagogies to action- and community-based learning environments.[5] Rather, I seek to focus on how contending notions of civic identities and occupied spaces direct students' learning experiences. While this approach may be more cerebral than models which incorporate direct activities, my intention is to respond to a need identified by Joel Westheimer and Joseph Kahne to integrate justice-oriented approaches into the classroom. In doing so, I heed their caution that instructors should "not aim to impart a fixed set of truths or critiques regarding the structure of the society. Rather they work to engage students in informed analysis and discussion regarding social, political and economic structures."[6]

My commitment to dialogue is one that is shared by the contributors to this volume and, I think, highlights the pedagogical principles set out in the first chapters of the book. Particularly, I seek to unpack for students the second component of the CLEA model introduced in chapters 1 and 2 by providing opportunities for students to reflect on the frames of reference that they employ as they participate in society. While, as I discuss later in the chapter, this course focuses on recognizing our own socio-economic locations and the effects that they have on our daily interactions with social spaces, it is my hope that students will also gain more general reflexive skills that they might draw on in a variety of intellectual and social spheres in the future.

In this article, I would like to promote a learner-centered model of pedagogy as going hand in hand with civic engagement models.[7] My interpretation of a learner-centered pedagogy is one that asks students to bring their strengths and weaknesses into the classroom. In doing so, I request that students contemplate the following questions: "What do I usually excel at in classes?" "What expertise have I already developed that I can contribute to classroom discussions and assignments?" "What do I find to be challenging or difficult?" Because the course is focused in part on examining the city of Toronto, on the first day I suggest to the students that they are already experts in our field of study and bring to the table their own unique experiences as citizens of the city of Toronto. Perhaps this is a bold move in the context of religious studies, where we ask students to check their personal religious and ideological stances at the door. Positioning the students as "insiders," however, serves my pedagogical aim of providing a venue in which the experiences of those who occupy the margins of the city are emphasized.

Civic engagement as a pedagogical practice has been defined in numerous ways.[8] It is often a response to a trend of ambivalence toward political and social engagement on the part of young people, and it is often classified under the auspices of the "bowling alone" phenomenon noted in contemporary American society.[9] At the most basic level civic engagement offers a collaborative and reciprocal interaction between students and the community at large. Civic engagement in the classroom promotes a framework of learning in which students are encouraged to understand themselves as agents or participants in their field of study and in relation to their object of study, both inside and (especially) outside the classroom. Ideally, civic engagement positions students to ask critical and meaningful questions about their own roles within their communities and social spheres of influence. There are a number of reasons why the study of religion serves as an ideal venue in which to make use of the civic engagement model. Primarily, I see the study of religion as one which draws upon a diversity of methodological and theoretical approaches in such a way that no one discipline and/or perspective is privileged. As such, civic engagement naturally lends itself to the subject matter in such a way that it becomes an additional conversation partner but does not overpower the discourse.

In employing this framework, I aspire to provide my students with nonconventional objects of study and to challenge them to include their own subjective experiences and epistemologies in their analyses of religion.[10] From the perspective of the Religion and the City course, a focus on civic engagement means the production of knowledge occurs not in an environment that is inaccessible, but rather one in which the students can take personal ownership over both their topic and their method of study. Extending out of the learner-centered focus, my approach tends to emphasize the individual experiences of each student as an independent agent in contrast to approaches emphasizing collective expressions and experiences.

Course Structure and Content: From Gilgamesh to the "GTA"

One of the primary components of this course offered students a chance to develop their own theories about religion and civic space that could then be applied across historical and cultural realms. Specifically, I was interested in encouraging the students to look at the ways that religious and secular narratives described and constructed categories of the "insider" and "outsider" within civic spaces. I emphasized that we can understand meaning-making as deriving from both official and unofficial narratives. My ultimate goal, as indicated previously, was to encourage students to break down boundaries erected by academic exercises, analyses, and critiques that restrict knowledge production to classroom activities. Rather, I wanted them to understand that their lived experiences outside of the classroom could also serve as primary sources or "texts" available for scholarly examination.[11]

The course texts—biblical passages, novels, poetry, essays, documentary films, and a field trip—provided case studies from which we, as a class, could develop a theoretical approach to non-conventional sacred spaces in both ancient and contemporary worlds. In the first half of the course we read, among other texts, the *Epic of Gilgamesh*, which we used as the model for exploring specific questions related to ontological constructions of the self and community. In the second half of the course we read Michael Ondaatje's *In the Skin of a Lion*, which is a modern retelling of the Gilgamesh narrative set in early twentieth-century Toronto.[12] Ondaatje's poetic novel combines fiction and reality to tell the unofficial history of the working-class immigrants responsible for the construction of Toronto. The crux of the novel reveals that the very individuals responsible for building the city of Toronto from the ground up are unable to access spaces occupied by the social elite, spaces which, for the purposes of our course, we identified as "sacred" sites. While officially excluded from these sites, the working-class protagonists of Ondaatje's novel employ several well-thought-out tactics to gain physical and figurative access to these spaces.

Alongside our readings of the Gilgamesh story in different settings and with a healthy dose of Foucault and Jonathan Z. Smith, we constructed a spatial theory that we applied to several case studies.[13] By working with the students to construct a theory, I hope that I am attending to Smith's insistence that we must reveal to students the hard work that goes into our pedagogical and intellectual endeavors.[14] I suggested to the students that in respect to the title of our course, Religion and the City, perhaps a religion of the city could be identified in Ondaatje's novel. The characters in the novel are forced to express their identity by investing in nonconventional spaces while opposing established authority structures. Our task then was to make similar inquiries into, and to relate the same theory to, contemporary Toronto. More specifically, students were asked to apply this theory by investigating who is included and excluded in the physical construction and cognitive imaginings of contemporary Toronto? In other words, what sites become nonconventional sacred sites to those who define themselves as citizens *non grata* in opposition to the establishment?

Field Trip

These questions were addressed in the major assignment for the course. I instructed students to select their own spaces within the city of Toronto that they determined/identified to resemble spaces described previously and to apply our theory to those sites. In order to guide them, I offered my own example, the Salvation Army's Gateway Shelter and Drop-in Centre, which provides support and shelter to people experiencing homelessness in downtown Toronto.[15] On a chilly March morning I took my class to the shelter, where they spoke first with Dion Oxford, the manager, who addressed the many challenges of urban homelessness. He then turned the class over to a Gateway staff member, Anthony, who runs walking tours of the inner city to provide community groups with insights into the ways in which individuals experiencing homelessness navigate, perceive, and experience Toronto's downtown core. One of the most profound points of our walking tour was that under Anthony's guidance we were led down the same streets and past the same civic structures described in Ondaatje's novel.

Each time that I watched Oxford present to my students, I was struck by how seamlessly he picked up the themes from the readings that I assigned in preparation for our visit, even without knowing it. Oxford, who grew up in a small rural town in Newfoundland, reflected upon themes of imagined communities and the invention of tradition as he explained the daily operations of the shelter and shared his own personal and theological reflections on the topic of homelessness. Using examples from his own conservative religious upbringing, which he contrasted to his young daughter's experiences growing up in multicultural Toronto, Oxford suggested to the students that homelessness is not only a problem affecting urban areas but also is rooted in broken relationships and cycles of abuse that precede someone turning to the streets. He argued that homelessness begins in the suburbs, small towns, and religious communities across North America. As he spoke with the students, his tone was gentle and unassuming. Despite the fact that Oxford spoke with compassion and empathy, each time I took my students to the Gateway, I found them to be uncharacteristically shy in his presence, and few hands were raised when he asked if they had any questions. In conversations later, several students reported that they were uncertain about how to contend with the notion that they might somehow be complicit in communities contributing to the problem of homelessness.[16]

Following Oxford's address, the students were introduced to Anthony, a former crack addict who had lived on the streets for eight years before coming to the Gateway to get clean. In contrast to Oxford's gentle tone, Anthony spoke rapidly and excitedly to the students, jumping from topic to topic and punctuating his points with curse words. Anthony's job was to give my class a tour of the city—*our* city—from the perspective of a person experiencing homelessness. Without hesitation we were off, and Anthony led our group through the downtown core, beginning with a rooming house adjacent to the Gateway that is—despite the city's best intentions—controlled by local drug dealers. Anthony explained how many of his friends who suffer from mental and physical disabilities reside in this building and struggle—often failing—to resist the temptations that accompany living in close proximity to substance abuse. From there we headed to City Hall and the city courthouse along with the adjacent city jail holding cells, about which Anthony has a handful of stories based on his own personal experiences.

Close to City Hall is the Toronto Homeless Memorial, which is hosted by a small Anglican church that caters to Toronto's homeless population. The Memorial is a small, unassuming sign typical of the signs that churches often place on their front steps to advertize service times and upcoming events. Standing just to the left of the Gothic-styled church, it lists the names of over five hundred homeless women and men who have died on the city of Toronto's streets. Anthony indicated to my by then wide-eyed students that they should be quiet and respectful as we gaze upon the names and take note of the many Jane and Joe Does unclaimed from the city morgue. In groups of two and three, my students huddled close around the glass to peer through the condensation at the list of typed names. In its simplicity the memorial is both modest and profound, and my students attended to it with an air of reverence. We did not stop for a lengthy time at the Toronto Homeless Memorial because, as Anthony explained, we were guests there and the space belongs to those who make use of the church's outreach services. As he ushered my students to move on I was struck by the fact that Anthony is able to achieve a balance between offering insight into the lived experiences of homelessness without objectifying members of Toronto's homeless community.

The most surprising part of the field trip occurred following the brief stop at the memorial. The church and memorial are just a few feet away from the Eaton's Centre—the heart of Toronto's shopping district. Anthony had us cut through the Eaton's Centre in order to get to Yonge and Dundas Square, a busy intersection which some call the "Times Square of Canada." The rapid transitions of moving, in less than five minutes, from the quiet and stillness of the Toronto Homeless Memorial through the crowded shopping center and onward out into the bright lights and busy intersection full of people took my breath away every time. On each occasion I noticed that, almost instinctively, the students reached for their cellphones to take a picture and capture the buzz of the city. And each time I thought to myself, "they live here; why do they need a photograph?"

I was somewhat surprised by their desire to capture this moment, as the students' interaction with this space stood in sharp contrast to Anthony's intimate knowledge of the site. This interlude raises important questions about the necessity of providing opportunities for civic engagement both inside and outside our classrooms. While I cannot speak with confidence about my students' motivations to capture that moment on film, I think that it is in part related to the fact that the tour offers them the chance to see their own civic spaces through a new lens. As we followed Anthony through the streets of Toronto, he paused frequently to shake hands in jovial camaraderie with men and women who are likewise a part of street culture. Anthony introduced the students to a space that many of them have occupied for years and offered a completely different perspective. At the city courthouse, where one of my students had served as an intern, Anthony told us about various fights in the basement holding cells. At the Eaton's Centre, where another student worked as a sales clerk, Anthony reported to us that he is often rudely asked to leave by mall security. Finally, in the park in front of the twenty-four-story apartment building in which I lived, Anthony reminisced about how in the 1990s he slept in the park for several weeks as part of an all-night "sleep-out" designed to draw attention to the need for more affordable housing in Toronto. After Anthony left, I pointed to my building and admitted to my students that I do not know my neighbors' names, and then concluded our tour by asking my students the following question: "Who is really at home and who is homeless in these spaces?"[17]

Reflections

In my view, the class trip to the Gateway provided students with an opportunity to learn within a framework of civic engagement. While the students understood themselves to be Torontonians, many of them later reported to me that this identity was one that they tentatively held because they felt uncertain about what the major issues and concerns are enveloping the city. In fact, because the city of Toronto is a so-called megacity with an ever-expanding metropolitan conglomeration of sizable suburban municipalities, the majority of my students reside in the suburbs and in a very real way are tourists in their own city. At least momentarily, our categories of insider and outsider were reversed.

In an attempt to have the students expand personal boundaries and better understand the city, I encouraged them in their final assignments to select and analyze sites that would challenge them to view the city from an unfamiliar perspective. Furthermore, I told them that they would be evaluated not only on their critique but also on their selection of data. Following my lead, many of the students selected sites that are central to specific subcultures and/or marginalized communities within the city (e.g., the Gay Village, Jewish or Muslim community organizations, Toronto's Occupy movement, domestic abuse care centers, the University's Centre for Women and Trans People, the "highway of heroes" leading into the city), whereas others chose to focus on what have traditionally been viewed as ethnic neighborhoods or locales within Toronto (Chinatown, Little Italy, Little Portugal, an Eritrean-Canadian restaurant) or neighborhoods that are notorious for violence and gang activity (Toronto's Flemingdon Park and Regent Park).

This assignment also asked the students to position themselves in relation to their chosen topic of study, through an ethnographically styled introduction. Many of my students began their papers by describing their commute—on the bus, subway, or streetcar—to their chosen location, recording their first impressions and preconceived assumptions about their field site. This practice simultaneously highlighted their proximity and distance from their chosen sites and echoed my instructions to the students that theirs was to be an approach that looked for new ways of interpreting familiar material rather than an investigation of brand new data. This practice of placing themselves physically on transportation systems that get them to their field sites is a striking metaphor for their roles as "resident experts" on the city. Already, they have mastered the technological and geographical know-how that takes them to their chosen sites. Too often in the study of religion we ask students to distances themselves—ideologically, analytically, and ethically—from their topics of study rather than to contend and wrestle with their proximity.

In the end, I was surprised by the number of students who selected sites in which they were personally invested. In their papers, students reflected on and problematized their own interactions with these selected sites. Since the focus of the assignment was on the way that spaces create narratives that include some while excluding others, the assignment provided an opportunity for students to challenge some of their own communities' practices regarding the construction of boundaries and the implementation of authoritative systems. While one might suggest that my own example of the Salvation Army Shelter paved the way for my students to adopt this methodology, the street walk is not in any way representative of a community in which I participate or about which I possess intimate knowledge. While Dion Oxford is a friend of mine and someone I admire greatly, my purpose in pointing to my own apartment building at the end of the tour was intended to emphasize the disconnect between Anthony and me, rather than any notion of shared community.

Shawn Ginwright's conclusions that youth in urban environments are often drawn to localized and alternative forms of civic engagement are helpful in thinking through my students' focus upon and critique of communities and spaces of which they possess intimate knowledge. In his study of civic engagement on the part of African American students in urban centers, Ginwright notes that traditional measures of evaluating civic engagement (i.e., volunteering, political campaigns, etc.) fail to adequately assess civic engagement on the part of urban youth. Ginwright calls on scholars and practitioners of teaching for civic engagement to seriously consider unrecognized acts of civic engagement such as political protests, civil disobedience, neighborhood involvement, and artistic expressions.[18]

Much of the research focusing on civic engagement promotes a classroom experience that compels students to be involved in political activities and social justice initiatives. As mentioned earlier, there is a concern that university-educated individuals are becoming less involved in civic responsibilities. In fact, there have been calls from student groups, community organizations, and university educators to integrate intellectual and practical venues for civic engagement.[19] To date, community-based learning initiatives are among the primary ways through which this integration has been successfully accomplished.[20] This initiative is a popular option for independent students with the means and aptitude for experiential learning. That being said, it is clear that in order to truly meet the demands for a cohesive integration of the concerns of civic engagement, universities must move beyond one-off courses and begin to integrate these themes into the curriculum and learning objectives of more established courses.

Teaching for civic engagement often carries an assumption that part and parcel of the higher education experience is one in which students are made aware of their responsibilities as community members. Courses can offer this community-oriented approach in a variety of ways that extend beyond service learning components, field trips, or the ethnography-like assignment I describe in this chapter. Discussions and integration of contemporary events and popular media are means that many instructors employ to promote civic engagement in a traditional classroom setting. Additionally, I've found it helpful to invite students into my own reflexive thinking about my pedagogical practices and techniques. In doing so, I hope to communicate to my students my expectations that we are all active participants in the learning experience.

I have left my definition of "civic engagement" intentionally broad. As a scholar of religion, I am sensitive to the reluctance of many of my colleagues to employ pedagogical practices that might be deemed ideological or values-driven. For example, in providing Anthony such a generous allocation of class time, one might assume that I am emphasizing my own personal (albeit fairly normative) commitments to reducing homelessness in Toronto. I have yet to resolve this concern, but I found it helpful to address the issue with the students in class as part of our discussion and reflection about the field trip. Throughout the term, I raised questions with the students about the purpose of higher education and asked them to be active participants in my own sorting through my motivations for selecting the readings, assignments, and activities. In a recent article, Ashley Finley asks whether civic engagement is a behavior or an attitude. She takes her inquiry one step further by seeking to distinguish between civic engagement as a program or an outcome.[21] Finley assumes some level of assessment that is not part of my objective in teaching the Religion and the City course. While it is my hope that the students in my class will gain an increased awareness concerning the ways in which civic spaces and structures are oppressive for those on the margins of society, and perhaps even feel compelled to address systems of inequality in the future, I at no point evaluate students based on behavior or attitude. In other words, I do not seek to ascertain whether or not my students have become "engaged" citizens. I feel that this type of assessment is not necessarily my role as an educator, but it does mean that many questions about the effectiveness and purpose of teaching for civic engagement remain unanswered—a conundrum that I think is the objective, rather than an obstacle, within this pedagogical practice.

In general my students reported that they enjoyed the field trip and were appreciative of the freedom granted to them in the written assignment, which allowed them to write about their own communities. This appreciation reflects trends noted by scholars about the so-called Millennial Generation. More specifically, as Angelique Davis and Brian Mello observe, members of this generation may be less likely to express interest in politics, but they are more engaged by issues that have a personal or local element to them.[22] The field trip, in certain ways, makes homelessness a personal issue to many of the students in the class. For example, one of my former students has since organized similar Streetwalks with the Gateway for his church group and friends. Another student later applied themes from the course in her Master's thesis on space in the Hebrew Bible. A third student emailed me to tell me that she was reworking her assignment as an opinion piece for submission to a local newspaper.

It is easy to identify all of the encouraging reasons that teaching for civic engagement is a positive venture, but I would be remiss if I failed to address some of the limitations that my experience with this method of teaching exposed. As an instructor, I often found myself pulled between competing priorities. As one student reflected after the course had concluded, the teaching methodology "surprised students out of the normal university learning environment." Certainly this is my intention, but teaching for civic engagement involves focusing on less traditionally academic subject matters, and I am concerned that it might be at the expense of scholarly exercises and the accumulation of knowledge. I attempted to compensate for these potential problems by assigning far too many readings, which in retrospect probably should have been culled. At times, I felt that the course was pulling students in too many directions at once. Some of my colleagues questioned whether teaching for civic engagement diminished the academic neutrality and scholarly rigor that the study of religion has promoted in distinguishing itself from theology.[23] Additionally, some of the students reported that initially they were uncertain as to whether or not it fit the model of education and evaluation with which they were more familiar. For example, one student explained to me in an email following the completion of the term, "I felt disassociated with the course for much of the term as I didn't find it was speaking to me academically. In writing the final exam however, I realized that the course did speak to me on a more personally and introspective manner and I have actually taken a lot away from it, regardless of the final mark I receive."

A Question of Expertise

It is important for scholars and teachers within our discipline to attend—both personally and academically—to debates concerning the role that personal values and commitments play in our pedagogical practices (in my case, a commitment to eradicating homelessness). In the classroom, this reflexive process can become a learning opportunity through which students are presented with the challenges that derive from a course of study that seeks to balance qualitative data and theoretical speculation.[24] My approach has been to draw on my own disciplinary home, anthropology, which as Sherry Ortner explains uses the body as an instrument of knowing.[25] Anthropological fieldwork involves the ability of the researcher to develop specific relationships and therefore is as contingent upon the personality and interests of the researcher as it is upon the theoretical approaches to study. While it certainly does not attend to all of the concerns that critics may have concerning the place of teaching for civic engagement within the religious studies classroom, I have found it helpful to unpack these concerns with my students alongside discussions of reflexivity that inform anthropological and ethnographic studies of religion.[26]

The editors of this volume have begun the important task of examining the practice and purpose of teaching for civic engagement within the disciplines of religious studies and theology. I suspect that, as with other disciplines, we will discover that while there are cross-disciplinary similarities with fields like politics, economics, sociology, and others, there are also challenges that are specific to our own areas of expertise and needs of our students. I have alluded to a couple of these challenges already in this chapter. In my experience it was optimal to combine teaching for civic engagement with a learner-centered pedagogy that uses the resources already available to students in the course. Students served as resident experts of Toronto and were able to identify objects of study within their own neighborhoods and communities. Assured that they were indeed already experts, and armed with a new method of looking at civic spaces from a different perspective, my students uncovered a city that was simultaneously less and more familiar to us all.

Notes

1. Robert Orsi, "Everyday Miracles: The Study of Lived Religion," in *Lived Religion in America: Toward a History of Practice*, ed. David D. Hall (Princeton: Princeton University Press, 1997).

2. I taught this course three times between 2009 and 2011 at the University of Toronto while I was completing my doctoral work. The course was originally offered in conjunction with the Religion and the Public Sphere Initiative at the University of Toronto (http://www.chass.utoronto.ca/rps/). The goal of the Religion and the City course was to incorporate some of the core themes of research focusing on public manifestations of religion, and it was made possible in conjunction with generous funding from the Jackman Humanities Foundation. An earlier version of this chapter appeared in *Spotlight on Teaching: AAR Religious Studies News* in October 2010.

3. CivicAction, *Breaking Boundaries: Time to Think and Act Like a Region* (Toronto: CivicAction, 2011), 14.

4. Diana Eck's work with the Harvard Pluralism Project is, of course, the most prominent example. William Closson James' Religious Diversity in Kingston project provided insight into shifting religious demographics from the Canadian perspective. See Diana Eck, *A New Religious America: How a "Christian Country" Has Become the World's Most Religiously Diverse Nation* (New York: HarperCollins, 2001) and William C. James, *God's Plenty: Religious Diversity in Kingston* (Kingston and Montreal: McGill-Queen's Press, 2011).

5. Joel Westheimer and Joseph Kahne, "What Kind of Citizen?: The Politics of Educating for Democracy," *American Educational Research Journal* 41 (2004): 241–42. Within the discipline of religious studies and theology, the essays collected by Devine, Favazza and McLain are foundational for thinking about community-based learning courses. See Richard Devine, Joseph A. Favazza, and F. Michael McLain (eds.), *From Cloister to Commons: Concepts and Models for Service Learning in Religious Studies* (Washington: American Association for Higher Education, 2002).

6. Westheimer and Khane, 243.

7. The term "learner centered" is one that is employed frequently with different meanings. My own understanding of the term follows closely to Maryellen Weimer's descriptions of the concept and its application, see Maryellen Weimer *Learner-Centered Teaching: Five Key Changes to Practice* (San Francisco: Jossey-Bass, 2002). Elsewhere, in an article co-written with faculty and undergraduate students, I outline a case study of learner-centered pedagogy: see Nicholas Dion, Rebekka King, Tyler Baker, Jingjing Liang, James McDonough, and Joshua Samuels, "Open Space Technology and the Study of Religion: A Report on an Experiment in Pedagogy," *Bulletin for the Study of Religion* 42 (2013): 28–32.

8. See, e.g., Richard M. Battistoni, *Civic Engagement across the Disciplines* (Providence, RI: Campus Compact, 2002); Ernest L. Boyer, *Scholarship Reconsidered: Priorities of the Professorate* (Princeton, NJ: The Carnegie Foundation for the Advancement of Teaching, 1990); and Thomas Ehrlich, "Civic Education: Lessons Learned," *Political Science and Politics* 32 (1990): 245–50. In addition, a special edited volume in the AACU's *Peer Review* in 2003 explored teaching for civic engagement and featured helpful articles on what we mean when we say "civic engagement" and, more prominently, its application under the title "Educating for Citizenship."

9. See Barry Checkoway, "New Perspectives on Civic Engagement and Psychosocial Well-Being," *Liberal Education* 97 (2011): 6–11; Angelique Davis and Brian Mello, "Preaching to the Apathetic and Uninterested: Teaching Civic Engagement to Freshmen and Non-Majors," *Journal for Civic Commitment* 18 (2012): 3; Robert Putman, *Bowling Alone* (New York: Simon & Shuster, 2000); and Westheimer and Kahne, 242.

10. Parker Palmer, *The Courage to Teach: Exploring the Inner Landscape of a Teacher's Life* (San Francisco: Jossey-Bass, 1998), 106.

11. See, e.g., Keith Morton, "Making Meaning: Reflections on Community, Service, and Learning" in *From Cloister to Commons: Concepts and Models for Service Learning in Religious Studies*, ed. Richard Devine, Joseph A. Favazza, and F. Michael McLain (Washington: American Association for Higher Education, 2002), 41–42.

12. Michael Ondaatje, *In the Skin of a Lion* (Toronto: Knopf Doubleday, 1997).

13. Readings included Paul's letter to the Romans, Augustine's *City of God*, Orhan Pamuk's *Istanbul*, Joseph Smith and The Book of Mormon, Jim Jones and Jonestown, and, on the third occasion that I taught the class, the Occupy movement.

14. Jonathan Z. Smith, "The Necessary Lie: Duplicity in the Disciplines," in *Studying Religion: An Introduction*, ed. Russell T. McCutcheon (London: Equinox, 2007), 73–80.

15. I mention the Salvation Army Gateway Shelter by name with permission from Dion Oxford. More information about the Gateway can be found on the shelter's website: http://www.thegateway.ca.

16. Marianne Delaporte's chapter in this volume uses the framework of hospitality to consider the ways in which we prepare students to think about civic engagement as a reciprocal relationship.

17. Steven Bouma-Prediger and Brian J. Walsh interrogate this point when they contrast the sense of place and fellowship possessed by those experiencing homelessness to an increased sense of displacement and malaise that they see afflicting modern culture; see Steven Bouma-Prediger and Brian J. Walsh, *Beyond Homelessness: Christian Faith in a Culture of Displacement* (Grand Rapids, MI: William B. Eerdmans, 2008).

18. Shawn Ginwright, "Hope, Healing, and Care: Pushing the Boundaries of Civic Engagement for African American Youth," *Liberal Education* 97 (2011): 34–39.

19. Edward Zlotkowski and Dilafruz Williams, "The Faculty Role in Civic Engagement," *Peer Review* 5 (2003): 9–11.

20. See n. 5.

21. Ashley Finley, "'Connecting the Dots': A Methodological Approach for Assessing Students' Civic Engagement and Psychosocial Well-Being," *Liberal Education* 97 (2011): 55.

22. Davis and Mello (see n. 9), 5.

23. Fred Glennon makes this point in his discussion of service learning courses; see Fred Glennon, "Service Learning and the Dilemma of Religious Studies: Descriptive or Normative," in *From Cloister to Commons: Concepts and Models for Service Learning in Religious Studies*, eds. Richard Devine, Joseph A. Favazza, and F. Michael McLain (Washington: American Association for Higher Education, 2002), 9.

24. Fiona Bowie, "Anthropology of Religion," *Religion Compass* 2 (2008): 862.

25. Sherry B. Ortner, "Resistance and the Problem of Ethnographic Refusal," *Comparative Studies in Society and History* 37 (1995): 173.

26. These questions, of course, are the cornerstone of all ethnographic fieldwork, not just that pertaining to the study of religion. When working with undergraduate students, I find the following texts to be the most accessible: James Clifford and George E. Marcus (eds.), *Writing Culture: The Poetics and Politics of Ethnography* (Berkeley: University of California Press, 1986); Don D. Fowler and Donald L. Hardesty (eds.), *Others Knowing Others: Perspectives on Ethnographic Careers* (Washington: Smithsonian Institution Press, 1994); and James V. Spikard, J. Shawn Landres, and Meredith B. McGuire (eds.), *Personal Knowledge and Beyond: Reshaping the Ethnography of Religion* (New York: New York University Press, 2002).

6

Engaging Media and Messages
in the Religion Classroom

Hans Wiersma

THE NOTION THAT advances in electronic communications technology are creating an increasingly interconnected "global village" has been around at least since
Marshall McLuhan popularized the term in the early 1960s.[1] It follows, therefore,
that educators desiring to incorporate civic engagement strategies may consider
using electronic communications tools to equip students to be engaged citizens
in the global village. Such media-enabled engagement implies new modes and
expanded environments for the academic study of religion.

In light of the foregoing, this essay rests upon two core pedagogical assertions:

1. Civically engaged teaching and learning in the academic study of religion
    equips learners to analyze and evaluate electronic communication media, in-
    cluding the way in which various media depict and influence persons, com-
    munities, institutions, etc. This assertion aligns particularly well with the
    first two elements of the CLEA model described in the opening chapters of
    this book.
2. Civically engaged teaching and learning in the academic study of religion
    equips learners to utilize electronic communication media for a variety of
    purposes, including activist purposes. This assertion is relevant to all four
    elements of the CLEA model.

This chapter illustrates several ways in which accessing, analyzing, evaluating,
and implementing various electronic media can enhance the religion class-
"room" that espouses broad—even global—civic engagement as one of its central
features.[2]

The fact that the word "room" has been rendered in quotation marks in the
preceding paragraph is a tip-off to one of the central observations of this chapter: namely, that the modern classroom is really no room at all but rather an

"environment" that can encompass the entire globe. For academic disciplines centered upon the study of religion, the advent of the "global classroom" holds much promise. That is not to say, however, that the opportunities afforded by an earth-encompassing educational space are immune to the limits and failings of the human condition. In other words, just because a classroom in, say, Kansas City can peer through a webcam mounted atop a building in Cairo and view—in "real time"—what is happening in Cairo's Tahrir Square, does not necessarily mean that peace and harmony will suddenly erupt in either Egypt or Missouri. The global classroom will not quiet all of the world's religion-fueled trouble spots. However, the fact that, today, individual human eyes and ears, and words and ideas, can more or less freely and instantaneously reach many, many people around the world implies certain consequences for the world's religions as it does for the study of the world's religions. The message is that the media-savvy, civically engaged classroom can impact not only the terrain of religious studies but perhaps also the formation of individual and communal religious identities.

Understanding Media

Since Marshall McLuhan and the "global village" have already been invoked, some additional introduction and exploration of McLuhan's insights are in order. Although his musings have sometimes been characterized as enigmatic or abstract, McLuhan was straightforward regarding the meaning of what has become his best known utterance: "the medium is the message." Clarifying his über-adage, McLuhan explained that "the 'message' of any medium or technology is the change of scale or pace or pattern that it introduces into human affairs."[3] Put another way, "'the medium is the message,'" wrote McLuhan, "because it shapes and controls the scale and form of human association and action."[4] As the foregoing quotations indicate, the content and uses of new media (technologies) were, according to McLuhan, less important than the new overarching communal realities wrought by technological developments. For instance, it is true that a light bulb contains light and can be used to make possible things like playing baseball at night. For McLuhan, however, the light bulb's "content"—light—was not its most important message. Rather, the most important message of the advent and development of the light bulb was the manner in which it changed the scope and form of human perception and communication.[5]

In the wake of the initial publication of *Understanding Media*, McLuhan encountered his share of critics.[6] With the advent of the third printing of *Understanding Media*, McLuhan was compelled to respond to any who were wary and/ or confused by his seminal idea. In the preface to the third printing, McLuhan offered a helpful elucidation of his famous contention: "The section on 'the

medium is the message' can, perhaps, be clarified by pointing out that any technology gradually creates a totally new human environment. Environments are
not passive wrapping but active processes."[7] This statement indicates what many
fail to understand about the main assertion behind the adage "the medium is
the message": namely, that the message is about the creation of new human
environments.

Although he initially referred to a change in "scale or pace or pattern," what
McLuhan wanted to emphasize was this: "the medium is the message" means
that the true significance of any new technology is the new human *environment*—
or space, or setting, or locale, or atmosphere, or milieu, or surrounding, or scene,
or situation, or landscape, or terrain, or territory—that such a new technology enables. In addition, McLuhan clarified that such new environments are not static
or passive but "active processes." In other words, those who find themselves in
new environments created by new technologies (media) are being *acted upon*.[8]

McLuhan went on to explain his vision that new, active environments necessitated the need for counterenvironments. In particular, he saw the arts and
education as best suited to providing such counterenvironments. As concerns education, McLuhan held that the study of media "opens the doors of perception"
so that human beings might evaluate and counter the onslaught of ever-newer
environments created by their proliferating technologies. In this way, "media
studies"—the critical assessment of technological development—offers an opportunity to teachers and learners to use technology in the creation of counter- or
"anti-environments." Such environments can mitigate, withstand, and even turn
back the technology-induced environments that are acting upon individuals and
communities. In other words, the classroom, by its nature, offers an exemplary
environment for creating counter/anti-environments vis-à-vis media. Applying
McLuhan's insight to college courses in religion, the class-"room" might just be the
best environment to counter a media-infused cultural environment that misunderstands and misrepresents a variety of religious/spiritual subjects, be it Islamic
history, Christian fundamentalism, or the tension between science and faith.

For McLuhan, the critical evaluation and implementation of new media
coincided with the fact that we "are entering the new age of education that is
programmed for discovery rather than instruction." In this light, McLuhan
commended "the new scene of electronic involvement," one in which media
is engaged in order "to enable us to see our situation."[9] For a scholar who was
writing in a day when the "new scene of electronic involvement" was, as far as
schools were concerned, limited to rolling a radio, television, or film projector
into the classroom, McLuhan's ability to see into the far-off future is to be appreciated. McLuhan, it can be claimed, intuited today's multimedia classrooms—
classrooms which give students the ability to see "our situation" through a variety
of lenses and from multiple vantage points.

With LED projectors, video disc players, computers, Internet access, and wireless connectivity present in many if not most college and university classrooms (not to mention teachers and learners wielding "smart" phones, laptops, and tablet computers), demonstrating the validity of McLuhan's decades-old observation about how technology alters human environments is a straightforward task. Today, a professor can, within the walls of his or her own classroom, show students a website containing information that supports a particular argument. At the same time, a resourceful student (sitting toward the back of the class, perhaps) can immediately search the Web for an article or blog post that counters the argument. And, if the professor confronts the student about surfing the Internet during lecture, the student can tweet a complaint or, worse, head for http:// ratemyprofessor.com, where comments and rankings are compiled. Implied in this "new culture of learning" is the notion that academic discovery can happen independently of the instructor even *while* the instructor is instructing.[10] Indeed, when one considers the modern-day classroom—a boundary-flexible, nonlinear, decentralized space no longer defined by walls or clocks or professors standing at the front of the room—one concludes that McLuhan prophesied aright. More than ever, the medium is the message. More than ever, technology—and the extent to which it is engaged and implemented, assessed and applied—determines the environment, including the pedagogical environment of college and university religion classrooms.

Religion, Media, and the Extension of Humanity

Individuals and communities have seemingly always relied on media when it comes to the transmission and spread of religious ideas. Even before the advent of written text, humans created media such as cave drawings, talismans, totems, and monuments—think Stonehenge—to communicate their conceptions of the gods and how the gods related to the human realm.[11] With the evolution of pictographic, cuneiform, and alphabetic structures of nonverbal expression, it became possible for humans to communicate their notions of the divine in increasingly sophisticated and efficient modes. The introduction of "portable" text—whether written on stone tablets, animal skin, or papyrus—provided an additional layer of sophistication and efficiency. The development of such communications media is, arguably, what made it possible for the Vedas to become foundational for ancient Indian culture and, more recently, for religions like Islam and Christianity—both of which were eventually aided by the invention of moveable type—to take hold around the globe. To apply McLuhan's idea that media are "extensions of man," religious texts make it possible to transmit and, more importantly, *broadcast* human religious ideas and speech.[12] It goes perhaps without saying, then, that in the age of digital electronic communication, such transmission and broadcasting can be maximized. And here it is worth taking note of the literal sense of the word "broadcast"—namely, the notion that, like a sower throwing seed, media make it possible for words and images to be cast and planted far and wide. The transition from oral to written tradition has been determinative in the evolution of human religious consciousness and experience. Therefore, it should not come as a surprise if and when the transition from written to digital tradition proves to be similarly determinative.

What, then, do the preceding observations imply for religion courses in twenty-first-century colleges and universities? Only this: The new learning environments enabled by the latest and ever-evolving advances in electronic (digital) communications media potentially allow for three interdependent possibilities:

1. Unprecedented access to information about religious subjects, religious leaders, and the members of religious communities.
2. More effective modes for analyzing and evaluating religious subjects, religious leaders, and the members of religious communities.
3. Greater opportunity to advocate for change in regard to religious subjects, religious leaders, and the members of religious communities.

What follows, then, is an exploration of each of these three possibilities, with an eye toward McLuhan's implication that the modern classroom is at its best when it functions as a "counterenvironment" or "anti-environment" set up and maintained in intentional contrast to the dominant cultural environments created by new communications media.

Access to Information and Technology in the Religion Classroom

Before considering the analysis and evaluation of media in the religion classroom, or strategies for advocacy and reform implementing media in the religion classroom, it will prove useful to describe the landscape made possible by the typical undergraduate institution's "information technology" (IT) department—a landscape to be explored by teachers and learners alike. At the same time, this description of the media landscape comes with a disclaimer: By the time you read this, this description will likely be inadequate or even passé, given the breakneck pace with which communications technologies alter and render the current version obsolete. The fact that the rapid evolution of electronic media is a fact of life can be (and has been) described in various ways, from Moore's Law (which holds that the capacity and speed of digital memory increases exponentially) to the "Rise of The Cloud" and the resulting redundancy of more tangible storage media such as CD-ROM, DVD, Blu-Ray, and portable flash drives. By the time you read this, it may very well be that nano-memory technologies have rendered Moore's Law a quaint artifact and "The Cloud" has been supplanted by something called "The Sky" or "The Air" or "The Wind." In short, by the time you read this, people may well be asking, "Remember Facebook?"[13] Therefore, as you read what's written ahead, keep in mind that it was written in 2014, the year Siri spoke on iPhones, Google eyeglasses hit the market, and working but mostly unused VHS players could still be found in most classrooms.[14]

Nevertheless, whatever the capabilities and brands of hardware and software available in the typical college classroom at a given point in technological history, there are two "givens" that, barring the collapse of the electrical grid, appear to be permanent:

1. Teachers and learners with access to the Internet have access to thousands upon millions of sources of information around the planet.
2. Moreover, teachers and learners with access to the Internet have access to thousands upon millions of people around the planet, including other teachers and learners.[15]

Note, however, a third apparently permanent "given": Political and/or commercial interests will continue to maneuver to control access to information. The notion of an entirely free Internet is a mythical one; increasingly, the digital communications landscape is becoming bounded by restrictive governments and corporations that seek to control access to information and people. Indeed, restriction and censorship are ongoing concerns. One's access to the Internet (and therefore to information and people) can be limited by a variety of factors, including economic, content-based, commercial, and political factors. A brief elaboration of each of these factors will prove useful in demonstrating that "equal access" in the global village is not a guarantee.

Economic factors: In 2012, 75 percent of U.S. households were connected to the Internet (up from 55 percent in 2003), leaving one-fourth of U.S. households without web access.[16] Seventy-eight percent of North Americans say they use the Internet, compared with 32 percent of the rest of the world.[17] For those who are Internet-disconnected, the reason is either economic or by intention.[18]

Content-based factors: Out of concern for digital piracy, many colleges and universities prohibit students from accessing peer-to-peer, file-sharing websites on school computers. Elementary, middle, and high schools filter certain types of web content and block certain websites on school computers, usually out of concern for exposure to inappropriate material or limiting distractions in the classroom and library. However, a social media site that might be a distraction for one student may also be an important research resource for another student. The ongoing debate concerning boundaries for Internet access in schools is similar to earlier (albeit continuing) debates about banned books.[19]

Commercial factors: The concept of "net neutrality" concerns the question of how much control should be tolerated or permitted in regard to the flow of information over the Internet.[20] Broadband corporations can and do control Internet access speeds, discriminating among users in the form of tiers of service, limiting users' upload and download capacities, or expanding bandwidth for certain preferred content providers.[21] It is possible that a day will come that teachers and learners will have to pay closer attention to the limits imposed upon their Internet usage from beyond the firewalls of their academic institutions.

Political factors: Closely related to the commercial factors concerning the viability of an "open Internet" are certain political factors. Beginning in October, 2011, the U.S. Congress considered passage of the Stop Online Piracy Act (SOPA). Supported by record companies and other entities, SOPA seeks, among other things, to permit individuals and corporations to request court orders barring access to certain websites (especially those sites suspected of trafficking in digital piracy). In protest, content providers, search engines, and browser-makers, including Twitter, Google, and Mozilla, facilitated user protests, while Wikipedia temporarily shut down, displaying only a banner that read, "Imagine a world without free knowledge."[22] The Internet-fueled backlash led to significant congressional back-pedaling; SOPA remains tabled.[23] Meanwhile, in China, Iran, and elsewhere, governments continue to limit access to websites that are deemed to pose a threat to governmental interests and overall political stability.[24]

With the preceding four factors in mind, teachers and learners—but especially teachers—designing environments and activities that implement digital communications media will want to consider questions of restriction and access. Do all students have reasonable access to the Internet? Do inequalities exist between course participants—Internet haves and have-nots—that need to be addressed? Which students can log on anytime at home and which students will need to arrange their schedules to log on at the school's library or computer lab or, in the case of "distance learning," a coffee shop or Internet cafe? Are some activities being conducted via a web-based service that may require an upgrade of service with the ISP? Are there participants who live in countries that block access to certain websites that will be required or at least desired for optimal course participation? In short, it will be important to keep in mind that "unlimited" global connectivity is more of an ideal than a reality.

While concern regarding access to technology and information is potentially important for any educator, the ante is upped somewhat for the civically engaged classroom seeking to expand the concept of "room." Moreover, the civically engaged religion classroom at a college or university may, in fact, find that the issue of access and connectivity has a religious dimension. That is to say, as teachers and learners seek to develop a classroom that functions as a "counterenvironment" (or counterculture), as indicated by McLuhan, the study of religion might help formulate a response to at least two questions:

1. How are concerns regarding inclusion and exclusion in the technological development of local and global communities analogous to concerns regarding inclusion and exclusion in the development of religious/spiritual communities?
2. How can specific religious (and non-religious) traditions and their ethical systems inform understanding and advocacy regarding digital communications technology, the flow of information, the privilege of access, and human rights?

Analysis and Evaluation of Media in the Religion Classroom

The two questions concluding the preceding section are examples of the type of inquiry that underlies the assertion that introduced this essay: "Civically engaged teaching and learning in the academic study of religion equips students to analyze and evaluate electronic communication media. . . ." This section highlights strategies designed to equip learners to analyze and evaluate the impact of media on religion and on the study of religion. Throughout the remaining sections of this chapter, keep in mind that all subjects invite the application of critical thinking strategies on at least three levels: (1) how media shapes the formation of religious understandings and traditions, (2) how media shapes the encounter with religious understandings and traditions, and (3) how media shapes the study of religious understandings and traditions. In regard to the strategies outlined herein, special attention is given to web-based content and to social media; examples are cited, and ideas for new directions are offered.[25]

What does it mean that a web-connected classroom has the "world at its finger tips"?[26] For one, it means that a classroom's collective exposure to, say, the Vatican's interior spaces or the Angkor Wat temple complex is no longer limited to the descriptions and images strictly curated by the typical "World Religions" text book. Instead, the wired classroom means that visiting, monitoring, and even

eavesdropping on religious sites and communities from within the typical college classroom is now as easy as booting a web browser and paying a virtual visit.
As mentioned previously, a classroom with a projector and Internet connection
opens up teachers and learners to a world of possible destinations pertinent to the
academic study of religion.

Consider the following example:

An instructor teaching about the "Holy Land" desires to go a bit deeper than
simply having students read and discuss an article or chapter about Jerusalem.
Consequently, the instructor has the idea to lead the class on a virtual tour of Jerusalem, an exercise that can be accomplished via Google Earth or some other
digitally based geographic imaging platform. Now let's say that the same instructor wonders how the tour might be democratized, that is, how to involve each
learner in determining which sites to visit. Such a goal might best be accomplished by engaging learners in a "crowd-sourcing" exercise that enables each
participant to search for, locate, and post words and images of Jerusalem's various contested holy sites using their own laptops, tablets, and smartphones.[27]
This strategy would permit students to describe landmarks and view images
via a common digital platform, whether that platform is the class's own desig-
nated social media page (created, say, with Facebook or Instagram), or a common
blog (using, say, Wordpress or Blogger), or a "wiki" module available through the
school's learning management system (such as Blackboard or Moodle). Finally,
with the information and image gathering completed and projected on the classroom screen, the instructor (or another participant) would facilitate an analysis
and evaluation of the collected data—data that might include the Western Wall,
Haram al Sharif, and the Church of the Holy Sepulchre, as well as the Knesset,
Augusta Victoria Hospital, and the West Bank Barrier ("security fence" or "separation wall"?). Such data is likely to reveal strong emotion, unfiltered bias, and
divergent interpretations of fairness, justice, and international law.

The example—a literal yet virtual engagement with Jerusalem as *civitas*—
serves to illustrate the extent to which digital communications technology can
alter and enhance the learning environment. Of course, before an instructor
would be able to create such an environment, he or she would need to be familiar
with the products and terms included in the preceding example: Google Earth,
crowd-sourcing, digital platform, social media, Facebook, Instagram, blog, Wordpress, Blogger, wiki, learning management system, Blackboard, and Moodle.
That is to say, there is a learning curve to this stuff. However, even where an
instructor possesses considerable grasp of the technological nomenclature and
expertise with the available digital tools, it does not mean necessarily that the
classroom will be magically transformed into the anti- or counter-environment
envisioned by McLuhan. That is, the instructor imagined in this example could
have implemented the available technology simply to do a little tourist-oriented

sightseeing in and around Jerusalem, without the deployment of the higher levels of critical assessment. Moreover, the instructor might have neglected to guide students in assessing how exploring Jerusalem virtually via the Internet is certainly not the same as exploring Jerusalem on the ground and in real time. The point is that no matter how sophisticated the technology and no matter how global the classroom's reach, it is still up to the instructor to equip and guide students in analytical and evaluative reflection upon all dimensions of the learning experience, including its limits.

In the interest of creating an environment in which such critical reflection is facilitated, consider a second example. Whereas the previous example concerning a virtual exploration of Jerusalem can be considered a macro-exploration—literally beginning with a bird's-eye view—the following classroom scenario serves as a micro-exploration, one that begins with the consideration of local or localized events and experiences. The setting for this example is an Introduction to Religion course with twenty-five students at a college in a mid-sized, mid-American city. As part of a two-week long unit on Islam, the instructor has the goal of equipping participants to learning about *salat*, the Second Pillar of Islam, and a key component of Muslim discipline and worship. To meet this goal, the instructor envisions an objective designed to enable learners to witness and reflect upon practices incorporated under the term *salat*. In addition, the instructor wishes to equip learners to analyze and evaluate the effectiveness of *salat* as a religious discipline. Finally, the instructor wants to challenge learners to compare what they've learned about Islam via the study of *salat* to what they've learned about Islam from various news and entertainment outlets.[28]

If the school is fortunate enough to be located near a mosque, then the assignment around *salat* might commence with a guest presentation by a local imam or a visit to a local Islamic center. However, such a presentation or visit, although useful, would offer participants a glimpse into merely one of the variety of settings and modes of *salat*.[29] In terms of the three objectives listed earlier, there remains more to discover. Yet it would not be practical, pedagogically speaking, to spend three additional class meetings on listening to other guest speakers or visiting other mosques, if indeed there are other mosques in the vicinity. Of course, depending on demographics, many schools will be nowhere near a mosque. Here is where the media-enabled learning environment can make a difference.

First, in order to meet the first objective, the instructor invites students to search for video footage of *salat* and post links to or embed the footage in a common platform, such as the online discussion forum module built into most learning management systems.[30] The instructor gives students some additional search terms—*Azan, Shahada, Jummah, Ramadan, Hajj*, Muslim prayer, Sufi meditation—in order to expand the connections to *salat*. Immediately, however, a problem presents itself. What if, despite the additional terms, each student executes the same YouTube search, "salat," and picks the first three videos that appear? The result would be a small sample of video footage. To anticipate this scenario, the instructor declares that any video that has already been posted may not be posted again, thereby rewarding those who attend to the assignment earlier and more or less ensuring a large sample of up to seventy-five videos.

To meet the second objective, the instructor splits students into online discussion groups, assigning each group a set of videos, and inviting them to enter and respond to comments and questions in the online forum and before the next face-to-face meeting of the class. In setting up the forum discussion, the instructor has directed students to compare what they learn about *salat* to their own worship traditions and practices around prayer or meditation.

Finally, the third objective is accomplished when the class meets again and the instructor projects the forum discussions for all to consider. The instructor highlights particularly astute observations, penetrating questions, and compelling comparisons. Students are invited to add commentary and questions. In addition, the professor may want to guide critical reflection regarding scope and import: for instance, the fact that it's on YouTube says nothing about whether the presentation of *salat* is more or less representative or controversial.

Next, the professor opens a new browser window and does a search for "Islam Mainstream Media." Students are invited to direct the instructor regarding which links to explore. Last, students are asked to write a 300-word reflection—about one page—upon the question, "In what ways do news and entertainment messages regarding Muslims support or contradict your own learnings about Islam via the study of *salat*?" The instructor could simply ask students to print out the reflection and hand it in the next time the class meets; however, in keeping with the digitally enhanced, collaborative environment, the professor might instead direct students to cut-and-paste their reflections into a new discussion thread on the forum. This step would invite one more layer of online feedback among participants. Here, the professor might also encourage students to post links to (or embed) additional examples of news and entertainment portrayals of Muslims.

The series of exercises and assignments described in the two examples just given comprise at least six significant learning outcomes:

1. By virtually engaging members of various religious communities—in the collecting of words and images relevant to Jerusalem mainly produced by Jews, Christians, and Muslims, or in gathering narrative video created by Muslim practitioners of *salat* in its various forms and contexts—students develop their ability to explore a religious topic from "within," that is, from the point of view of the creators of the websites and videos accessed.
2. Students develop their ability to engage with one another in collaborative analysis and evaluation not only in person but also online.

3. Students develop their ability to critically reflect upon the ways in which media—websites, news programming, entertainment—influence the way religious communities are perceived.

4. Students develop their ability to create a "counterenvironment" with the intention of providing a corrective narrative in response to the narratives offered by more dominant media environments—yes, McLuhan would be pleased.

5. Students develop their ability to critically engage the new media itself. That is, they learn to ask questions like: How does a Facebook site prejudice one's understanding or limit one's exposure? How does a YouTube video only tell part of the story? What are the disadvantages of a website that does not substantiate its claims by linking to trusted sources? And, for that matter, what makes for a trusted source?

6. As a sort of unwitting end result, students develop their ability to crowd-source or "wikify" their learning and to collaborate on the creation of a potentially permanent online record and repository of data (texts, images, video, discussion and reflection, analysis and evaluation, and more).

All told, these six learning outcomes demonstrate the power and potential afforded by new technologies and the resulting learning environments.

Advocacy and Reform with Media in the Religion Classroom

And yet, in terms of civic engagement, the two examples and six learning outcomes described in the previous section go only so far. While it is true that the preceding sample exercises involving Jerusalem and *salat* civically engage with religious media, issues, communities, and individuals at a certain level, both exercises represent a form of second-order discourse. That is, both examples involve participants in the exercise of collecting data *about* something, of talking *about* something, of interpretation and commentary. Missing, then, is the performative aspect of civic engagement, the element of civic engagement that seeks to have a more direct effect upon a given medium, issue, person, community, or institution.[31]

As the section title indicates, engaging media and messages in the religion classroom includes the potential for advocacy and reform. In connection with this theme, it was asserted at the beginning of this chapter that "civically engaged teaching and learning in the academic study of religion equips learners to utilize electronic communication media for a variety of purposes, including activist purposes." This assertion has in mind a kind of media usage not unlike Martin Luther's posting of *The Ninety-Five Theses* or the publication of Charles Moore's

1963 photographs depicting civil rights demonstrators being attacked by police dogs and fire hoses.[32] The communications media implemented by Luther and Moore "went viral" in their respective fashions and helped inspire the deep shifts in social and religious understandings of their respective eras. Chances are low that the two examples that follow will inspire full-scale social change on par with the sixteenth-century church reformations or the 1960s' civil rights movement. Nevertheless, the examples are intended to inspire teachers and learners to conceive new ways to utilize communications media to effect change in understandings, attitudes, and practices related to religion (and non-religion).

Example One: Internet-Based Media and Interfaith Conversation

Anyone who has ever taken the time to read the comments posted beneath a YouTube video featuring the prominent biologist and atheist Richard Dawkins, or the prominent Christian and creationist Kenneth Ham, knows that productive dialogue regarding the "religion vs. science debate" is in short supply—on YouTube at least. The "conversations" featured in, say, the comments section of a video titled "Richard Dawkins—'What If You're Wrong?'" are marred by the kinds of name-calling and *ad hominem* attacks characteristic of conversations in which participants are anonymous and unaccountable.[33] Even ten minutes of reading such "dialogue" is enough to cause one to despair completely of finding online sources for constructive and effective discussion of the issues in question.[34]

Ideally, college religion courses can serve as strong counterenvironments to settings that do not lend themselves to responsible speech, accountability, civility, or, for that matter, Bloom's "Taxonomy of the Cognitive Domain."[35] The Interfaith Youth Core (IFYC) is an organization that believes that "college students, supported by their campuses, can be the interfaith leaders needed to make religion a bridge and not a barrier." IFYC's goal is the building of "a world characterized by [1] respect for people's diverse religious or non-religious identity, [2] mutually inspiring relationships between people of different backgrounds, and [3] common action for the common good."[36] Religion professors who recognize those three components as worthy outcomes may already be facilitating and modeling interfaith conversation in support of such outcomes. At the same time, new technologies make it possible to expand the impact of such outcomes beyond the boundaries of the classroom and campus.

Consider again the religion and science conversation mentioned earlier. It is possible that a college classroom might have an adequate balance of worldviews to foster a decent dialogue, one that contributes to increased mutual understanding between, say, the secularists and religionists enrolled. On the other hand, at some schools and in some classes, it may be that some voices are missing, or that the conversation is one-sided. Here is where social media and an online website creation platform can help bring others into the conversation and empower students to be part of effecting reform in communities beyond the campus.

One relatively obvious way to implement digital communications tools for the sake of interfaith dialogue is to bring outside individuals and communities into the course space. Programs like Skype or FaceTime can be used to "beam in" dialogue partners—theist and humanist alike—from almost anywhere on the globe. Audio- or video-conferencing tools can be used to enable a panel discussion featuring panelists drawn from, say, the local council of churches and a regional association for atheists. A live, text-based conversation can be facilitated simply by booting an instant messaging platform, such as iMessage or similar programs available via Skype or Facebook.[37] Even such a "minimum" investment in set-up efforts could have the effect of creating among students and the other involved parties the type of pluralism advocated by the IFYC and the Harvard-based Pluralism Project.[38] However, adding an additional component to such dialogue will create a more lasting and potentially far-reaching resource for constructive conversation. This additional component involves the creation of a website that would feature a course's science and religion conversation—or a "Does God Exist?" conversation, or any conversation featuring disparate religious viewpoints—in highly distilled form.

Step One for such a project would be the actual dialogue itself. Conversation events involving outside groups of believers and nonbelievers would take place under the auspices of leaders who can guide a civil conversation. A student or group of students would be deputized to document the conversation on paper and with photos if not also video. *Step Two* would be to ask participants this question: "Which arguments made by 'the other side' bore some validity or had the most merit? Which arguments had the least merit?" *Step Three* would be to challenge and empower students to create a single website that would feature the dialogue in its critically assessed form. Online "WYSIWYG" website builders such as Weebly or WordPress make it possible for novices to create websites of quality appearance and depth.[39] A website documenting the critical outcomes of the aforementioned religion and science conversation would feature (a) a description of the conversation's participants, (b) highlights from the conversation, (c) a listing of the arguments that participants found most useful, and perhaps (d) participants' "testimonies" regarding how the conversation informed or altered their understanding and regard of "the other." The documentation described in Step One would provide ample imagery to lend the website visual data and appeal. The outcome: an online destination cataloguing the fruits of one classroom's engagement with other persons and communities around a constructive conversation concerning religion and science. The URL (link) to the website could then be repeatedly dropped into the comment section of the "Richard Dawkins—'What

If You're Wrong?'" YouTube video, and similarly contentious comment sections. Who knows? Such guerilla implementation of the student-created website could go viral and bring about (slight) shift in the tenor of the (ongoing) debate.

Example Two: Internet-Based Media and the Revision of History

This final example borrows from the strategies of an existing web-based resource. The resource, the Historyapolis Project, can be viewed at historyapolis. com.⁴⁰ The Historyapolis Project "seeks to illuminate the history of Minneapolis. Inspired by the idea that history is a powerful tool for community-building, we are working to unearth stories that can explain how the city took shape. We hope to entertain and engage the broadest possible audience. But our central mission is to challenge popular assumptions about our city's bygone days."⁴¹ Historyapolis represents a process of historical record-making that is community-based, democratized, and appreciative of oral tradition. Even a cursory investigation of the Historyapolis website, beginning with its invitation for viewers to log on as participants, will demonstrate the promise that a similarly constructed resource might have for a college religion course.⁴²

Specifically, professors who challenge and empower students to tell their own stories, to relate the formation of their own religious formation and identity, might also consider enlisting these very same students in a project that empowers such story-telling among members of communities beyond the edges of campus. What would it take for students in a religion course to connect with and enable the members of, say, a local (or distant) immigrant group to share publicly their own faith narratives in light of arriving in and adapting to a new religious landscape?⁴³

Consider again the example of the history of Minneapolis, especially its religious history. Thanks in part to Garrison Keillor's tales of Lake Wobegon, a popular conception is that the region's religious make-up is dominated by Scandinavian Lutherans who bring Jell-O salads to church potlucks and who speak the dialect featured in the movie *Fargo*.⁴⁴ While Minneapolitan history is clearly informed by the waves of Scandanavian Lutheran immigrants that arrived to the area beginning two centuries ago, the popular conception will be challenged and corrected by the faith stories of more recent immigrant groups, especially of Hmong and Somalia immigrants. These two groups have brought, respectively, Shamanist and Muslim religious traditions to Minnesota's Twin Cities. The Historyapolis Project offers, potentially, a virtual locale where the new faith stories can be shared, so that the history might be more accurately revised.

Certainly, each university's city and each college town has an under-recognized and under-reported religious story to tell, whether that story belongs to the most recent immigrant group or to the indigenous group that lived and worshipped on the land originally. New communications technologies make it possible to engage with the members of such communities, to hear and record their stories, and to share those stories with the world. The outcome for students is a learning experience that empowers them to become civically engaged teachers and, in a small way, religious reformers.

Conclusion

When Marshall McLuhan prophesied the "Global Village" he also saw the potential for the college classroom to serve as an important environment for critical reflection and truth-telling within the Village. Developments in modern communications technologies have confirmed both McLuhan's prophesy and his vision for teaching and learning in the university setting. Religion professors committed to pedagogies of civic engagement will do well when they consider and implement strategies made possible by the ongoing development of the Internet and the digital electronic media that make the "World Wide Web" a reality.

Notes

1. "The new electronic interdependence recreates the world in the image of a global village." See Marshall McLuhan, *The Gutenberg Galaxy: The Making of Typographic Man* (Toronto: University of Toronto Press, 1962), 31.
2. It is possible that a religion instructor will design a course that intentionally avoids all electronic media *and* practices civic engagement. Such a course might, in the spirit of "disconnecting," eschew using the Internet for research or cell phones for communicating across distances, but nevertheless lead students into the neighborhood for various projects. "Civic engagement" in such a course would be necessarily local rather than broad and global.
3. Marshall McLuhan, *Understanding Media: The Extensions of Man* (New York: McRaw-Hill, 1964), 8.
4. Ibid., 9.
5. Ibid. Here, McLuhan chastised General Electric for believing at the time that it was in the business of making light bulbs rather than in the business of moving information.
6. Cultural critic Dwight MacDonald, writing in 1964, characterized *Understanding Media* as "impure nonsense, nonsense adulterated by sense," an "accumulation of contradictions, non sequiturs, facts that are distorted and facts that are not facts, exaggerations, and chronic rhetorical vagueness. . . ." Writing a few months later, author Christopher Ricks criticized McLuhan for denying that "content plays any part at all" in the analysis of media, before dismissing

Understanding Media as "a viscous fog, through which loom stumbling meta-
phors." Both essays were republished, along with other reviews of McLuhan's
work and responses from McLuhan himself, in Gerald Stearn (ed.), *McLuhan:
Hot & Cool: A Primer for the Understanding of & Critical Symposium with a Rebuttal by McLuhan* (New York: Dial Press, 1967), quotations at 205, 212, 215. See
also Raymond Rosenthal (ed.), *McLuhan: Pro & Con* (New York: Funk and Wagnalls, 1968).

7. McLuhan, *Understanding Media*, vi (in "Preface to the Third Printing").

8. As another communications theorist put it, "The environments set up by
different media are not just containers for people; they are processes which
shape people." Quoted from John M. Culkin, "A Schoolman's Guide to Marshall McLuhan," *The Saturday Review*, March 18, 1967. Culkin's article provides a helpful and accessible overview of McLuhan's systematic thought. See
http://www.unz.org/Pub/SaturdayRev-1967mar18-00051 (accessed on June
15, 2014). More Culkin: "We become what we behold. We shape our tools
and our tools shape us." Quoted in Marshall McLuhan, Quentin Fiore, and
Jerome Agel, "The Medium Is the Massage: With Marshall McLuhan," audio
recording, produced by John Simon, Columbia Records, 1968. See http://www.
themediumisthemassage.com/the-record/ and http://marshallmcluhan.com/
downloads/the-medium-is-the-massage-reissue.mp3, 35:05 (accessed on June
15, 2014).

9. McLuhan, *Understanding Media*, vii–x.

10. "In the new culture of learning, the classroom as a model is replaced by learning environments in which digital media provide access to a rich source of information and play, and the processes that occur within those environments
are integral to the results" and "the new culture of learning focuses on learning
through engagement *within* the world" (italics in the original). Quoted from
Douglas Thomas and John Seely Brown, *The New Culture of Learning: Cultivating the Imagination for a World of Constant Change* (Lexington, KY: Thomas and
Brown, 2011; printed by CreateSpace Independent Publishing Platform), 37–38.
This volume offers much insight and abundant examples of the kinds of teaching and learning environments enabled by new media. To illustrate the kind of
decentralized and interdependent processes advocated in the book, the authors
intentionally avoided publishing through the established academic press—an
example, perhaps, of the medium being the message. See Goldie Blumenstyk,
"Manifesto for a New Culture of Learning," *The Chronicle of Higher Education*,
online edition, May 15, 2011, http://chronicle.com/article/Understanding-the-
New-Culture/127459 (accessed June 15, 2014).

11. For an ambitious, erudite, and interdisciplinary consideration of the evolution-
ary bases of human religious expression, including the technologies (media)
humans developed to create such expression, read Robert N. Bellah, *Religion
in Human Evolution: From the Paleolithic to the Axial Age* (Cambridge, MA:

Harvard University Press, 2011). Throughout the tome, Bellah underscores the human inclination to represent religious ideas symbolically and iconically, whether through spoken word, writing, painting, music, statuary, monument, and so on—that is to say, via media.

12. Interestingly, the extent to which McLuhan's ideas about media were influenced by his deeply held Roman Catholic faith is a matter that continues to be debated. See (or hear), for instance, "Marshall McLuhan, Man of Faith," *Encounter* radio program, Australian Broadcast Company, broadcast May 19, 2012. http://www.abc.net.au/radionational/programs/encounter/marshall-mcluhan-man-of-faith/4005998 (accessed August 15, 2013). According to one scholar interviewed, Michael W. Higgins, McLuhan was a daily communicant at St. Michael's College in Toronto. McLuhan, says Higgins, viewed the visually oriented Roman Catholic Mass as "undamaged" by the technological shifts represented by Gutenberg's printing press and, later, electronic mass communication.

13. Remember MySpace?

14. On the same day that this footnote is being written, a librarian at Augsburg College in Minneapolis, MN, sent an e-mail to all faculty asking for their input regarding a proposal to (a) remove VHS tapes from the library's reserve shelves and (b) convert video from certain tapes so that the data can be digitally streamed to classroom computers.

15. Whether the connection is synchronous (as with a "live chat," "webinar," or other online gathering platform) or asynchronous (as with email, SMS/text message, postings to an online forum), the Internet allows people to connect with people, and teachers and learners to connect with each other, in ways that have been heretofore too costly and/or too slow. This fact alone implies a truly new classroom environment—a "global classroom," as it were.

16. United States Census Bureau, "Computer and Internet Trends in America," *Measuring America,* https://www.census.gov/hhes/computer/files/2012/Computer_Use_Infographic_FINAL.pdf (accessed January 7, 2014). Although the report says "America," the numbers reflect U.S. households only.

17. "Internet Users in North America, June 30, 2012." http://www.internetworldstats.com/stats14.htm (accessed June 15, 2014).

18. For example, in 2012, 12.2 percent of U.S. households reported they did not have an Internet connection because they did not want it, while 10.1 percent reported having no home web access because it was too expensive or because they lacked a suitable computer. Ibid.

19. See, e.g., Winnie Hu, "A Call for Opening Up Web Access at Schools, for Learning's Sake," *New York Times,* September 29, 2011.

20. See, e.g., the work of legal scholar Tim Wu, especially Jack Goldsmith and Tim Wu, *Who Controls the Internet: Illusions of a Borderless World* (New York: Oxford University Press, 2006). Wu is credited with coining the term "network neutrality."

21. See, e.g., "Comcast and Netflix Reach Deal on Service," *New York Times*, February 24, 2014.
22. See Wikipedia's own, ongoing page devoted to keeping users current on the status of SOPA: http://en.wikipedia.org/wiki/Wikipedia:SOPA_initiative (last accessed January 8, 2014).
23. A similar bill (called "Preventing Real Online Threats to Economic Creativity and Theft of Intellectual Property Act," a.k.a. PROTECT IP, a.k.a. PIPA) under consideration by the U.S. Senate remains in a similar state of limbo.
24. See, e.g., Jonathan Kaiman, "Tiananmen Square Online Searches Censored by Chinese Authorities," *The Guardian*, June 4, 2013. http://www.theguardian.com/world/2013/jun/04/tiananmen-square-online-search-censored (accessed June 15, 2014).
25. This chapter offers specific examples of teaching and learning exercises strongly supported by digital communications technologies. For a highly useful, well-designed framework for thinking about and strategizing for media-enhanced courses and classrooms, consult Diana Lauillard, *Rethinking University Teaching: A Conversational Framework for the Effective Use of Learning Technologies*, 2nd ed. (London and New York: Routledge, 2004). The four major examples of teaching and learning exercises described herein fall under the various rubrics elaborated in Lauillard's work.
26. It has been widely and variously observed that the World Wide Web offers "the world at one's fingertips." In the case of the classroom, consider these words: "Greater accessibility to information means that our current generation of children has the world at its fingertips. Texts and documents from distance libraries are available instantaneously. Audio recordings of great speeches can instill passion in ways that textbooks may not. Classrooms in different states—or countries—can communicate instantly." Quoted from Todd Tarpley, "Children, The Internet, and Other New Technologies," in *Handbook of Children and Media*, ed. Dorothy Singer and Jerome Singer (London: SAGE Publications, 2001), 548. Regarding this source, published in 2001, it's worth noting that most of the book's thirty-nine chapters deal primarily with television; only two of the chapters, including Tarpley's, specified "online" or "Internet" as the primary subject matter. A second edition was published in 2011, with several new articles devoted to online concerns; in addition, Tarpley's article was moved from chapter 29 to chapter 3.
27. Of course—and here's an example of the concern treated in the "Access to Information and Technology" section earlier in the chapter—it should not be assumed that each student will have his or her own portable Internet-connected device. On the other hand, many schools have computer labs, with a bank of computer stations—one for each student. Such a resource might be the most expedient way to "equalize" access to the needed technologies.

28. An exercise such as this one will provide varying types and levels of challenge for Muslim and non-Muslim students alike. Good pedagogy requires that the instructor attend to the dynamics created when the religious subject under consideration is familiar and even holy to some but not to all students.

29. This is not to say, of course, that a site visit or field trip is not highly worthwhile or effective. See Marianne Delaporte and Hans Wiersma, "Site Visits and Civic Engagement," *Religious Studies News*, October 2010. http://www.rsnonline.org/index.php?option=com_content&view=article&id=252&Itemid=333 (accessed January 21, 2014).

30. Or consider using Voicethread, Prezi, or a class-designated YouTube channel (to name three web-based resources not yet named) as a platform for collecting video data.

31. Here, the notions of civic engagement's "performative aspect" and "direct effect" correspond with part of the definition of civic engagement offered by Barbara Jacoby: "Through civic engagement, individuals—as citizens of their communities, their nations, and the world—are empowered agents of positive social change for a more democratic world." Barbara Jacoby, "Civic Engagement in Today's Higher Education," in *Civic Engagement in Higher Education: Concepts and Practices*, by Barbara Jacoby and Associates (San Francisco: Jossey-Bass, 2009), 8–9. Of course, part of the challenge in a college religion course will be to assess competing claims regarding what constitutes "positive social change" and a "more democratic world." For further discussion of this challenge, see chapter 1 of this volume.

32. There are numerous renditions of the manner in which the invention of moveable type made possible the quick spread of Luther's ideas. See for instance, "Social Media in the 16th Century: How Luther Went Viral," *The Economist*, December 17, 2011. http://www.economist.com/node/21541719 (accessed June 15, 2014). The story of how Charles Moore's photos brought national attention to civil rights in the American South is told by Moore in *Charles Moore: I Fight with My Camera*, DVD, directed by Daniel Love (Pittsburgh: Kenneth Love International, 2005). This half-hour documentary is available at https://www.youtube.com/watch?v=dob40602LzA (accessed July 1, 2014).

33. "Richard Dawkins—"What If You're Wrong?'" https://www.youtube.com/watch?v=6mmskXXetcg (accessed July 23, 2014; on this date, the video had more than 3.8 million views and more than 285,000 comments).

34. A more civil conversation—one featuring Dawkins and fellow biologist Francis Collings— can be found in David Van Biema, "God vs. Science," *TIME*, November 5, 2006. http://content.time.com/time/magazine/article/0,9171,1555132,00.html (accessed July 23, 2014).

35. Benjamin Bloom, ed., *Taxonomy of Educational Objectives: The Classification of Educational Goals: Book 1. Cognitive Domain* (White Plains, NY: Longman, 1956).

36. See http://www.ifyc.org/about (accessed July 24, 2014). Consider also Diana Eck, head of the Pluralism Project at Harvard University, who contends that interfaith work is a civic issue: "Creating pluralistic societies . . . will require the energies of citizens who participate in the forms of public life, political life, and civic bridge-building that make diverse societies work. Generating new thinking adequate for the twenty-first century and its religious life will also require the best of theological reflection in every religious tradition, new theological thinking that is responsive to the challenges of both secularism and religious pluralism." Quoted from Diana Eck, "Prospects for Pluralism: Voice and Vision in the Study of Religion," 2006 Presidential Address, *Journal of the American Academy of Religion* 75 (December, 2007): 773; also available at http://jaar.oxfordjournals.org/content/75/4/743.full.pdf (accessed July 27, 2014).

37. Using a messaging application to record interfaith conversation has advantages, including the fact that it makes possible the retention of a transcript. Consider an assignment that directs students to (1) find a conversation partner among their Facebook friends, (2) make screenshots of the Facebook conversation so that they might be shared in class (with the conversation partner's permission), and (3) reflect upon and assess the conversation after the fact.

38. http://pluralism.org.

39. WYSIWIG stands for "What You See Is What You Get"—a reference to the visual interface that sits atop the underlying html code. An application that facilitates the creation and maintenance of a website or blog is called a "Content Management System" or CMS. Such applications allow for a high degree of collaboration among participants.

40. http://historyapolis.com (accessed July 24, 2014).

41. Ibid.

42. As of this writing, the Historyapolis Project in fact lacks entries regarding the history of churches, mosques, synagogues, temples, lodges, covens, etc. in Minneapolis. Persons with connections to such histories—and who may have stories to tell—are invited to sign-up and contribute!

43. This is a rhetorical question. It would take at least the kind of website-building application discussed in the previous example. In the case of Augsburg College, which hosts the Historyapolis Project, an ongoing grant from the city of Minneapolis made possible the appointment of a new faculty member and the funding of resources, including staff, of the school's IT department.

44. See, e.g., Garrison Keillor, *Lake Wobegon Days* (New York: Viking, 1985). Regarding the film *Fargo* (1996), see Mary Ann Beavis, "*Fargo*: A Biblical Morality Play," *Journal of Religion and Film* 4.2 (October, 2000). http://www.unomaha.edu/jrf/fargo.htm (accessed July 24, 2014).

7

Service and Community-Based Learning

A PEDAGOGY FOR CIVIC ENGAGEMENT
AND CRITICAL THINKING

Philip Wingeier-Rayo

IS DEMOCRACY REDUCIBLE to discourse? An old television advertisement for a fast-food chain criticized the paltry size of its competitor's hamburgers with the question "Where's the beef?" This phrase took on a political meaning when Walter Mondale repeated it during the 1984 Democratic presidential primaries as a critique of the lack of substance in the platform of competitor Gary Hart. This criticism could also be valid of academics who reduce democracy to discourse without "walking the talk" and who do not provide students with practical civic engagement skills. How can we encourage critical thinking and civic engagement without modeling it? If students merely read about civic engagement, will this skill be transferable and implemented in the everyday lifestyles of our students? Can we teach civic theory and expect students to be engaged in their communities? The answer is probably not. This chapter discusses service-learning (or, as more generally described in this volume, "community-based learning") as a pedagogical strategy that educators can use to both meet learning objectives and practice civic engagement skills.

Definitions of Service-Learning

According to Andrew Furco, there are more than two hundred published definitions of service-learning.[1] For example, the Center for Civic Engagement at Oregon State University defines service-learning as "the integration of meaningful learning, community service, and reflection. Service-learning requires partnership and collaboration between students, community partners, and faculty/staff to address community identified needs while engaging students in hands-on, experiential learning about issues of local concern."[2] A popular definition offered by Thomas McGowan is "a pedagogical strategy that utilizes authentic community service to enhance academic learning."[3] For the purposes of our focus in this book on civic engagement, I use the definition of the Learn and Serve National Service-Learning Clearinghouse that defines service-learning as "a teaching and learning strategy that integrates meaningful community service with instruction and reflection to enrich the learning experience, teach civic responsibility, and strengthen communities."[4]

A similar term that some prefer to use is "community-based learning." This term implies less of a power differential between the students who carry out the service and the recipients of the service. Community-based learning also implies that there are resources within the community that can be accessed by the students for pedagogical purposes without any service at all. This is an important distinction within the field, because many college students come from a privileged background. Service-learning, on the other hand, can imply that they are offering a benevolent service to an underserved and underprivileged community—which somehow makes them superior. Service-learning can also imply that the receiving community is just that: passive recipients of the generosity of well-meaning, affluent students. Certainly there are power imbalances in the world, and universities are often places of privilege. Community-based learning is a term that emphasizes the educational resources and opportunities that communities have to offer and that they are equal partners with the university. In this chapter I primarily use "service-learning" because this is the term used by my university and in my syllabi in the courses and experiences to which I refer. It is also the more common term in higher education. But it should be apparent that the term "community-based learning" complexifies the conversation and offers a viable alternative name for this pedagogical strategy.

Some academics hastily disregard service-learning or community-based learning as not academically rigorous and therefore do not include it as a teaching strategy. While this critique has its merits, service-learning often has been confused with mere community service without the structured instruction and reflection that enhance learning. The difference between service-learning and mere community service is found in the alignment of service-learning activities with the course learning objectives.[5] One could make a similar argument for lab within a science class. A science instructor would not require a lab experiment on a topic unrelated to learning outcomes of the course. A lab experiment is only appropriate when it complements the competencies that students are mastering. Similarly, this analogy could be extended to many academic disciplines. The rule of thumb is whether or not the stated learning outcomes or competencies can be advanced by a service-learning activity; if so, then it is a valid teaching strategy.

Does Service-Learning Contribute to Civic Engagement?

The point of this book is to offer pedagogies that enhance civic engagement. This chapter argues that service-learning is one of the best teaching strategies to actually practice civic engagement. Of course, my co-authors in this volume are presenting many wonderful theories and pedagogies to teach civic engagement in the classroom. Here I would like to use the analogy of a medical student who goes on to specialize as a surgeon. Would you like to be the first patient of a surgeon who has only studied human anatomy and surgical procedures in the classroom? Or would you prefer to be the patient of a surgeon who has had hours of experience in the operating room assisting, receiving feedback, and reflecting on the outcome with experienced surgeons? Service-learning can be that laboratory where students practice the classroom theory in the real world, get feedback from the community partner and their professors, and reflect on the experience.

The U.S. Department of Education had this to say about the relationship between classroom learning and community-based learning for developing democratic principles:

> A good understanding of the democratic principles and institutions embodied in our history, government, and law provide the foundation for civic engagement and commitment, but the classroom alone is not enough. Research shows that students are more likely to have a sense of social responsibility, more likely to commit to addressing community or social problems in their adult lives as workers and citizens, and more likely to demonstrate political efficacy when they engage in structured, conscious reflection on experience in the larger community.[6]

The broad conclusions of this study can be replicated each time an instructor employs service-learning as a pedagogical tool in a course and assesses its effectiveness for meeting civic engagement as a competency. Of course, when a student is completing an assignment for a grade, then this is not an objective evaluation of an ongoing commitment to civic engagement. In fact, the student is being encouraged—or even coerced—to perform in exchange for a grade in a course. However, by practicing civic engagement in a safe environment such as a class and reinforcing the behavior, it increases the likelihood that the behavior will stick. As training wheels are to riding a bicycle, as braces are to straight teeth, so is the service-learning pedagogy to civic engagement. Civic engagement, as with any learned behavior, must be practiced and reinforced in order to increase the likelihood that it will become a habit, as the U.S. Department of Education research just cited appears to indicate.

Given the heavy emphasis of getting outside the classroom in service-learning, its critics claim that it is not academic enough for an institution of higher learning. However, Alexander Astin, emeritus professor and founding Director of the Higher Education Research Institute at UCLA, argues that service-learning is not only academic but is also a powerful tool to advance the traditional goals of a liberal arts education:

> I would submit that there is currently available to all of us who teach the liberal arts a simple but extremely powerful tool that not only promises to make liberal learning more "pragmatic" in addressing our myriad social problems, but that also provides us with an opportunity to strengthen the most important features of a classical liberal education. I am speaking here for "experiential learning," and the special form of it that has come to be known as "service learning."[7]

There are two factors that can contribute to making service-learning a valuable teaching strategy: adequate preparation beforehand and critical reflection afterward. When a service-learning project is introduced into a course, students require instructions on how to have a meaningful experience and direction on what skills or competencies they are expected to practice. Also essential is reflection following service to make connections between theory and practice. Some instructors point out the student learning outcomes and literally draw connections between the syllabus and the service-learning exercise. In David Kolb's book *Experiential Learning: Experience as the Source of Learning and Development*, he offers a helpful framework for connecting theory to practice. Kolb believes that the learning process should go through a cycle of four key stages: (1) concrete experiences, (2) reflective observation, (3) abstract conceptualization, and (4) active experimentation.[8] While these four stages are helpful, I would add a prior stage of introduction to prepare the students for the service-learning experience; I explain my rationale in the next section.

Selecting a Service-Learning Project

So far in this chapter we have seen service-learning from the perspective of the instructor and student, but we have not dealt with how the service will benefit the community partner. Service projects are not merely for the student but also are meant to meet the needs and advance the goals of the community partner. I can remember projects that have been more for the benefit of the students, and the community organization has felt used or that its needs were not being met. An appropriate project must be a win-win with all sides having their goals met. This is important: otherwise, an instructor can abuse a community organization or a population as a means to an end. This may shut the door the next time the instructor (or a subsequent well-meaning group) attempts to partner with the organization. On the other hand, the community partner may be perfectly fine welcoming groups of students whether or not they are productive, as some organizations see education or *conscientizacao* as part of their mission.

So when deciding which service-learning project or what community organization would make an appropriate partner, it is helpful to not answer this question on your own but rather to ask the community partner if you and your class can be of assistance. The community partner should be treated as an equal at all times during the planning, implementation, and evaluation process. It is a fairly safe assumption that if the class is comprised of typical eighteen- to twenty-two-year-olds then the students will have a limited skillset. The students may have experience playing with children, setting up a computer lab, or painting, so if the community partner is expecting highly skilled laborers then the hosts will undoubtedly be disappointed. Many times the community organization will realize ahead of time that the students do not really have what they need and will be too embarrassed to say "no" and will therefore assign a menial task to keep the students busy. I have had this happen on several occasions, and the students go away feeling that this was a waste of time—both for the hosts and for themselves. For example, I have taken students to a thrift store where they sorted and folded used clothes in a back room for a few hours and didn't really have any meaningful contact with people in the community. Although this is not ideal, it is still better than the other option of attempting a more difficult task for which they are unprepared. This has happened to me on several occasions when the community partner had lined up projects like masonry, carpentry, or electrical wiring that neither I nor my students had the skills to accomplish to the hosts' satisfaction. This can be dangerous both for the students and for the future occupants of the building if not done correctly, and it can be a waste of time and materials if the work has to be redone. On one occasion, after spending all morning laying block to build a wall in Nicaragua, our hosts encouraged us to take the afternoon off to go sightseeing. We came back to the project the next morning to find that our hosts had torn down our wall and rebuilt it while we were away.

On the other hand, I have been pleasantly surprised on service projects to find students with very handy skills that I never imagined—you would never know it by looking at them. On one occasion, I took a class to an old church building that was being transformed into a Spanish-speaking mission and discovered that a couple of students had electrical wiring skills. While I asked the other students to shampoo the rugs, these two students re-wired the building and changed outdated lighting fixtures, saving the church hundreds of dollars in electrician fees. Over time, in order to go into service-learning projects better prepared and avoid misunderstandings with the hosts, I have developed a questionnaire that students can complete with a checklist of their levels of competency in a variety of areas such as masonry, electrical, plumbing, painting, computer, language, and music skills. This helps the community partner and me choose a project that is both realistic and within the area of expertise of the students, thus increasing the chances of both the students and the hosts feeling that the service project met real needs and was not a waste of time.

Of course, not all the skills needed to be successful in a community organization are technical in nature, as there are also "people skills" needed to relate to the hosts. If we are dealing with students who come from a rural background or an isolated area (as is the case at my institution) and are being asked to relate to people of different ethnic backgrounds, then the young people may not have the cultural competencies to be effective. On the other hand, if one of your course objectives is for students to acquire cultural competencies, then a cross-cultural service-learning project will give students the opportunity to practice new skills. This was the case with sixty undergraduate nursing students from Clemson University who took a cultural assessment test (Transcultural Self-Efficacy Tool) before and after serving in cross-cultural settings and demonstrated clear improvement after their service project.[9] Of course, it is not fair for the students or for the hosts to throw students into a situation where they are unprepared to succeed.

Whether the project is domestic or international, a thorough introduction to the project before leaving campus can greatly increase its success. Any type of photos, video, talk from previous students who served with the community partner, or a visit from the partners themselves in class can help prepare the students. The class should be fully aware of what to expect and what will be expected of them before beginning the project. No matter how much orientation is given ahead of time, the students must have basic human relation skills, empathy, and a willingness to expand their horizons for the service-learning experience to be successful.

It is always amazing to me to see competencies in students that they had not exhibited in the classroom emerge in the service-learning experience. For me, this really emphasizes the point of this whole chapter, namely, the value of service-learning. I have had students that were quiet, reserved in class, or quite frankly not very good students. Yet when I took these same students off-campus into a marginalized community they were in their element. The students themselves were from similar communities and they felt at home. This could be the case for some ethnic communities that are a very small minority on campus, yet just down the street they represent the majority in the community. These students thus had the survival and the relational skills, and sometimes the language skills, to communicate with the hosts that the other students lacked. Sometimes the ethnic minority students felt more at home in the community than they did on campus. Therefore, unbeknown to me and to their classmates, they communicated with ease with the hosts and took on leadership roles that they had not previously exhibited in the classroom.

For example, I recently taught a class on Christianity and Culture based on H. Richard Niebuhr's classic book *Christ and Culture*. We spent the whole semester debating how Christianity should engage civically on issues like homosexuality, patriotism, pacifism, and civic disobedience, among others. Then we went on a service-learning outing in a trailer project where the residents were primarily Hispanic. The lone Latina in the class was able to use her bilingual skills to greet our hosts in their native tongue, to be culturally sensitive, and to translate back and forth for the rest of the class. Being bilingual did not help this student read, discuss, and write papers on very difficult theological material in the classroom setting; however, her unique language skills were invaluable for successful communication with the Hispanic community.

Another invisible skill that an instructor can never know that a student possesses is working with children and youth. This is an area that surprises me every time I take students out of the classroom. It always amazes me to see a student who I have encountered as quiet or reserved in the classroom take initiative on a service-learning project. By looking out over my class, I never know who has younger siblings, nieces, and nephews, who has worked with children or youth, or who is an only child and completely unprepared to work with children. Yet when I take students outside the classroom into a community, a few students emerge with the skills and charisma to work with children and youth. For example, when I lead service trips to Latin American, there are inevitably hundreds of children around the project. The average age in many Latin American countries is around 16—so these are countries of children. If our assignment involves heavy labor, I will ask our hosts if it would be appropriate to create a program for the children in the community. So, before leaving the United States we will prepare to take both the tools necessary for the construction project and the materials needed for a children's program. This makes for a welcome change of pace for students who are tired and sore from heavy construction to play with children. We can take some simple supplies from a hobby store in the United States and create some fun crafts that are accompanied by a lesson plan on civic values. The danger is replicating colonial and paternalistic habits of the *gringos* teaching or doing for the racialized locals. Therefore, it is always important to work with the hosts to create a lesson plan that is appropriate for the local culture and to model partnership while carrying out the lesson. My point is, however, that some students will emerge as having the human relation skills and overcome language barriers to have meaningful encounters with our hosts. This is something that I could never detect or predict before going on the service trip.

On one occasion, we were repairing an old, abandoned church in Gautao, Cuba, and the group started a game of street soccer with the children. The great thing about playing soccer is that it is an international game that does not require oral communication and helps to break down language barriers and build bridges. The game extended up and down the street with many kids laughing and smiling. At the time we thought that breaking down barriers between the United States and Cuba was a good use of our time and a valuable lesson. After all, on the inside humans are all the same. However, the next day I received a phone call from the Bishop of the Methodist Church in Cuba. Apparently, a neighbor had reported to the state security that the group was neglecting the service project and wasting time "goofing around." This is a valuable lesson about having clarity in what is the objective of the service-learning project. The host and the class may have differing understandings of the end goal. Apparently, the host did not perceive playing soccer and breaking down barriers to be advancing their goal of repairing the building; however, it was meeting the learning objective of acquiring cultural sensitivity skills. In fact, it helped to overcome stereotypes and to build bridges and lasting friendships that will help counterbalance the negative images presented in the U.S. media about communist Cuba. I reflect more on this point further ahead in this chapter.

If one does choose international service-learning, there are obviously many more factors such as cost, time, academic credit, and how to choose your community partner. This is a more in-depth and specific topic than what we can cover in this chapter. However, I will digress enough to reiterate what international travel writer Rick Steves states in his book *Travel as a Political Act.*[10] Steves emphasizes that travel helps to break down barriers and provides opportunities for people to learn from the solutions that other countries offer to the world's basic challenges of food, transportation, health care, education, and government. Moreover, he discourages travelers from going to tourist traps, such as those offered on commercial cruise lines; rather, he suggests that we choose alternative destinations that place us into contact with the ordinary residents and citizens of the host country. Just as the title of Steves' book suggests, when travel and international service-learning is done well, it is an exercise in civic engagement.

This brings us to the opening question in this chapter: Is democracy reducible to discourse? Is it possible to teach civic engagement in a classroom setting and have the students come away with competencies? Yes, I could have taught a semester-long class and read about Cuban history, culture, and current realities. At the end of the semester I could have assessed the students' ability to articulate the material. I could even give them an assignment to write their senator or congressperson to stop the economic embargo and travel ban to Cuba. Would this make them any better at engaging civically? However, from the point of view of an instructor, there is not anything better for learning a skill than going into the setting, practicing those skills, and reflecting on those experiences. The next section discusses how service-learning contributes to civic engagement.

Implementing Service-Learning in College or University

If you are reading this chapter, then I assume that you have used or are considering using service-learning to instill civic engagement. Service-learning has been used by instructors from different institutions, with varying sizes, student bodies, financial resources, and surrounding communities, so these pedagogies would need to be adapted to one's particular context. Much of my experience with service-learning was at Pfeiffer University, a small private institution with 800 undergraduate students and 1,200 graduate and adult degree completion students. Many prospective students choose Pfeiffer with its quiet rural campus over the vast diversity of the larger state universities. They elect a college close to home that is not a radical change from their current lifestyle, because change is scary. This is particularly the case at this institution, where 50 percent of the undergraduates are first-generation college students, and 80 percent of the students come from within a fifty-mile radius of North Carolina's central Piedmont region. The students would like to acquire job skills without challenging underlying assumptions. By definition this makes the parents and students who choose a school for this reason relatively conservative because they want to preserve their way of thinking and being. However, in my undergraduate religion classes, I included course objectives that encourage critical thinking and civic engagement. When attempting to teach these skills, it is necessary to encourage students to examine their assumptions, and so this course objective is in tension with many of the students' reasons for being in school in the first place.

Pfeiffer prides itself on volunteer service, and between June 2012 and June 2013 the students collectively gave 35,000 hours of community service. Our students are very eager to serve others, but it is mainly charity work. Ten years ago, Pfeiffer created the Francis Center for Servant Leadership to coordinate voluntary service. The mission statement of Pfeiffer is "to be the model church-related institution forming servant leaders for life-long learning." In spite of encouraging students to be involved with service, there is little understanding of systemic injustice. The students generally do not understand that benevolent charity, without a systemic analysis about how poverty and injustice are created, could, in fact, perpetuate the very wrongs they hope to right. They are content to give a person a fish and see her or him eat for a day instead of doing the deeper analysis of asking why she or he is hungry.

In 2013 Pfeiffer adopted a new Quality Enhancement Plan (QEP) emphasizing critical thinking and engaged learning. Historically, Pfeiffer students have scored low on the former, while most of the majors require some type of internship or practical to fulfill the latter. This new QEP opens the door for service-learning as a teaching strategy to encourage students to be civically engaged and to think outside the box. For example, the Religion and Intercultural Studies major in which I taught encourages students to move from giving a fish (charity), to teaching a person how to fish (sustainability), to asking who owns the water rights to the river (systemic analysis). Pfeiffer is not content to allow the current charity paradigm to perpetuate the problem by giving a hand-out; rather, we would like to educate young people to challenge unjust systems that create inequality and perpetuate poverty.

As part of the Religion and Intercultural Studies major, Pfeiffer encourages students to take advantage of mission and service opportunities. It does not emphasize mission and service as benevolent charity but rather as engaging the "other" in order to learn about another person's experience. Many of the students at Pfeiffer have had limited exposure to other cultures outside of their own, and most have not traveled outside of the United States. So if your students come from similar backgrounds as Pfeiffer students, service-learning is a pedagogical method to encourage students to encounter others in a thoughtful and reflective manner. I have used this methodology to encourage students to get outside the classroom and open their eyes to the experience of those different from themselves.

On one occasion, while teaching an introductory course for first-year students, I arranged a visit to a homeless shelter where the students facilitated "ice breaker" activities to engage the guests at the center. The students led and participated in a game called "the big picture" where each individual is given one or two cards— each with one small part of the larger picture. Without showing one's card to the others, the group must place the cards in a sequence. Once a card is laid on the floor, it cannot be moved. So the group went around the circle with each individual describing the image on his or her card. Finally one of the guests said that he thought he had the first card and laid it on the floor, thus exposing it to the group. Then another person said that he had the next card. Still another suggested that we not place the cards too close together because they should leave a gap to leave room for mistakes. One by one the residents and the students laid their cards on the floor, creating the big picture. When the last card was laid, everyone took a step back and saw that the picture began with an up-close picture of a chicken on a farm. As one moved back and gained perspective, it turned out the farm was on a billboard, which was on the side of a bus, which was in the middle of a big city. Eventually the picture zoomed out to space with an image of the world.

During a debriefing time following the exercise the guests and the students commented that at the beginning of the exercise each one thought that he had the key card to the puzzle. Each participant thought that his card was the most important one. But only when they were laid down on the floor together, and the participants could take a step back to gain perspective, did they realize that their card was not the most important one. If fact, there is a bigger picture. Through this service-learning opportunity the students were forced to relate to homeless people who had a very different life experience than they did. However, if we were to draw a picture of life in the United States, then no individual's experience would be accurate without the others. Similarly, college students can be lulled into believing that their experience as a traditional eighteen- to twenty-two-year-old college student is normative; however, there are many people who do not go straight to college. When college students are confronted by the experience of marginal communities they realize that there are other perspectives on life. In order for us to gain the big picture we need to learn to encounter and listen to others who come from different backgrounds to broaden one's perspective. Service-learning provides a pedagogical tool to encourage students to go beyond their personal experience to encounter others.

Such stretching of personal boundaries can be even more dramatic in the case of international service-learning. While boarding an airplane for Cuba, for example, one of my students turned to me and said that this was her first time on an airplane. Then another said, "Me, too," and yet another, "Same with me." Not only was this the first time out of the United States for all but one of these nine undergraduate students, but it was the first time on an airplane for three. Right there on the jet-bridge, I whipped out my camera to document this historic occasion. The flight attendant welcomed the first-time fliers onto the plane and even posed for a snapshot. Suddenly I felt a heavier weight of responsibility on my shoulders to chaperone inexperienced travelers on an international service trip, especially to a country like Cuba! But I also saw an incredible window of learning opportunities. This context makes recruiting students for international service trips all the more challenging but, at the same time, all the more rewarding. As mentioned earlier, the background of my Pfeiffer students placed my course objectives directly at odds with my students' goals (and perhaps in line with their parents' fears).

While it is possible to teach critical thinking and civic engagement in the classroom through reading, case studies, and videos, I find that there is nothing like service-learning to experience the skills that one is trying to teach. The objective of this particular international service trip was for the students to challenge their assumptions and prejudices through personal interaction with Cubans in the context of a service project. The firsthand knowledge of the Cuban situation, enhanced by personal encounters with Cubans, facilitates cognitive dissonance in which original assumptions are challenged with the acquisition of new information.

The process leading up to the actual trip lasted a full year. First, we recruited students through information sessions and presentations by students who had traveled on previous service-learning programs. Then we began orientation sessions in the fall with guest speakers, videos, and readings. Finally, in the spring semester immediately prior to our departure, the intensity turned up a notch with background reading on the history, culture, and politics of Cuba. We also collected medical supplies to donate to the medical commission of the Methodist Church in Cuba, which was our host and community partner. I required the students to keep journals to reflect on their reading: They were required to continue this exercise during the trip. While actually in Cuba, in spite of a full in-country schedule of service in the form of building an apartment structure for retired pastors in the central province of Las Villas, as well as encounters with Cubans and visits to historical and cultural sights, we also held nightly reflection sessions. I constantly came back to the question "Is what you are seeing and hearing different from your expectations?" Typical answers included "I thought there would be a lot more poverty" or "I thought that the houses would have dirt floors and that there wouldn't be running water or electricity."

Naturally, we did see hardships and shortages of basic commodities like medicine, which led to good discussions about the Cuban health care system, and eventually to the topic of the United States' trade embargo. We hand-carried our donations of medicines into Cuba and were able to distribute them to medical personnel. One disturbing fact that students wrestled with is that the embargo includes medicine. Even at the height of the Iraq war, the United States never restricted medicines to Saddam Hussein. This and other troubling facts about United States foreign policy contributed to cognitive dissonance regarding what our government has told us about Cuba. The next step is to move from critical thinking to civic engagement. Upon returning, most students were committed to writing to their elected representatives and to seeking speaking engagements in churches and civic organizations.

When I began this service-learning program to take students from rural North Carolina to Cuba—most traveling outside the United States for the first time—I started a year-long orientation about Cuban history, culture, and politics. I was also able to use this service-learning project in Cuba to allow students to learn more about their own reality. For example, in one assignment designed to prepare for our time in Cuba, I told the students that Cubans would ask them about their reality. I asked them, "What was the form of government, economy, culture, and history of North Carolina?" Initially they could not answer the question in a meaningful way, so it became a research project to prepare them for dialogue in Cuba. Through learning about their own context, they learned how much the economy had changed since the passage of the North American Free Trade Agreement (NAFTA) in 1994. This is something they knew on a personal level, since a major textile facility, Pillowtex, closed in nearby Kannapolis, laying off 5,000 workers in 2003—including a parent of one of the students. My students (average age twenty) have lived the effects of NAFTA upon the North Carolina economy, exacerbating the decline of textiles, tobacco, and furniture production and forcing a transition to the financial industry, wineries, Google, Dell, and food research. Marking a transition in the economy, David Murdock, CEO of Dole Foods, has recently opened a $1.5 billion North Carolina Research Campus in Kannapolis. Students have felt these changes in the local economy, but they were not aware of how much North Carolina had changed during their lifetime—especially as a result of NAFTA—until they did research to prepare for their international service.

Similarly, the actual service project in Cuba challenged their understanding of reality when they realized, for example, that Jesse Helms, a Republican senator from North Carolina, was the author of the Helms–Burton law that tightened the U.S. embargo on Cuba and made it illegal for foreign companies trading with Cuba to trade with the United States. This law had the effect of extending the U.S. embargo to other countries and making it a de facto blockade. When the students saw the effects of this policy on the personal lives of Cubans, and understood the personal involvement of Helms, they were motivated to write to their elected representatives upon returning to the United States. In this case, students exhibited transformational learning; they drew upon new personal experiences to develop a more inclusive worldview and, hopefully, greater autonomy as persons. My principal objective in taking the students to Cuba was to encourage critical thinking and civic engagement, inspired by the theoretical framework of Paulo Freire's liberatory pedagogy of critical consciousness through dialogue with reality.

Theoretical Dialogue Partners

The late Brazilian pedagogue Paulo Freire encouraged learners to be empowered and move from being (passive) objects to (active) subjects of their own history.[11] He challenged what he called the "banking concept" of education in which students are treated as passive learners waiting for the instructors to "deposit" information in them. Freire attempted to revolutionize the educational process, and in turn society, by replacing this teacher/student dichotomy with a liberatory pedagogy where both the teacher and the student gain critical consciousness, with a greater awareness of reality, through a dialectic relationship with one another and with a greater awareness of reality.[12] Freire states that this pedagogy has two stages; the first stage requires a discovery of the oppression: "In the first, the oppressed unveil the world of oppression and through the praxis commit themselves to its transformation."[13] Service-learning is one strategy for students to go beyond the classroom to discover oppressive situations. In the experience of my students this came in the form of learning about the Cuban reality and also researching their own socio-economic situation in North Carolina. Another important element to

Freire's libertory pedagogy is the connection between reflection and practice, or praxis. For Freire, education cannot only be in a classroom; rather, there must be a practical component or action combined with reflection. Only when one is confronted by reality can one truly enter into the learning dialectic.

Subsequently Jack Mezirow developed a similar pedagogy that he called transformational learning.[14] Just as in Freire's theory, Mezirow begins with the student's life experiences, and through reflection on new experiences, students themselves produce a paradigm shift leading to a more inclusive worldview and greater autonomy as persons.[15] Through Freire's and Mezirow's pedagogies we are able to use a service-learning opportunity, such as this one, to enable the students to learn more about their own reality.

How to Resource a Service-Learning Project

You might be thinking to yourself: "service-learning projects take resources that my institution doesn't have," or "Where am I going to get resources to implement service-learning?" I delivered a paper on service-learning at a conference on Global Education at Isabella Thoburn College in Lucknow, India. Just before it was my turn to speak the moderator announced that the students had created a display of their service-learning projects, and we took a break to view their posterboards. The education, science, and health care students in Lucknow had been involved in service-learning by going to poor rural villages around the city, paying their own transportation, and had created a puppet show on nutrition and hygiene that they presented to the villagers on Saturday mornings. After viewing these student projects I realized that I had more to learn than to offer! What could I say in that paper? Well, I delivered my paper with some of the points that I am making in this chapter, but I came away with a lesson that I would like to share with you: If the students at Isabella Thoburn College can find the transportation and materials to offer puppet shows in rural villages in India, then surely you can find the resources at your institution for a service-learning project.

As you can see, service-learning pedagogy does not have to be just an exercise in charity or deal only with local issues. It easily adapts and expands to global issues. Richard Kiely developed a pedagogy for global service-learning that encourages reflection on the service-learning experience. He encourages participants not only to expand horizons but to transform them. Kiely's work warns educators against colonizing patterns of global service-learning.[16] In recent years Pfeiffer University has offered opportunities to travel and serve in Guatemala, Nicaragua, and Cuba, and, thanks to the United Methodist Women, students have been sent to participate in the Young Women's Leadership Program in South Korea.

In sum, using Freire's liberatory pedagogy as a basis for service-learning or community-based learning, one can encourage students to reflect on their own life experiences and contexts to see how the people whom they travelled across international borders to serve are not dissimilar to themselves. In a sense, the community that the students are going to serve becomes a mirror in which to see themselves in a different light. After all, the effects of globalization and the global economy are much more far-reaching than we all realize. And, on the inside, we are all basically the same.

Conclusion

Returning to the ad slogan mentioned in the introduction: Where's the beef? This question could also be used to critique pedagogies that only teach about civic engagement in theory but have no practical application. Service-learning provides students with the opportunity to add some beef, or put meat on the bone. It allows them to answer the question "Is this real?" It affords the student opportunities to get outside the classroom into real-life situations and to put into practice what they are learning about civic engagement. This practice must be reinforced by reflection on the service.

One of the criticisms of service-learning is that it is not academic enough. Students are not studying the classics, economic theory, or the latest nuclear physics equations. This may or may not be the case, as there is nothing that would impede the service-learning pedagogy to be used in one of these academic disciplines. In fact, I once attended a Carolina Campus Compact conference on service-learning and sat down at a lunch table with the vice president from Georgia Tech who said that they are encouraging international service-learning campus-wide and are internationally certifying students who meet the requirements on their diplomas. Such students are applying their learning to real-life situations. They acquire real-world experiences and, to reiterate a point made by Charles Strain, they are offering a reality check to the course material.[17] Moreover, they are learning to be engaged citizens and relate their skills to underprivileged communities with real-life problems. The desired outcome of Freire's and Mezirow's pedagogies is that students acquire the skills to become engaged citizens. In other words, they offer pedagogies that do not just offer discourse about democracy but rather teach, practice, and reinforce civic engagement—it is my hope that it will be retained as a lifelong habit.

Notes

1. Andrew Furco, "Institutionalizing Service-Learning in Higher Education," *Journal of Public Affairs* 3 (2002): 209–24.
2. "Service Learning," *Center for Civic Engagement*, Oregon State University, http://sli. oregonstate.edu/cce/ways-be-engaged/service-learning (accessed January 31, 2015).

3. Thomas G. McGowan, "Toward an Assessment-Based Approach to Service-Learning Course Design," in *From Cloister to Commons: Concepts and Models for Service Learning in Religious Studies*, ed. Richard Devine, Joseph A. Favazza, and F. Michael McLain (Washington, DC: American Association for Higher Education, 2002), 83.

4. Cited in Joe Bandy, "What Is Service Learning or Community Engagement?" *Center for Teaching*, Vanderbilt University, http://cft.vanderbilt.edu/guides-sub-pages/teaching-through-community-engagement/ (accessed January 31, 2015). The website of the National Service Learning Clearinghouse is https://gsn.nylc.org/clearinghouse.

5. Andrew Furco, "Service Learning: A Balanced Approach to Experiential Education," in *Introduction to Service Learning Toolkit: Readings and Resources for Faculty* (Boston: Campus Compact, 2000), 9–13.

6. Cited in John Saltmarsh, "The Civic Promise of Service Learning," *Liberal Education* 91:2 (2005): 54.

7. Alexander Astin, "Liberal Education and Democracy: The Case for Pragmatism," *Liberal Education* 83.4 (1997): 5.

8. David Kolb, *Experiential Learning: Experience as the Source of Learning and Development* (Englewood Cliffs, NJ: Prentice-Hall, 1984).

9. Roxanne Amerson, "The Impact of Service-Learning on Cultural Competence," *Nurses Education Perspectives* 31.4 (2010): 18–22.

10. Rick Steves, *Travel as a Political Act* (New York: Nation Books, 2009), viii.

11. Paulo Freire, *Pedagogy of the Oppressed* (New York: Continuum Publishing Company, 1970), 20, 54, 57.

12. Ibid, 52.

13. Ibid, 40.

14. Jack Mezirow, *Transformative Dimensions of Adult Learning* (San Francisco: Jossey-Bass, 1991), 198.

15. Jack Mezirow, *Learning as Transformation* (San Francisco: Jossey-Bass, 2000), 22.

16. Richard Kiely, "Transformative International Service Learning," *Academic Exchange* 9.1 (2005): 275–81.

17. See Charles R. Strain, "Creating the Engaged University: Service-Learning, Religious Studies, and Institutional Mission," in *From Cloister to Commons: Concepts and Models for Service Learning in Religious Studies*, ed. Richard Devine, Joseph A. Favazza, and F. Michael McLain (Washington, DC: American Association for Higher Education, 2002), 25–39.

8

Religious Diversity, Civic Engagement, and Community-Engaged Pedagogy

FORGING BONDS OF SOLIDARITY THROUGH INTERFAITH DIALOGUE

Nicholas Rademacher

MANY COLLEGE-LEVEL EDUCATORS in the area of religious studies and theology seek new ways to engage students who arrive on campus from diverse religious backgrounds. Today, religious diversity includes not only students from various religious traditions but also an increasing number of students who claim no religious affiliation, the so-called "nones." Complicating matters further, students frequently bring with them very limited religious literacy, even among those who are active members of a religious community. In this context, facilitating learning around religion or theology is difficult enough; coupling such learning with civic engagement may seem impossible.

I highlight here three questions that have proven central and recurrent in my encounters with students who represent the kind of diversity just described. First, "How do religious studies and theological educators address religious diversity in their classrooms?" This diversity increasingly includes students from various religious and denominational backgrounds, students who have no religion, and students from particular religious traditions who are in need of basic formation in their own tradition. Second, "How do religious studies and theological educators move beyond the traditional boundaries of classroom learning so that students can become active in discipline-specific civic engagement while promoting broader social change?" Finally, "How do professors of theology and religious studies accomplish the aforementioned goals while at the same time sustaining adequate academic rigor?"

Reflecting on their extensive practice of justice education in the discipline of theology, both Bradford Hinze and Suzanne Toton have brought to our attention the foundational importance of building relationships with those who are poor and the victims of injustice. As Toton explains, "it is essential to venture beyond the walls of our institutions to build relationships of solidarity with communities struggling for justice."[1] Likewise, Hinze proposes, "one of the most basic pedagogical ingredients is to cultivate a disciplined attentiveness, an affective sensitivity, to the lives and life stories of those with whom one is involved."[2] The pedagogical practice presented here takes this call to solidarity as its starting point while simultaneously addressing religious diversity and religious literacy around the Christian tradition.

The pedagogy described in this chapter represents a form of community-based learning insofar as it is designed to build relationships of solidarity through community engagement—in the form of interfaith dialogue—and to stimulate action for structural change. Community-based learning, like service-learning, has proven to be notoriously difficult to define, and most scholars readily admit that there is no one definition of either pedagogical approach. Writing about the latter, Robert Bringle, Patti Clayton, and Julie Hatcher explain, "Service learning is a socially embedded practice . . . and therefore, different words are used—and avoided—in reference to it, reflecting the different assumptions, ideologies, norms, and identities of different personal, organizational, and cultural contexts."[3] Taking these variations into consideration, their definition of service-learning corresponds, in part, to the community-based learning practice that I describe in this chapter:

> A course or competency-based, credit-bearing educational experience in which students (a) participate in mutually identified service activities that benefit the community, and (b) reflect on the service activity in such a way as to gain further understanding of course content, a broader appreciation of the discipline, and an enhanced sense of personal values and civic responsibility.[4]

Indeed, the pedagogy that I relate in this chapter unfolds within a three-credit course, in consultation with the membership of two community partners. The collaboration is designed to encourage in the students and, ideally, the participating members of each community, a greater awareness of their personal values and a commitment to civic responsibility, which is to say, recognition that we are all truly responsible for all. With regard to the students, this community-based learning project is also designed to enable them to better understand religious studies and theology as an interdisciplinary field and to master key terms and concepts in the scholarship that they encounter throughout the course.

Just as Toton and Hinze have challenged educators in the areas of theology and religious studies to take solidarity as a starting point for their teaching, so do critics of service-learning call for social justice foundations in their field. These challenges to service-learning inform the model of community-based pedagogy described in this chapter. For example, Barbara Jacoby, surveying the landscape of critical responses to service-learning, asks whether service-learning actually challenges or merely reinforces existing behavioral and structural injustice.[5] Furthermore, she asks, "Can campus–community partnerships ever be reciprocal partnerships among equals?"[6] Along with other practitioners, Jacoby cautions that such collaborations are frequently caught in the snare of "doing for" rather than "doing with."

In response to such critiques, Marshall Welch explains that "new models of community service and service-learning" that "emphasiz[e] civic engagement, social change, and social justice" are emerging. In these new models, writes Welch, "activism and politics move from the margins to the center of learning as students and educators seek creative ways to move from service to civic engagement."[7] Service and civic engagement, however, are not necessarily mutually exclusive. They can inform one another.

Along these lines, Dan Butin describes his term "justice-learning" (service-learning with "justice-oriented goals") as a practice that "open[s] up the possibility that how we originally viewed the world and ourselves may be too simplistic and stereotypical."[8] While my approach emerges from different philosophical grounds, I agree with Butin's characterization of a particular approach to service-learning that, he argues, makes justice-oriented education possible. This kind of service-learning, he explains,

> provides a space where students are confronted with the ambiguity, noise and disruption of their way of thinking about and engaging with the world [that, in turn,] forces a reconsideration of the taken-for-granted quality of the structures and practices that, beforehand, seemed all too normal.[9]

This justice-oriented service-learning approach coheres with the challenge that Toton and Hinze present to teaching and learning in the field of theology. The community-based learning practice that I explore here attempts to facilitate relationships of solidarity and the development of a justice-oriented disposition that counters prevailing practices and structures that reinforce poverty.

Accordingly, this chapter emerges from reflection on an ongoing, multi-year campus–community collaboration between residents of a local homeless outreach center, members of an ecumenical, intentional-living Christian community, and students in two distinct classes that I teach on an annual basis: "Faith and Justice" and "Catholic Social Thought and Practice." Ultimately, this chapter offers an overview of a pedagogical practice that expands the definition of faith so as to welcome students of all backgrounds; asks students to clarify their own faith commitments and attendant attitudes and behaviors; and engages each student, his or her classmates, and community members in interfaith dialogue on relevant social justice topics. This program is set against a backdrop that includes theoretical readings on the importance and relevance of interfaith dialogue, interdisciplinary perspectives on the meaning of faith, and Catholic social teaching as an introduction to key terms and concepts from the Christian theological tradition.

The four civic capacities defined in the CLEA model, as described in earlier chapters of this book, provide a reference point that may help to clarify the outcomes that, ideally, emerge from the pedagogical practice presented here. The scholarly engagement of religious studies theory and the theology of Catholic social teaching within the framework of interfaith dialogue foster "intellectual complexity" from both traditional and liberatory perspectives. Interfaith dialogue in and with the community—which requires movement from the campus to the community and back again—generates solidarity, which corresponds to "empathic accountability," as students enter into relationship with community members from different backgrounds, including but not limited to individuals from varying socio-economic locations and different belief systems. The multiplicity of views and voices that students encounter during these dialogue sessions expands their basic "frames of reference and social location." Finally, the pedagogical practice outlined here has the potential to lead to "motivated action," including both direct service, as a response to immediate suffering, and action for structural change that will fundamentally alter the way in which members of society relate to one another. In the conclusion, I address several limitations to this practice and chart a course for further research and pedagogical development.

The Context: Acknowledging and Respecting Religious Diversity in the Classroom

Three words. "I hate religion." This short, brutally honest, anonymous disclosure was written by a student in an introduction to Christianity course at a Catholic liberal arts college located in the Northeast region of the United States. While dramatic when compared to his/her peers' responses, this attitude is typical of young people in the so-called "Millennial Generation."[10] Such anecdotal evidence could be multiplied exponentially. Around the proverbial water cooler at religious studies, theology, and ministry conferences, not to mention at home institutions, scholars, educators, and activists frequently lament the religious illiteracy and apparent indifference to religious traditions that seems to be ubiquitous among young people.

Beyond the anecdotes, which some observers may dismiss as little more than educators grousing over the challenges presented by underprepared and noncooperative students, the reality of a religiously illiterate and tradition-less generation has been well documented by scholars.[11] According to a Pew Research Center study of this generational cohort, Millennials—those born between 1982 and 2002—"are considerably less religious than older Americans."[12] Like most Americans, this generation tended to score low on a 2010 survey of religious knowledge conducted by Pew Research Center's Forum on Religion and Public Life. Furthermore, 25 percent of Millennials do not affiliate with any religion, joining the rising tide of so-called "nones."[13]

When it comes to education, Millennials are accustomed to knowledge acquisition for improved performance on standardized tests. They prefer an organized and predictable educational experience to one that is fluid and subject to change. Many Millennials have been introduced to and have participated in community service or other forms of volunteerism at the local and even global levels. These experiences, of course, have been tightly organized in ways that leave little room for serendipity. Research indicates that classroom learning and community service have focused more on acquisition of knowledge and experience than simultaneous or even delayed reflection on the meaning and purpose of learning and doing.[14]

Instead of looking at what is missing, a review of the positive dimensions of the Millennial generation's relationship with religion reveals a firm foundation for engaging questions around faith, belief, and religious traditions. The *majority* of Millennials affiliate with a religious tradition. Even if they do not have a familiarity with basic knowledge of their tradition, 68 percent of Millennials identify as Christian, and another 6 percent identify with the Jewish, Muslim, Buddhist, or Hindu tradition.[15] Even the majority of Millennial "nones," those individuals who do not affiliate with a particular religious tradition, *still* believe in God and report an active prayer life.[16] Millennials are trained in content acquisition. Most Millennials are practiced in and eager to participate in action for social justice.

These general trends are broadly confirmed at the institution where I teach, a Catholic college of higher education, which is located in suburban Philadelphia and welcomes learners of all faiths, cultures, and backgrounds.[17] The college places significant emphasis on education for justice. The core curriculum is called "Justice Matters." Traditionally, the roughly 1,300-member student body has self-identified as Catholic. While these students continue to represent the majority of students at the college, following national trends, the students increasingly identify their religious affiliation as "none" or otherwise do not admit to a particular religious affiliation. Over a five-year period, an average of 58 percent of students self-identify as Catholic; 11 percent self-identify as Protestant, 2 percent as Jewish, and 13 percent as "other"; while over that same period an *average* of 17 percent of total students do not indicate a religious affiliation. The number of students who do not self-identify with any religious tradition or otherwise refuse to report their religious affiliation has risen from 13 percent to 29 percent over five years; this is higher than the national average.[18]

Every semester, I encounter anew courses full of Millennials who, with few exceptions, fit the general characteristics of their cohort. The pedagogical practice that I outline here emerges from ongoing reflection and refinement on my encounters with these students. I have learned much from them; I am indebted to them for helping me understand how to mediate religious studies in a meaningful and more sensitive way.

Broadening the Definition of Faith to Enter the Conversation on Religion

I begin the course by asking students to define the term "faith." Many students associate religion with institutional expressions of specific religious traditions such as Christianity, Judaism, Islam, Buddhism, or Hinduism and, in turn, associate these traditions with their more obvious expressions, such as their sacred texts and worship practices rather than the spiritual dimension of these traditions.[19] Before turning to a more nuanced understanding of the term "faith," we go on to discuss the contemporary urgency to study religion by reading about and discussing the scope of religious illiteracy and assessing the ways that religion tends to appear in the media. Many of the students are relieved to know that they are not alone in their lack of knowledge about their own or any religious tradition, and they tend to agree that religion is rarely represented favorably in the media.

The students encounter an interdisciplinary and inclusive definition of faith in the first three chapters of the now-classic text *Stages of Faith: The Psychology of Human Development and the Quest for Meaning* by theologian and human development theorist James W. Fowler.[20] Many students are surprised to discover a distinction between faith and religion, just as they are challenged to comprehend the breadth of Fowler's definition of "faith." His definition of faith is broad enough to include nearly everyone.

In defining the term "faith," Fowler draws on the work of theologian Paul Tillich, ethicist H. Richard Niebuhr, and comparative religion scholar Wilfred Cantwell Smith. Drawing on the work of Tillich and Niebuhr, Fowler calls faith a "universal human concern" that is "prior to our being religious or irreligious."[21] We are engaged in questions of "faith" even before our religious identity takes shape. Drawing on Smith, Fowler uses religion to refer specifically to any "cumulative tradition" with its "texts of scripture or law, including narratives, myths, prophecies, accounts of revelations, and so forth . . . symbols, oral traditions, music, dance, ethical teachings, theologies, creeds, rites, liturgies, architecture, and a host of other elements."[22] These elements are "expressions of faith," both individual and communal. The symbolic, ritual, and abstract renderings of theology are not to be confused with "faith" itself.[23]

"Faith," as I present it to the class, can be regarded as a dynamic dimension of human existence—a verb rather than a noun—according to which we make sense out of and give meaning to our various experiences—in relationship with other people—according to shared values and a shared, developing narrative. It is an imaginative process. Faith is the process by which we make sense out of our experiences through images and concepts. We belong to multiple "faith communities," comprised of relationships that have a share in and contribute to the evolving expression of our experience through symbols, rituals, and stories. These communities include our various networks of friends, our family, our school, later our workplace, our political identity, and religious commitments, if any. Fowler calls the evolving expression of our experiences-in-relationship a "Shared Center of Value and Power."

Fowler explains that we place our trust and allegiance—that is, we "faith"—in relation to those groups, organizations, and people that confer value and meaning on us. He writes,

> We value that which seems of transcendent worth and in relation to which our lives have worth. Further, in a world of powerful forces that have an impact on us, enlarging and diminishing us, forming and sometimes destroying us, we invest loyalty in and seek to align ourselves with powers that promise to sustain our lives and to undergird "more being."[24]

Together, individually and in community, we continually create and renew our sense of self and our communities—our faith—aligning ourselves with those people and groups that confer meaning upon us. We challenge and are challenged by these multiple communities. It is incumbent upon us to take ownership of our role in this process—or face certain alienation.

It is instructive, in light of this understanding of faith, to listen anew to the reasons that students give in explaining why they do not affiliate with, let alone participate in, religion. A significant reason for their lack of affiliation with institutional religion emerges from their feeling that they do not feel valued by those institutions; and that they do not feel a part of the meaning making that is meant to be a fundamental dimension of religious institutions.

Once the students see and understand the distinction between "faith" and "religion," our conversation in the classroom about faith shifts. Even those students who do not affiliate with a particular religious tradition begin to see they have "faith" and that they "faith" when understood in this way. The focus turns on questions related to *value* and *meaning.* What provides us with "worth"? Where do we "invest loyalty"? What "powers . . . promise to sustain our lives"?[25] What people, groups, and institutions are important to us, give us meaning? Reflecting on these "big questions," the students begin to think and talk about faith using Fowler's language of Shared Center of Value and Power in more detailed and expansive ways.

Encountering Difference: Putting Theory into Practice through Interfaith Dialogue

This conversation becomes more explicit and intentional as we read about the meaning and significance of interfaith dialogue, paying special attention to the highly accessible book *Encountering Other Faiths: An Introduction to the Art of Interreligious Engagement* by Maria Hornung, a Medical Mission Sister who serves as an Adult Learning Consultant with the Interfaith Center of Greater Philadelphia.[26] Interfaith dialogue can be a powerful tool as a college-level pedagogy. According to Hornung, who speaks with reference to adults in general, "It enables a growth in maturity as a full human being" and imparts an appreciation for the challenge of finding common ground but also the possibility for doing so.[27] I would add that one of the objectives of this interfaith pedagogy, as I have adapted it to my teaching, is to help students to become conscious co-creators of their faith identity through dialogue with one another, the community, and the tradition.

According to Hornung, interfaith dialogue is a tool for building the common good. She explains, "The aim of interfaith dialogue is to search together for what is true and good, convinced that none of us knows all truth and goodness and that interacting together we can reach a greater ability to live the truth and goodness we discover."[28] Hornung calls the contemporary period a Kairos moment: This age is ready for interfaith dialogue, given both widespread religious cooperation and the pervasive division within and among religious traditions across the globe. She encourages not more dialogue among the "experts" but rather dialogue in the classroom, by the public, at the grassroots level both in the form of conversation and joint action for justice.[29] I agree with Hornung that, given the urgency, this activity should not be limited to the "intellectual upper echelons" and that it belongs in our classrooms.

Interfaith dialogue is especially important and relevant because it can lead to solidarity by taking a participant into broader and broader circles of relationship. As Hornung explains, it "generates belief in the possibility of a positive outcome without violence . . . enables the sacrifices that ensure that all the chances for justice and peace are taken."[30] The ultimate objective, she continues, is "the cultivation of global ethics and solidarity," which emerges through a lifelong process that this practice intends to initiate.[31]

The curricular practice that I describe here best matches the "neighborly dimension" and the "practical or 'making common cause' dimension" among the multiple modalities of interfaith dialogue summarized by Hornung. The first modality focuses on forging friendships in the "places where we live, work and socialize together, thus creating a culture of welcome for ourselves . . . and for tasks we undertake."[32] The second modality focuses on collaborating with all people of good will "to help humanity and to address human problems and issues."[33]

There are a number of "ground rules for interfaith dialogue" that we use in class, derived from Maria Hornung's program. In my experience, the students frequently invoke certain ground rules for creating safe-space, including: "come to the dialogue with sincerity and honesty"; that "each participant must be allowed to offer his or her unique self-definition"; that we should check "preconceived ideas" at the door; and that mutual trust coupled with a healthy self-criticism of one's own faith tradition is essential. These ground rules are helpful for facilitating challenging conversations in the classroom as well as in the community and in engaging challenging content from the tradition.

Filling the Hole at the Center of the Cube: Catholic Social Teaching as Common Vocabulary

Up to this point, the discussion of faith has been more or less content-less, as far as the "faith" perspective of the course as a whole is concerned. The students know that the course has a certain "shared center of value and power" (SCVP) given the learning objectives and reading assignments, but we have not spent much time clarifying it yet. Naming the SCVP of the course means addressing one of the criticisms of Fowler's definition of faith, namely that there is no "core of the cube."[34] In my model, Catholic Social Teaching serves as a "core" at the center of the cube, as a basis for critical dialogue with the students' own faith commitments. The theological basis of the various themes or principles provides an introduction to and an anchor in the Catholic theological tradition while the wideness of the individual themes provides overlap with the social justice commitments of other religious and non-religious traditions.

Once the students begin to clarify their own Shared Center of Value and Power and have become comfortable discussing their position and listening attentively to their peers, the principles of Catholic Social Teaching provide a common language for our ensuing conversation on justice topics, specifically poverty, homelessness, and hunger not only in the classroom but in the community as well. After practicing interfaith dialogue among ourselves, we leave the classroom and invite guests into the classroom on a rotating basis. Catholic Social Teaching becomes intelligible in the encounter with flesh-and-blood people rather than words on a page alone, especially such principles as the sacredness of life and the dignity of every person; rights and responsibilities; and solidarity, to name just three.

Moving Beyond the Traditional Boundaries of the Classroom

Indeed, although important and significant, the conversation in the classroom does not prove sufficient to animate the practice of interfaith dialogue or the meaning and significance of the key terms and concepts—from "faith" through the principles of Catholic Social Teaching. Instead, the course content and engagement with the material become real the moment we leave the classroom and enter into conversation with members of the community, including residents of a nearby homeless outreach center and members of an intentional-living, ecumenical Christian community.

Over several weeks in a given semester, each party hosts the other in turn for dialogue and joint relationship-building activities. Sessions are held on the college campus, at the homeless outreach center, and at the Christian community house. Each community has the opportunity to extend hospitality to the other. Likewise, each community leaves its space and enters into the others' spaces for intentional dialogue around faith and social justice topics. We engage in activities that build community together, we share stories from our lives, and we have conversations around specific social justice topics.

The structure of the community collaboration is fairly simple in concept, yet it is here that this practice advances in innovative directions. The collaboration strives for equality and reciprocity among the partners in the planning and implementation of the project. Furthermore, this collaboration promotes solidarity through the practice of interfaith dialogue, which fundamentally undermines the perennial temptation of service-learning to "do for" instead of "doing with." Dialogue levels the status distinctions and lays the foundation for serious conversation about the structures and systems that promote inequality in the first place.

At the start of each semester, the instructor of the course, the director of the homeless outreach center, and leaders of the Christian community house gather to map out meeting dates and a general overview of the programming for the semester. Nevertheless, the particular activities vary not only from semester to semester but also frequently from week to week as we respond to feedback from participants in our respective communities. In all cases, dialogue is at the heart of our encounters. This dialogue is frequently stimulated by or finds expression through art. For example, we have read and discussed prose poems related to particular social justice topics as prompts to conversation; we have started sessions by working in small groups to draw images or write our own poems related to our shared vision for social justice; and we have used photography, pictures taken by participants, to discuss the various ways we see the world both now and as we would like it to be.

Through this process, members from each community consistently report a moment when they begin to feel part of a whole. It is difficult to describe what they mean. Victor Turner's discussion of "liminality" and "communitas" provides the closest approximation to what I have heard reported. In his classic text, *The Ritual Process: Structure and Anti-Structure*, Turner describes the liminal state as a place where "secular distinctions of rank and status disappear or are homogenized" and where a sense of communitas or solidarity emerges. As Turner explains, "It is rather a matter of giving recognition to an essential and generic human bond. . . ."[35] The passage he borrows from Jewish philosopher Martin Buber is an apt description of the experience of this partnership. Buber wrote:

> Community is the being no longer side by side (and, one might add, above and below) but *with* one another of a multitude of persons. And this multitude, though it moves towards one goal, yet experiences everywhere a turning to, a dynamic facing of, the others, a flowing from *I* to *Thou*. Community is where community happens.[36]

In fact, that description, were it somehow measurable, would make a good learning outcome for this pedagogical practice.

This engaged pedagogy—rooted in movement from the campus to the community and back again—has the ability to generate something like communitas because, to borrow again from Turner, "it transgresses or dissolves the norms that govern structured and institutionalized relationships."[37] In this case, the transgression is not radical. It takes place through literal and metaphorical movement to the margins such as: interdisciplinary conversation about faith, the practice of interfaith dialogue, and decamping to a neighboring, economically distressed community. Through this activity, we find ourselves at the "edges of structure," namely a college classroom where everyone's voice is equal; and "beneath structure," because we find ourselves at what many people in our society would call an "inferior" location, namely a homeless outreach center; or a Christian community in an economically distressed urban district. Taken together, the experience that emerges from our interaction in these spaces is profound.

The Catholic Social Teaching principle of "solidarity" represents another way to talk about this experience. Catholic Relief Services describes this concept in the following way: "We are all part of one human family—whatever our national, racial, religious, economic, or ideological differences—and in an increasingly interconnected world, loving our neighbor has global dimensions."[38] The sense of solidarity that emerges through this project clarifies the interdependence among the members while revealing the ways in which their political and economic destiny is joined. Students learn of the hardship endured and the hope expressed by the temporary residents at the homeless outreach center just as the students share their fears of crippling student debt and the prospect of work in a decimated job market. This pedagogical practice forges bonds of solidarity, highlights the significance of the "rights and responsibilities" of everyone, and underscores the "sacredness and dignity of the human person."

From the assessment perspective, this community collaboration hones students' skill in the practice of interfaith dialogue in the real world. Their knowledge and understanding of the principles of Catholic Social Teaching is more substantial because they see it in practice. When compared to a parallel section of the same course, the students in the section with the community collaboration perform better in their oral and written communication in terms of their knowledge and understanding of key terms and theoretical concepts.[39]

Conclusion

The flowering of this partnership—between and among students, residents of a homeless outreach center, and members of an intentional-living Christian community—can be quite beautiful, in terms of the relationships forged between and among community members; student and community member generosity; and increased levels of student achievement. Yet, a fifteen-week semester limits the scope of transformation that might occur for the community or any one student in any one course. In December or May, depending on the semester, once the final exam period expires, we are all scattered to the winds.

The critical research on service-learning, considered at the start of this chapter, suggests areas where this community-based learning practice can be improved. In his assessment of service-learning, Dan Butin advocates for a "political perspective of social learning" to augment a "technical perspective of service-learning." The latter is limited because it focuses exclusively on the "best practices" for implementing a service-learning-based course. He argues that a technical perspective must be joined to a political perspective in order to develop a comprehensive approach to social justice. The political perspective uncovers the limitations of service-learning. Butin explains:

> In doing so [linking the technical and political perspectives], service-learning becomes revealed to be almost universally located within the context of a specific academic course beholden to specific structural constraints: there is a short-term, one-semester time frame to complete activities; there are a limited number of engaged students; there is a

complete turnover of the "service" population; the goals of the course are student-centered to the extent that academic learning is a key requirement within the course; service-learning is positioned as an add-on that can easily be put in or taken out of a course; there is a limit to the time that students and teachers can be involved; and the service-learning on the academic side is ultimately associated with a particular individual (namely the professor supporting the service-learning).[40]

These limitations are relevant to the practice described in this chapter. The short duration of a single semester may be the most glaring deficiency. The limited number of hours available in a three-credit course inhibits the type of sustained critical analysis and action for social justice that might be possible beyond one or even two semesters.

These limitations are a challenge not only to individual courses but also to the entire university. From Butin's perspective, service-learning cannot be limited to a "course-based, credit-bearing, educational experience" but must find an "academic home" in higher education and thereby reshape its very foundations.[41] Likewise, Toton cogently counsels,

> If educators and their educational institutions are to do more than proclaim or talk about justice, if they are truly committed to the creation of justice, then they must come to terms with the limits of their own institutions, theories and methods. In short, they need to take risks . . . like the UCA [University of Central America], they need to seek out new relationships, new teachers, new theories and methods, and new sites from which they can, not only learn about, but participate in the creation of a more just and compassionate social order.[42]

When viewed from the perspective of the students' total educational experience, ideally she or he will encounter elements of social justice education in multiple courses—in the core, in majors, and minors—and extra-curricular activities that promote justice theory, social analysis, and practice while enabling them to synthesize the various parts into a comprehensive whole. Likewise, ideally, different areas of the institution would be working in the community from multiple angles—curricular and co-curricular—to promote social change; all the while seeking ways to help students and the community move into solidarity and work together to promote the common good.

The community-based learning practice described in this chapter is a step toward that ultimate objective by forging bonds of solidarity between and among community members. In doing so, it models an approach that overcomes some limitations of traditional service-learning practice while remaining beholden to other, institution-wide constraints. Nevertheless, this approach attempts to cast campus and community collaborators as co-workers rather than unequal partners. As Janet Poppendieck contends, "We need to imagine and create a movement that will reduce poverty by helping us all, a movement that will integrate rather than segregate poor people, that will cast them in the role of fellow workers for the greater good rather than grateful recipients of our exertions on their behalf."[43] While providing direct service is an important and necessary practice, a response to immediate suffering, it must be joined to practices that strive to create structural change as well. Interfaith dialogue is a way to initiate that process.

The pedagogy presented in this chapter is one approach that strives to promote the transformation of social structures by welcoming college students into an ongoing conversation about the meaning and significance of faith, in general, and Christian social thought and practice, in particular. This approach encourages a process of lifelong learning that instills a scholarly examination of the Christian tradition, acknowledges and respects multiple faith perspectives, and fosters ongoing interfaith dialogue and relationship-building among neighbors in the community who come together from disparate backgrounds. The practice seeks to engender hope and solidarity in the students and community members through interfaith dialogue while laying the foundation for and contributing to the creation of a broader movement for social change.

Notes

1. Suzanne C. Toton, *Justice Education: From Service to Solidarity* (Milwaukee: Marquette University Press, 2006), 105.

2. Bradford E. Hinze, "The Tasks of Theology in the *Proyecto Social* of the University's Mission," *Horizons* 39 (2012): 301.

3. Robert G. Bringle, Patti H. Clayton, and Julie A. Hatcher, "Research on Service Learning: An Introduction," in *Research on Service Learning: Conceptual Frameworks and Assessment: Volume 2B: Communities, Institutions, and Partnerships,* ed. Patti H. Clayton, Robert G. Bringle, and Julie A. Hatcher, IUPUI Series on Service Learning Research (Sterling, VA: Stylus, 2012), 337. They cite J. Conway, E. Amel, and D. Gerwein, "Teaching and Learning in the Social Context: A Meta-Analysis of Service-Learning's Effects on Academic, Personal, Social, and Citizenship Outcomes," *Teaching of Psychology* 36 (2009): 233–45.

4. Bringle, Clayton, and Hatcher, "Research on Service Learning," 338.

5. Barbara Jacoby, "Facing the Unsettled Questions about Service-Learning," in *The Future of Service-Learning: New Solutions for Sustaining and Improving Practice,* ed. Jean R. Strait and Marybeth Lima (Sterling, VA: Stylus, 2009), 98–99.

6. Ibid., 97

7. Marshall Welch, "Moving from Service-Learning to Civic Engagement," in *Civic Engagement in Higher Education: Concepts and Practices*, ed. Barbara Jacoby and Associates (San Francisco: Jossey-Bass, 2009), 175.

8. Dan W. Butin, "Justice-Learning: Service-Learning as Justice-Oriented Education," *Equity and Excellence in Education* 40 (2007): 180.

9. Ibid.

10. For scholarship on the "Millennial Generation," see Neil Howe and William Straus, *Millennials Rising: The Next Great Generation* (New York: Vintage Books, 2000); Robert A. Bongiglio, "Shorthand or Shortsightedness? The Downside of Generational Labeling," *About Campus* (July/August 2008): 30–32; Helen Fox, *Their Highest Vocation: Social Justice and the Millennial Generation* (New York: Peter Lang, 2012). Broad characteristics of this generational cohort are repeated frequently throughout the scholarship on this population. I echo here the caution of many scholars who warn against the use of generational monikers that advance sweeping generalizations about an entire group of people wherein many individual differences inevitably obtain. At the same time, I agree that the practice has a certain utility for the purposes of setting a framework or context. As I hope to explain in this section, my own experience has confirmed that many students, though not all, fit many of the characteristics presented in the scholarship on the Millennial generation.

11. Prominent examples of research in the area of religious literacy include: Stephen Prothero, *Religious Literacy: What Every American Needs to Know—and Doesn't* (New York: Harper Collins, 2008); Robert D. Putnam and David E. Campbell, *American Grace: How Religion Divides and Unites Us* (New York: Simon & Schuster, 2010); *Millennials: Confident. Connected. Open to Change: Executive Summary*, Pew Research Center's Social and Demographic Trends Project, February 2010. http://www.pewsocialtrends.org/2010/02/24/millennials-confident-connected-open-to-change/; *U.S. Religious Knowledge Survey*, Pew Research Center's Forum on Religion and Public Life, September 2010. http://www.pewforum.org/U-S-Religious-Knowledge-Survey.aspx; and *"Nones" on the Rise: One-in-Five Adults Have No Religious Affiliation*, Pew Research Center's Forum on Religion and Public Life, October 2012. http://www.pewforum.org/Unaffiliated/nones-on-the-rise.aspx.

12. See chapter 9, "Religious Beliefs and Behaviors," in Pew Research Center, *Millennials*.

13. Paul Taylor and Scott Keeter (eds.), "Millennials: A Portrait of Generation Next, Confident. Connected. Open to Change" (24 February 2010), 86. http://www.pewsocialtrends.org/files/2010/10/millennials-confident-connected-open-to-change.pdf.

14. The data in this section is derived mainly from the first chapter of Helen Fox's "Who Are the Millennials?" in her book, *Their Highest Vocation* (see n. 10). She supplements statistical data on the millennial generation with ethnographic

research culled from interviews with students, staff, and faculty at her institution, University of Michigan.

15. Pew Research Center, *Millennials*. See chart "Religious Composition of Age Groups" on page 87.

16. Pew Research Center, *Millennials*, 85.

17. See the Cabrini College mission statement via www.cabrini.edu/about/mission (accessed November 3, 2013).

18. See the Cabrini College Fact Book 2012–13, published November 26, 2012, by the Office of Institutional Research at Cabrini College.

19. This response evokes the now-popular "spiritual but not religious" distinction. According to the Pew Forum studies noted previously, the majority of Millennials tend to be "spiritual but not religious," which is to say that they report belief in God and a regular prayer life but they do not affiliate with a particular religious tradition. Although this distinction between spiritual and religious identity is commonly accepted, some scholars are calling into question the facticity of this separation. In his *Spiritual, But Not Religious: Understanding Unchurched America* (New York: Oxford University Press, 2001), Robert C. Fuller sees the words "spiritual" and "religious" as synonyms. Nevertheless, he explains that, popularly, things spiritual have become associated with private life and personal experience. Spirituality thus has become distinct from religion, which, again, popularly, has been limited to public expression of a particular institution according to prescribed rituals and doctrine (5). Reid Locklin in *Spiritual But Not Religious? An Oar Stroke Closer to the Farther Shore* (Collegeville, MN: Liturgical Press, 2005) challenges the religious–spiritual distinction by exploring religious institutions in a way that is "distinct from those with which most us are familiar . . . grounded not upon some abstract principle or hierarchical structure" but upon recognition, namely, in terms of "spiritual seekers continually receiving guidance from those teachers they encounter on the way" (9). In *Belief without Borders: Inside the Minds of the Spiritual but not Religious* (New York: Oxford University Press, 2014), Linda A. Mercadante describes the distinction as a "popular conceptual separation" that "is more rhetorical device than a true divorce" (6). Drawing on her hundreds of interviews with people who see themselves as spiritual but not religious, she discovers an emerging consensus of belief among people who identify in this way.

20. James W. Fowler, *Stages of Faith: The Psychology of Human Development and the Quest for Meaning* (New York: HarperCollins, 1981).

21. Ibid., 5.

22. Ibid., 9.

23. W. C. Smith's definition of religion via Fowler is employed as a heuristic device for the discrete pedagogical purpose of stimulating broader conversation on the topic. Nuanced conversation on the limits of W. C. Smith's and James Fowler's conceptions of religion would be pursued in a different course, such as

an upper level course on the scope and method of the study of religion for advanced students. There, we would examine countervailing conceptions of the meaning of "religion" in the work of such scholars as Jonathan Z. Smith's *Imagining Religion: From Babylon to Jonestown* (Chicago: University of Chicago Press, 1992); Tomoko Masuzawa's *The Invention of World Religions: Or, How European Universalism Was Preserved in the Language of Pluralism* (Chicago: University of Chicago, 2005); and Brent Nongbri's *Before Religion: A History of a Modern Concept* (New Haven: Yale University Press, 2013).

24. Fowler, James W. *Stages of Faith: The Psychology of Human Development and the Quest for Meaning.* New York: HarperCollins, 1981. 18.

25. Ibid., 3.

26. Maria Hornung, *Encountering Other Faiths* (Mahwah, NJ: Paulist, 2007).

27. Maria Hornung, *Workbook for Encountering Other Faiths: An Introduction to the Art of Interreligious Engagement* (Philadelphia: Interfaith Center of Greater Philadelphia, 2007), 33.

28. Ibid., 33.

29. Ibid., 16.

30. Ibid., 33.

31. Hornung, *Encountering Other Faiths*, 71.

32. Hornung, *Workbook for Encountering Other Faiths*, 37.

33. Ibid.

34. J. Harry Fernhout, "Where Is Faith? Searching for the Core of the Cube," in *Faith Development and Fowler*, ed. Craig Dykstra and Sharon Parks (Birmingham, AL: Religious Education Press, 1986), 65–6.

35. Victor Turner, *The Ritual Process: Structure and Anti-Structure* (Ithaca, NY: Cornell University Press, 1977), 97.

36. See ibid., 127; quoting Martin Buber, *Between Man and Man*, trans. R. F. C. Hull (London: Fontana Library, 1961), 51.

37. Turner, *Ritual Process*, 128.

38. See http://crs.org/about/guiding-principles.cfm (accessed June 28, 2013).

39. These results have been documented in a number of ways: through written exams, in which students are asked to define and integrate key terms and theoretical concepts in response to a performance task–based prompt and through formal observation of student practice of interfaith dialogue in the classroom. Additionally, learning in the community collaboration section of this course is rated more highly by students than other aspects of the course, based on results of both quantitative and qualitative assessment tools.

40. Dan W. Butin, *Service-Learning in Theory and Practice: The Future of Community Engagement in Higher Education* (New York: Palgrave MacMillan, 2010), 15.

41. Butin develops this position throughout *Service Learning in Theory and Practice*. For the specifically noted two points, see ibid., 17 and xiii–xiv.

42. Toton, *Justice Education* (see n. 1), 117.

43. Janet Poppendieck, *Sweet Charity? Emergency Food and the End of Entitlement* (New York: Penguin Books, 1999), 316. I am grateful to Suzanne Toton for sharing this resource with me as a way to understand the political implications of this project.

9

Stopping the Zombie Apocalypse

ASCETIC WITHDRAWAL AS A TOOL FOR LEARNING CIVIC ENGAGEMENT

Elizabeth W. Corrie

AT THE HEIGHT of the news cycle focus on macabre assaults on individuals that resembled "zombie attacks," a "meme" that came across my Facebook newsfeed titled "Zombie Apocalypse" included two photos. On the left was a photo of zombies, dressed in rags, covered in blood, and obviously slouching toward the viewer menacingly *en masse*. Over this photo were the words: "What we think it looks like." On the right was a photo of four young adults, dressed in current fashionable clothing, slouching against a wall, casually ignoring each other, each absorbed in interactions with their smartphones. Over this photo were the words: "What it really looks like." It turns out that, indeed, the "Zombie Apocalypse" has arrived, but not in the form of flesh-consuming undead. Rather, they have arrived in the form of gadget-consuming un-citizens.

This sentiment is not new, of course. The use of zombies as a metaphor for humans as mindless consumers dates back to George Romero's *Dawn of the Dead* (1978). The film is set in a shopping mall, which begins as a place of safety with seemingly unlimited supplies to protect the living against the coming undead hordes but becomes a living hell of boredom, disconnection, and meaninglessness. Yet, even while the Living discover that the mall is a trap, the Undead cannot resist its pull. At one point, Fran, one of the characters, asks, "Why do they come here?" Steve, another character, replies chillingly, "Some kind of instinct. Memory. What they used to do. This was an important place in their lives." As religious studies scholar Kim Paffenroth notes:

> Again, the horror for human beings lies not just in being torn to pieces and eaten alive by zombies, but in becoming one of them, a mindless mallgoer, never again able to conceive of anything higher or more interesting to do than wander about with a vacuous look of contentment,

punctuated by longing, lustful stares at windows and racks and displays full of useless, worthless stuff.[1]

If the Facebook "meme" is correct, then the zombie apocalypse has already arrived in the form of mass consumer culture. We have met the Undead, and they are us.

This, in any case, is the conclusion of a number of sociologists, economists, and cultural observers focused on our current cohort of youth and young adults. Their research reveals a disturbing correlation between participation in consumerism and levels of civic engagement. In this chapter, I look at this literature and propose one strategy of resistance, the Ascetic Withdrawal Project. Combined with other assignments that deepen students' understanding of particular global issues and encourage them to apply this knowledge by teaching it to others, the Ascetic Withdrawal Project helps students make connections between personal choices and their global impact. This, I argue, is a critical first step in learning civic engagement. I then place this project within my context of theological education, and suggest the role this type of assignment can play in training students for civic engagement as persons of faith.

Consumerism and the Rise of Civic Schizophrenia

In his book, *Lost in Transition: The Dark Side of Emerging Adulthood*, sociologist Christian Smith draws on the data from the National Study of Youth and Religion to conclude that:

> Very many of the emerging adults [ages 18–23] we interviewed . . . dedicate major portions of their educational, work, career, and leisure lives to securing their positions as consumers of material goods, experiences, and services. For that is what primarily defines a genuinely good life for them. What is important is not civic life but shopping, not good political decision making but smart consumer choices, not a more fully realized common good but higher consumer satisfaction, not enhancing public life but increasing purchasing power. That is a simple fact of life among nearly all emerging adults, which has been borne out by solid surveys conducted among young adults over many decades.[2]

This should not come as a surprise, given the fact that marketers are clear that children are their most valuable current and future consumers, and have dedicated their research and resources to cultivating children, even infants, to become brand-loyal customers for life.[3] Although North Americans are deeply immersed in consumer culture, the emerging adults we teach in undergraduate and graduate classrooms were quite simply "born to buy," as economist Juliet Schor frames it.[4] As the symbol for consumer culture more generally, "the mall" (including the online versions they access through their smartphones) is indeed an important place in their lives, and the pull it has operates on a level deeper than rationality. As Steve explains it in *Dawn of the Dead*, it is "some kind of instinct."

To be sure, sweeping assessments that portray consumerism as a totalizing and irresistible force before which we are powerless are neither accurate nor constructive. My experience of working with youth and young adults for nearly twenty years in high schools, youth groups, colleges, and seminaries regularly presents counterexamples. Many young people I work with are aware of the downsides of consumerism, and they try to live their lives in critical relationship to it as best they can. Consumers are "branded," yes, but they also engage in what Benjamin Barber calls "cultural creolization," in which they adopt and adapt brands for their own uses, even shaping the brands themselves through their interactions. Those committed to more conscious resistance engage in "culture jamming," which aims to topple existing power structures through subversive use of the tools of marketing itself.[5] A growing movement of "radical" or "political consumerism" suggests that forms of activism and resistance using the power of the purse are also developing.[6] As Tom Beaudoin points out, "brands do not control us, but they do strongly influence us. It is important to keep in mind that young adults—and all consumers—are not robots. We all act with a certain degree of freedom." Nonetheless, "that freedom always takes place within a specific context or situation," that is, within the "brand economy."[7] We are free, but we enjoy that freedom within a limited range of movement.

Evidence of resistance notwithstanding, those of us attempting to teach civic engagement—that is, "acting on a heightened sense of responsibility to one's communities that encompasses the notions of global citizenship and interdependence, participation in building civil society, and empowering individuals as agents of positive social change to promote social justice locally and globally"[8]— cannot ignore the largely negative impact consumer culture has on our students and on ourselves as citizens. Smith's survey statistics and interview narratives provide concrete evidence of a larger phenomenon that Barber calls "civic schizophrenia," in which the "private me" (the side focused on my individual consumer choices: what "I want") is fragmented from and opposed to the "public me" (the side associated with my capacity and desire to engage in collective deliberation and democratic decision-making: what "we should"). This tension causes a sense of contradiction and dissatisfaction because we falsely assume that the sum of all the freely made decisions of "private selves" will result in a collective common good, when in fact the aggregate of our private choices outweighs and often negates what we say we want as a society.[9] Using the example of public education,

Barber points out that the sum effect of individual parents exercising private "choice" through vouchers and other forms of opting out of the public education system results in an inferior education system that impacts us all.

> Of course no one really wants a country defined by deep educational injustice and the surrender of a public and civic pedagogy whose absence will ultimately impact even our own private choices. . . . As citizens, we would never consciously select such an outcome, but in practice what is good for "me," the educational consumer, turns out to be a disaster for "us" as citizens and civic educators. . . . [10]

This "civic schizophrenia" creates a context in which the individual understands himself or herself (and all others) to be entitled to perfect freedom *from* constraints on personal choice while blinding him or her from the cumulative impact these choices have in the public sphere, and ultimately preventing the individual from exercising his or her freedom *to* engage in democratic decision-making.

The emphasis Barber places on our current notions of "freedom" helps explain why consumer culture negatively impacts civic engagement. For Barber, North Americans are particularly focused on "personal freedom"—freedom to have or do whatever we like—and we have lost a sense of "social freedom" that can only come through engagement in the public sphere.[11] Christian Smith notes the strong correlation between consumerism and political disengagement: those classified as "materialists" (those who stated "they saw no problem with consumerism, thought it was a good thing, and participated in mass consumption themselves") made up 90 percent of those who were apathetic about politics, 84 percent of those who were distrustful of politics and the government, and 71 percent of those who felt disempowered and therefore did not want to engage in politics.[12] It appears that the more one is entrenched in the private world of consumption and earning money to support consumption, the less likely one is to see the importance of—or even be aware of—a public sphere that might seek the common good.

If a core challenge to teaching civic engagement with emerging adults consists in the fact that they are too immersed in their "private selves" to see the connections between their individual consumer choices and the impact these have in the public sphere, locally as well as globally, then perhaps an exercise in exploring one's personal participation in consumerism is needed to prepare students for learning civic engagement. In my course "Empowering Youth for Global Citizenship," a course for seminary students interested in youth ministry, this is precisely what I have attempted to do. By introducing a project that encourages students to make direct connections between their personal consumer habits and the global issues they are studying, I seek to overcome the civic schizophrenia that makes civic engagement unintelligible to so many emerging adults. By building into the curriculum a learning activity that pushes students to change behavior in small but concrete ways, a shift in thinking also becomes possible.

Overcoming Civic Schizophrenia: The Ascetic Withdrawal Project as Preparation for Civic Engagement

The context of my teaching is a university-based school of theology in a large, diverse urban center in the Southeastern United States, with an historical connection to the Civil Rights movement and a pervasive cultural Christianity.[13] The students in the school of theology come largely from this region, thus representing primarily African- and European-American heritages, with the notable exception of a large Korean and Korean-American population. The median age of the student body is 28, and the youngest segment of these students dominates the youth ministry courses I teach. Many are in a similar place in life: single or recently partnered, preparing for a first career, and both excited and anxious about the future. Their lives are full and overscheduled. They juggle relationships, jobs, ordination processes, and a demanding curriculum that requires four to eight weekly hours of contextual work in churches and non-profit agencies during their first and second years. The effects of our globalized world are all around them, but many do not realize this as they struggle to finish graduate school.

The title "Empowering Youth for Global Citizenship" suggests the course goal: to encourage young people to engage in the world as "faithful global citizens" (a concept explored from several perspectives throughout the semester). It also suggests the course's primary assumption: that young people are largely disempowered and disengaged in this form of interaction with the world.[14] The syllabus thus begins with the following essential questions: "What does it mean to be a 'global citizen,' and why should a person of faith seek to become one? How can we overcome the barriers to engagement in society, so that we, and our youth, are empowered to work for the common good, to live out our calling to love our neighbors—and our enemies?" Implied in these questions are theological, ethical, and pedagogical assumptions, namely, (1) that individuals are part of and responsible to an interdependent global network of institutions and people; (2) that this same global network discourages individuals—particularly North American youth and young adults—from engaging in acts that might counter or transform the destructive aspects of it; and (3) that education can intervene in this discouragement and make globally conscious action more likely. Embedded yet deeper in these assumptions is a hope that students taking this course will not only come to understand themselves as global citizens but also will become actively engaged in social transformation, through their own lives and through work with youth that awakens young people to active global citizenship.

These assumptions shape the design of the assignments. The midterm project asks students to research a particular social justice issue arising from or impacted by our globalized context. I then ask them to present it to each other as a means of broadening the awareness of their classmates. The final project then builds on this research, asking students to design a religious education curriculum that would encourage youth to explore this topic and relate it to their lives and their religious beliefs. The Ascetic Withdrawal Project, in parallel with these more traditional assignments, requires students to spend six weeks of the course fasting from some daily activity that contributes, whether directly or indirectly, to a negative aspect of global consumerism. In my vision for the course, I see the midterm and final projects combining to increase students' understanding of a particular issue through research and application of this research to the design of a teaching event, and the Ascetic Withdrawal Project as an educational experience aimed at raising awareness of personal consumer habits.

The Ascetic Withdrawal Project (AWP) goes beyond personal practice, however. As a means for creating a community of support and accountability, the assignment calls for students to post weekly to the class blog a reflection that considers:

1. A particular instance or set of instances in which you were made conscious of your ascetic withdrawal practice. This might be a time you were "tempted" or fell into "temptation," breaking your practice. It might be a time in which you realized later that you had forgotten your practice and had accidentally broken from it out of prior habit. Or, it might be a time in which you had to explain to others your practice and how they reacted to it.
2. Something unexpected that you noticed or learned by engaging in your practice (e.g., about yourself, about others, about society).
3. How well you feel you're doing that week on your practice.

In addition, students are asked to read and write a comment on the posts of two others in the class each week. These comments could offer encouragement, compare their classmate's experience with their own, offer suggestions or ideas, raise questions, or note observations. They need only to be a few lines, but could be longer. I encourage students to respond to the postings of different classmates each week, to ensure that every student receives some feedback from their peers over the course of the project. As the instructor, I participate in the project as well, post my own reflections, and read and respond to others in the same way as the students, with students reading and responding to my posts as with any other participant.

I try to signal the importance of the exercise by preparing the class for it on several levels.[15] I introduce the idea of the project on the first day of class, and in the weeks leading up to the start of the project I remind students to reflect carefully on their choice of ascetic withdrawal practice. In class, we talk about the unique ways in which we are all "branded," and I bring into class some of the artifacts that reveal my own "branding," in an act of transparency about my own process of discerning a fast appropriate to my particular attachments.[16] Some students spend significant time mulling over possible consumer habits from which to practice withdrawal. Those who have trouble discerning a practice can seek suggestions from the class or from me (where we usually engage them in questions that help them think about specific consumer goods or habits to which they are most connected or would find challenging to give up). On the start day, the students post their first blog entries, declaring their practice and reasons for choosing it. The practices have ranged from giving up fast food, ready-made grocery store meals, or Starbucks drinks; fasting from media sources such as television, or from particular networks such as NPR and cable news; resisting "impulse shopping" in buying magazines and make-up; abstaining from "high fructose corn syrup" or meat; reducing waste from packaging or water usage; and abstaining from sending text messages in favor of more direct and personal communication, whether by phone or face to face. In each case, students identified a personal and significant reason for their choice.

The questions I ask students to consider in their reflections each week aim not only to raise their awareness of how deeply entrenched their own consumer habits are, but also to highlight how deeply countercultural—even threatening—abstaining from any aspect of consumerism can be. In asking about moments in which they became conscious of their fasts as they had to make different choices from their regular routine, and in encouraging them to think about what they are learning about others and about society as they engage in their practices, I seek to draw their attention to the ways in which their actions impact—and may be resisted by—those around them.[17] Invariably, students discover that some of their peers actively oppose their fasts. Those who give up meat find themselves in arguments with others who want to convince them that eating meat is essential to a healthy diet. Those who give up television find they are excluded from social gatherings around popular shows. Roommates try to "tempt" them by waving junk food in front of their noses. When students go home for Thanksgiving holidays, parents and other family members not only question but also criticize their chosen fasts, even indicating that it offends them. Again and again, students find themselves having to explain and justify their actions to a suspect and sometimes hostile community. As students post these experiences on our class blog, we are able as a class to reflect on what might be so upsetting or threatening by their fasts. Encountering firsthand societal resistance to their countercultural choices

underscores for them that something more powerful than personal transformation is at stake—the exercise of personal choice that goes against consumer culture is not quite as "free" as they might have realized. Personal choice becomes
an act of personal resistance . . . and public witness.

The students from these courses have since graduated, and for the most part
now work in local churches as religious educators, youth ministers, and pastors.
Occasionally, I hear from some of these students and they are excited to tell me
about the ways in which they continue to work on and teach about topics they
explored in our midterm and final projects in their local church contexts. Most
also remember well what they did—and learned—from their Ascetic Withdrawal
Projects. When all three assignments complemented one another, however, students appear to have had the greatest insights about their role as global citizens.
In those cases, they were able to connect their personal practices of consumption
directly to global issues of justice that they felt passionate enough about to engage
in after the completion of the course.

From the first iteration of the course, I designed the midterm and final projects to build upon each other.[18] In order to discern a topic relevant to the lives of
the youth, the midterm asked students to consult with a group of youth in order to
identify a "generative theme" related to a particular aspect of "brokenness of the
world" the youth found compelling. After identifying a topic, students conducted
research into the political and economic factors driving it, whether any church-
related institutions took a position on or engaged the issue, what organizations
were addressing it (and how), the students' own theological reflection connecting the issue to the work of Christians as "global citizens," and what actions the
students recommended in response. For the final, students had to design a detailed educational event—a weekend retreat, a series of classes for Sunday School
or weekly youth meetings, a conference, workshop, etc.—that would teach what
they had learned through their midterm research, using pedagogical strategies
appropriate for a youth audience and workable within a specific church, school,
or non-profit setting. The midterm allowed students to develop some expertise in
content; the final allowed students to apply this while developing some expertise
in content delivery.

Over the years, the projects have been wide-ranging. Students, in consultation
with their youth, developed topics such as mountain-top removal in Appalachia
as related to the dependence on coal for local energy, the Israeli–Palestinian conflict inspired by the heated debates youth experienced in school during the bomb-
ings of Gaza in 2008–2009, the food system and its relationship to local farmers
and food insecurity in Atlanta, the prison-industrial complex and its relationship
to high incarceration rates of youth, the production practices of Apple and its connection to youth culture around Apple products, the global economy connected
to the death penalty in the wake of the widely reported Troy Davis execution,

access to clean water worldwide, domestic and international sex-trafficking and its particular prevalence in our city, and explorations of the dynamics of race and discrimination on both local and global levels.

In my original design of the course, I assumed that the midterm and final projects, research-based and practically applicable to the professional settings for which my students are seeking preparation, would form the "backbone" of the course, with the Ascetic Withdrawal Project serving as an ancillary activity related to personal transformation. However, in reviewing the relationship of the Ascetic Withdrawal Project to the midterm and final, a more apt metaphor is that of the "heart" (AWP) connecting the "head" (mid-term) and "hands" (final). All three were connected, yet it was not until students engaged in their ascetic withdrawal practices that they became enlivened to the possibilities of applying what they were learning to their professional lives. For example, the student who did her mid-term research on the Israeli–Palestinian conflict—not because of her own interest but because her youth group members identified this as *their* interest—discovered through her practice of conserving water the political dimensions of water access in Georgia, which led her to research the role of control of water aquifers in the West Bank in the conflict. Her own consciousness of water squandered by some and desperately needed by others made the conflict on another side of the world real for her, and this drove the urgency with which she developed her final project—a youth mission trip to the Holy Land, which she now hopes to lead in her current ministry context.

Another student presented her midterm research on the farm bill and the production of corn, and explored eating organically and locally as her practice. The markets, produce, and resources she discovered during her personal practice became the building blocks of her final project, a summer-long curriculum with her youth group on food and faith. A student already interested in mountain-top removal in Appalachia discovered during his fasting from red meat the environmental, health, and economic costs of meat production. This awareness shaped the way he proposed to make connections between the environmental, health, and economic struggles of the communities served in the Appalachian Service Project mission trip he developed for his final project, and enacted with his youth later that summer. While the midterm and final projects were designed to build on each other, with research (head) informing action (hands), the AWP gave this work a depth and personal connection (heart) not originally anticipated at the beginning of the semester.

Perhaps the combination of these three assignments helps to bridge the gap between the "private self" and the "public self," overcoming, or at least showing a way to overcome, the "civic schizophrenia" that Benjamin Barber identifies.[19] This becomes clear when personal choices of how long one takes a shower become connected to global water policies, when one realizes how difficult it is on a daily basis to avoid eating foods with corn as an ingredient and connects this to the U.S. Farm Bill and to the devastation of livelihoods of Mexican corn farmers, or when one attempts to stop watching television only to discover televisions permeating every space one enters, whether restaurants, hotels, or other homes. When they try something on a personal level that goes against the dominant culture enough to expose the fallacy that personal choices are disconnected to the larger context of society, students begin to reconnect the "private" to the "public." The "freedom" felt within the private sphere—the freedom to choose to do and have whatever you want within the limited menu of choices provided—finds a new freedom within the public sphere: the freedom to make conscious choices as an individual (perhaps even controversial ones) that participates in a vision of a common good.

Faithful Global Citizenship: Teaching Civic Engagement in a Seminary Context

As presented herein, the Ascetic Withdrawal Project can work in both undergraduate and graduate courses as a complement or preparation for other civic engagement learning. In my context in a school of theology, we are intentional about making connections to the theological dimensions of this experience. The first two iterations of this course were taught in the spring semester, and thus corresponded with the season of Lent. This moment in the liturgical calendar, marked by practices of reflection and asceticism, created a meaningful context for exploring our identities as consumers and citizens theologically. Although the following discussion offers a theological lens for considering the significance of the Ascetic Withdrawal Project, those teaching in other contexts might extrapolate from these insights the importance of seeing the change of daily habits in the face of cultural pressures as an ongoing process that requires patience, support from peers or a learning community, a willingness to persist despite setbacks and pressures to conform, and a larger vision compelling enough to make the struggle "worth it."

In *Branded: Converting Adolescents from Consumer Faith*, Katherine Turpin places the project of moving away from uncritical consumerism within a context of faith and religious education. For Turpin, consumerism has itself become the "ultimate concern" for most Americans, particularly youth. It has become, she maintains, the source of our meaning-making, the core of our identity.[20] For this reason, she argues in favor of the term "consumer faith" and insists that any attempt to engage critically and transform our habits as consumers must be understood as a process akin to "conversion."[21]

In her discussion of the process of "conversion" from "consumer faith," Turpin outlines a four-part movement drawn from John Wesley's theology of sanctification and Christian formation. In working with young people to help them move away from an ultimate concern centered on material wealth as the path to happiness and toward a more authentic Christian formation, educators can employ a process in which they: (1) *awaken* youth to the structures of oppression and destruction that shape their lives and deform their spirituality (showing how the "private self" is not immune to the impact of the aggregate decisions of all "private selves"); (2) engage in *repentance* with them through practices of self-reflection and dehabituation; (3) encourage *justification* through the introduction of more deeply satisfying ways of living out Christian vocation; and (4) support *regeneration* by fostering small groups accountable to and supportive of each other for the long-term process of what Turpin terms "ongoing conversion" or sanctification. In this way, educators can walk with youth along the challenging path of shifting slowly away from consumer faith in the midst of a deeply and unapologetically consumerist society, a journey that will help young people attend to and grow into who God calls them to be.[22] In connecting the Ascetic Withdrawal Project to the liturgical context of Lent, I hoped to ground this assignment within this theological framework and to prove Turpin's point that changing consumer habits is a process best understood as conversion.

Although Turpin's book was not originally intended to be the central text in the class, it has become a central pedagogical foundation because I repeatedly observed that, as students learn about the complexities of this interconnected, globalized world and their role within it, their reactions prove much of her thesis. Throughout our course, but particularly in the beginning weeks, students view films and read articles about the complex and often destructive nature of globalization on the environment, on nations in the "two-thirds" world, and on children and people of color. The films, including *The Corporation* and *Consuming Kids*, not only characterize global economic systems as pervasive and often beyond the reach of governmental authority, but they also make direct connections to the ways in which children and youth are "branded" from infancy through a ceaseless onslaught of media images that follow them throughout the school day, into their homes and even their bedrooms. Effective in "awakening" my students to the seriousness of the problem they and the youth with whom they work face, these films tend to have the more immediate impact of creating despair and alarm. These films have enormous educational value because they effectively communicate complex realities. However, if they stand alone, they form what Turpin calls the "shock, inform, and convert" pedagogy, which "assumes that if a person is exposed to a sufficiently compelling version of reality, they will desire more knowledge about that version of reality and subsequently change their behavior in response to this new knowledge."[23] As Turpin notes, such methods by themselves "lack the staying power to maintain a change in life habits and commitment over time," because they do not "address the deep change aspects of the faithing self, who depends on the existing meaning system for making sense of life."[24] For Turpin, a "fuller pedagogy of conversion," one that more effectively empowers young people to make deep and lasting change, must couple awakening with repentance, justification, and regeneration.

The Ascetic Withdrawal Project seeks to embody at least part of this "fuller pedagogy." Turpin defines the next phase, *repentance*, as "self-knowledge." Drawing on Wesley, she characterizes repentance as based not in fear or guilt but within a context of grace that allows people to identify the ways in which they are still committed to "sin" (consumer culture) and are invited to set out on what she terms an "adventure in partnership with God" to move toward a life more fully expressive of the love of God.[25] Turpin introduces the concept of "practices of dehabituation" such as pilgrimage and ascetic withdrawal. These are aimed at allowing the believer to step outside [his or] her current context and "to see herself and her belief system in a new light, a form of repentance that increases self-knowledge and fuels ongoing conversion."[26] The Ascetic Withdrawal Project thus intends to be an "ascetic withdrawal from sites of consumption."[27] I encourage students to choose a practice to take up and/or give up a practice that would help them withdraw from consumer faith and focus more intentionally on their Christian faith. The goal, as explained in the assignment guidelines, is "to engage in a practice that aims at conversion away from consumer faith and towards a richer Christian faith through the tradition of observing the fasting period of Lent." As a season explicitly connected to reflection upon sin as preparation for the celebration of God's gracious act on Easter, Lent opens up space for students to connect these theological concepts with the very specific and personal interactions with consumerism they experience in the Ascetic Withdrawal Project.[28]

While I originally envisioned the AWP project as a practice of repentance, the second part of Turpin's process, I witnessed elements of her concept of a "fuller pedagogy," including *justification*, as we moved through the project. Turpin describes justification as "the gasp of wonder, the moment of 'that's awesome' in response to the fundamental sense that something is so right it is worth staking your life on."[29] She goes on:

> We become justified when we find something that's beautiful enough and powerful enough to make sense of all that we are and that we hope for in life. This "gift of faith" allows us the freedom to imagine ourselves differently, and thus to live differently in light of this new imagination.[30]

This experience is primarily aesthetic—we see a beautiful vision of a new way of being in the world, of the possibilities into which we begin to imagine ourselves living. At the same time, the attractiveness of this new vision causes the old ways to lose their appeal. This is a different form of critical consciousness—rather than a "shock, inform, and convert" approach, we see something more worthy of our love, and we step toward it rather than merely away from the old faith.[31]

As my students moved through the six weeks of Lent, many of them did catch a glimpse of something more worthy of their love, something attractive enough to invite them to move away from a blind consumerist lifestyle toward a life aligned more closely to their own faith commitments. What began as an exercise of ascetic sacrifice became for many students a source of joyful insight and meaningful living. Several students described moments during their projects that enriched their lives by pointing to something deeper and more satisfying than consumer culture. One student gave up fast food as part of his desire to slow down the pace of his lifestyle. He began cooking meals at home with his wife, who had joined him in giving up fast food as well. By the end, he noted that one of the greatest gifts the experience gave him was the meaningful time he spent cooking with his wife. Another student, a wife and mother of two young children, gave up "grab and go" food from Whole Foods out of a desire to cook from scratch for her family. Despite the significant time commitment and strong temptation to "give in" on particularly stressful days, she felt that "there is no love in the pre-cooked food" and that cooking, and teaching her husband how to help with the cooking, gave her a new way of expressing love for her family. A student who gave up watching cable news remarked on the positive impact it had on his temperament. He also shared that his fiancée had made particular note of this change, something he took quite seriously in light of his preparations to begin a lifetime commitment with her. Another student remarked on how she had lapsed into a "guilty pleasure" of daydreaming in the shower when she was supposed to be conserving water, only to discover that her showers—even with the reverie— took less time than the showers she used to take. She had become able to enjoy a shower while still using less water. Another student noted that after giving up fast food, he lost fifteen pounds and felt much healthier, in addition to learning how to cook. Another student, having committed to buying only locally grown food, discovered Swiss chard for the first time, trying several different recipes that she then proudly described in her posts. In each case, students sensed that, even in the midst of ongoing "temptation" to break their fasts, they were gaining something more wonderful than what they were losing—something money couldn't buy.

The theological concepts of conversion, sin, grace, justification, and regeneration/sanctification that Turpin uses offer a unique response to the pedagogical problem of teaching civic engagement. Such concepts acknowledge the pervasive and overwhelming power of consumer culture to shape our lives and identities. They make it clear that no single educational event—a documentary screening, a lecture, a service project, a research project, or even, for that matter, a multiweek practice of ascetic withdrawal—can magically transform self-absorbed, smart-phone-obsessed, mall-going young people into active citizens overnight. Overcoming civic schizophrenia is a lifetime process, requiring "ongoing conversion" within communities of accountability and support. Along the way, we find ourselves constantly retreating back into the isolated "private self," but this is no reason to give up. As sinners, grace remains ever available, ever enlivening and inviting us to enter into a life that goes deeper, and broader, than our branded existence can give.

In the process of engaging this assignment, I have discovered, with and through my students, that practices of ascetic withdrawal do *more* than contribute to "ongoing conversion" of the individual away from "consumer faith." They also become a means of public witness and even evangelism. Our private fasts turn out to be unavoidably public, and when students have gone beyond the awkwardness of defending their fasts to their peers, they have sometimes stumbled upon opportunities for public—arguably prophetic—witness. Within a theological context, explaining why one is not eating a certain food, watching cable news, sending text messages, or buying products with unrecyclable packaging is an opportunity not only to educate others about the global ramifications of these consumer choices but also to articulate the relationship this has to one's faith. For example, a student who fasted from television could not avoid explaining to his peers why he needed to leave the room where a television was on, and when pressed why this was something appropriate to do *for Lent*, he found himself offering a theological justification that made clear that for him part of what it means to be a Christian is to be actively engaged in personal transformation not merely for one's own sake but for the sake of building God's Kingdom. The private self that would engage in practices of personal holiness finds that it cannot but unite with the public self that would engage in works of social holiness.[32]

Conclusion: Raising Lazarus with Seminary Students

For my teaching context, the training of ministers and religious educators charged with teaching this Gospel, the attempt to "convert" away from "consumer faith" addresses the "zombie apocalypse" of consumerism by transforming it. The theological insights of sin, grace, justification, and public witness that come from connecting the Ascetic Withdrawal Project to the season of Lent helps to stem the tide of the growing hordes of disconnected, materialistic, "undead" un-citizens, at least a little. In the Gospel of John, Jesus raises his friend Lazarus from the dead, in a scene that begs adaptation for a "Christian Zombie" movie: the "dead man" comes out of the tomb, "his hands and feet bound with cloth," while a crowd of people stand amazed (John 11:44). Of course, Lazarus is *not* a zombie, but a sign of the Resurrection, of God's power over death and the promise of life beyond the death-dealing "powers and principalities" that oppress us here and now. This sign is so powerful and so threatening to the religious authorities that they decide they must put Lazarus to death as well as Jesus (John 12:9–11). Lazarus comes back from the dead not as an isolated, mindless consumer but as a prophetic witness to the countercultural Gospel of Jesus that insists that we are not what we buy but, rather, adopted children of God (Romans 8:12–17). We are no longer zombies following our instincts back to the mall, but church leaders following a call to radical discipleship.

To teach civic engagement today, educators must first address the split between the private self and the public self that allows many of us, but particularly the emerging adults we teach, to live in a bubble of extreme individualism that limits freedom and agency to consumer choice and blinds us to the social impact of our disconnected, self-interested choices. As one pedagogical strategy for this, the Ascetic Withdrawal Project attempts to overcome this split, reconnecting personal experiences of engaging consumerism with researched knowledge of the social impact of those consumer choices. When this particular activity is combined with assignments that encourage research and the application of that research for educating others, it reconnects the private and public selves, deepens the civic engagement learning, and prepares students for leadership in society. When you tie this particular assignment to a liturgical and theological context, such as Lent, it reconnects personal and social holiness, deepens theological reflection, and prepares students for prophetic leadership in the church. If the zombie apocalypse really is the pervasive phenomenon of young adults absorbed in individual pursuits of consumerism to the exclusion of civic engagement, then perhaps it is time to put down the zombie survival guides and turn inward, so that we can prepare ourselves to turn outward.

Notes

1. Kim Paffenroth, *Gospel of the Living Dead: George Romero's Visions of Hell on Earth* (Waco, TX: Baylor University Press, 2006), 56.
2. Christian Smith with Kari Christoffersen, Hilary Davidson, and Patricia Snell Herzog, *Lost in Transition: The Dark Side of Emerging Adulthood* (Oxford: Oxford University Press, 2011), 217. James Roberts cites several studies of college students since the 1960s that document the trends in their stated life goals, which increasingly name "being well-off financially" as their highest goal, far surpassing goals like "helping others in need" or "raising a family." See Roberts, *Shiny Objects: Why We Spend Money We Don't Have in Search of Happiness We Can't Buy* (New York: HarperOne, 2011), 137ff. Sociologist Zygmunt Bauman has devoted significant study to the sweeping cultural changes that have occurred as we have moved from a "society of producers" to a "society of consumers," and

he considers active citizenship a "collateral casualty of consumerism." While Smith et al. explain that emerging adults consistently report being too over-whelmed by the tasks of getting on their own feet as they leave home to pay at-tention to politics and community service, Bauman describes a more pervasive problem—the constant effort it takes to maintain oneself as a "marketable com-modity" in order to survive an economic system that "disposes" of flawed com-modities and consumers. See Zygmunt Bauman, *Consuming Life* (Cambridge, UK: Polity Press, 2007), 147–49.

3. Juliet B. Schor, *Born to Buy: The Commercialized Child and the New Consumer Cul-ture* (New York: Scribner, 2004), 99–117; and Allisa Quart, *Branded: The Buying and Selling of Teenagers* (Cambridge, MA: Perseus Publishing, 2003), 3–16.

4. Though "born to buy," not all children come from social contexts that allow them to fulfill this demand. Elizabeth Chin explores the complex dynamic of consumerism practiced in marginalized communities in *Purchasing Power: Black Kids and American Consumer Culture* (Minneapolis: University of Minne-sota Press, 2001).

5. Benjamin R. Barber, *Consumed: How Markets Corrupt Children, Infantilize Adults, and Swallow Citizens Whole* (New York: W. W. Norton & Company, 2007), 257–90. See also Katherine Turpin, *Branded: Adolescents Converting from Consumer Faith* (Cleveland, OH: Pilgrim Press, 2006), 35–37; and Kalle Lasn, *Culture Jam: How to Reverse America's Suicidal Consumer Binge—And Why We Must* (New York: Harper Collins [Quill], 1999), xi.

6. See, e.g., Jo Littler, *Radical Consumption: Shopping for Change in Contemporary Culture* (New York: Open University Press, 2009); Michele Micheletti, *Politi-cal Virtue and Shopping: Individuals, Consumerism, and Collective Action* (New York: Palgrave MacMillan, 2003); and Michele Micheletti, Andreas Follesdal, and Dietlind Stolle (eds.), *Politics, Products, and Markets: Exploring Political Consumerism Past and Present* (New Brunswick, NJ: Transaction Publishers, 2004).

7. Tom Beaudoin, *Consuming Faith: Integrating Who We Are with What We Buy* (Lanham, MD: Sheed & Ward, 2003), 59.

8. Caryn McTighe Musil, "Educating Students for Personal and Social Respon-sibility: The Civic Learning Spiral," in *Civic Engagement in Higher Education: Concepts and Practices*, ed. Barbara Jacoby and Associates (San Francisco: Jossey-Bass, 2009), 59.

9. Barber, 128.

10. Ibid., 132. For a concise discussion of how the idea of "citizen" has been eclipsed by the idea of "consumer" in public life, see Yiannis Gabriel and Tim Lang, *The Unmanageable Consumer*, 2nd ed. (London: Sage Publications, 2006), 172ff.

11. Barber, 36. Barber locates the origins of this problem in the decline of the Prot-estant work ethic and the rise of an "infantilization ethos" as a result of the deformities of late stage capitalism. Many other cultural critics find blame in

other areas as well. Henry Giroux, an educational theorist, worries particularly about the diminished role of higher education as the place for teaching a sense of civic duty, democratic values, and critical thinking, in the wake of the corporatization of education. But the result is the same: "In a society where knowledge is instrumentalized, commodified, fragmented, and privatized, it becomes difficult for everyone, not just students, to connect private troubles to public problems." See Henry A. Giroux, *Twilight of the Social: Resurgent Publics in the Age of Disposability* (Boulder, CO: Paradigm Publishers, 2012), 16–17. This inability of students to connect the private with the public, with a near total immersion in the private, is what I hope to address in my teaching.

12. Smith et al. (see n. 2), 274.

13. Portions of this section draw on a previously published work. See Elizabeth W. Corrie, "From Civic Engagement to Circles of Grace: Mid-Range Reflection on Teaching for Global Citizenship," *Teaching Theology & Religion* 16 (2013): 165–81.

14. A. Kiesa, A. P. Orlowski, P. L. Levine, D. Both, E. H. Kirby, M. H. Lopez, et al., *Millennials Talk Politics: A Study of College Student Political Engagement* (College Park, MD: Center for Information and Research on Civic Learning and Engagement, 2007). David White also cites this as an essential challenge in youth ministry in *Practicing Discernment with Youth: A Transformative Youth Ministry Approach* (Cleveland, OH: Pilgrim Press, 2005).

15. Although loosely applied in this context, the principle of "backward design" informs this approach. Beginning with the desired result of cultivating self-awareness of one's personal engagement in consumer practices, I determined that the acceptable evidence would be written and oral comments that demonstrated insight into personal habits as a result of a practical activity. I consequently planned an introductory "hook" of using my own consumer habits as an example, explained the connection between the activity and the essential questions guiding the course, and modeled the type of self-reflection I hoped to see in the student work. I then returned to the topic several times to reinforce the connection between the assignment and the course goals as a way to underscore the importance of engaging the assignment thoughtfully in order to gain the most learning from it. See Grant Wiggins and Jay McTighe, *Understanding by Design, Expanded Second Edition* (Alexandria, VA: Association for Supervision and Curriculum Development, 2005), 191ff.

16. The concept of being "branded" is used here to describe the phenomenon of being deeply committed—often unwittingly, almost always unreflectively—to the symbolic meaning corporate brands and logos communicate, and our use of them for our own identity expression and development. See Turpin, *Branded*, 11–28; and Quart, *Branded* (see n. 3), xiv.

17. Years of personal experience and observation informs this assumption, but a fascinating field of research in consumer behavior provides some social

scientific data to support the prediction that students will encounter social pressure when they engage in practices that challenge the norms of their social groups. See, e.g., Wendy Wood and Timothy Hayes, "Social Influence on Consumer Decisions: Motives, Modes, and Consequences"; Jeffrey Simpson, Vladas Griskevicius, and Alexander J. Rothman, "Consumer Decisions in Relationships," *Journal of Consumer Psychology* 22 (2012): 304–14, 324–28; Mary Douglas, "Why Do People Want Goods?" in *Consumption: Critical Concepts in the Social Sciences, Volume 1,* ed. Daniel Miller (London: Routledge, 2001), 262–71; M. Venkateson, "Experimental Study of Consumer Behavior Conformity and Independence," *Journal of Marketing Research* 3 (1966): 384–87; and D. N. Lascu and G. Zinkhan, "Consumer Conformity: Review and Applications for Marketing Theory and Practice," *Journal of Marketing Theory and Practice* 7 (1999): 1–12.

18. By encouraging students to go back to what they learned in their midterm projects and extend this understanding in their finals, I am following the principle of a "spiral curriculum" discussed in Wiggins and McTighe, *Understanding by Design,* 296–300.

19. See Barber, 128.

20. Turpin, 37–41.

21. Ibid., 45.

22. Ibid., 15–17.

23. Ibid., 73.

24. Ibid., 73, 108.

25. Ibid., 113.

26. Ibid., 116.

27. Ibid., 118.

28. In the comments students write to each other in response to blog reflections, they frequently make sense of their struggles to maintain their fasts in terms of their "fallenness" but also in terms of the value of being reminded of one's humanity for further spiritual growth, the development of humility and compassion for others, and the reminder of one's dependence ultimately upon God.

29. Turpin, 136.

30. Ibid.

31. Ibid., 143.

32. This discovery extends beyond Turpin's work and comes to the forefront when put in conversation with the discussion of civic engagement in relation to consumerism.

What Are the Theoretical Issues and Challenges in Teaching Civic Engagement in Religious Studies and Theology?

10

Thinking about the "Civic" in Civic Engagement and Its Deployment in the Religion Classroom

Carolyn M. Jones Medine

THE SENSE OF what constitutes the "civic" and how we participate in it is chang-ing. With the emergence of the new secularism and other re-imaginings of communal space[1] and the acknowledgment of globalization as a force for both forming community and generating further marginalization, we find ourselves rethinking what it means to engage in action in the public, civic sphere. Martha Nussbaum connects secularism to action and to meaning in *Creating Capabilities: The Human Development Approach*, offering a clear sense of what secularism, which is part of liberalism, should offer. In terms of her Capabilities approach, which focuses on human development, particularly the development of women, she writes that

> Such values, however, either are or can become a part of the many compre-
> hensive doctrines that citizens reasonably hold. If they are articulated in a
> calculatedly "thin" way, without grounding in controversial metaphysical
> notions (such as the idea of the immortal soul), epistemological notions
> (such as the idea of self-evident truth), or thicker ethical doctrines (such
> as Kantianism or Aristotelianism), they can potentially command the ap-
> proval of a wide range of citizens subscribing to different religious and
> secular positions.[2]

Citizenship and participation in the public sphere are at the core of Nussbaum's thinking. These constitute key elements in much of the thinking on civic engage-ment in the classroom.

Here, I want to think through what the "civic" in "civic engagement" might be. I begin with the impact of Robert P. Putnam's *Bowling Alone: America's*

Declining Social Capital, which was one impetus for the emergence of civic engagement elements of higher education. With Putnam's framework in mind, I first want to ask: What do we mean when we use the term "civic"? I argue that, if we mean participation in citizen political roles, the "civic" is understood to be disintegrating in America. Second, I want to look at the likely formation these disengaged citizens received in school, focusing on *Magruder's American Government*, the most widely used civics textbook. Third, I want look at a broader notion of the "civic" in college and university programs and at how the notion of civic engagement is understood in relation to traditional curricula, particularly, for professors who use this kind of work, for promotion and tenure. Fourth, I want to look at how engagement with the particular/local opens a perspective on the global and, using the work of Chandra Mohanty, to look at the possible missteps we, as teachers, can make as we construct civic engagement learning activities. Finally, I want to speculate about why the work of religious studies is work that potentially makes civic engagement effective.

Bowling Alone

Robert Putnam, in *Bowling Alone*, reminds us that Alexis de Tocqueville, when he visited the United States in the 1830s, was struck by American participation in civic associations. Putnam writes that scholars who research de Tocqueville's claim agree that public life and social institutions, when they function well, are influenced by active civic engagement. Putnam found, in the 500,000 interviews that he conducted, a decline in civic engagement in America. Involvement in union membership, PTA, volunteering, and other traditional forms of association have declined. Disengagement from the public sphere, Putnam asserts, leads to psychological disengagement as well. Americans who do not participate in civic life trust their government less, for example. More important for Putnam is the decline in "social capital," which he defines as "social connectedness." He finds as reasons for this decline several elements, including the movement of women into the workforce, the mobility of the population, and the impact that technology has had on our leisure time.[3]

Putnam does qualify his own claims, recognizing that there are new forms of association that are vibrant—for example, environmental and feminist organizations, AARP, and even soccer—but he does not think that these associations generate the same social capital as older organizations, because the members generally do not meet and/or exchange views.[4] He also admits that he "overlooked three important factors" in his analysis: the growth of inequality, the growth of diversity, and the decay of mobilizing organizations.[5]

Though his book was criticized for its methodology and its uses of data, Putnam's argument still made an important impact. As Howard Richards, Professor of Peace and Global Studies at Earlham College in Richmond, Indiana, put it, what Putnam writes matters, because lack of civic engagement "negatively impacts measures of child welfare, it makes neighborhoods less safe to live in, it reduces prosperity, it makes people less happy and less healthy, it saps the vitality of democratic institutions."[6]

Perhaps Putnam's work might have faded into obscurity except for the September 11, 2001, attacks on New York City and Washington, D.C. In "Pedagogy and Political (Dis)Engagement," K. Edward Spiezio argues that the September 11 attacks "played the perversely functional role of cauterizing the consciousness of this heretofore politically disengaged generation," catapulting them into a greater desire to participate in democracy.[7] It is not that democracy and education had not been linked before; the prolific and insightful Henry Giroux, for example, had already made this connection before 9/11, and continues to write extensively about democracy and education.[8] What Spiezio saw was an urgency, and he responded by suggesting that colleges and universities could help to organize and to promote civic engagement. He writes:

> The purpose of this essay is to suggest that educators can play a decisive role in transforming this teachable moment into an enduring encounter with the theory and practice of participatory democracy if we are willing to embrace some potentially far-reaching curricular and institutional innovations in regard to how we teach students about political engagement.[9]

Spiezio specifically wants civic engagement activities to be tied to political processes. He writes that just placing students in voluntary positions, through service learning, does not lead to a sense of civic duty. Data supports his concern. For example, a survey by the Higher Education Research Institute 2000 found that student volunteerism was at an all-time high but that political participation, particularly among first-year students, had fallen to an all-time low, particularly since civics courses suggest that citizenship is about relying on the state and elected representatives to "promote their individual welfare."[10]

With Spiezio's argument in mind, let us look at the likely civic formation that high school students bring with them into colleges and universities and how that does and does not lead to civic participation.

Magruder's American Government and the Formation of the Citizen

Rob Walker, in a *Slate Magazine* article, commented on the significance (and size and cost) of the best-selling high school government and civics textbook:

Magruder's American Government. Its publisher, Prentice-Hall, "has claimed that the book has held at least 70 percent of the civics-text market since it was first published in 1917."[11] We begin with *Magruder's*, which is continually updated, because its influence on defining the civic and citizen participation spans almost one hundred years, because it is the most used textbook in high school civics courses, and because of its categories. We should also note that it is more than a bound textbook: There is a large web page for the text that includes online activities that, in a civic engagement model, puts the information into use, and there are summaries of the text's information.[12] As one critic wrote:

> *Magruder's* is an institution unto itself: by 1993, it had undergone 76 editions. It is so easily identified by *"Magruder's"* that finding the original author's name—Frank Abbot Magruder—and his intent—"to portray the fluid and dynamic nature of U.S. democracy"—involved a bit of a search.[13]

Magruder's includes topics like "Foundations of American Government" and "Political Behavior (of the American People)." It includes chapters on the branches of American government, comparative political and economic systems, and, finally, participation in state and local government. Concluding with the local, it explains and suggests online learning activities like this one:

Local Government

· Learn about the population, economics, and government of your own county (or a county of your choosing if you live in a region without counties).
· Summarize your findings in a table or series of graphs.
· Printable Worksheet: Print this worksheet and use it to report what you've learned from this Internet activity.[14]

The text also suggests modes of participation in those structures, like writing letters. This local concentration supports Spiezio's claims about how civics participation is defined for young people and how that definition might suggest leaving the hard work of the civic space to elected officials.[15] The web page and textual features, however, do encourage critical thought and personal action. Walker, in the *Slate* article, notes that the "Skills for Life" section

> . . . aims, I gather, to teach practical lessons, including one on "Filing a Consumer Complaint" and another on "Taking a Poll." Other elements include . . . political cartoons, and results of polls in which . . . the Close-Up Foundation asked high-school students which characteristics of a presidential candidate might influence their vote.[16]

Magruder's offers an ongoing contribution to the formation of American political consciousness, yet it seems to have little effect, if we look at that most basic action of citizenship: voting.

While voter turnout increases and decreases, many Americans choose not to vote: About 93 million Americans, according to the *Examiner*, did not vote in the 2012 election.[17] President Barack Obama's entry into the scene in 2008 galvanized young voters: They voted for him 4 to 1 over President George W. Bush.[18] This trend continued in the 2012 election, with Obama getting 60 percent of the youth vote. Yet, this does not signal increased participation overall.[19] As Scott Jaschik reports in "Political Engagement 101," "Survey after survey reports that American students—while concerned about the world around them—are apathetic about politics. Events like Katrina or Darfur spark activism and voluntarism. . . . But voter registration (and voting), turnouts at town hall meetings and knowledge of the political process remain embarrassingly low."[20]

Some elements of the recent election, however, demonstrated a change in the American civic space that also belies some of Spiezio's claims. In the most recent presidential elections, as the preceding statistics suggest, the youth vote demonstrated increasing power in the American political scene. Also, while white voters remain the majority, the 2012 election indicated how important Latino/a and other racial-ethnic voters are and will be in the future. The *New York Times*, for example, reported that while "Hispanic" voters are about 17 percent of the population, the influence of this voting demographic was significant for President Obama. Mitt Romney secured 59 percent of the White vote, the largest percentage in history, but lost the election. In addition, scholars suggest, the "location" of these elections in our post-9/11 world changes the face of democracy and, thereby, the face of civic engagement.

Global America

I cite this information on voting to suggest that America, like the rest of the world, finds itself not just participating in but also experiencing the effects of globalization[21] and, through global development, a change in what constitutes the civic space. September 11th, I would argue, though some would argue against me, highlighted for Americans that we had entered "a fundamentally new era,"[22] making us recognize that the American *polis* and our participation in it is influenced perhaps, conditioned by, and located in global forces. To make some sense of the effect of this, let us turn to the work of Arjun Appadurai.

Arjun Appadurai, in *Fear of Small Numbers: An Essay on the Geography of Anger*, offers a lucid explanation of globalization as an institutional and structural matter.[23] Appadurai argues that in the new geography created by globalization, once settled ideas like freedom, the market, democracy, and rights do not operate in the same way and do not stay in place.[24] He uses the terms "vertebrate" and "cellular" to show how the nation-state experiences the effects of global systems and the unsettling of its terms. The vertebrate and the cellular are presented in Table 10.1.[25]

I set this information into a binary chart for ease of reading, but Appadurai is clear that the two overlap and are interdependent. The modern nation-state is a hybrid, and the gray areas of the vertebrate are complicit with the cellular. While information, technology, and the rapid movement of people, ideas, and capital are key in both the vertebrate and the cellular, cellular groups multiply as these global elements "roam" without license or limit.[26] This movement across boundaries opens interstitial space in which, for example, terrorist networks, which are cellular, Appadurai argues, can work. They function, he tells us, in the opportunistic spaces created by the "fantasy" of the nation-state that it is sovereign.[27]

Yet, for Appadurai, the vertebrate and the cellular can both clash and complement. While terrorism is one face of the cellular, "deep democracy" is another.[28] Appadurai himself is most interested in how global networks put resources into the hands of those at the local level—particularly women—such that local problems can be tackled "one issue and one alliance at a time."[29] Appadurai calls this use of global attributes "deep democracy" or "cellular democratization" and sees it as a form that builds capacity and creates partnerships.[30] In addition, since

Table 10.1 The Vertebrate and Cellular in Arjun Appadurai's Thought

Vertebrate "Complete"	Cellular Not complete
SYSTEM	LABORATORY: alternative global polity
nation-state order	mobile, recombinant, opportunistic
norms, protocols, institutions, hierarchy	de-nationalized networks, transnational action
semiotic symbols: flags, stamps, consulates, ambassadors	fed by information technology and financial transactions
spinal system: international balances of power, treaties, legislation, sovereign territory, national patriotism.	parts multiply by association and opportunity
fantasy is that the nation-state assures a sovereign economic space	global capitalism wants to roam without license or limit

ideas, goods, and people cross boundaries quickly, "international action networks" can form that can have influence and change policy on multiple levels.[31]

"Participation," rather than classical notions of citizenship, then, is located in this complex of actions and ideas. Looking at Spiezio's and Appadurai's arguments together, one might argue that civic engagement can be defined as more than just voting patterns; indeed, it can work in this interstitial space as well. What begins on the local level might have international impact. We must also recognize that our students are engaged, already, in this international community, though not always consciously as citizens. A facility with technology may open students to a larger community than the American one, but it is a community that they, largely, do not engage face to face. Blogs, Tweets, and Facebook may generate spaces in which students safely can practice identity without facing tensions and disagreements. In addition, world events like Darfur or Hurricane Katrina do mobilize action—in the form of donations, for example. So, it is not that young people are disengaged, just that they are, perhaps, differently engaged.

I see the issue of engagement in a global world as complicated by the characterization of being "spiritual" but not "religious."[32] To be sure, religiosity does not guarantee the desire to be engaged; as a student wrote on an examination of mine many years ago, "I am so happy to be a Christian who only has to believe, not do anything else." Religious practice, like citizenship, does have prescribed paths for civic action, including exposure to difference and activities like meditation or self-reflection.

What does this configuration of concerns—lower voting patterns, globalization with its attendant elements, and being differently engaged—mean in the classroom and for the professors who are incorporating civic engagement activities into their classes?

The Pedagogy and Politics of Civic Engagement

In response to calls like Spiezio's, many educational institutions have instituted civic engagement curricula. Many, over 200, public and private colleges and universities joined the American Democracy Project, which started in 2003 as "a non-partisan, multi-campus initiative that seeks to create an intellectual and experiential understanding of civic engagement for undergraduates in institutions that belong to the American Association of State Colleges and Universities."[33] Its goal is to create a greater intellectual understanding of and commitment to participation in the civic life of the United States. Other organizations have become active partners on college and university campuses as well.[34] All in all, civic engagement has strong public backing.

Civic Engagement programs at many institutions, like my home, The University of Georgia, both reinforce the vertebrate and engage the cellular. "Civic engagement" is a transdisciplinary, "umbrella" term for a multitude of activities: volunteering, participation in service-learning courses on campus and abroad, advocacy, and community work-study.[35] It may, at other institutions, include "servant leadership" and terms like "character education." This expansion of civic engagement beyond, but inclusive of, democratic participation supports Thomas Ehrlich's definition in *Civic Responsibility and Higher Education*, of civic engagement as both political and non-political, as seeing oneself as part of a community in which the problems of the whole are one's own problems.[36]

The University of Georgia Center for Leadership and Service defines itself as empowering "students to internationally engage in leadership learning and practice active citizenship," suggesting a combination of the *Magruder's* citizenship model with Appadurai's deep democracy cellular model.[37] The Center offers both opportunity for work and information, through the "Russell Forum for Civic Life in Georgia."[38] Service-learning opportunities are both local and international, with about one-fourth of study-abroad courses incorporating service-learning options.[39]

The University of Georgia Office of Service-Learning is more local: "Service-learning at the University of Georgia is *the application of academic skills and knowledge to address a community need, issue, or problem and to enhance student learning.* Service-learning helps integrate two core aspects of UGA's mission—teaching and service—and is explicitly recommended in UGA's 2010–2020 Strategic Plan."[40] There is also an emphasis on scholarship: professors can apply to become service-learning fellows.

This combination of teaching, service and engagement, and scholarship signals a shift in, perhaps an extension of, the models of the scholar for large institutions like mine, particularly in the Humanities. While we are used to scientists producing products for the public use and good, holding patents, and (most importantly) bringing in money through them, the large universities at which I have taught have emphasized scholarship above all other activities for advancement. Therefore, it remains to be seen how a scholar-teacher-activist identity will be rewarded.[41]

More important is what pedagogical strategies are utilized in civic engagement and service-learning courses. Most institutional statements that I read as I researched this chapter mirror that of the University of California system statement that any civic engagement work must be integrated with the campus mission and the current curricular structure, as well as community needs. It goes on to say that the engagement must be rigorous, integrated with a scholarly agenda.[42] Civic engagement scholarship is understood *to enhance* traditional scholarship, not to replace it, according to the University of California report, and, I would suggest, therefore is not understood to be service, which counts very little in large universities. The University of California report, in comparing Traditional Scholarship and the Scholarship of Engagement, simply adds the appeal to the public and public issues. For example, Traditional Scholarship "breaks new ground," while Scholarship of Engagement also breaks new ground but with application to "broader public issues." Traditional Scholarship is reviewed and evaluated by peers in the discipline, while in the Scholarship of Engagement, the scholarship must also be validated by members of the community.[43] In sum, Traditional Scholarship's movement into engagement involves applying knowledge to address social issues in particular communities.

The scholarship of engagement is, ultimately, *scholarship*—hence, easy to evaluate in tenure and promotion criteria—but with an additional practical application. The University of California emphasizes that engaged scholarship is low- or no-cost, if embedded in the existing curriculum. The report goes on to say, "It is important to emphasize that rigorous research reconnects the academy to its public purpose."[44] What might this mean for the Humanities classroom, or for pedagogical practice in the Religious Studies classroom?

Civic engagement clearly enhances college learning. An Association of American Colleges and Universities (AAC&U) report in *Diversity and Democracy*, "Civic Engagement and Student Success: A Resonant Relationship," argues that civic engagement activities—called "High Impact Practices"—generate outcomes that colleges and universities are particularly interested in: higher grade point averages and graduation rates, preparation for employment, meeting learning outcomes, and diversity. In addition, civic engagement increases the personal and psychological well-being of students.[45] Christine Cress, in "Student Engagement and Student Success: Leveraging Multiple Degrees of Achievement," argues that students learn more academic content, learn higher-order skills, as they have to apply their knowledge to complex situations, and grow in emotional intelligence and conscientious community activity.[46] Does this effect last?

The long-range civic engagement work seems to be less persuasive. There is, as yet, little data to measure the outcomes of civic engagement over time. The AAC&U distributed a brief in 2012 for its annual meeting to examine the issue in "A Crucible Moment." While we must recognize, as Kathleen Ferraiolo reminds us, "Many of the skills and attitudes of citizenship defy easy quantification, and much of the work of assessment is in creating and testing appropriate indicators of progress,"[47] the report was not encouraging. While over 70 percent of college students reported participation in some kind of active learning, and "despite a wealth of positive evidence related to service-learning experiences, finding on a range of civic measures and social responsibility outcomes compared over time suggest that students' civic learning is neither robust nor pervasive."[48] The report argued that there is a need for more evidence on how pedagogies of engagement build "capacities for success in an increasingly global and diversifying nation," and it emphasized that, over all, low percentages of students engage in study-abroad experiences that might lead to global thinking.

A Higher Education Research Institute (HERI) report on "Understanding the Effects of Service Learning" (2003) looked at the impact of service learning, in particular, on recent college graduates. It surveyed students in a variety of ways.[49] These students, they argue, are "'fast-trackers' and high achievers."[50] HERI wanted to understand three categories of behavior, values, and belief that they believe contribute to civic engagement:

· Community/civic engagement: civic leadership, working with communities, volunteerism, charitable giving, and involvement with alma mater.
· Political engagement: general political engagement and its four subfactors: political activism, political expression, commitment to political/social change, and voting behavior.
· Civic values/goals: pluralistic orientation, self-efficacy, and the goal of promoting racial understanding.[51]

The HERI study showed a steady decline in participation over time: "while 80.3 percent of the students surveyed had participated in community in the year prior to entering college, this figure declined to 74.4 percent by the senior year of college and to 68.1 percent six years after completing college."[52] In addition, the values of helping others in difficulty, participating in a community action program, becoming a community leader, or influencing social values also declined.[53] Is what we see here a pattern of what we might call "strategic altruism," as fast-trackers realize that they need activities to gain admission to the best colleges and, later, to the best graduate and professional schools? If this is so, it might support Eric Uslaner and Mitchell Brown's contention that what they call "particularlized trusters"—people who "have faith only in their own kind" and who will participate in groups with people like themselves—do not develop, necessarily, "generalized" trust of others.[54] They also argue that the small amount of time that persons spend in civic engagement activities is not enough to "shape, or reshape, an adult's values such as trust."[55] Given this reality, what might be happening in our classrooms, and how do we address this self-interested altruism?

Obstacles and Achievements

Service learning, the HERI report concludes, has its most powerful effect when it is combined with "a larger collection of college experiences."[56] It appears to have a "unique impact" on civic leadership[57] when combined with "courses and experiences which likely expose students to diverse and new perspectives," like ethnic studies and interdisciplinary courses.[58] These allow for reflection on the self in relation to the "other." Yet, this is dangerous territory, which we must traverse consciously.

Chandra Mohanty, in "'Under Western Eyes' Revisited: Feminist Solidarity through Anticapitalist Struggles," recognizes that pedagogy is, in a real sense, the scholar's mode of civic engagement. Speaking about feminist pedagogies in particular, Mohanty warns us that we should avoid two pedagogical modes: tourism and exploration. The classroom that involves tourism might see civic engagement as an "add-on": add an activity and stir.[59] In this case, civic engagement reifies difference: The engagement is in contrast to the normative classroom experience, and it reinforces the distances between classroom and public space, rather than integrating them. It can also, to cite Mohanty's notion of the "Third World Difference," re-inscribe nationalist and normative categories and assumptions, as well as self-interests.

The explorer mode separates civic engagement in another way. It suggests that the civic engagement project is about "others," both local and global. In feminist pedagogy, Mohanty calls this the "women in ____" way of teaching, which suggests that Two-Thirds World women, wherever they live, are equal, but remain separate from "us."[60] While civic engagement might correct the idea that the "other" is not here, it still might not complicate internal issues. Going "out" to work for the "other" may not become working with the other, which would generate—indeed, demand—thought and reflection on issues like our own racism, sexism, etc., for example.

Mohanty argues for a model of teaching based on feminist solidarity and co-implication. This model, she argues, enforces the reality that the local and the global exist simultaneously in our local, as well as national, spaces and constitute each other; this takes us back to Appadurai's formulations, but in the classroom space.[61] This solidarity model, as Mohanty calls it, stresses interconnections and requires us to formulate questions about connections and disconnections, forcing a struggle in teaching to open the world in all its complexities.[62]

How can we try to militate against the exoticizing and use of the "other" for the self? Key elements that HERI and other studies emphasize for cultivating success are sustained interaction—with professors and other students as well as community partners; an institutional commitment to particular values that civic engagement highlights; and student reflection.[63] For professors, this means integrating the service project into the student's lives (student interest is a major predictor of success); the goals and content of the course material, including assessment that includes evaluation; and into the institutional mission.[64] This level of scaffolding includes the rigor that institutions desire, and it signals gravity to the students participating in civic engagement. In addition, there must be, as HERI suggests, ongoing reflection, which is the key, in civic engagement, to pedagogical success.

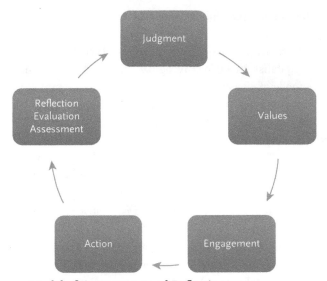

FIGURE 10.1 Model of Engagement and Reflection.

In 2010–2011, the Wabash Center for Teaching and Learning in Theology and Religion held a colloquy on "Religious Commitments in the Undergraduate Classroom." For that colloquy, Joseph Favazza, Kathleen Skerett, Daniel Deffenbaugh, and I generated a model through which to explore commitment, engagement, and reflection on these (see Fig. 10.1).[65]

As one can see, these elements build on one another: One engages in an action, reflects on (or in a classroom setting, evaluates or assesses) that action's meaning, makes a judgment, and, thinking critically, discerns how that action challenges, enhances, or changes one's values. This cycle is one we must inculcate in pedagogical structure and scaffolding by offering students categories for thinking critically and structures in which to deploy those categories—that is, crafted assignments—to think through the meaning of what they have done and what it means to and for self and other. Our model suggests a sustained and deepening of a pattern of being, one that would generate a lifelong habit not just of learning but of reflection on self and world.

Religious Commitments or Commitments in the Religious Studies Classroom

What Favazza, Deffenbaugh, Skerrett, and I came to think about engagement is that the *kind* of commitment is less important than the fact that there *is* commitment that becomes ongoing and that becomes self-conscious through reflective practice. What reflection might open up for students, keeping in mind Mohanty's warnings, is the recognition that the national and, now, global civic space is not one that is fully open and equal, that some have greater resources than others. Uslaner and Brown note that, "More inequality leads to less trust and less caring for people who are different from oneself. Where there is less trust, there are fewer acts of kindness towards others."[66] Uslaner and Brown find that there is "less likely to be an effect from civic engagement to trust than from trust to civic engagement."[67] How, then, can we instantiate trust? To this and other issues I (re)turn in some concluding remarks.

Conclusions

Civic engagement in the classroom is one element of a larger configuration of desires and needs that have entered the classroom—I would argue, on all levels of learning—in the last few years. The rethinking of the place of religion (and other disciplines) in the secular world,[68] and the turn to ethics (via the work of Emmanuel Levinas)[69] with its accompanying (re)turn to the affective dimensions of learning (recovering the work of Piaget),[70] along with the recognition that inculcating these theories into active learning models, including civic engagement, help students achieve academic and worldly success, is changing the higher education classroom. The turn to ethics and affective theory accompanied the resurgence in an interest in practice, fueled by the work of Michel Foucault and others, and thought about in a postcolonial mode by thinkers like Edward Said.[71] The question is what the place of religious studies can and should be in this reconfiguration of the academic landscape—and, indeed, of the civic space.

If what we desire is only to form political actors, civic engagement in the religious studies classroom might not be the path for such development, though politics plays a role in the practice of religion territorially, making both religion and politics contentious "in place." If, however, we desire that our students come to trust and work alongside the neighbor, religious studies (as an interdisciplinary field) is good ground for such work.

If trust "is the subjective probability by which an individual, *A*, expects that another individual, *B*, performs a given action on which [her] welfare depends,"[72] what we are asking students to learn is cooperation toward future goals with fellow citizen/neighbors. Trust asks that, at the very least, we tolerate the "other" and, at the best, that we have compassion with and for "others." The practice of civic engagement suggests that, in addition, we come to work toward common goods we see as vital.

Much of what I do as a teacher is to think about "selves" embedded in, standing in tension with, and leaving and entering community. This issue of movement across and within boundaries is one that suggests a form of struggle that serves, I think, to de-exoticize the "other" and the "self," whatever we believe those to be, and to think about relationship "formed" and "de-formed" in a matrix of influences. In my teaching, I hope that students will come to understand those they "other"[73] as not necessarily just like the "self," but as on parallel and viable life paths.

I am, as I teach religion, concerned with the impact of social location and dislocation and what those generate and repress. In my questioning of normative categories—even that of "religion," I unsettle issues that, in more stable forms, might allow us to become Mohanty's "tourists" or "explorers" without being changed and, as the language around teaching has suggested, "transformed."

The recognition, in the work I cited throughout this chapter, that writing is a key element of making the lessons of civic engagement "stick," so to speak, means that what we *already do* as educators does matter. Perhaps it does not matter so much that students who have graduated from college and university decline in active participation in civic engagement work. What might matter more is a habit of being—the intellectual habit of engagement—that has been developed in those students by the work that they have done and the stories they have heard, read, and written about and toward. In other words, the act of inter-pretation may make young people able to translate the values they learned in civic engagement effectively into the secular roles they inhabit, whether they continue to volunteer or not. This involves an openness to the "other."

Eboo Patel suggests that telling and hearing stories may be the root of social change—in that sense, the foundation of civic engagement pedagogies. He writes, utilizing Marshall Ganz's "Why Stories Matter," that there are three—I would suggest, interconnected, overlapping, and interfolding—stories: the story of self, the story of us, and the story of now.[74] The first is the story of the "self," "interpreting to others your reasons for being engaged in a struggle." The second tells the story of the multiple religions, races, ethnicities, and nations in which "selves" are embedded, particularly of those in different locations who, neverthe-less, fight for the same causes. Finally, the story of "now" brings these factors into "the reason for action, sacrifice, movement, and urgency at this moment above all others."[75] These may come together in creative ways.

Elaine Scarry suggests, in her recent work, that the multi-level action of story, which we encounter in the Liberal Arts and Humanities, develops "generous imaginings" and is a counteraction to the story that allows injuring others.[76] Such "generous imaginings" can open the way to justice and fairness, which Scarry defines as creating "symmetry" in our relations to others. John Randolph LeBlanc and I thought about this issue in our co-authored work, *Ancient and Modern Religion and Politics: Negotiating Transitive Spaces and Hybrid Identities*,[77] using, particularly, the work of Robert Detweiler. Detweiler argued that story lets us do two things: to tell the difference that may make the difference and, in what he called the erotic power of narrative, to make community among non-related "selves" such that I can no longer tell or understand my story without telling or understanding yours.[78] This recognizes that a "self" is a network of relations and keeps open, as Edward Said writes, the access to a set of values different from those of the modern, professional world, forcing us to continue to raise complex moral questions.[79]

Perhaps what we, in the study of religion, offer to civic engagement activities is not just the doing of them, but the interpretation, the storytelling around that affective and ethical engagement that internally unsettles norms. This capacity helps the student who majors in religion become ready to engage in the political activities suggested in Magruder's textbook, making her or him a good local citizen. But, she or he may also develop a critical interpretative capacity that opens her or him to, and makes her or him able to address the realities and complexities of, Appadurai's hybridized and global world. The work of civic engagement, along with thinking and writing about it, is all a method and practice, as Edward Said suggests in his work on the amateur and on worldliness, through which we give up mechanical notions of right and wrong and enter communities that necessarily include a variety of people, so that we do not find ourselves huddling "in some tiny, defensively constituted corner of the world," but able to dwell in a "large many-windowed house of human culture as a whole."[80]

Notes

1. For additional thought on secularism in the postmodern world, see Don E. Eberly (ed.), *The Essential Civic Society Reader: The Classic Essays* (Lanham, MD: Rowman and Littlefield, 2000), which offers a large selection of essays by key thinkers, including Robert Bellah and Peter Berger. Other key thinkers in this area include Amatai Etzioni in works like *Spirit of Community: The Reinvention of American Society* (New York: Touchstone Books, 1993). Other sources include Michael Walzer, *Politics and Passion: Toward a More Egalitarian Liberalism* (New Haven: Yale University Press, 2006) and Michael J. Sandel, *Public Philosophy: Essays on Morality in Politics* (Cambridge: Harvard University Press, 2006). Also, Stephen Eric Bronner, *Reclaiming the Enlightenment: Toward a Politics of Radical Engagement* (New York: Columbia University Press, 2004) argues that there is an idea of political engagement in the Enlightenment project that, when practiced, can revitalize political community and the Enlightenment project itself. The arguments range from the communitarianism of Etizoni to Walzer's call for a "thick" interpretation of community, one that moves beyond mere legal categories.

2. Martha Nussbaum, *Creating Capabilities: The Human Development Approach* (Cambridge, MA: Belknap Press, 2011), 90.

3. Robert Putnam, *Bowling Alone: The Collapse and Revival of American Community* (New York: Simon and Schuster, 2000), 74. Television, in terms of leisure time, Putnam argues, makes our communities "wider and shallower" (75).

4. Ibid., 71.

5. Robert Putnam, "The Civic Enigma," *American Prospect* (June 1, 2005): 33. Cf. Robert Putnam, *Bowling Alone,* 71, and Austin Gordon's several articles, available at www.saddleback.edu/faculty/agordon (accessed February 21, 2013).

6. Howard Richards, "Letter to Douglass Bennett." http://howardrichards.org/peace/content/view/21/74/ (accessed February 21, 2013).

7. K. Edward Spiezio, "Pedagogy and Political (Dis)Engagement," *Liberal Education* (2002): 14–19.

8. See, e.g., Stanley Aronowitz and Henry Giroux, *Postmodern Education: Politics, Culture and Social Criticism* (Minneapolis: University of Minnesota Press, 1991). Giroux has been consistent in his thought about educating for democratic critical citizenship.

9. Spiezio, "Pedagogy and Political (Dis)Engagement," 14.

10. Ibid., 17.

11. William A. McClenaghan, *Macgruder's American Government* (New York: Prentice Hall, 2013). The book has been in print since 1917. Rob Walker, "Magruder's American Government," *Slate Magazine* http://www.slate.com/toolbar.aspx?action=print&id=2,070,583 (accessed September 20, 2012).

12. See Pearson's page for this book at http://www.pearsonschool.com. A web accessible copy is at: "Resource Center," *Magruder's American Government Homepage.* http://www.phschool.com/webcodes10/index.cfm?fuseaction=home.goto WebCode&wcprefix=mqk&wcsuffix=1000 (accessed 1 February 2015).

13. Civic Education, http://www.thenationalforum.org/Docs/PDF/Civic_Education. pdf, 19 (accessed August 24, 2011).

14. "Go Online Activity," *Magruder's American Government Homepage,* http://www. phschool.com/webcodes10/index.cfm?fuseaction=home.gotoWebCode&wcpre fix=mqd&wcsuffix=7251 (accessed February 1, 2015).

15. See Spiezio, "Pedagogy and Political (Dis)Engagement," 17.

16. Walker, "Magruder's American Government," 3.

17. Mike Delrio, "93 Million Eligible Voters Did Not Vote in 2012," *The Examiner,* November 12, 2012. http://www.examiner.com/article/93-million-eligible-voters-did-not-vote-2012 (accessed February 1, 2015).

18. David Von Drehle, "Obama's Youth Vote Triumph," *Time,* January 4, 2008. http://www.time.com/time/politics/article/0,8599,1700525,00.html (accessed February 21, 2013).

19. In our most recent election, e.g., only about 58 percent of eligible voters cast a vote. For data, go to http://www.census.gov/compendia/statab/cats/elections/voting-age_population_and_voter_participation.htm, (accessed January 17, 2013).

20. Scott Jaschik, *Political Engagement 101*. Inside Higher Education, August 24, 2011. http://www.insidehighered.com/news/2007/08/30/political (accessed March 3, 2013).

21. We recognize that "globalization" does not have one stable definition. The trends recognized as global—economic globalization; issues of political authority, with a new interest in the question of sovereignty; and technology and culture—are ones that Appadurai considers and that we will consider here.

22. See, e.g., Eric Brahm, "Globalization." *Beyond Intractability*, July 2005.http:// www.beyondintractability.org/bi-essay/globalization (accessed February 27, 2013). Brahm argues that we have seen economic restructuring because the "scale and magnitude of global economic interaction" is larger and greater than in the past. In addition, the power of the nation-state is influenced by "non-state actors," from organizations like the United Nations to corporations. With technological and actual human migration, culture also travels more quickly. Brahm writes: "There was some discussion after 9/11 whether the need for security would bring an end to the era of globalization. In some areas, such as educational exchanges, there has been an impact. Overall, however, the flow of goods, people, and messages of peace and war continue unabated some four years later. In many respects, therefore, globalization is not going away. The challenge for humanity, then, is to direct these forces in peaceful and beneficial ways."

23. Arjun Appadurai, *Fear of Small Numbers: An Essay on the Geography of Anger* (Durham, NC: Duke University Press, 2006).

24. Ibid., 39.

25. Ibid., 20–28.

26. Ibid. 30.

27. Ibid., 129.

28. Ibid., 134.

29. Ibid., 136.

30. Ibid., 134.

31. See, e.g., Shahzad Ansari and Kamal Munir, "Letting Users into Our World: Some Organizational Implications of User-Generated Content" in *Technology and Organization: Essays in Honour of Joan Woodward*, ed. Nelson Phillips, Graham Sewell, and Dorothy Griffiths (Bingley, UK: Emerald Group Publishing Limited, 2010), 88 (Whole essay 79–106). The authors argue that a "digitalized common" has worked both from experts down and from consumers up. They argue that users do not want just choice but more "say."

32. See, e.g., the work of the Higher Education Research Institute of the University of California, Los Angeles (HERI), http://spirituality.ucla.edu/ (accessed February 1, 2015). The whole report is available as a PDF at: http://spirituality.ucla.edu/docs/ reports/Spiritual_Life_College_Students_Full_Report.pdf. Their seven-year

study culminated in Alexander W. Astin, Helen S. Astin, and Jennifer Lindholm's *Cultivating the Spirit: How College Can Enhance Students' Inner Lives* (San Francisco, CA: Jossey-Bass, 2010). HERI's findings are organized around ten spiritual and religious measures: The spiritual measures are equanimity, spiritual quest, ethic of caring, charitable involvement, and ecumenical worldview; the religious ones are religious commitment, religious engagement, religious/ social conservatism, religious skepticism, and religious struggle.

33. See http://www.fgcu.edu/ADP/mission.html. The *New York Times* lists participating colleges at http://www.nytimes.com/ref/college/collegespecial2/coll_aascu_part.html (accessed February 21, 2013).

34. The Association of American Colleges and Universities lists over 25 organizations that have some impact on college campuses, including the Campus Compact, the Pew Partnership for Civic Change; the Saguaro Seminar, launched by Robert Putnam; the National Society for Experiential Education, and others. See http://www.aacu.org/resources/civicengagement/organizations.cfm (accessed February 21, 2013).

35. The University of Georgia, Northwestern University (http://www.engage.northwestern.edu/about/index.html), IUPUI (http://life.iupui.edu/osi/civic-engagement/), and other, larger institutions offer these kinds of options. See also the CIC Committee on Engagement Report for information on Michigan State, Ohio State, and other large institutions' definitions of civic engagement (http://www.scholarshipofengagement.org).

36. Thomas Ehrlich, *Civic Responsibility and Higher Education* (Westport, CT: Oryx Press, 2000), vi.

37. See the University of Georgia web page for the *Center for Leadership and Service*: http://cls.uga.edu/ (accessed February 1, 2015).

38. The Russell Forum is the civic engagement program of the Russell Library for Political Research and Studies. It hosts discussions, such as a recent topic, "The Divided State of America: How Can We Get Work Done Even When We Disagree?" It has also hosted a community forum on how to build a vibrant community and on the challenges to meeting this goal, guided by nonpartisan moderators. See http://rbrl.blogspot.com/.

39. University of Georgia Office of Service-Learning. http://servicelearning.uga.edu/international-service-learning/ (accessed January 17, 2013).

40. Ibid.

41. For a wealth of articles on this issue, see the Campus Compact website: http://www.compact.org/initiatives/trucen/trucen-toolkit/trucen-section-b/ (accessed January 17, 2013).

42. "Promoting Civic Engagement at the University of California: Recommendations from the Strategy Group on Civic and Academic Engagement." http://cshe.berkeley.edu/publications/docs/StrategyReport.2.06.pdf (accessed January 17, 2013), 6.

43. Ibid., 6.

44. Ibid., 11–12.

45. Kathryn Peltier Campbell (ed.), Theme Issue on "Civic Engagement and Student Success: A Resonant Relationship," *Diversity and Democracy* 15:3 (Fall 2012): 1.

46. Ibid.; Christine M. Cress, "Student Engagement and Student Success: Leveraging Multiple Degrees of Achievement," *Diverstiy and Democracy* 15:3 (Fall 2012): 3.

47. Kathleen Ferraiolo, *Is It Working?: Three Universities Take on Assessment.* Pew Partnership. www.pew-partnership.org/pdf/new_directions/5_assessment. pdf, 101 (accessed January 21, 2013).

48. Ashley Finley, "A Brief Review of the Evidence on Civic Learning in Higher Education." Paper presented at the annual meeting of the Association of American Colleges and Universities, January 24–28, 2012, Washington, DC.

49. A. W. Astin and Lori J. Vogelgesang, *Understanding the Effects of Service Learning: A Study of Students and Faculty.* Higher Education Research Institute, July 2006. http://www.heri.ucla.edu/PDFs/pubs/reports/UnderstandingThe EffectsOfServiceLearning_FinalReport.pdf (accessed January 21, 2013).

50. Ibid., 57.

51. Ibid., 24.

52. Ibid., 58.

53. Ibid.

54. Eric M. Uslaner and Mitchell Brown, "Inequality, Trust, and Civic Engagement," *American Politics Research* (November 2005): 868–94.

55. Ibid. They also recognize that all civic engagement is not the same. Political involvement, which is about mistrust and contest, is not the same as other kinds of engagement, like charitable donations and volunteering—which build on trust and might lead one to encounter others unlike the self (874).

56. Astin and Vogelgesang, "Understanding the Effects," 72.

57. Ibid., 88, 130.

58. Ibid., 132.

59. Chandra Talpade Mohanty, "'Under Western Eyes' Revisited: Feminist Solidarity through Anticapitalist Struggles," *Signs* 28.2 (2003): 499–535, esp. 518–19.

60. Ibid., 519–20.

61. Ibid., 521–22.

62. Ibid., 530.

63. Ibid., 7. See also: Richard Arum, Josipa Rosaka, and Melissa Velez, *Learning to Reason and Communicate in College: Initial Report of Findings from the CLA Longitudinal Study.* The Social Science Research Council. http://www.ssrc. org/publications/view/C6153FC0-6654-DE11-AFAC-001CC477EC70/ (accessed January 21, 2013).

64. HERI (see n. 32), 55.

65. Carolyn M. Jones Medine, Kathleen Skerett, Joseph Favazza, and Daniel Deffenbaugh, facilitators, The Wabash Center for Teaching Theology and Religion, Colloquy on Religious Commitments in the Classroom, 2010–2011.

66. Uslaner and Brown (see n. 54), 888.

67. Ibid., 889.

68. See n. 1 and, e.g., Bob Connor, "How Adequate Is Secularism as a Basis for Liberal Education?" The Teagle Foundation. http://www.teaglefoundation.org/Resources/Additional-Resources/How-adequate-is-secularism-as-a-basis-for-libe (accessed February 1, 2015).

69. See, e.g., Marjorie B. Garber, Beatrice Hanssen, and Rebecca L. Walkowitz (eds.), The Turn to Ethics (New York: Routledge Press, 2000).

70. See, e.g., Patricia Ticineto Clough and Jean Halley (eds.), The Affective Turn: Theorizing the Social (Durham, NC: Duke University Press, 2007).

71. Michel Foucault, The History of Sexuality: Vol. 3. The Care of the Self, trans. Robert Hurley (New York: Random House, 1986), and Edward Said, Reflections on Exile (Cambridge, MA: Harvard University Press, 2000). See also Michel de Certeau, The Practice of Everyday Life, trans. Steve F. Rendall (Berkeley: University of California Press, 1988).

72. Diego Gambetta (ed.), Trust (Oxford: Basil Blackwell, 1990), quoted in Cirstiano Castelfranchi and Rino Falcone, "Social Trust: A Cognitive Approach." PDF available at www.agent.ai/doc/upload/200408/cast03_1.pdf (accessed February 1, 2015).

73. Here, I choose to put "self" and "other" in quotation marks, recognizing—in my own thought—that the "other" is a creation of colonialism and Enlightenment understandings that map the world in ways that some modes of thinking might not recognize.

74. Eboo Patel, "Storytelling and Social Change," Sojourners, February 2013, posted by the Leading Change Network at http://leadingchangenetwork.com/2013/01/31/storytelling-and-social-change-by-eboo-patel/ (accessed September 10, 2013). Marshall Ganz, "Why Stories Matter: The Art and Craft of Social Change." Sojourners, March 2009. http://sojo.net/magazine/2009/03/why-stories-matter (accessed September 10, 2013).

75. Patel, "Storytelling."

76. Harriet Rubin, "Elaine Scarry: Using Art to Encourage Empathy," http://NBCNEWS.com. http://www.nbcnews.com/id/23397625/ns/us_news-giving/t/e . . . #.Ui9Xd4Uic9c (accessed October 29, 2012). Scarry argues in "Poetry Changed the World" Boston Review, July 1, 2001, that engagement with literature, with story, can generate empathy that gives rise to new social institutions. In our interiority as readers and writers, we potentially become "labile," able "actively to re-consent each day" to our commitments and to open ourselves to new ones. http://www.bostonreview.net/poetry-arts-culture/poetry-changed-world-elaine-scarry (accessed October 29, 2012).

77. John Randolph LeBlanc and Carolyn M. Jones Medine. *Ancient and Modern Religion and Politics: Negotiating Transitive Spaces and Hybrid Identities* (New York: Palgrave Macmillan, 2012).

78. Ibid., especially 31–42.

79. Edward Said, *Representations of the Intellectual: The 1993 Reith Lectures* (New York: Vintage Books), 82, 88. I recognize that this may not be a value for all. In Henri J. M. Nouwen, Donald P. McNeill, and Douglass A. Morrison, *Compassion: A Reflection on the Christian Life* (New York: Doubleday, 1996), the authors quote Sir Peregrine Worsthorne, British journalist and political writer, who argues that this kind of engagement is unhealthy: "No healthy society should allow itself to see the world through the eyes of the unfortunate, since the unfortunate have no great interest in perceiving, let alone exploiting, the highest value of civilization: individual freedom" (4–5).

80. Edward Said, "The Politics of Knowledge," in *Reflections on Exile and Other Essays* (Cambridge: Harvard University Press, 2000), 383.

II

More than Global Citizenship

HOW RELIGIOUS STUDIES EXPANDS PARTICIPATION IN GLOBAL COMMUNITIES

Karen Derris and Erin Runions

PREPARING STUDENTS FOR civic engagement has come to mean more than prepar-ing them for involvement in local or national issues and civic structures.[1] The idea that students must learn what it means to act as citizens within a global context is widely promoted, as diffuse as the concept of global citizenship may be.[2] The term "global citizenship" evokes the language of rights and duties, but global citizens have no legal status and no democratic access to institutions that could ensure that those are met.[3] Rather, global citizenship arises from initia-tives that connect individuals around shared concerns and goals whether they are corporate, activist, or otherwise.[4] Global citizens form communities based around these shared interests or goals; when goals are attained or abandoned, the global community may disband or transform around a new agenda. In broad-est terms "global citizenship" evokes an awareness that globalization has cre-ated connections—voluntary or not, explicit or implicit—that transcend national boundaries. Civic engagement on a global scale, by its very nature, must expand beyond all particular formations of the civic.

In many liberal arts contexts, emphasis is now placed on preparing students for global awareness.[5] Mission statements and learning objectives of liberal arts institutions variously articulate this vast goal. The global responsibilities envi-sioned in descriptions of the outcomes of a liberal arts education suggest uphold-ing a humanistic ethic, or yet again, serving a multinational corporate bottom line. Common to all, however, is an awareness of responsibilities and opportunities for its students. The mission statements of the private liberal arts institutions where the authors teach are no exception in imagining well-formed global citizenship as an important goal of education. They include statements such as, "We gather stu-dents . . . into a small residential community that is strongly rooted in Southern California yet global in its orientation" (Pomona College) and "Education goes beyond training to embrace a reflective understanding of our world; it proceeds from information to insight, from knowledge to meaning" (University of Redlands). The open-ended challenges of creating a global or worldwide orientation suggested in these statements serve a goal of forming global citizens. These institutions further describe central outcomes of a liberal arts education as follows: "Students are able to make examined, principled decisions that guide their actions as responsible global citizens" (University of Redlands) and "Pomona's liberal arts curriculum and residential community prepare students for lives of personal fulfillment and social responsibility in a global context."

In this chapter we wish to consider how the question of mobility in the world—with what ease and to what end—might present a challenge for equal footing within global initiatives and for pedagogies of civic engagement aimed at global citizenship. We suggest that interrogating issues of mobility, whether abstractly as intellectual movement (an exposure or willingness to consider a multiplicity of worldviews) or more concretely as literal movement between contexts, can critically inform the discourse and development of global civic engagement. The academic study of religion may be uniquely positioned to interrogate the concept of global citizenship, to think about mobility differently, and to help students and institutions of higher learning to understand their own positions within unequal global power relations so that they can begin to foster more equitable global relationships. This work allows students to participate in global communities with an ethic of care that seeks to undo hierarchies of power and their damaging impacts, rather than uncritically maintaining them.[6]

Three experiences in our own classrooms and campuses inform our discussion. One of the authors (Karen Derris) led a group of University of Redlands students to India for three weeks of intensive conversation with His Holiness the 17th Karmapa, one of Tibetan Buddhism's highest spiritual teachers and the leader of the oldest of its four Buddhist lineages. The other (Erin Runions) is part of a collaboration in which students travel to a local women's prison to participate in a writing workshop led by Runions and two other professors of the Claremont College consortium (of which Pomona College is a part). In these two situations, students have the privilege of traveling to places where many, or all, from their host environment do not. While this difference is highly evident in entering and leaving the prison, it also factored into the invitation to study with the Karmapa. In the third example, mobility takes a different turn. Both authors work on campuses where service work is primarily done by Latina/o and Chicano/a workers, who have traveled, or whose parents have traveled, to the United States to work. Some of these workers may be undocumented, making their situation precarious and allowing wages to remain low. In this instance, movement is not for educational purposes, but in service of students' experiences. Relatively recent events at Pomona College have made the difference in security for students and service workers painfully clear: Seventeen workers were fired in December of 2011 for not being able to present proper documentation at short notice.

These differentials in mobility say much about global power relations, as shaped by transnational corporate globalization. How, then, do we make our students aware of their privilege of mobility, if we are going to teach them to be civically engaged in a global context? In order to explore what the academic study of religion can bring to this question, we first explore where Religious Studies fits within pedagogical discussion on fostering global citizenship. We then begin to nuance the notion of global citizenship by interrogating differences in mobility among global citizens, drawing on the examples of the Pomona College seventeen and the prison writing workshop. Finally, we turn to thinking about other ways of being in global community, drawing on the University of Redlands trips to India to meet with the Karmapa.

Pedagogies for Global Citizenship

Pedagogical discussions on how to prepare students for global citizenship frequently focus on the importance of instilling skills of democracy, dialogue, and self-critique. Democracy is assumed as a vital good for global citizenship. When used to refer to the nongovernmental sphere, democracy tends to refer to something along the lines of "human wisdom deployed toward the goal of harmonious coexistence."[7] Pedagogical skills considered vital to this project are: conflict resolution, problem solving, open and equal dialogue, participation in projects, and self-awareness of contexts and biases. So for instance, in a study on the contribution of one-unit seminars to "democratic learning and global citizenship," Jodi Anderson, Marc Levis-Fitzgerald, and Robert Rhoads show that "literature on democratic education tends to describe five key elements of student-centered learning environments: meaningful and egalitarian dialogue, problem-based inquiry, inclusion of the self (including individual student experience and self-reflection), a recognition of the co-construction of knowledge, and situating teaching and learning within the larger socio-political context."[8] Along similar lines, Martha Nussbaum has promoted education for global citizenship and democracy, suggesting three vital skills: the ability for self-critique, a sense of being a citizen of the world, and a "narrative imagination" that can empathize with others' positions.[9] Andria Wisler has emphasized conflict resolution as an important skill to teach students for a democratic global citizenry.[10] These scholars suggest that if students can learn to interrogate their own positions, to harmoniously co-exist, to productively dialogue, and to resolve conflict within the classroom, they can do it outside of the classroom, in local and global contexts. For this reason, the development of intercultural skills is also advocated.[11] To this list we would add the importance awareness of privileges of mobility.

A critical engagement with issues of mobility necessitates rethinking the long-promoted tradition of study-abroad as the fullest experience of cultural diversity for liberal arts undergraduates. By moving into a different national, cultural, and/or linguistic context, students are promised an immersive experience that will enable them to experience another way of being in the world. Delivery of this promise has been critically assessed by scholars of travel education who question the kinds of encounters study-abroad offers when experiences are purchased and encounters with hosts are affected by differentials in wealth, nationality, and mobility. Reflecting on her own study-abroad experience as an undergraduate, Talya Zemach-Bersin offers a critique of immersive study-abroad programs that fail to evaluate issues of power that shape students' experience. She argues, "An international education that focuses on American-based discursive ideals rather than experiential realities can hardly be said to position students in this country for successful lives of global understanding. Rather, such an education may inadvertently be a recipe for the perpetuation of global ignorance, misunderstanding, and prejudice."[12] Others suggest that "study abroad in and of itself does not lead to the development of global citizenship," but only when the pedagogy carefully incorporates experiential learning, in which students can develop intercultural appreciation and collaboration and "develop a new kind of global citizenship in which issues of power and privilege are addressed in a healthy way."[13] Along these lines, it is important to recognize that the ability of students to travel to places where there is less freedom of mobility is symptomatic of a global hierarchy of power. There is a danger that this power dynamic can go unexamined and therefore reproduce these hierarchies in individual interactions.

When the privilege of mobility is not critically assessed, travel education—whether study abroad, shorter visits, or field trips—all too easily becomes an entitlement that ignores responsibilities or is focused on students' goals and achievements[14] more than on the kind of global relationships they might learn to foster. An immersive experience should place demands upon students that question their privilege of easily leaving their own milieu and entering another cultural environment. Such demands may dictate their behavior and may limit personal, intimate choices such as dress, food, and personal conduct. Travel education can give students the opportunities to experience the responsibility of entering another culture without imposing their own cultural norms.[15]

Many of the more generalized discussions of education for global citizenship do not highlight, or even mention, religion. The exclusion of religion from discussions of democracy, particularly in the context of liberal arts education, obstructs not only an important avenue for studying global communities but also pedagogical resources for preparing students to responsibly participate in global communities. As Natalie Gummer argues, "Discussions of world citizenship (or even U.S. citizenship) that elide the challenge of grappling with religious worldviews expose a covert intolerance at the very core of secularism, calling into question the 'liberality' of liberal education."[16] A focus on multiplicity of worldviews, both as a theoretical construct and as particular negotiations of truth and meaning held by religious traditions, in the academic study of religion often forms the basis for dialogue across difference.[17]

The study of religious worldviews within the academic classroom, or of dialogue between religious communities (and secularists and atheists too) on college campuses or in local communities, are seen to nurture an ethical disposition of humility that Gummer terms "a profound unknowing." This kind of pedagogical work shifts intellectual expectations from comprehension, that is mastering a body of knowledge, to a dialogical process that aims to understand not only one's own particular perspective but what a different vantage point has to offer.[18] In Religious Studies classrooms, examples of inter-religious dialogue, past or present, are often examined as sites in which assumptions about reality, oneself, and the world might can be negotiated.[19] Diana Eck's long-term study of religious pluralism in the United States raises the possibility of moving beyond tolerance of religious differences to actively engaging diversity with respect.[20] Respect can evolve into more intensely personal reactions, a disposition Lee Yearley terms "spiritual regret." Yearly describes spiritual regret as deep feelings of admiration one might feel for another religious worldview, cognizant of the fact that commitment to one's own religious traditions makes it impossible to adopt those newly encountered beliefs and practices from the other religious tradition.[21] These dispositions of humility, respect, and spiritual regret enable students to recognize and take seriously the perspectives and contexts that motivate action and beliefs that differ, sometimes radically, from their own.

Furthermore, it is important also to help students see the role of religion in political and civic action. Promoting dialogue as an end in itself may ironically relegate religion to the private sphere and, like secularist biases, discount or ignore the role of religious commitments in civic arenas. In other words, focusing on dialogue does not attend to the actual civic work in which religious groups engage. In her study of immigrant religious communities in the Boston area, for example, Peggy Levitt terms their engagement in civic issues "religious citizenship" to emphasize the role of religious identities in civic spheres.[22] Grounded in the pedagogical sphere, Gummer advocates for ethical *action* as a next step that follows from students' understanding and reflective interrogation of their own limitations as actors.[23]

Building upon these insights, we suggest that Religious Studies offers at least four key methodological possibilities for thinking about global citizenship. First, it interrogates the relationship between ontologies and ethics. In other words, it allows students to pay close attention to the way in which people's actions are shaped by their beliefs about foundational questions of what it means to be human in relation to the world and the cosmos. In other words, Religious Studies allows students to see other ontologies than their own, and to see how they shape ideals, ethics, and actions. It also helps students to consider their own ontology as it affects their ethics. Students can see that their orientation toward the global is shaped by their own ontology and that if they are to engage in serious dialogue across cultures, they will have to understand the role that religion plays in shaping political and ethical positions (so also Gummer). If global collaborations tend to be goal-driven, as noted earlier, students must consider the ontological constraints on the formation of goals, as well as the possibilities opened up for different modes of collaboration by other ontologies.

Second, Religious Studies provides a theoretical perspective that helps to do the work of self-critique that Nussbaum suggests. The academic study of religion urges students to understand religious ideals and also the "political, institutional, and material interests" which shape and complicate these ideals and the very category of religion.[24] Religious Studies asks students to understand religion as part of, not separate from, the culture in which it engages. In other words, it asks students to understand the constructed nature of religion. Interrogation of the relation between ideal and power structures is by no means limited to Religious Studies; but because religion often articulates ideals, it is a particularly apt subject matter through which to explore these dynamics. Applying this kind of questioning to the issue at hand, we can think about the ideals that pedagogical discussions of global citizenship seek to instill (harmonious co-existence, democracy, dialogue, conflict resolution, self-awareness) in relation to the power relations that shape them. These ideals imagine partnerships of equally distributed power and resources. But if we think for a minute about the mobility required for global collaborations, we quickly see a set of global power relations in which this ideal turns out to be intentionally or unintentionally extended more readily to those from the global north and those who are educated.

Third, Religious Studies affords the possibility to talk about mobility precisely because students often do travel in our courses, either physically or conceptually in terms of encountering other worldviews and ontologies. Religious studies is not unique in this respect, by any means: Many fields do this kind of work. When we take students to visit religious sites, we have the opportunity to discuss the various kinds of movement around the site, as well as its meanings locally and diasporically. We also have the opportunity to discuss our own privileges of mobility. Moreover, because Religious Studies attends to differences in worldviews, ontologies, and ethics, it allows us to talk about our own assumptions and the possible conflicts that emerge if we go into a space assuming that our way is better, more rational, or more desirable. Students are given an opportunity to learn what Bennett calls intercultural competence; that is, they have to move from responding to cultural difference by denial, defensiveness, or minimization to responding to it with sensitivity, adaptation, and integration.[25]

Fourth, Religious Studies draws particular attention to the embodiment of ideals. Students learn in our courses that religion is as much a set of cultural *practices* as it is a belief system,[26] and they are asked to think about how practice and belief are related to ideals as they are embedded in larger structures of power. When we ask students to investigate the constructed nature of religion, we must hold this perspective together with a second that acknowledges that, for many people in the world, religion is a primary operative reality for living. Religions may be socially constructed, but they are nonetheless very real for many adherents. Thus, as we will discuss, when students travel to participate in other religious and cultural traditions, for instance, during their time in India, or even when they travel to the prison, they often have to make changes to particular embodied practices: there are restrictions on what they wear (in the prison, for instance, no jeans, open-toe shoes, or short skirts), what they eat (in India, no meat), and how they comport themselves (for both places, restraints on sexual expression and/or touching). These are clear parameters in which they must accede to the demands of another culture. There are also less clear parameters that may be unstated and have to be negotiated as they are observed and experienced.

In these changes or limitations, students experience different ideals and power structures in their own bodies. Students should be aware of and observe the responsibilities that come with visiting mosques, temples, or churches on field trips to local religious communities that are a part of many introductory courses in Religious Studies. Demanding that students observe etiquette of behavior and dress challenges them to negotiate difference and the demands placed upon them that come with taking up the privilege of mobility. Sometimes it makes them angry or uncomfortable. But if they can be asked to assess the structures of power in which their own embodied practices are formed, and if they share embodied practices with others, they can move toward interrogation of their own identity and empathetic engagement with others.

Mobility as a Complicating Factor

The implicit egalitarianism of "citizenship" often masks tremendous inequalities in terms of access to the planet's global resources. The ability to exercise the rights of global citizenship (however those are negotiated in any given instance of global interaction) is obviously not equally open to all. In actual practice, the designation "global citizen" functions as a privileged identity, available to those who have the personal wealth to explore and benefit from the wider world and who can claim protection of a powerful government as they do so. Issues of mobility illuminate this critique by tangible experience. The legal right to physically move across national boundaries is open only to those holding certain national passports, visas and airplane tickets. As such, despite its best impulses, global citizenship easily becomes a matter of having the "right" to move into others' spaces as well as the right to refuse entry into one's own.

Here it might be important to consider the power relations of mobility in the context of what Michel Foucault has called "biopolitics." In *History of Sexuality* and in his posthumously published lectures given at the Collège de France in the late 1970s, Foucault argues that beginning in the seventeenth century, power operates less and less by the threat of death and more and more through the control of life, hence the term "biopolitics".[27] Biopolitics enables the smooth functioning of capital throughout and between populations. Within secular liberalism power is mobilized so that *populations* are produced, regularized, and classified as different kinds of human capital.[28] As economies expand in the twentieth century, biopolitics functions globally, allowing populations to be "regularized" through the control of birth rates, mortality rates, and longevity.[29] Populations are cultivated *as capital* via mobility, racialization, sexual regulation, and securitization. In the context of globalization, some populations are positioned as disposable, some as commodity-labor forces, and some as investors. Workers' skill becomes a form of capital to be moved around.[30] Migration becomes a tightly controlled biopolitical investment. Political decisions are made about which populations are of most worth, in terms of capital.[31] Although power may seem to be dispersed across cultures in globalization, biopolitics still works to secure geographic hierarchies of domination.

Within the context of biopolitics we need to reorient the ways in which mobility and travel are used in the cultivation of global citizenship. In contrast to the ideals of democratic learning, which generate the promotion of student travel, many global citizens do not have the privilege of travel and enrichment through mobility. Given this difference, we might think about what role our students are being prepared for within a global context. Are college-level students in the global north being prepared to manage capital or access to capital in some form or another? Does their encouraged mobility help them step into a hierarchized role in terms of global capital? What does such a role mean for ethical engagement in global communities?

Two case studies illuminate the power dynamics that allow, control, and prohibit travel, depending on global citizens' placement in the global hierarchy. In stark contrast to students' privilege to travel to and experience other religions and cultures, in these cases, those with whom students interact do not have the same freedom of mobility. Our pedagogical interventions should be to make students aware of their own positioning within global biopolitics in relation to others and to understand how the category of religion might be used to produce, engage, or resist the systems, limitations, and embodied differentials that comprise biopolitics.

First, the Pomona College decision to fire seventeen dining hall workers on December 1, 2011, illustrates clearly the legalized constraints on mobility and security for immigrant workers through the threat of deportation. The firings were the result of an anonymous complaint, filed by an employee of the college against the college administration, stating that the college was not verifying its employees' immigration status. In the investigation that followed, the college hiring practices were ultimately exonerated. As part of this investigation, however, the large corporate law firm retained by the Board of Trustees (Sidley Austin) took it upon themselves to review the immigration status of every employee across the college. Many faculty have argued that this step was not required by the original complaint and showed lack of Trustee oversight of the investigation and lack of concern for employees. Eighty-four staff, faculty, and students, some of whom had provided service to the college community for decades, were given three weeks to provide proof of their right to work in the country and to correct anomalies in their files. Sixty-seven employees presented acceptable documents; seventeen were terminated. It has not been disclosed what precise deficiencies the fired workers' documents held. The College administration claimed that they were only following the law and that noncompliance would be cause for the federal government to take action against the College (withdrawal of federal funding, investigation by ICE, and so on). Although the College governance firmly denies any ulterior motives, it seemed to many faculty and workers rather suspect that the administration did not take into consideration that those fired were engaged in a union drive and that such an act would be a form of intimidation, whether intended or not. In effect, the pursuit of better working conditions was shut down through legal avenues that depend on the constraint of immigrants' mobility.

This case raises the more generalized issue of the disparity between the kinds of mobility afforded to students and faculty and to mostly Latino/a workers. Immigrant workers travel to the United States to work in low-paying jobs, including dining halls and residence halls of college campuses. Even if institutions like colleges do not habitually employ undocumented workers, they benefit from the surplus of inexpensive labor that undocumented immigration produces. As Pardis Mahdavi has pointed out in her study of intimate labor by immigrant workers in another context, states frequently foster insecurity and "deportability" for immigrants in order to keep labor costs low.[32] The specter of deportation and threat to security is felt by all non-naturalized immigrant workers and is intensified for those with the least protections. In contrast, non-naturalized students and faculty have more options for visas and more options for institutional sponsorship and security, both legally and in terms of political will.[33] According to present regulations, nonspecialized workers cannot be sponsored by institutions for documentation, nor can they begin the application for documentation from inside the United States. Within the context of biopolitics, immigrant workers are mobile insofar as they can support the production of life and education for citizens. While students from the global north travel to have their lives enriched by other cultures, workers from the global south travel to enrich the lives of those on college campuses.

We can bring these kinds of issues into our Religious Studies classrooms by asking students to analyze the hidden ways that religion is deployed around labor rights. For instance, religion may be a factor in shoring up various labor pools and markets. Junaid Rana has shown how the stigmatization of Muslims in the war on terror works with markets to create a disposable workforce of surplus labor; one that can be policed and regulated via the threat of deportation. The fear of the "Muslim terrorist" means that Muslim immigrant men are marked as non-citizens, living constantly under the threat of detention and deportation.[34] Or, from another angle, we might consider how religious groups themselves engage the civic sphere around issues of labor injustice. For example, in Claremont, religious groups from the surrounding community led a concerted effort to protest and condemn Pomona College's treatment of workers. Along similar lines, religion can be used by bosses or workers as a way of dealing with poor work conditions, either to accept them or to mobilize and raise consciousness about changing them. In the United States, the Interfaith Worker Justice coalition "advances the rights of workers by engaging diverse faith communities into action, from grassroots organizing to shaping policy at the local, state and national levels."[35] Labor is just one of the places in which we might ask students to observe the role of religion in the public sphere, as it relates to issues of mobility.

The second case study, the travel of students from the Claremont Colleges to the California Institute of Women (CIW) shows even more dramatically the disparity in mobility between privileged and less privileged global citizens. Women's prisons are disproportionately filled with people from lower economic brackets and non-white ethnicities, who are convicted of *nonviolent* crimes (many on drug charges).[36] Whole segments of society are institutionalized, forming a new caste system.[37] Their mobility is completely constrained, with respect to the larger world and within the prison itself. In terms of the biopolitical relations of capital, prisoners are a captive labor force, working for less than $1.00/hour in the prison, in agriculture, on fire crews, on diving crews for underwater repairs, and so on.[38] Moreover, segregating large segments of lower economic populations also does the work of making invisible economic disparity and unemployment. The unincarcerated are therefore free to enjoy their lives unhindered by extreme reminders of economic disparity and the disenfranchisements of democracy.

Students from the Claremont Colleges are made patently aware of this disparity in mobility, partially by the physical barriers of the prison and partly by the framing we faculty give them in the several courses in which the writing work-shop is embedded.[39] Students are confronted by the process of getting into the prison (they have to be cleared prior to arriving, and the entrance process itself is lengthy), and by their own freedom in coming and going, versus the CIW students' lack of mobility. The faculty responsible for the workshop have been concerned to construct the experience so that Claremont students become further aware of power structures in which incarceration becomes an acceptable means of dealing with social issues. Faculty have also tried to ensure that students become aware of their own privileges without becoming either tourists or charity workers. For this reason, Claremont students and CIW students are positioned on the same level, as students of the workshop. They are given the workshop syllabus at the same time and are required to do the same assignments. All students are encouraged to consider how relationships can be constructed as mutual sites of listening, creating, and skill sharing. One section of the workshop requires a group writing experience, with students from inside and students from the outside contributing equally. Faculty do spend extra time with Claremont students, helping them to debrief their experiences and challenging notions that they are there to share their privilege or teach the women inside.

How then do these disparities in mobility relate to the ideal of training students for global citizenship? The challenge is to build analysis of freedom of mobility into *Religious Studies* courses seeking to facilitate civic engagement. The method of interrogating ideals in relation to power taught in Religious Studies helps students to see how the very notion of global citizenship could uncritically facilitate the mobility of managerial and professional classes. It would seem that the ideal of global citizenship is embedded within an economic and power structure in which full, mobile privileges are only given to a small segment of global citizens. Making students aware of this disparity seems to us to be an important part of self-critique (as per Nussbaum's suggestion), as does understanding whose lives this disparity serves.

New Forms of Global Communities

Interrogating mobility as a defining condition of global citizenship motivates us to explore other models that would consciously work to create equality among all members of global communities. Traditional areas in the study of religion, particularly the connections between ontologies, ethics, and embodied practices, can be oriented toward considering alternative beliefs of what makes us a part of global communities and how those global communities are defined. We can investigate how these beliefs about the world and our place in it inform ethical systems and advocate acting according to ethical ideals. The study of religion, we believe, can therefore challenge students and faculty alike to consider the underlying assumptions of what makes us a part of global communities and how we can ethically live within them.

Our third case study, a travel course to Dharamsala, India, to study with His Holiness the Seventeenth Karmapa, illuminates how to broaden our commitments to global civic engagement. In this particular situation, issues of power and authority are complex. Within the Tibetan sphere and Buddhist communities that span ethnic/national identities, the Karmapa is one of the most revered Tibetan Buddhist spiritual leaders, in part because he is invested with the authority of a nine-hundred-year-old lineage. He is widely seen as the likely spiritual successor to His Holiness the Fourteenth Dalai Lama, his close mentor. Tibetan Buddhists perceive the Karmapa as a living Buddha, an enlightened being, and they treat him with the highest forms of etiquette and respect dictated by tradition and devotion. Geopolitics, however, limits the Karmapa's mobility. He lives in India as a refugee having fled Tibet at the age of fourteen in order to escape increasing control by Chinese government officials who sought to manipulate his role in Tibetan society for their own ends. While receiving invitations from Buddhist communities and scholarly institutions in Asia, Europe, and North America, the Karmapa has only traveled abroad on two occasions when the Indian government granted him permission to do so. These conditions limiting his movements in spite of, or perhaps because of, his authority within Tibetan Buddhism form the background of an invitation Derris received from the Karmapa's office to bring a group of her college students to Dharamsala, India, for three weeks of conversation with the Karmapa.

The opportunity originated from a larger project of sharing the Karmapa's teachings with an international audience in early adulthood on common concerns for the world and their place in it. The Karmapa's interest in the project is manifold: While esteemed as one of the highest lamas in Buddhism, at the time he was just 25 years old (a peculiarity of the tradition of reincarnated lineages in Tibetan Buddhism). In meeting with a group of American college students, the Karmapa was thus seeking out his generational peers for explicitly global conversation. The students were invited to his home, in part, because he could not travel to meet with people like them in theirs.

The importance of traveling with an invitation cannot be underestimated. In this particular instance, access to the Karmapa would be absolutely impossible without a direct commitment from his office; but traveling with an invitation, to be an invited guest, reorders the power hierarchy implicit in study abroad. When students travel as invited guests their experience is dictated not only by their own agenda but that of their host as well. As such, demands and expectations are placed upon them that are the conditions of being hosted. In this course, the stakes were very high; the privilege of being guests of the Karmapa meant that any rupture of protocol would be highly offensive to our hosts; in actual fact more to those surrounding the Karmapa than to him, as he extended himself to the students with warmth and kindness, inviting a relaxed and friendly exchange while in his company.

A set of rules governed the students' dress and behavior for the entirety of the course. If they were to participate, they had to commit to following the Buddhist five precepts, the foundational moral prohibitions against taking life, stealing, using harmful speech, taking intoxicants, or engaging in sexual misconduct (that is, relationships that are harmful). They explicitly followed the Karmapa's teachings on the first two precepts: not taking life necessitated a vegetarian diet; not stealing demanded intentional use of natural and material resources. Intentionality in our speech supported cooperative and consensus-based decision-making within our daily group work. Refraining from consuming any alcohol and drugs removed obstacles to deepening mental awareness. Broadly interpreted, avoiding sexual misconduct encouraged compassionate care in our relationships. For all of the students, taking up this invitation meant changing their personal behaviors in concrete and embodied ways. Many later reflected that the transformative effects of following the precepts continued after their return home.

Tibetan cultural norms for being in a monastic setting dictated modest, respectful dress. The men in the group were expected to wear dress shirts and pants, even ties on particular occasions, and women covered their bodies with long skirts and blouses. The students had several heated exchanges among themselves about their embodied experience of personal and sexual politics. No one attempted to rewrite the terms of inclusion—if these rules weren't followed they would be asked to leave immediately—but they disagreed among themselves about the implications of their experience and their reactions to it.

The Karmapa spent twelve multi-hour sessions with the students, each focusing on a particular topic that had been originally suggested by the professor and the co-facilitator, an American Buddhist nun, Venerable Lhundup Damcho, based upon an informal survey sent to Derris' students on the questions they would want to ask a spiritual leader if they had that opportunity. The common themes that emerged shaped the twelve topics considering social issues (greed and consumerism, food justice, social activism, environmental resources, and gender politics) and also interpersonal ones (meaningful livelihood, healthy relationships, spirituality, compassion, conflict resolution) that often overlapped. A central theme of concern for compassionately transforming the world and oneself wove the sessions together.

The Karmapa's teachings on all of these topics challenged the students to investigate their own foundational assumptions about the world and, from there, how they might approach addressing global problems and inequities. Using common examples, the Karmapa invited the students to question their assumptions about the factors that govern our behavior. Are human beings naturally greedy? The students, particularly those majoring in economics, thought yes, but the Karmapa took them through a series of arguments that supported the counterclaim that greed is a habit that can be unlearned and need not govern personal behaviors or economic processes. The teachings emphasized the value of sharing ordinary experience for deepening awareness of our place in the world, for bridging very real differences in identity, and also for working for change.

The Karmapa's starting premise, grounded in Buddhist ontology, is one of interdependence. All things in the world—people, animals, and the natural world too—are interconnected and dependent upon one another for their existence. In one discussion the Karmapa pointed to a student's backpack as a vehicle for seeing interdependence and its implications for us. Inviting the students to consider the long chain of human and material resources that went into creating an ordinary backpack, step by step they imaginatively made visible the human and environmental suffering that they carry when they wear that backpack. The point was not to wallow in guilt, nor to refrain from consuming, but to consume consciously with intention, and to act where possible, no matter how small an act, to build compassionate connections around the world to counter inequalities. Students began to see that they were implicated in those inequalities by what they consume and even in their freedom of mobility. By critically reflecting on their own position in global communities, students deeply felt the responsibilities they bore toward others, both visible and invisible, in their daily lives.

Interdependence is the starting assumption of how we exist in this unbounded global community. When we understand our ultimate connection to all other things, and our dependence upon them too, we can identify our experiences of suffering and happiness with theirs. As we have discussed, when we view global citizenship through the lens of mobility, much of the planet is excluded. In the Karmapa's teachings the global in envisioned as unbounded: It encompasses animals, the natural world, and even space. A broader vision of the global and of our place in it, is the basis for developing empathy for others and responsibilities to them. Finally, when we empathetically recognize our connection to the well-being of others we are motivated to correct our own implication in their suffering.

The Karmapa offered these students an orientation for living in global communities that might be termed a "global community of care." As connections are unbounded, so is the temporal dimension of global communities. We can never opt out of it, and we can never relinquish our responsibility to ethically participate in it. The permanence of connection makes interrogating power relations within those connections all the more vital. This orientation differs significantly from the more limited rights and responsibilities of global citizenship that are defined to a significant extent by goal-oriented endeavors; once goals are attained or abandoned, communities of global citizens are reconstituted by the next set of concerns that extend beyond national boundaries. A global community of care might be assessed (and all too easily dismissed) as an expression of religious ideals; and yet a pedagogical counterargument could retort that while it is an expression of an ideal, it is an ideal that imagines a very different set of power relations than ones that the students might have previously encountered. As such, it opens up powerful new possibilities for living ethically, and more equitably, within global communities. While this orientation may arise from a Tibetan Buddhist worldview, there is no demand that one be a Buddhist to examine the world through this lens. It is a universal vision, yet not an exclusivist one, that all can evaluate and place alongside other possible orientations for building ethical global communities.

While the experience was certainly unique, we believe the lessons learned suggest a broader pedagogical connection between the study of religious traditions and preparing students for global civic engagement. What other models for living in global communities might students discover in their study of religious worldviews? Religious worldviews can be investigated to imagine how a religious tradition defines a global community and how that shapes its ethical ideals. These explorations can lead to questioning how these ethical ideals inform intentional action in particular social-historical contexts.

Conclusions

We began by questioning the centrality of global citizenship to liberal education and asked how varying privileges of mobility might complicate this engagement with the global. We have argued that Religious Studies is a vital arena for this project. Just as the study of religion insists that worldviews are always multiple and that ideals are always constructed by the particular conditions in specific contexts, so too can the study of religion contribute to the discourse and debate on global civic engagement by insisting that global citizenship be repositioned as one model of engaging in global community. Likewise, by recognizing the articulation of positions from which global ideals are articulated and the structures of power that manufacture and manipulate these ideals, the study of religion can challenge students to critically assess their own roles in the contests of agendas and values that are operating globally.

Whether we define mobility as crossing national borders (for study or for labor), moving regionally (such as to a local mosque or Hindu temple), or thinking about ideational exploration of other worldviews, the biopolitical location of the various actors must be acknowledged. Travel to other cultural, religious, or institutional sites is a valuable part of fostering global civic engagement, but only when it is done with intellectual rigor, with self-awareness and critique, and with attention to differentials of power and to corresponding differences in mobility. Without these forms of critical reflection, travel education reinforces unquestioned privilege. Therefore, it is important to integrate theoretical questions of mobility into the classroom and to make students aware of their own global positionality before traveling, whether locally or abroad. Simple exercises can integrate these issues with students' experiences, thereby challenging them to apply theoretical insights to their own positions in global power dynamics. The Karmapa's exercise to make visible the effects of globalization, described earlier, can be easily replicated in the classroom using any number of examples from the things they consume (lunch in the cafeteria, gas in their cars, etc. . . .) as a means of asking them to locate themselves and their roles in global mechanisms of movements of resources, capital, and labor. It can also encourage students to experience these connections to others in the world by acknowledging their dependence on others—those visible to them and also those invisible—in their daily lives. Developing this kind of awareness could then lead to a greater intentionality in how they choose to participate in these global dynamics.

Further, as also discussed herein, Religious Studies pedagogy commonly includes embodied experiences of visiting religious communities, more often in local contexts but sometimes abroad. Experiencing other ontological perspectives grounded in religious (or humanist, atheist, secular) worldviews allows students to challenge their own centrality in the world, their own unquestioned values and beliefs, and the power structures that undergird them. Embodied experiences allow students to experience and experiment directly and empathetically with models of participating in global communities. Ideally they would have the opportunity to co-author these models in dialogue with people in their host environment.[40] Hopefully, the outcome is a lifelong commitment to making visible those whose immobility renders them unseen and thereby excluded from the privileges of defining the terms for global engagement.

Students can be asked to make visible these patterns on their own college campuses. In many parts of the country, as on the Southern California campuses where the authors teach, the facility and cafeteria workers who maintain students' environments are likely immigrant workers from the global south, often exploited and mistreated. An informal survey conducted in a class session will likely show that a significant number of students have never talked to the people who work in their living spaces. Encouraging students to do so, through an appropriate assignment or just as a suggestion, creates another opportunity for students to directly consider the different impacts of mobility in their own communities, how they benefit from them, and how they might act in order to better unequal conditions. Students can also be encouraged to inform themselves about the governmental and economic mechanisms that noncitizens in their community must navigate in order to teach, study, or work on their campus.

Cultivating reciprocal relationships with host communities, as discussed by Marianne Delaporte in terms of hospitality elsewhere in this volume, is another way that we can reorient hierarchies in mobility. This takes ongoing commitments on the part of faculty and institutions to build reciprocal relationships with local or foreign communities where both host and guest participants are enriched by their encounters. As both the writing workshop in the CIW prison and the India travel course attest, when students experience embodied demands as a part of the responsibilities of mobility, they directly experience patterns of global power dynamics and the potential to resist and redirect inequities.

Finally, to return to the question of global citizenship, where we started, we see global responsibility—a central value of global civic engagement—as cultivated through consciously and ethically sharing the terms of engagement in different host communities. The aspiration to create a global citizenry and communities of equality will realistically always remain an aspiration, and yet there is great value in working toward that aspiration knowing full well that the goal will always be beyond reach. With awareness of systemic, biopolitical differences, the students of Religious Studies are far more able to participate responsibly in moving toward global communities of equality. We have tried to show the many ways in which Religious Studies can contribute to this process, from interrogating ideals, to understanding religious investments in sustaining or countering existing power relations, to encountering different ontologies and ethics as the basis for developing models of global civic engagement. In order to best prepare students for global civic engagement we need to allow for and then describe a multiplicity of models for living in global communities. It is not enough that students simply recognize their own global privilege, but rather that they actively work to equalize global dynamics; such an endeavor requires encountering and learning from other ways of conceptualizing the world and intentionally sharing the constraints, demands, *and* possibilities that those locations afford.

Notes

1. Many thanks to Rina Sadun for her excellent research assistance for this article.
2. See Nigel Dower, "Global Citizenship: Yes or No?" in *Global Citizenship: A Critical Introduction*, ed. Nigel Dower and John Williams (New York: Routledge, 2002), 30–39.
3. See David Held, "The Transformation of Political Community: Rethinking Democracy in the Context of Globalization," in Dower and Williams, *Global Citizenship*, 92–99; and Roland Axtmann, "What's Wrong with Cosmopolitan Democracy?" in Dower and Williams, *Global Citizenship*, 101–13.

4. See Nigel Dower, "Global Ethics and Global Citizenship," in Dower and Williams, *Global Citizenship*, 146–56; and Geoffrey Stokes, "Global Citizenship," *Ethos* 12:1 (March 2004): 19–23.

5. See Kevin Hovland, *Shared Futures: Global Learning and Liberal Education* (Washington, DC: Association of American Colleges and Universities, 2006).

6. As expressed here, it should become apparent that the idea of mobility has important implications for the facets of complexity and location, which make up the first two parts of the CLEA model outlined in the beginning chapters of this book.

7. Daisaku Ikeda, "The University of the 21st Century: Cradle of World Citizens," *Schools: Studies in Education* 7:2 (Fall 2010): 251.

8. Jodi L. Anderson, Marc R. Levis-Fitzgerald, and Robert A. Rhoads, "Democratic Learning and Global Citizenship: The Contribution of One-Unit Seminars," *The Journal of General Education* 52:2 (April 2003): 87.

9. Martha Nussbaum, *Cultivating Humanity: A Classical Defense of Reform in Liberal Education* (Cambridge, MA: Harvard University Press, 1997); "Education for Citizenship in an Era of Global Connection," *Studies in Philosophy & Education* 21:4/5 (July–September 2002): 289–303; "Cultivating Humanity in Legal Education," *The University of Chicago Law Review* 70:1, Centennial Tribute Essays (Winter 2003): 265–79; "Liberal Education & Global Community," *Liberal Education* 90:1 (Winter 2004): 42–47; and *Not for Profit: Why Democracy Needs the Humanities* (Princeton, NJ: Princeton University Press, 2010).

10. Andria K. Wisler, "'Of, By, and For Are Not Merely Prepositions': Teaching and Learning Conflict Resolution for a Democratic, Global Citizenry," *Intercultural Education* 20:2 (April 2009): 127–33.

11. Milton J. Bennett, "Becoming Interculturally Competent," in *Toward Multiculturalism: A Reader in Multicultural Education*, ed. J. S. Wurzel (Newton, MA: Intercultural Resource Corporation, 2004), 62–77; Nussbaum, *Not for Profit*, 79–94.

12. Talya Zemach-Bersin, "American Students Abroad Can't Be 'Global Citizens,'" *The Chronicle of Higher Education*, March 7, 2008, A34. http://www.yale.edu/yalecol/international/predeparture/pdf/GlobalCitizens.pdf (accessed February 8, 2015).

13. Ann Lutterman-Aguilar and Orval Gingerich, "Experiential Pedagogy for Study Abroad: Educating for Global Citizenship," *Frontiers* 8 (Winter 2002): 43, 66. Along similar lines, Sutton and Rubin show in their study of the results of study abroad in the University System of Georgia that while students may have many personal benefits from study abroad, and they may gain more knowledge about other cultures and global dynamics, there are no measurable differences in cultural sensitivity or interpersonal accommodation—two factors that would be important in establishing more equitable global relationships. See Richard C. Sutton and Donald L. Rubin, "The GLOSSARI Project: Initial Findings from

a System-Wide Research Initiative on Study Abroad Learning Outcomes," *Frontiers* 10 (Fall 2004): 73.

14. See Benjamin F. Hadis, "Why Are They Better Students When They Come Back? Determinants of Academic Focusing Gains in the Study Abroad Experience," *Frontiers* 11 (August 2005): 57–70, which explores why students' intellectual curiosity increases after study abroad. Students may have increased "independence," "global mindedness," and "open mindedness" in many cases, all of which make them better students. He does not, however, consider how it might better prepare them to be in equitable global relationships.

15. Indeed, the most beneficial experiences for learning may turn out to be those when a student is excluded because of the limits of participating in host communities. An excellent example can be found Amitav Ghosh's memoir, *In an Antique Land* (London: Granta Books, 1994), when his offer to participate in the observance of Ramadan is kindly rejected by his Egyptian host community (whose invitations to attend Friday services at their mosque he repeatedly declined) because, as they explain to him, the observance of Ramadan is a privilege that is earned through one's life commitments.

16. Natalie Gummer, "A Profound Unknowing: The Challenge of Religion in the Liberal Education of World Citizens," *Liberal Education* 91:2 (Spring 2005): 44–49; see also Peggy Levitt, "Religion as a Path to Civic Engagement," *Ethnic & Racial Studies* 31:4 (May 2008): 766–91.

17. Nussbaum, *Not for Profit*, 83–84.

18. Gummer, "A Profound Unknowing," 47–49.

19. Ann Marie B. Bahr, "Interreligious Dialogue, Community Cohesion, and Global Citizenship: The Role of a Religion Program in a Rural, Land-Grant University," *Journal of Ecumenical Studies* 46:2 (Spring 2011): 242–50; and Levitt, "Religion as a Path," 766–67.

20. Diana L. Eck, "Prospects for Pluralism: Voice and Vision in the Study of Religion." *Journal of the American Academy of Religion* 75:4 (2007): 743–76; "What Is Pluralism?" The *Pluralism Project*, Harvard University. http://pluralism.org/pages/pluralism/what_is_pluralism (accessed 10 July 10, 2012).

21. Lee Yearley, "New Religious Virtues and the Study of Religion," Fifteenth Annual University Lecture in Religion, Arizona State University, February 10, 1994.

22. Levitt, "Religion as a Path," 787.

23. Gummer, "A Profound Unknowing," 49.

24. Elizabeth A. Castelli, "Women, Gender, Religion: Troubling Categories and Transforming Knowledge," in *Women, Gender, Religion: A Reader*, ed. Elizabeth Castelli with Rosamond Rodman (New York: Palgrave Macmillan, 2001), 4.

25. Bennett, "Becoming Interculturally Competent" (see n. 11).

26. For a theoretical discussion of the importance of thinking of religion as more than just belief, as well as the Christian influence on the study of religion,

see Richard King, *Orientalism and Religion: Postcolonial Theory, India and "The Mystic East"* (New York: Routledge, 1999).

27. Michel Foucault, *The History of Sexuality* (Vol. 1), trans. Robert Hurley (New York: Vintage, 1990 [1976]), 135–45.

28. See Michel Foucault, *Society Must Be Defended: Lectures at the Collège de France, 1975–76*, ed. Mauro Bertani and Alessandro Fontana, trans. David Macey (New York: Picador 2003); *The Birth of Biopolitics: Lectures at the Collège de France 1978–1979*, trans. G. Burchell (New York: Palgrave Macmillan, 2008).

29. Ibid.

30. Foucault, *Birth of Biopolitics*, 224.

31. Foucault, *Society Must Be Defended*, 254–63.

32. Pardis Mahdavi, "'But We Can Always Get More!' Deportability, the State, and Gendered Migration in the United Arab Emirates," *Asian and Pacific Migration Journal* 20 nos. 3–4 (2011): 413–30. See also Gabriel Thompson, *Working in the Shadows: A Year of Doing the Jobs (Most) Americans Won't Do* (New York: Nation Books, 2010).

33. For instance, David Oxtoby, President of Pomona College, stated the College's support for undocumented students and the Dream Act initiative in his "Charge to the Class of 2010" speech to Pomona College's graduating class, May 16, 2010. http://www.pomona.edu/events/commencement/files/2010-commencement-oxtoby.pdf, (accessed February 8, 2015).

34. Junaid Rana, *Terrifying Muslims: Race and Labor in the South Asian Diaspora* (Durham, NC: Duke University Press, 2011), 158.

35. Interfaith Worker Justice, "Mission & Values," *Interfaith Worker Justice*. http://www.iwj.org/about/mission-values (accessed June 19, 2012). See also American Labor Studies Center, "Labor and Religion," *ALSC*, October 15, 2010. http://labor-studies.org/by-education-area/global-studies/labor-and-religion/ (accessed June 29, 2012); and Kim Bobo, *Wage Theft in America: Why Millions of Working Americans Are Not Getting Paid—And What We Can Do about It* (New York: The New Press, 2009).

36. A Sociologists for Women and Society factsheet gathers together statistics on women in prison in the United States. See Jodie M. Lawston, "Women and Prison: Sociologists for Women in Society (SWS) Fact Sheet." *SWS*, Spring 2012. http://www.socwomen.org/wp-content/uploads/2010/05/fact_1–2012-prison.pdf (accessed February 8, 2015). As Lawston points out, "Imprisoned women are disproportionately racial and ethnic minorities. At year end 2010, Black women (133 per 100,000 Black female residents) had an imprisonment rate almost three times higher than that of white women (47 per 100,000); Latinas' rate of imprisonment fell between that of Black women and white women (77 per 100,000 Latina residents)." Lawston gathers her statistics from Paul Guerino, Paige M. Harrison, and William J. Sabol, "Prisoners in 2010," *Bureau of Justice Statistics*, December 15, 2011,

http://www.bjs.gov/index.cfm?ty=pbdetailamp;iid=2230 (accessed February 8, 2015).

37. Michelle Alexander, *The New Jim Crow: Mass Incarceration in the Age of Color-blindness* (New York: The New Press, 2010).

38. According to the California Prison Industry Authority, it "operates over sixty service, manufacturing, and agricultural industries at twenty-two prisons throughout California." For further details on prison labor in California, see Ruth Gilmore, *Golden Gulag: Prisons, Surplus, Crisis, and Opposition in Globalizing California* (Berkeley: University of California Press, 2007); Robbie Brown and Kim Severson, "Enlisting Prison Labor to Close Budget Gaps," *New York Times*, February 24, 2011. http://www.nytimes.com/2011/02/25/us/25inmates.html?_r=1&pagewanted=all (accessed February 8, 2015).

39. Other faculty are Sue Castagnetto, Chris Guzaitis, and Valorie Thomas. The courses in which we embed the workshop are differently framed; all include critical analysis of the prison industrial complex, along with other framing theory. Courses include: Women, Crime and Punishment; Literatures of Incarceration; Feminisms in Community; and Religion and Civic Engagement.

40. See Lutterman-Aguilar and Gingerech, "Experiential Pedagogy" (see n. 13), 58–59, on the importance of cooperation and dialogue with host community members for teaching students problem solving in a global context.

12

Political Involvement, the Advocacy of Process, and the Religion Classroom

Swasti Bhattacharyya and Forrest Clingerman

KNOWLEDGE MAKES FOR *better citizens*—this statement resonates with many who teach religion and theology. What draws us to study religion is a desire to have a deeper understanding of the different ways of comprehending what it means to be human, and in turn to uncover how this knowledge might contribute to the public good. In other words, the desire to *teach* religious studies and theology often is founded on a certainty that our discipline can benefit both individuals and society.

While there are many ways that our field is beneficial, we wish to focus on one in particular: *religious studies can play a role in preparing people to be citizens, who are responsibly engaged in the political sphere*. In this chapter, we investigate political involvement in the classroom as a particular form of civic engagement, insofar as "students draw a clear conceptual distinction between political engagement and other forms of civic engagement."[1] Like other forms of civic engagement discussed throughout this book, informed political involvement has immense value for the public sphere, whereas a lack of informed involvement leads to a disintegration of a flourishing society. This insight is at the heart of the CLEA model of teaching civic engagement, which is explained in the introduction and first two chapters of this book (political involvement is especially connected with the tasks of empathy and motivated action, which form the third and fourth component of the CLEA model). Therefore, fostering *political* engagement in our religion classrooms is one way the academy can be part of teaching *civic* engagement.

At the same time, politics in the classroom presents a difficulty. Although many wish education to be apolitical, students and faculty alike have political commitments. In some cases these commitments are self-conscious and explicit, but in others they are unacknowledged and uncritically accepted. To teach political involvement means we must recognize that we all stand within a political tradition, with certain perspectives on what is good and true. This dynamic is familiar to scholars of religion, because we already contend with our own personal religious (or nonreligious) stances and those of our students. Thus we in religious studies are well suited to foster political engagement: We regularly deal with the ethical and pedagogical challenges that exist in teaching *about* a tradition while avoiding standing exclusively within the tradition. These challenges are similar to those that exist when political worldviews are allowed into the classroom.

To address the proper place of political engagement in the classroom, we first suggest the need for "informed involvement in the political sphere." Second, we reflect on the relationship between our role and responsibility as educators, on the one hand, and advocates, on the other hand. Proper advocacy in the classroom is at the heart of our argument. The appropriate form of advocacy for the classroom centers on fostering informed political involvement through an "advocacy of process." This includes creating a space for reflection and self-critique, for the development and articulation of the student's own perspectives, and for challenging views and social discourse when appropriate. Finally, we consider the challenges that can occur when including political topics in the classroom, including the perception of indoctrination, the possibility of classroom tension over competing viewpoints, and the limits of assessment.

Informed Advocacy in the Political Sphere
Defining the Political Sphere

In the context of higher education, political involvement and civic engagement have an uneasy relationship: Civic engagement is broader than political involvement. However, for many students political advocacy might be the most recognizable and explicit form of civic engagement. We wish to focus on political discourse, acknowledging that it is only one form of civic engagement in education.

How might we define "political," especially as it is relevant to teaching civic engagement? A political science colleague suggested a useful vernacular definition: The "political" can be defined as "acts with consequences for large numbers of people." Even though this is not particularly exact, it is a helpful starting point for identifying the political sphere of life. The political is irreducibly communal, and it consists of actions that are animated by ideas and values. These acts invariably include conflict over what to do, because it is sometimes unclear what the correct course of action ought to be. In other words, politics is where we handle situations of public concern that address competing needs, interests, and rights. The political realm includes governance and basic oversight of a society's common goods and services. The political is framed by attempts to address more complex concerns, such as issues of difference, belonging, power, and justice. A modern democracy uses a large degree of public participation to maintain the political realm—but this means that more controversies will arise, and the political sphere must be able to adjudicate these differences.

Everyone has a certain understanding of the political realm—one's politics is simply an individual perspective on the values and narratives that animate the society's political sphere. For educators and scholars, this presents a pedagogical and ethical issue: We must wrestle with how our personal politics relates to our professional obligations to advance appropriate discourse. To use the terms of Kant, we must interrogate the relationship between our "private reason" bestowed by our positions with the "public reason" that is our right as members of society.[2] We cannot confuse the advancement of personal political beliefs with the advancement of institutional, disciplinary, and societal educational expectations. *Whatever our politics, a proper balance between public and private reason is difficult.*

Yet balance them we must. For political tensions find their way into the classroom, and they have a place. This place rests on how these competing views share a certain set of values, rooted in a concern for the common good. Whether Democrat or Republican, Progressive Conservative, Liberal or NDP, Congress or BJP, pro-life or pro-choice, pro-UN or isolationist, etc., *everyone* ought to be concerned with active involvement aimed at promoting a good society. For the classroom, this raises an issue: While some forms of advocacy are appropriate, how does one foster political engagement without simultaneously injecting an inappropriate advocacy of any particular political perspective?

Informed Involvement and the Civic Skills of Political Life

In order to ascertain the limits of appropriate advocacy, we wish to suggest the need to clarify what constitutes the ideal of political involvement. Even though everyone is part of the political realm, a clear difference exists between haphazard dabbling and informed engagement in politics. Thus, part of fostering political engagement in religious studies and theology classrooms is oriented toward *informed* involvement, which should take on a specific meaning in political life and thus also in the classroom. If political involvement has a place in the classroom, the ideals of critical reflection and the pursuit of truth should remain— that is, higher education should admit only informed political involvement inside the classroom walls.

To be considered informed involvement, there is a need to incorporate *civic knowledge* with *civic skills*. The civic knowledge that is required involves a basic understanding of the political process, as well as the facts surrounding the controversy. Most commonly, civic knowledge is taught in political science and civics courses. However, the relationship between religion and politics means that a basic "religious literacy"[3] is an important element for civic knowledge. Yet there is more to political involvement in religious studies than simply correcting mistaken perspectives and providing detailed facts. It also requires a process of knowing. Certain abilities and skills of critical reflection are needed to navigate the tensions between religious traditions in a pluralistic society, as well as to engage in dialogue and debate in respectful ways. Our contemporary political life thirsts for critical reflection on religion, not only in cases that deal directly with religious freedom and conflict, but also in cases wherein religion has a more subtle influence. Certainly a straightforward way that religious studies participates in political engagement is through advancing understanding and insight into the ways religion works in society.

In political activity, civic skills complement civic knowledge. For example, Mary Kirlin reports that Verba, Schlozman, and Brady found that three components are "needed for adults to participate in public life: a) interest or motivation, b) a connection to the networks of individuals involved (usually by invitation), and c) resources (time or money) and the civic skills to use the resources effectively."[4] Conceptual knowledge is not enough for civic engagement; there must also be interest, aptitude, resources, and a lived knowing of how one fits into the political realm. Kirlin herself suggests four categories of skills needed for civic life: organizational, communication, decision-making, and critical thinking skills.[5] Education might only indirectly influence students' interests. However, education has a large role to play on the acquisitions of connections, civic skills and attitudes. Therefore, just as civic knowledge finds its way into religious studies classrooms, fostering civic skills should also be part of our pedagogical strategy.

Fostering Informed Political Advocacy in the Classroom

Certainly, fostering informed involvement is not a controversial pedagogical goal: The original mission of many colleges and universities in the United States was to educate its people so they could participate in the democratic process.[6] But we wish to take this a step further: In teaching informed involvement, religion professors are practicing a form of advocacy related to *political* positions and debates. This is because what we study is irreducibly political: Religious commitments influence the public sphere and political discourse. For instance, religion factors into lobbying efforts, political rhetoric, and policy statements. The volatility of these connections requires analysis and critique, but this is itself a process of political involvement. In other words, pedagogies of informed involvement inevitably involve different levels of political *advocacy*.

Advocacy in the classroom can be controversial, especially when, in the words of Jordy Rocheleau and Bruce Speck, that advocacy "involves professors not simply providing alternative positions for student consideration, but rather attempting to cultivate correct student conclusions about class material—particularly moral, political, and religious issues."[7] Rocheleau and Speck also indicate that some scholars assume advocacy is not an issue if they announce their position explicitly. However, according to these authors, "It is the intent and active effort to persuade, not the announcing of one's position, that defines advocacy." To resist *illegitimate* advocacy in the classroom, we see the need to promote a specific, legitimate form of advocacy: the movement of persuading students to hold a position and being engaged in a manner consonant with reflective and humanistic learning.

The Advocacy of Process

If we are correct that advocacy has a place in the academy, what specific form does such advocacy take? In the first chapter of Patricia Meyer Spacks' edited volume *Advocacy in the Classroom: Problems and Possibilities*, Myles Brand provides a theoretical framework for our discussion regarding advocacy in the classroom. In his juxtaposition of the "Unbridled Absolutist" to the "Unbounded Relativist," and "normative or value judgments" to "empirical judgments," Brand establishes some boundaries that fit well within the context of religious studies and theology.[8]

On one extreme is the caricature of the Unbridled Absolutist, one who believes there is a unified set of truths in each field and it is his or her job to get as close to that truth as possible. In this case, the obligation of the professor in the classroom is to present the truths, and appropriate methodologies to understand them. In the case of religion and theology, the stance of the absolutist is not simply to correctly identify the "facts"—for instance, the dates when the Prophet was in Medina or the outcomes of the Council of Trent. This position goes further, to include positions about the "Truth" of one religion, set of doctrines, or theological interpretations. From this side of the discussion, advocacy would be inappropriate and prohibited.

The Unbounded Relativist provides the opposing caricature. For someone who fits this category, there is no set of truths regarding any field of study, but only an indefinite number of interpretations with no one being correct, or even more correct than another. In this case there is no professional obligation toward "truth." So a professor is free to advocate for any version of reality he or she prefers: or, in the case of religious studies, to advocate for the futility or absurdity of all religions.

Using the distinction between normative judgments and empirical judgments, Brand presents a middle ground between these two extremes. Advocacy is simply a normative judgment on an issue: taking a side in a debate and arguing for it. This does not contain any kind of threat against students to enforce a position, because it is tempered by one's professional obligation toward critical and open-minded inquiry. *Such a stance is political, not because it uses the content of politics but because it seeks to further what we judge to be an effective and necessary form of political discourse.* That is, part of the task of religious studies is to strongly advocate for a civic structure that is hospitable to a range of political positions and outcomes. We might call this an *advocacy of process*—an advocacy of political skills in the academy—rather than an advocacy of position.

To state our point in a different way, the process of teaching one form of engagement in civil discourse over another is *itself* a political position. The position that is most often advocated for in religious studies holds to ideals of pluralism, democracy, and critical reflection as essential for making sound political choices as a society. More importantly, the advocacy of process resolutely fights against the anti-intellectualism and the claims of "elitism" that higher education must contend with in some quarters. The advocacy of process asserts that everyone participates in the political realm, and that certain ways of deliberating and debating social actions are better than others.

The advocacy of process happens in the classroom all the time—it begins by the very topics we choose to teach and the texts we select for the course. Significantly, when we make clear the context and methodology behind knowledge, students are better able to evaluate and to understand the issues (that is, not merely to proselytize for a particular position). Our pedagogical choices frame and define the subject matter, and therefore we need to be intentional and transparent in our advocacy of certain intellectual perspectives. We also need to acknowledge how our choices inform and further a political process we are implicitly advocating.

Being open to multiple interpretations is not the same as saying that all interpretations or positions are equal or even acceptable. Allowing for dialogue in the classroom provides students with the opportunity to hear and critique different perspectives being expressed. The study of religion is rooted in our ability to assess the adequacy of our approaches and perspectives. Unlike the Unbounded Relativist, we readily acknowledge that the norms of our discipline offer a measure and standard for how to investigate and discuss religion, and what conclusions might be appropriately drawn for academic discourse.

This advocacy does not simply end at the classroom doors. The classroom necessarily includes the possibility of informing political action beyond the walls of the academy. When a student has engaged in classroom material appropriately, the outcome is that she or he has learned skills and knowledge that can influence her or his ongoing political activity. In terms of an advocacy of process, this outcome is desirable, rather than something to be minimized and avoided. The knowledge and skills learned in the classroom are valuable. They can inculcate a perspective that promotes individual responsibility and agency, advances an ideal of reasoned and respectful discourse, and persuades society on a whole to have a deeper and more thoughtful engagement with the public square.

This view of advocacy allows us to move past the difficulties of academic freedom and issue advocacy. In his chapter in Spacks' book, "A Full Circle: Advocacy & Academic Freedom in Crisis," Richard Mulcahy discusses how advocacy is a "libertarianism within the academy that allows the professor the freedom to inquire, teach, and research what he or she sees fit. The only limitation imposed is . . . work be dedicated to seeking 'the truth.'" He goes on to say, "If truth cannot be defined, the professor would be expected to show a healthy respect for fact."[9]

So, in the name of academic freedom, Mulcahy supports advocacy in the classroom. As with Brand, this is an advocacy of process; it is not unrestrained, and it is coupled with a respect for factual information.

The advocacy of process is not simply a possible teaching tool, but it can be a part of our identity as educators. If so, then attacks on advocacy in the classroom could be reflecting a different understanding of the term. Michael Bérubé, in "Professional Advocates: When Is 'Advocacy' Part of One's Vocation?," points out how "advocacy" is often the label for "whatever practice seems to violate the professional protocols." Or, as Judge Jeffery Neary suggested in a personal conversation, "an activist judge is one who ruled against your position." However, at the conclusion of his discussion, Bérubé indicates that the appropriate question to ask is *not* whether advocacy has a place in the classroom; rather, "our task is to ask each other across the disciplines, from the natural sciences to the human sciences to the professional schools, what kinds of 'advocacy' are legitimate—and, in fact, required—by the standards of responsible professional behavior."[10] The advocacy of process, in other words, is the criterion for assessing all other forms of political advocacy in the classroom.

This vision of advocacy in the classroom fits in many disciplines, specifically into religious studies and theology. It is grounded in a goal of the academic study of religion: to critically examine presumptions and perspectives. This applies to all positions, including one's own. There is social and intellectual value in being better informed about one's own tradition. However, such value only emerges when one is both intellectually critical of one's home tradition and respectful of other traditions. One of the foremost aims of the academic study of religion is to work out how religious commitments coexist in the public sphere, in light of the diversity of individual, private commitments. More concretely, the religion classroom becomes a place to learn and hone civic skills. *This means working against hegemonic, intolerant, or ignorant approaches to religion in the classroom—for the sake of a student's involvement in political life.* It means religious studies must foster political involvement by advocating appropriate forms of political engagement, without advocating a single political end.

The Limits of Knowledge for Knowledge's Sake

If we are correct, then the religion classroom is the location for informed involvement—what the CLEA model refers to as "motivated action"—and our task as educators is to advocate a political process rather than a specific political solution. But to say that educators should foster political involvement is contentious because it means that our positions in society are not limited to "pure" knowledge. This latter position is illustrated by Stanley Fish in his book *Save the World on Your Own Time*. Fish argues that professors ought to "teach materials and confer skills, and therefore don't or shouldn't do a lot of other things—like produce active citizens, inculcate the virtue of tolerance, redress injustices, and bring about political change." He goes on to say, "civic participation is a political rather than an academic goal."[11] Obviously, for Fish, educators have no business taking on this type of responsibility. Our response to Fish is: of course, one of the most important roles of the academy is to provide students with an opportunity to learn material, that is, to learn the content and methods of various fields of study. However, equally important is for them to develop the skills of critical thinking, to understand the meaning, importance, and implications of the material—all with an eye toward how they will choose to utilize what they have learned as they move forward in their lives.

In this context, educators in higher education (particularly in religious studies and theology) have a responsibility to promote student involvement in political life, from local to global communities. Against claims that we should exclusively teach "knowledge for knowledge's sake," there are a number of reasons to implement political and civic engagement pedagogies in the classroom. First, Fish is correct in saying that the business of the academy is the production of knowledge. Being politically engaged within a variety of community contexts is important because this engagement deepens our knowledge and understanding; it provides new perspectives and tools to interpret knowledge. Put simply, political engagement can further the production of knowledge. Experience is a producer of knowledge in its own right. This type of engagement involves the four dimensions outlined by the Pedagogies of Civic Engagement Workshop project through the CLEA model: (1) being attentive to the meaning of knowledge, its potential, and its implications (intellectual complexity); (2) engaging in a process of self-discovery and understanding one's own location vis-à-vis the knowledge (frames of references); (3) engaging in the process of listening to people expressing alternative perspectives, and learning to think in the place of others (empathetic accountability toward others); and (4) judging and/or choosing a course of action (motivated action). These four capacities are elements that can be developed and practiced through this engaged pedagogy.

Second, there is a direct correlation between the degree to which a student is involved and the student's actual learning.[12] "Engaged," "student centered," and "active learning" are just a few of the terms that describe these practices for student learning. Involvement is not simply on the level of knowledge acquisition— it also occurs at the intersection between our academic life and our place in the public sphere: *involvement is application.* Civic engagement projects require the students not only to learn particular material but also to understand it on a level that they can then apply it to particular situations that are outside of the classroom and in the public sphere. This requires students to actively engage the content, learn and understand it, and then take it a step further. This type of educational environment provides opportunities for deep learning.

Third, by employing engaging, learning-centered types of pedagogical strategies in the classroom, students are prepared for complex, multidimensional situations facing them outside of the academy. Elizabeth Minnich said it well in *Transforming Knowledge*:

> There is nothing "merely academic" about how we think and what we think we know. We are creatures and creators of meaning. Among the many meanings that interweave our varied worlds, the meanings of *human being* are central. They can sustain us in peaceful, caring, just relation with others and with the earth we share. They can divide and rank us within systems of dominance. They can open us to love, friendship, respect, justice, nurture. They can enable us to enslave, exploit, rape, kill those who have been defined as less than fully human. We are called by inspiring and by disturbing meanings of *human being* to keep thinking, to hold horizons open. We, who are conscious creatures and creators of meaning, remain responsible.[13]

Minnich clearly rejects Fish's division of academic content and critical reasoning from how we choose to utilize this knowledge in our daily lives. Pedagogies of civic engagement acknowledge that we are indeed "creatures and creators of meaning." They enable students to learn and develop the necessary skills to be intentional and critical in their application of their knowledge in the world around them. In other words, politically engaged classrooms allow students to take the first step as political agents within a social setting.

Challenges to Fostering Appropriate Political Advocacy in the Religion Classroom

If we are correct, then a religion classroom is not simply a place for civic engagement in general, but also the site of open and honest *political* debate. In the present section, we explore how this political advocacy is addressed in a concrete way in the classroom. In fact, a number of important questions are raised by politics in the religion classroom:

- How do we talk about religion in society? How do religious language and ideas influence the world?
- How do we model the difficult conversations of religion and morality—especially in a pluralistic society—so that we are equipping leaders of our civic society?
- How do we equip students with the ability to identify and critique the hidden religious dimensions of political discourse, especially as it occurs in local, national, and global issues?
- How do we study another tradition in a way that maintains its fundamental integrity while also acknowledging its possible shortcomings? How do we study our own traditions in this way?
- What mechanisms for assessment are appropriate and possible, in light of the political and social dimensions of the study of religion?
- How do we approach political positions that are abhorrent to a minority, if the majority remains unaware or dismissive?

These questions (and numerous others) point to the fact that the relationship between religion, politics, and the classroom is messy, complicated, and difficult to assess. Because of this, there are several challenges to fostering political engagement in religious studies. In light of our discussion of an advocacy of process, we wish to address some of the most pressing of these challenges.

Indoctrination and Students as Pawns of a Non-Pedagogical Agenda

While political *advocacy* in the classroom is important, political *indoctrination* has no place in the classroom. That is to say, there is a clear difference between fostering informed involvement and manipulating students to act in uninformed ways.

Why is indoctrination fundamentally different from the advocacy we are proposing here? Rocheleau and Speck suggest a definition of "indoctrination" that differentiates it from other ways educators influence students:

> Indoctrination, unlike the attempt to persuade through reasoned argument, attempts to get individuals to accept beliefs as true without regard to reasons or evidence. Indoctrination can be identified by the intention of a speaker to cultivate acceptance of a belief resistant to rational reflection or criticism.[14]

According to Rocheleau and Speck, this view of indoctrination uses "non-rational means" or "irrational persuasion"—lies, distortions, intentional ambiguity, or other tactics that go against fair and even-handed treatment. Along with indoctrination, using students as pawns to further a professor's ideological perspective is another charge one can face when bringing political advocacy into the academy.

An example might illustrate this difficulty. Two colleagues (one from religious studies and the other from theater) at one of our institutions created an interdisciplinary civic engagement assignment. Working in groups, students were asked to research material on a student-chosen topic and create some kind of performance that required them to take what they learned from the course and present it to a community of their choosing. Based on the assignment, several student groups chose to perform what amounted to guerilla theater on topics ranging from hunger and poverty to violence against women to war. One of the projects, highlighting issues of racism, raised concerns for an administrator. The administrator interpreted the project as being a means by which the faculty were "using the students as pawns in what could be a dangerous game."

Was this indoctrination or appropriately informed involvement? Certainly the project provided a powerful critique of racism (pushing a number of buttons of those in power), but this could have occurred through indoctrination. What makes it an example of appropriate advocacy is that the idea, its development, and its execution were entirely those of the students, not the instructors. In contrast, the role of the professors consisted of careful consideration into the design of the assignment and the creation of appropriate space for students to "try on" political debate. What was being advocated, in other words, was the normative claim that students must develop their own voice on issues of importance to them. But such a voice must always take the form of informed involvement, which arises from sustained critical reflection, civic knowledge, and the appropriate application of civic skills learned in the classroom.

In this context, it is imperative that educators be explicit and avoid confusing student learning of the *practice* of political engagement with the students' adoption of a particular political *position*. The ultimate goal is student learning: students developing and honing the skills of critical thinking with others, clearly articulating their carefully thought-out ideas, and engaging the political realms on any number of levels. As Rocheleau and Speck indicate, "Open and rational inquiry is also thwarted if educators use their authority to silence debate."[15] Rather than silencing debate, we encourage it. We foster environments where students are encouraged to critically analyze issues, to look for the underlying presuppositions upon which stances are built, and critique both. We want open and rational inquiry, as that is one of the only ways to expose the hypocrisy and inconsistencies seen in so many of our current public political debates.

Because of this, even the *perception* that one is indoctrinating or using students as political pawns is problematic. Faculty and students alike need to keep in mind that when issues of race, class, gender, sexual orientation, and so forth are challenged, people get upset and respond. Even when there is a clear differentiation between the process of political engagement and the content of political engagement, the classroom can become a site of emotional conflict. In our illustration, accusations of indoctrination and using students to our own ends is one way of mitigating the challenge, of silencing the voice of opposition. In extreme cases, jail and other legal repercussions could be the consequence. In any event, issues of responsibility are very important to consider when embarking on political engagement projects. While one can never know how others will react, both the students and faculty members have responsibilities and need to be prepared.

To properly appreciate this need for responsibility, one must consider the risks involved with these types of projects. It is essential to be explicit and to provide enough context for the issues and process in order for effective learning to occur. The assignment itself needs to be closely tied to learning objectives. Faculty should have multiple checkpoints for student work to ensure that controversial material is appropriately handled; institutional policies on controversial topics should also be well known to faculty and students. Finally, the instructor must provide an explicit description that identifies what responsibilities students should be expected to take upon themselves, as well as the responsibilities of the faculty member. While it is impossible to anticipate all of the risks and challenges that might face those involved with civic engagement assignments, it is incumbent upon the faculty member to take precautions, and to prepare themselves and the students.

Competing Viewpoints, Tensions, and Classroom Incivility

In January 2011, the shooting of Representative Gabrielle Giffords, several of her staff members, and a number of others made national news. Almost immediately, the press turned to the question of the tone of political discourse in the United States. Increased acrimony between those who disagree and the overall polarized political discourse in the country were initially seen as the context for the shootings. This was only one episode in a larger history of a contentious public square. Too often the divisive nature of these debates has them teetering on the brink of violence, sometimes giving into it.

The classroom is not immune to these tensions. As multiple political positions are allowed, the emotional and intellectual investment made in competing viewpoints can often bring us to a point of strife. Because of the sensitive nature of religion for many, we are familiar with these tensions and incivilities in our classrooms. It can arise with an off-handed comment by students such as "I think Mormonism is a cult." Or honest but misguided questions, such as an evangelical Protestant student asking a Catholic student, "Why is it a big deal if I chew gum while taking communion?" Religion is at the core of self-identity for many. When politics is added to the mix, the tensions between beliefs can threaten to derail positive political engagement.

Combating incivility not only defines the ideal of the public square, but it is the reason for promoting an advocacy of political process in the classroom. The public sphere is where maintaining a level head, critically examining the materials, and carefully making decisions is of utmost importance. But this is certainly possible. For example, in his examination of the Cuban missile crisis, Graham Allison peels back the layers of rhetoric and demonstrates how careful listening, actually hearing the "other," and critical analysis worked to avert the catastrophe that could have been.[16] In Trita Parsi's *A Single Roll of the Dice*, he too carefully examines the complex, multifaceted relationships between the United States, particularly the Obama administration, and Iran.[17] Both of these authors demonstrate more than the importance of having thick skin; they also demonstrate the absolute necessity of our political representatives to have a mastery of the skills we have been talking about throughout this chapter.

The classroom is a real space, albeit one that is contrived, where these skills can be learned and honed precisely because the stakes are lowered in the spirit of inquiry. It is a safe place to try out new ideas, learn how to really listen, and challenge solutions that are too simplistic. However, maintaining civility in this context can prove to be just as challenging. How do educators effectively balance competing viewpoints? How might tensions disrupt the educational process? In what ways might classroom incivility arise? More importantly, how might educators use the tensions inherent in political debates as part of a transformative education?

In *When Students Have Power: Negotiating Authority in Critical Pedagogy* (Chicago: University of Chicago Press, 1997), Ira Shor presents an in-depth discussion on the challenges he faced when he truly opened his classroom to a democratic process. Along with the challenges, Shor discusses how he resolved them. How can we maintain a balance between welcoming all voices while at the same time trying to contain a student's sometimes vitriolic monologue? One strategy to creating a safe environment where engaging, productive, and informative discussions thrive is establishing ground rules from the first day of class. Students are asked to write down responses to the following:

1. Briefly jot down things/behavior/responses that encourage and foster your learning.
2. Briefly jot down things/behavior/responses that inhibit or shut down your learning.
3. Having listed the above, write out two or three ground rules you would like the class to consider adopting.

After students work independently, they spend a few minutes discussing their findings with one partner. Then together the students establish the ground rules by which the class will be run. After they have their list of rules, each member of the class commits to upholding and enforcing them. This stage is important to stress: They created the rules, they are to abide by them, *and* they enforce the rules; this job ought not to be the exclusive responsibility of the faculty. In this way, the students have a stake in the rules they established, they are invested from the beginning, and they share in the responsibility of maintaining civility in the classroom.

While incivility is not acceptable, discomfort and tension can be. It is the very tensions that accompany controversial political debates that can be used for transformative education. The very process of moving beyond mere mastery of the reading material to experiencing the material can make for very challenging and uncomfortable situations. When contemporary, controversial issues are discussed in the classroom, passions are heightened and tempers flare—not unlike in the political realm, as alluded to in Gifford's case. However, it is these very, real situations that can lead to transformative learning, as David Concepción and Juli Thorson Eflin have suggested.[18]

As our students learn how to deal with incivility and conflict in the classroom, they will be better prepared to deal with it in the political realm. While this type of pedagogical strategy can sometimes make for disruptive, messy, and confusing class sessions, we argue that this adds to the learning of our students. Life can be disruptive, messy, and confusing. Why should the classroom be otherwise? We want our students to be prepared for what awaits them outside of the walls of the academy. Therefore we humbly, sometimes with fear and trembling, welcome the disruption that can occur when real issues are tackled within class.

Assessment

A third challenge is assessment. As Rocheleau and Speck ask, how might we "grade virtue" or otherwise assess a student's political engagement? Unlike the mastery of content, grading for involvement in the political process does not seem to have explicit, semester-length outcomes. Rather, political involvement rests on individual perspectives and long-term personal growth. In the worst cases, grading suggests a reward structure that is related to one's agreement with a certain position. Students could easily feel pressured to take up a political stance in order to improve their class performance (or use our wariness of favoritism to manipulate their grade, as John Barbour pointed out in his essay "Grading on the Guilty-Liberal Standard"[19]). Furthermore, different types of political engagement cannot be easily compared on a single spectrum, especially when taking the diversity of student positions into account. Finally, the most difficult issue is the fact that political advocacy—unlike a paper or other homework assignment—is not meant to be finished in a particular time in the semester.

These problems are not insurmountable. Rocheleau and Speck present two responses. First, "it isn't necessary to have everything which is taught be graded."[20] In other words, it is acceptable to acknowledge that some student outcomes are not part of their classroom grade. This sentiment is implicitly found across religious studies: For example, Barbara Walvoord's *Teaching and Learning in College Introductory Courses* discusses acknowledged and unacknowledged outcomes of religious studies classes. Certain outcomes are hoped for by professors but not explicitly assessed for the course.[21] Some course goals are not easily graded, and perhaps grading is not required in some circumstances. By removing the grade from the learning of political engagement and civic skills, the professor can circumvent some of the problems of pressure and the limitations imposed by the timeline of the term.

A second response balances the lack of assessment. For Rocheleau and Speck, "it is sometimes of value to grade students for their display of virtue."[22] In fact, there are several instances in which professors grade for dispositions and attitudes; they mention grades for "good participation" as one such case. Likewise, professors sometimes grade for the application of, or growth in the ability to use, methods of study. They go on to argue that we can—in certain circumstances— judge a student's moral, theological, and political stance. In fact, this claim naturally emerges from the sense of advocacy we discussed previously. We are not grading content but ways that the student *approaches* political engagement, including how to understand the context, knowledge, and skills required to be involved. A position that fails to be delivered with a firm ground, clear reasoning, or sense of mutual respect, for example, can be identified, and a rubric can be structured to explain the different levels. We can likewise develop markers for what it means to carefully reason political positions, or the ability to critique assumptions of privilege and presumed authority. In each of these cases, there is a sense of objectivity: We are not assessing the student's personal position but rather we are advocating a certain vision of the political process, which includes the ability to practice a certain skill or mode of thinking.

With explicit parameters of what political skills and attitudes are being taught, it is possible to create a fair and reasonable assessment that results in a student grade. An example comes from a class on environmental theology, when students had a two-part assignment related to environmental policy. Students were asked to write a letter to an elected official (a member of Congress was recommended) on an environmental issue of their choosing. In order to complete the letter, students were required to research the chosen issue and to present their position in a persuasive way through the letter. Students were not required to actually send the letter, though many did. The second part of the assignment was a reflection paper, in which students deliberated on ways that religious commitments might influence their perspective on public policy. Grades were not based on the position the students took but on how well the positions were researched and presented. And to avoid indoctrination, such transparency is essential: Students must have a clear idea of the goals of the assignment, as well as the mechanisms for assessment. They must also have the opportunity to voice concerns—and a safe space to do so. As educators, we should be wary of any grading mechanism that seeks to diagnose the content that informs behaviors and attitudes in order to correct presumed "deficiencies."

Here we can open ourselves to another dimension of assessment: namely, assessment used to improve teaching effectiveness rather than student achievement. In classes that include a component of political involvement, assessments that do not filter into student grades can and should be present, in order to better understand what is occurring in the classroom around controversial and sensitive topics. In other words, there might be a different use for assessments in this case: namely, to inform our teaching success and limitations. An example of this might be helpful. In a discussion of teaching peace and justice, Katherine Turpin identifies what she calls "five characteristic temptations" in how students of relative privilege approach justice education: the temptation to run, to defensive anger, to neutralize conflict, to "fix it," and to despair."[23] In each of these, a student is having a reaction to uncomfortable material that confronts personal and intellectual dimensions of the student's self-conception. It would be wrong to use this as part of a grading scheme—falling into one these five temptations should not automatically be cause for a lower grade. However, these five temptations might form the basis for an assessment of classroom practice and teaching techniques. If a particular lecture elicits a response of despair, then changes might be warranted, for example.

Professors are placed in a position that demands a careful balance of limiting or foregoing assessment, on the one hand, and ensuring clear and reasonable parameters, on the other. But something else must be highlighted: In religious studies, this balance is complicated by the fact that one's political and civic views are sometimes intertwined with one's religious and ethical commitments. We have a dual professional responsibility of respect toward students' religious commitments and toward objective, critical examination of the subject. When introducing the issue of political engagement, we add a third dimension to the equation. We must acknowledge that, for example, some students will not wish to engage certain political skills or debates on religious grounds. Providing alternatives for classroom assignments is imperative. Most importantly, maintaining an attitude of sensitivity and flexibility is key. To clearly identify the outcome desired—and to continually remind oneself that there can be many different ways of achieving any outcome—will help balance the competing demands of professional ethics in the field.

Conclusion

We have sought to encourage professors of religion and theology to embrace the need for political advocacy in the classroom. But our desire is not to demand that students adopt a particular political position. Rather, we think the classroom is vitally important for students to learn how to successfully navigate individual religious and political commitments in the midst of a pluralistic public square. We echo Helene Moglen's rejection of the declared dichotomy between advocacy and responsible teaching. According to Moglen, the "crucial distinction that needs to be made is not one between a politically neutral classroom and the classroom that is political, but rather one between classrooms that are political and those that are politicized. In politicized classrooms, teachers deploy their institutional authority in order to impose their own intellectual agendas on students whom they perceive to be passive and incapable of intellectual reciprocity."[24] In contrast, the political classroom is a place where students mature in their own political agency.

To do this effectively means to uphold the tasks of our vocation. Education around political engagement, like all forms of teaching, exists with a set of ethical professional obligations. In this, teaching for political engagement has a great deal in common with transformative education. Dorothy Ettling writes, ". . . the educator's engagement of transformative learning theory demands a conscious, ongoing examination of the appropriateness of methods that are used and the implications of outcomes that are fostered. This is, in fact, the ethical demand."[25] This ethical demand is found when approaching issues of political advocacy and involvement.

Notes

1. Edward K. Spiezio, "Pedagogy and Political," *Liberal Education* 88 (2002): 15.
2. Immanuel Kant, "An Answer to the Question, What Is Enlightenment?" in *Practical Philosophy: The Cambridge Edition of the Works of Immanuel Kant* (New York: Cambridge University Press, 1996): 11–22.
3. Stephen Prothero, *Religious Literacy* (San Francisco: HarperSanFrancisco, 2007).
4. Mary Kirlin, "The Role of Civic Skills in Fostering Civic Engagement," *Circle Working Paper* 06 (June 2003): 5.
5. Kirlin explains these four categories in the following way. First, there are organizational skills such as planning, implementation, and the ability to hold

civic responsibilities. Second, communication skills include language abilities, as well as skills related to specific modes of communication (writing, speeches, and interpreting political communication). Third, collective decision-making requires skills such as listening, understanding the interests of others, working with others, making difficult choices, and building cooperative relationships. Finally, critical thinking (about political and social life, taking positions and defending them, and synthesizing positions).

6. Eric Fretz, "Teaching Liberty and Practicing Deliberative Democracy in the Classroom," *Campus Compact Reader* (2004): 2–3. http://www.compact.org/reader/winter04/article2-print.html (accessed Dec 16, 2008).

7. Jordy Rocheleau and Bruce W. Speck, *Rights and Wrongs in the College Classroom: Ethical Issues in Postsecondary Education* (Bolton, MA: Anker, 2007), 25.

8. Myles Brand, "The Professional Obligations of Classroom Teachers," in *Advocacy in the Classroom: Problems and Possibilities*, ed. Patricia Meyer Spacks (New York: St. Martin's Press, 1996).

9. Richard Mulcahy, "A Full Circle: Advocacy and Academic Freedom in Crisis," in *Advocacy in the Classroom: Problems and Possibilities*, ed. Patricia Meyer Spacks (New York: St. Martin's Press, 1996), 154.

10. Michael Bérubé, "Professional Advocates: When Is 'Advocacy' Part of One's Vocation?" in *Advocacy in the Classroom: Problems and Possibilities*, ed. Patricia Meyer Spacks (New York: St. Martin's Press, 1996), 195.

11. Stanley Fish, *Save the World on Your Own Time* (New York: Oxford University Press, 2008), 66–67.

12. Ken Bain, *What the Best College Teachers Do* (Cambridge, MA: Harvard University Press, 2004); George D. Kuh, Jillian Kinzie, John H. Schuc, et al., *Student Success in College: Creating Conditions that Matter* (San Francisco, CA: Jossey-Bass, 2005).

13. Elizabeth K. Minnich, *Transforming Knowledge* (Philadelphia: Temple University Press, 2005), 1.

14. Rocheleau and Speck, *Rights and Wrongs in the College Classroom*, 35.

15. Ibid., 36.

16. Graham T. Allison, *Essence of Decision: Explaining the Cuban Missile Crisis* (Boston: Little, Brown and Company, 1971).

17. Trita Parsi, *A Single Roll of the Dice* (New Haven: Yale University Press, 2013).

18. David W. Concepción and Juli Thorson Eflin, "Enabling Change: Transformative & Transgressive Learning in Feminist Ethics & Epistemology" *Teaching Philosophy* 32 (2009): 177–98.

19. John D. Barbour, "Grading on the Guilty-Liberal Standard," *The Chronicle Review* 53, no. 42 (June 22, 2007): B16.

20. Rocheleau and Speck, *Rights and Wrongs in the College Classroom*, 47.

21. Barbara Walvoord, *Teaching and Learning in College Introductory Course* (Malden, MA: Blackwell Publishing Ltd., 2008).

22. Rocheleau and Speck, *Rights and Wrongs in the College Classroom*, 47.

23. Katherine Turpin, "Disrupting the Luxury of Despair: Justice and Peace Education in Contexts of Relative Privilege," *Teaching Theology and Religion* 11 (2008): 144ff.

24. Helene Moglen, "Unveiling the Myth of Neutrality: Advocacy in the Feminist Classroom," in *Advocacy in the Classroom: Problems and Possibilities*, ed. Patricia Meyer Spacks (New York: St. Martin's Press, 1996), 209.

25. Dorothy Ettling, "Ethical Demands of Transformative Learning," *New Directions for Adult and Continuing Education*, no. 109 (2006): 60.

13

Religious Studies, Theology, and Pedagogies of Civic Engagement

Thomas Pearson

REID LOCKLIN AND Ellen Posman do us a great service in the opening chapters of this book by grounding the pedagogies of civic engagement in the most hallowed purpose of the undergraduate curriculum: critical thinking.[1] Drawing on Jack Mezirow and the Women's Ways of Knowing collaborative, they argue that critical thinking is most fully realized when it includes "active formation and articulation of personal commitments."[2] Further, to truly "complexify" thinking requires making judgments that lead to action. Critical thinking is consummated in engaged democratic participation in civic life, grounded in reflective self-analysis of one's own epistemological and social position. Therefore, cognitive development of undergraduates must entail students discovering, articulating, and developing their values—and then acting on them.

Similarly, Carolyn Medine's chapter at the far end of this book diagrams education as a continuing cycle of steps in which the student

> engages in an action, reflects on (or in a classroom setting, evaluates or assesses) that action's meaning, makes a judgment and, thinking critically, discerns how that action challenges, enhances, or changes one's values. This cycle is one we must inculcate in pedagogical structure and scaffolding by offering students categories for thinking critically and structures in which to deploy those categories—that is, crafted assignments—to think through the meaning of what they have done and what it means to and for self and other. Our model suggests a sustained and deepening of a pattern of being, one that would generate a lifelong habit not just of learning but of reflection on self and world.[3]

These chapters, bookending this volume, provide a student- and academic-centric justification for the pedagogies of civic engagement. Their arguments complement the institution- and civic-centric arguments made by Martha Nussbaum and others who have argued that democracy requires a civically engaged citizenry and that academic institutions have historically understood their mission as the preparation of democratic citizens.[4] These arguments place the pedagogies of civic engagement at the heart of the mission of the academy and undergraduate education. They challenge and expand a narrower view of academia as simply the discovery of new knowledge and the preparation of skilled workers.

This chapter asks a specific question from the space that several of the foregoing chapters have cleared for us: How are the pedagogies of civic engagement complicated by the historic divide between religious studies and theology? Are the learning goals of the pedagogies of civic engagement appropriate only on the theological side of this contentious spectrum? I will think through this question using the various learning designs and implicit and explicit student learning goals presented in this book's disparate chapters (each of which describes and analyzes different pedagogies of civic engagement). This chapter does not provide a reliable summary of the carefully nuanced arguments and evidence contained in these chapters. Instead it paints in broad strokes, sketching out caricatures of various positions in order to juxtapose them to one another and draw out contrasts, similarities, and the larger contours of what's at stake in the question.[5]

Religion and Theology

One of the most prominent and strident voices articulating the difference between theological and religious studies is Russell McCutcheon.[6] As a shortcut, I rely here on a statement linked from McCutcheon's University of Alabama Department of Religious Studies website, apparently intended to explain the department's understanding of the academic study of religion to various constituencies (students, parents, colleagues, the broader academy, trustees, and legislators). The short essay answers the question posed in its title: "What Is the Academic Study of Religion?"

> It is fundamentally an *anthropological enterprise*. That is, it is primarily concerned with studying people . . . their beliefs, behaviors, and institutions, rather than assessing "the truth" or "truths" of their various beliefs or behaviors. . . . It is not concerned to make *normative judgments* concerning the way people *ought* to live or behave. To phrase it another way, we could say that whereas the anthropologically-based study of religion is concerned with the descriptive "is" of human behavior, the theological study of religion is generally concerned with the prescriptive "ought" of the gods.[7]

To pose my question using broad and crude caricatures to simplify and clarify positions: Should "McCutcheonites" dismiss any and all of the pedagogies of civic engagement because they are inevitably and inappropriately theological in orientation—concerned with the personal transformation of students, with discerning and acting for justice, with the "prescriptive ought" rather than with the "descriptive is," and therefore inappropriate to the undergraduate classroom? In this chapter I show that many of the pedagogies of civic engagement presented in this book stop well short of this level of normative prescription. However, the chapters by Medine, Locklin, and Posman (as well as that of Swasti Bhattacharyya and Forrest Clingerman) seem to praise the pedagogies of civic engagement precisely because they teach students to make "normative judgments concerning the way people ought to live or behave." Then by what license do religious studies faculty teach it, a McCutcheonite might ask? A scholar trained to read and analyze ancient Mediterranean texts, a Sanskrit scholar, an American historian, an anthropologist—what is the professional credential by which they are qualified to teach college students to critique contemporary social phenomenon, to help them clarify their own values on a social or political issue, to make normative judgments, and to take action? As Stanley Fish provocatively argues, they ought to be arrested for operating without a license.[8]

Fish's polemical position provides my first foothold for traction. There are, of course, many credentialed professors with training in normative academic disciplines: not just theology and ethics but also economics and any number of policy-driven and pre-professional fields. These are legitimate academic disciplines. They are grounded in academic methods requiring critical thinking, evidence, argument, citation, and peer review. That McCutcheonites would not want theology to sully or confuse the discipline of religious studies does not thereby ban it from the academy. Theology must at least be granted its own wing of the academic study of religion, if perhaps entirely separate from the discipline that McCutcheonites themselves would pursue. Just because one scholar studies life forms through the discipline of biology does not invalidate another scholar from studying physical processes through the discipline of chemistry, or another from studying literature in an English department, or incarceration policy in some other department.

Yet ought the normative theological study of religion comprise the undergraduate curriculum (most pointedly, in state universities protected by the separation of church and state)? I cannot plumb the depths or complexity of this wide-ranging and contentious debate here, but it should be uncontroversial to say that the goals for student learning in *any* course ought to align with the clearly stated learning goals for the course and the mission of the institution where the course is being taught. It should not be controversial to argue that different kinds of academic study of religion might be appropriate in different kinds of teaching

contexts. Russell McCutcheon's statement about what constitutes the study of religion fits well with the University of Alabama's mission regarding the "creation,
translation, and dissemination of knowledge"—although some who disagree
with his position may dispute how well religion courses thus construed contribute to the university's mission of "enhancing the quality of life."[9] On the other
hand, Carolyn Medine, teaching at the similarly secular, state-supported University of Georgia, hopes that "students will come to understand those they 'other'
as not necessarily just like the 'self,' but as on parallel and viable life paths."[10]
Her chapter articulates robust goals for student psychological and cognitive development in a course that ought to be in service of the University of Georgia's
rather conventional mission statement focusing on "academic achievement" and
"research knowledge."[11]

I needn't resolve here the historical debate about the appropriate goals of the
academic study of religion. When it comes to educating college students, there
would seem to be plenty of room in higher education to engage a broad range of
student learning objectives under the moniker "the academic study of religion."
Clearly, the academy is spacious enough to provide room for novelists as well as
literary theorists, room for artists as well as art theorists, and room to "be religious" (academically), as well as to study religious people—that is to say, there is
room in the academy for pedagogies of civic engagement that would make normative arguments about how society ought to be and require students to act on
their judgments.

Various departments, and various institutions, can decide their own curricula without prohibiting other departments and other schools from making
other decisions. McCutcheonites can choose not to be conversation partners with
scholars constructing normative arguments about religious phenomenon and
experience, human relations, social justice, and "the prescriptive ought of the
gods," just as they are similarly not conversation partners with poets, or chemists.

But the question remains: Is there a normative and prescriptive "ought" at
the heart of pedagogies of civic engagement, and are they thereby appropriate for
some brands of the academic study of religion and not others? In fact, there is
a broad range of normative positions represented in the pedagogies and assignments described in the various chapters in this book. Intentionally so. I now turn
to review some of them.

Some Strong Cases

I will start with an extreme case to help clear some ground from which to organize
the rest. The goal of Elizabeth Corrie's "Ascetic Withdrawal Project" is "to raise
[students'] awareness of how deeply entrenched their own consumer habits are"
and "to highlight how deeply countercultural—even threatening—abstaining

from any aspect of consumerism can be." These are the sorts of normative positions that many of the authors in this volume could well endorse personally.[12] However, they would probably not adopt her articulation of such overtly Christian sectarian learning goals for their students. Corrie writes: "The goal, as explained in the assignment guidelines, is 'to engage in a practice that aims at conversion away from consumer faith and towards a richer Christian faith through the tradition of observing the fasting period of Lent.'"[13] Furthermore:

> the theological concepts of conversion, sin, grace, justification, and regeneration/sanctification that [the author, Katherine Turpin,] uses offer a unique response to the pedagogical problem of teaching civic engagement. . . . As sinners, grace remains ever available, ever enlivening and inviting us to enter into a life that goes deeper, and broader, than our branded existence can give. . . . Practices of ascetic withdrawal do *more* than contribute to "ongoing conversion" of the individual away from "consumer faith." They also become a means of public witness and even evangelism.[14]

Corrie, however, is teaching at a Christian theological school (Emory University's Candler School of Theology), and her task is to prepare students to serve the church by becoming Christian educators. The assignment is designed so that it "prepares students for prophetic leadership in the church," and that seems entirely appropriate in her context.[15]

It is interesting to note that Marianne Delaporte, teaching undergraduates, seems to share Elizabeth Corrie's explicitly Christian sectarian learning goals. She shows no reticence in unpacking with her students the components of biblical hospitality. "Hospitality, as our faculty tell students, is one of the basic and necessary duties of religious life."[16] Apparently, these sorts of learning goals are appropriate in this particular undergraduate curricular context: a Catholic institution, Notre Dame de Namur University. In her teaching context, she can provide her students (and her colleagues in the academy) a reasoned, academic analysis that connects hospitality to a "mutual relationship" with underprivileged members of the community, and thereby construct a normative social justice position for her students that provides a framework and grounding for a progressive liberal Catholic social justice pedagogy of civic engagement and social activism.

> We discuss the components of biblical hospitality . . . the creation of community, advocacy for the marginalized, mutual welcome, and the hidden face of the divine. Hospitality in this sense is radical and dangerous. It requires a leap of faith.[17]

It is interesting to see how a normative Catholic position such as this becomes more complicated in the chapter by Nicholas Rademacher, similarly teaching undergraduates in a Catholic institution, Cabrini College. His civic engagement project is

> designed to encourage in the students and, ideally, the participating members of each community, a greater awareness of their personal values and a commitment to civic responsibility, which is to say, recognition that we are all truly responsible for all. With regard to the students, this community-based learning project is also designed to enable them to better understand religious studies and theology as an interdisciplinary field and to master key terms and concepts in the scholarship that they encounter throughout the course.[18]

There is no difficulty locating these learning goals squarely within an academic theology of a social justice bent. Interestingly, the course also emphasizes "respecting multiple faith perspectives" and bringing people together from "disparate backgrounds." Although in this context these values are located within a particular confessional tradition, they also give expression to the ethic of inclusion and diversity that have emerged as central values and organizing principles of the academy (and contemporary American society). These academic values are not at all limited to pedagogies involving normative theological positions and can even be observed, arguably, in the approaches undergirding many of the supposedly neutral academic nontheological approach to comparative religions and religious studies.

In contrast to the chapters by Corrie and Delaporte, Rademacher shows carefully nuanced concern for the diversity of students in his classroom and the faith traditions they represent, including many who would claim no faith tradition at all. This diversity makes him uncomfortable about imposing Catholic social teaching as a normative system. This problem does not arise in the chapters by Corrie and Delaporte. Clearly, Rademacher does not want to say that students are required to adopt these meanings and values in order to do well in his course. That would be "indoctrination." It might be appropriate for the formation of Catholic priests, but not for undergraduate students. So he draws on James Fowler's book *Stages of Faith* to provide students a broader understanding of "faith" by analyzing it through stages of cognitive development. "What provides us with 'worth'? Where do we 'invest loyalty'? What 'powers . . . promise to sustain our lives'? What people, groups, and institutions are important to us, give us meaning?"[19] Rademacher seeks to expand the definition of faith so as to welcome students of all backgrounds, and he does this by asking them to clarify *their own* faith commitments and attendant attitudes and behaviors. He teaches them to engage their classmates and community partners in interfaith dialogue and social justice topics.

The chapter takes pains to demonstrate that this requirement for "engagement" is not particularly normative. Thus, we are told that the course promises to "respect multiple faith perspectives" and to create in students a "greater awareness of their personal values." But how do these commitments and learning goals fit with the course's much more normative goal to foster "a commitment to civic responsibility"—"which is to say," he tells us, "recognition that we are all truly responsible for all"?[20] Does the course succeed if students gain greater clarity of their own personal values, or does it succeed even more if they bring their personal values into alignment with traditions of Catholic social teaching?

Despite the emphasis on diversity, inclusivity, and the development of students' *own* commitments and values, Rademacher's pedagogy of civic engagement is clearly oriented toward normative transformation of students toward specific social justice analyses and commitments to justice and justice-oriented action. The course seeks to "facilitate relationships of solidarity and the development of a justice-oriented disposition that counters prevailing practices and structures that reinforce poverty."[21] Fostering dispositions is clearly central to what Rademacher values in this pedagogy. It is not sufficient to "learn about" justice (or religion, for that matter). Students in this course should "learn to"—they should act in the world, they should *be* religious. But this normativity is tellingly couched or softened by emphasizing students' own cognitive-religious development rather than normative theological positions.

Four Degrees of Normativity

There are several degrees of normativity displayed in these chapters. The first level is a McCutcheon-like delimiting of religious studies pedagogy to an "objective" anthropological study of religion and religious people—not "assessing 'the truth' of their various beliefs or behaviors."[22] At this level, contemporary socio-anthropological accounts of religion are treated as normative. First-degree normativity operates in the assumed difference between studying what people do and say versus studying what they *ought* to do and say. It gets complicated when the object of study is not an ancient rite or exotic belief but is instead contemporary social structures and power. But we can set that complicating case aside for the moment, as well as the familiar epistemological problems with "objectivity" identified by philosophy and discourse-analysis.

Many of the chapters in this book describe courses with learning goals oriented to this first degree of normativity. For example, Philip Wingeier-Rayo describes the goal of his immersion trip to Cuba as an opportunity to expose students to another culture:

> The objective of this particular international service trip was for the students to challenge their assumptions and prejudices through personal interaction with Cubans in the context of a service project. The firsthand knowledge of the Cuban situation, enhanced by personal encounters with Cubans, facilitates cognitive dissonance in which original assumptions are challenged with the acquisition of new information.[23]

The objectives in his civic engagement assignment analyzed in Melissa Stewart's chapter in this book focus on the exploration of power dynamics and tensions between a new religion and pre-existing cultures and religions:

> The specific assignment was to find three articles about Christianity or another religion and its struggle with culture. Students wrote three one-page reflections on how religion related to culture in these news stories.[24]

Another project described in Stewart's chapter involves students critically assessing the representations of religious traditions in media.[25] Presumably, in this case, the teacher would assign readings that provide an authoritative analysis of how representation works in the media—much as a McCutcheonite might assign, say, John Comaroff or Christian Smith to provide an authoritative academic account of a religious belief or rite (and, it should be noted, it is for this first-level normative purpose that Nicholas Rademacher assigns James Fowler's *Stages of Faith* as an authoritative reading for his course).

Also included in this first degree of normativity are learning goals involving the development of reading, writing, and critical thinking skills. But notice that the chapters by Locklin and Posman have exploded the boundary between critical thinking and the development of a students' normative orientation to the world and even the requirement to take action. I return to this point later in the chapter.

The second degree of normativity is best illustrated by Barbara Walvoord's widely cited study of *Teaching and Learning in College Introductory Religion Courses.*[26] Her empirical study of "highly effective teachers" names and quantifies what those teaching in the undergraduate classroom have known all along: Regardless of how rigorously one teaches courses in the first degree of normativity, many students will come into the classroom with existential questions about their own faith and values and judgments of others'. However inchoately or incoherently understood and articulated, students will, to some degree, inevitably be "religious seekers" (or debunkers) in the classroom.

What should we do with students' personal religious interests in the content of a course? We might decide to include learning goals that involve students' reflection on their own values and faith. Or, if this makes us uncomfortable, we might decide to leave students' own religious discernments out of the content of the course but find pedagogical strategies to leverage their heightened interest in existential meaning-making questions for our own, somewhat different (perhaps what we might understand as "more academic"), pedagogical purposes. I call this strategy the second degree of normativity: the strategic pedagogical intention to use the "inappropriately religious" questions students bring into the classroom to draw them into the course material as we construe it, to accomplish *our* learning goals (presumably located securely in first-level normativity). I think any smart first-degree-normative teacher ought to be open to this pedagogical strategy— although some might be uncomfortable when drawn into existential discussions with students, or they might worry about students offending or alienating each other through inappropriate comments, and will probably therefore feel called upon to occasionally disabuse these religious questions in an academic course on religion.

Second-degree normativity acknowledges that students enter with existential meaning-making questions and seeks to leverage them to achieve first-degree normative learning goals. Civic engagement pedagogies often escape down to this level of normativity when challenged. More troubling, it is where a civic engagement course that intends to be more normatively oriented might operate if students are not adequately prepared with authoritative academic readings that help them articulate their own commitments from their community-based learning experience: Students are allowed to or even encouraged to reflect on their commitments, but this remains outside of the normative content of the course. The chapters in this book all agree that this is not effective or responsible civic engagement pedagogy.

Third-degree normativity—also encompassed in Barbara Walvoord's analysis of what the most effective undergraduate religion faculty do—includes students' reflection on existential questions as one goal among other phenomenological-anthropological (first-level normative) learning goals. Course content might include examples of philosophers, theologians, poets, novelists, or others reflecting on existential meaning-making questions of value and judgment. This course material demonstrates to students the wide range of compelling responses that are possible for such questions, and it models a properly rigorous and academic method for this kind of reflection.

Third-degree normativity does not require students to arrive at specified answers to these questions. Students are not evaluated according to the degree to which they adopt the professors' or the authors' position, although they probably need to learn to think and express themselves using the language and categories presented by the authors and professor. However, students often believe that they cannot disagree with what they discern as the normative position of the course. And professors often stack the deck by including a preponderance of readings that lead students to the clear conclusions that the professor has already reached.

Typically, third-degree learning goals are lodged in courses that otherwise are more thoroughly oriented toward first-degree learning objectives regarding others' religious beliefs and behaviors. This can give rise to the sense that these third-degree goals are added on or exist outside the proper scope of the course. Recall the frequent admonitions in this book that the community-based learning component of a course must align with and contribute to the learning goals of the course. A course presenting first-degree normative analyses of social and political issues can easily bleed into second-degree normativity (although students' private judgment and meaning-making with the material might just as often be in opposition to the professors' own, scrupulously bracketed, political and ethical judgments). Just as easily, the learning objectives in a first-degree normative course can enter third-degree normativity when the content it objectively describes includes an analysis of power and social relations. It is hard to find analyses of social and political inequality that do not involve normative judgments of how the world *ought* to be. Faculty not trained in normative discourses of theology, ethics, or social analysis must answer the Stanley Fish objection that we ought to stick within the bounds of our academic training if we do not have a license to teach meaning-making and ethical judgment of social relations.

Consider how first-, second-, and third-degree normativity intermingle in the learning goals articulated in Reid Locklin's civic engagement assignment placing students in conversation at a local medical and long-term-care facility, as glossed in Melissa Stewart's chapter.[27] The goals include: level three ("to develop greater sensitivity to the complexity of their own social identities"), level one ("stronger skills in cross-cultural and interreligious communication"), level one again ("a richer sense of the important role played by diverse religious persons and institutions in Canadian society"), and level three again ("empathy for religiously diverse others and framing their own social identities").[28]

This easy movement between the various levels of normativity is a reflection of the robust and expansive understanding of critical thinking so well articulated for us in the CLEA model of teaching civic engagement: critical thinking and communication skills (first-degree normativity) are only completed when the thinker gets to the point of understanding and articulating his or her own social location as part and parcel of the analysis, and making a personal judgment of value and meaning—which is clearly third-degree normativity.

We also see this movement in Melissa Stewart's gloss of Clark Chilson's civic engagement pedagogy project.

> As expressed in both the goals of the class and the grant project, Chilson's main objective in the classroom is to foster critical inquiry by teaching students to identify the complexity of different social, political, and cultural situations and to recognize other frames of reference. Chilson, as he articulated it several times during the grant workshops, argues that "this is the proper purpose of university education, and that the civic virtues such as empathetic engagement and motivated action for the good of society can and should emerge naturally from critical inquiry."[29]

Critical thinking requires analysis of political society and the recognition of a variety of frames of reference, which leads to empathetic engagement and motivated action, and to the common good.

Stewart's gloss of the assignment depicts third-level normative goals emerging out of what otherwise appears to be a course lodged in first-degree normativity. Chilson's "Religion in Asia" survey course goals require students to demonstrate historical knowledge of major events, people, texts, doctrines, concepts, and practices, and to improve critical thinking skills (that is, to "improve your ability to summarize different points of view, analyze texts, evaluate arguments, and discover new ideas").[30] Students read the *Analects* of Confucius. In later iterations of the course, in order to create a civic engagement aspect to the pedagogy, Chilson added an essay assignment requiring students to think about their own role in society from a Confucian perspective. The goal of understanding the complexity of social and political forms enlarges into "recognizing other frames of reference" and then to an engagement with Confucius about how people can best serve the society in which they live.

Presumably, students need not adopt the Confucian position on such matters, but may merely use Confucius as a conversation partner (that is, demonstrate knowledge of Confucian ideas) as they explore their own values and commitments. In contrast, a fourth degree of normativity becomes visible in the chapter by Marianne Delaporte in which there is apparently an implicit normative position that students must approximate in order to succeed in the course. "Hospitality . . . is one of the basic and necessary duties of religious life."[31] It would seem that students who fail to recognize and articulate this position have not fully grasped the content of the course. Elizabeth Corrie's seminary course clearly operates at this fourth level of normativity as well.

This is why the nuancing in Nicholas Rademacher's chapter is so fascinating. Much of the rhetorical energy of the chapter is devoted to explaining how the goal of the course is to help students recognize, articulate, and develop their own existential meaning-making (second-degree normativity). He does this by (normatively) invoking James Fowler's cognitive development theory, which broadens the idea of faith and theology to encompass any articulation of value and power. Rademacher is quite concerned with inclusivity. He wants to bring diverse positions and understandings into the conversation—both the diverse students in the classroom, and the diverse community partners they will encounter. Thus he seems to be operating in the registry of third-degree normativity. And yet, he also seems to provide Catholic social teaching as normative content in the course, such that it becomes the normative lens through which students are to interpret their encounters with their community partners and their "shared center of value and power." This constitutes fourth-degree normativity. It is confusing because the first-degree normative course content (such as Fowler, but also the key theological concepts that comprise the content of the course) also functions to inform students' third-degree normative exploration of their own faith perspectives and thereby moves it toward a fourth-degree normative course in which adopting specific analyses and judgments constitutes successful learning in the course.

This is a central tension running through undergraduate learning goals for civic engagement: Is the goal to expose students to social realities by prescribing a service activity of some sort (first-degree normativity); to hope for, but not require, their personal reflection on these conditions (second-degree normativity); to require them to reflect on and judge these conditions (third-degree normativity); or does the goal reach all the way to successfully learning a normative understanding of what a just intervention should properly entail (fourth-degree normativity)? To what extent is the correct judgment and intervention part of the content of the course? For example, must Marianne Delaporte's students profess hospitality at the heart of Catholic social teaching to do well in her course? In Philip Wingeier-Rayo's course, must students recognize that charity for the poor is an inadequate response compared to working to establish justice and sustainability?

Note too that the move beyond judgment to actually take action is justified by the particular characteristics of the normative system through which the judgment is made. In such systems, the judgment to be made is that a particular kind of action must be taken. But note as well that just as third-degree normativity (making a personal judgment) is already contemplated in Locklin and Posman's expansive definition of first-degree critical thinking as found in the CLEA model, so too is the fourth-degree of normativity (which would require social action as the necessary outcome of proper judgment) also anticipated in this robust definition of first-degree critical thinking that requires not just personal judgment but finally action as well. One must ask, then, whether this expansive understanding of critical thinking is itself a creature of fourth-degree normativity.

Empirical Judgments Versus Normative Judgments

A remarkably robust fourth-degree normativity emerges from the chapter contributed by Karen Derris (trained as a scholar of Buddhist scripture) and Erin Runions (trained as a Bible scholar). It is remarkable in part because their doctoral "licensing" was not in the normative fields of theology, or ethics, but they have broadened their academic interests since graduate school to acquire expertise in the normative fields of social analyses and critique. Their first-degree normative approach to religious studies leads them to a critique of the concept of "the global." Their normative positions emerge from materialist, cultural studies and Marxist theory—not theology or ethics as practiced by a religious tradition.[32]

Derris and Runions locate their scholarly work in the field of religious studies, clearly not theology. Their analysis of the production of privilege and power through the trope of mobility in the sites of campus cafeteria workers and a women's prison are grounded in materialist cultural studies analysis, not theological concepts. This is political, not theological critique. So one must wonder if the McCutcheonite allergy to making "normative judgments concerning the way people ought to live or behave"[33] holds true when the judgment is grounded in materialist cultural studies critique, rather than what could be confidently dismissed as the "prescriptive 'ought' of the gods." These pedagogies of civic engagement teach students to analyze the real material relations and discursive constructions that produce privilege and inequality in society.

This project would seem to be quite comfortable within the human sciences rather than theology. And yet even though teaching students that we are all inevitably implicated in these power relations would claim to be an empirical analysis, it is remarkably congruent with the normative theological judgment that a McCutcheonite approach would reject when it appears in Marianne Delaporte's course. Additionally, the authors' pedagogical project to help students "locate themselves"[34] would seem to be the same movement employed by third-degree normativity (having the goal of helping students articulate, critique, and develop their own faith perspective). How different this looks when grounded in a materialist analysis of society as opposed to Christian theological categories.

This is where the McCutcheonite aversion to "normative judgment" appears narrow-minded and parochial. It is preoccupied with distinguishing itself from the normative judgments of religious subjectivities and religious phenomenon that constitute the object of their study. But this McCutcheonite position can appear oblivious to similarly normative socio-political judgments emerging from neo-Marxian analysis. One has to wonder why a McCutcheonite is comfortable thinking with the normative traditions emerging from Foucault, or the Frankfurt School, but not Barth or Catholic social ethics. When is an "ought" a religious ought? What counts as religious discourse—especially as McCutcheonites are wont to problematize the very category of "religion" as a modern invention of the scholars' study?[35]

The difficulty arises when the object of study is not some ancient rite or exotic belief but instead is a critical analysis of contemporary social structures and power. If the professor is trained in a normative discipline, then there would seem to be an equivalence between students reading, for example, Comaroff's explanation of religious behavior and Gramsci's explanation of political power—even though Gramsci would seem to be making *"normative judgments* concerning the way people *ought* to live or behave."[36] McCutcheonite contestation seems to emerge only when the analysis is based on "the ought of the gods" (identified as religious discourses) rather than "empirical analysis of material relations" (presumably *not* religious discourse). A McCutcheonite delimiting of religious studies to anthropological empirical phenomenon would not seem to have a complaint against a social justice–focused course—to the degree that the course remains focused on empirical analysis of social conditions and political power. It gets complicated when the course inevitably introduces discussion of how conditions *ought* to be. In religious studies the "ought" has been relegated to the category of what the religious people we are studying do and believe. The unquestionably academic pedigree of the normative sciences of social analysis complicates a McCutcheonite dismissal of the pedagogies of civic engagement. What seems to matter is not the presence of the normative "ought" in a course but whether that "ought" emerges from the gods or from empirical science (that is, whether it is construed as religious or not).

Learning About, Learning From, and Self-Reflexivity

The chapter by Derris and Runions is grounded in two fields of religious studies. First, there is the social scientific critique of material relations in the cafeteria workers and the women's prison, which has just been discussed. But then the chapter shifts to a third case in which Karen Derris brings her students to India for a long series of conversations with a Tibetan monk. This engagement seems to be lodged in a more conventionally religious studies approach: the course content exposes students to phenomenological understanding of the religious other. However, the orientation shifts when the chapter explains that "a central theme of concern for compassionately transforming the world and oneself wove the sessions together."[37]

This is precisely the kind of religion scholarship that McCutcheonites would reject—for it seems to constitute "learning to be religious" rather than "learning about religion." I would designate this as a fifth degree of normativity, characterized as learning *from*, not just *about* the religious other. And, whereas third- and fourth-degree normativity could be thought of as the students' development within his or her own theological tradition (helping them to become more religious as a stage in their cognitive development), this fifth degree is characterized by cognitive development through encounter with the religious other—a "learning about" for sure, but also a "learning *from*." Fifth-degree normativity contemplates the possibility that it is not just Aristotle, Augustine, or Martin Luther that might contribute to students' cognitive development and exploration of meaning and value—but also the traditions of the religious other.[38]

> The Karmapa's teachings on all of these topics challenged the students to investigate their own foundational assumptions about the world and, from there, how they might approach addressing global problems and inequities. Using common examples, the Karmapa invited the students to question their assumptions about the factors that govern our behavior. Are human beings naturally greedy? The students, particularly those majoring in economics, thought yes, but the Karmapa took them through a series of arguments that supported the counterclaim that greed is a habit that can be unlearned and need not govern personal behaviors or economic processes. The teachings emphasized the value of sharing ordinary experience for deepening awareness of our place in the world, for bridging very real differences in identity, and also for working for change.[39]

This is where the first-degree normative religious studies project to study about the other is merged with the third- and fourth-degree theological project to develop and refine one's own theological position. It is telling that the authors reach this point at the end of their chapter, having traversed through the more academically respectable materialist empirical studies grounding of their normative judgment and ethics.

This dynamic is even more explicit in Rebekka King's chapter. She appears to want to locate her course in first-degree normativity:

> As a scholar of religion, I am sensitive to the reluctance of many of my colleagues to employ pedagogical practices that might be deemed ideological or values-driven. . . . I at no point evaluate students based on behavior or attitude. In other words, I do not seek to ascertain whether or not my students have become "engaged" citizens. I feel that this type of assessment is not necessarily my role as an educator.[40]

Like Karen Derris, she exposes her students to the religious and socio-cultural other—this time in the form of a social worker's critique of the social relations productive of homelessness, and a tour of downtown Toronto as it is perceived by homeless people. King worries that the course might emphasize her own normative commitments to reducing homelessness in Toronto—a classic McCutcheonite concern for first-degree neutral objectivity rather than normative judgment. She addresses her concern by making the postmodernist self-reflective epistemological move that has become a hallmark of a certain brand of the humanities since the late twentieth century, a move not unsympathetically regarded by McCutcheonites in many cases. She writes:

> I have yet to resolve this concern [whether she is imposing her own normative judgments], but I found it helpful to address the issue with the students in class as part of our discussion and reflection about the field trip. Throughout the term, I raised questions with the students about the purpose of higher education and asked them to be active participants in my own sorting through my motivations for selecting the readings, assignments, and activities.[41]

King addresses the normativity at the heart of the pedagogies of civic engagement through this metacognitive and self-reflexive pedagogical strategy. This is the opposite of requiring students and professor to "bracket" all preconceptions and values, which seems to be required for first-degree dispassionate and nonjudgmental phenomenological study of the religious other. Instead, if there is a fear of normativity, then the response is to involve students in self-conscious reflection on this dilemma, to reveal the multiple possibilities of interpretation and experience, and to explore the positionality of the self as one such perspective. This breaks down the students' and the McCutcheonite assumption that we are "outsiders" to the phenomenon we are studying. King's students live in the city which is the object of their investigation. Their reflections on their perspectives are part of the inquiry, not separable from it.

> Because the course is focused in part on examining the city of Toronto, on the first day I suggest to the students that they are already experts in our field of study and bring to the table their own unique experiences as citizens of the city of Toronto. Perhaps this is a bold move in the context of religious studies, where we ask students to check their personal religious and ideological stances at the door. Positioning the students as "insiders," however, serves my pedagogical aim of providing a venue in which the experiences of those who occupy the margins of the city are emphasized.[42]

Thus we return to third-level normativity—requiring students to reflect on their own values and meaning-making, to make judgments. Once again, we have come full circle and can see how the expansive definition of critical thinking provided by the chapters of Locklin and Posman infuse each successive degree of normativity. It resides in first-degree normativity because it is the central cognitive development skill at the heart of the academic enterprise to educate students. Its insistence that critical thinking is not complete until the thinker has recognized his or her own social location and made a personal judgment undergirds both second- and third-degree normativity. The same is true for fourth- and fifth-degree normativity (which are developments, essentially, of the third degree). And here again, in King's self-reflexive turn on third-degree normativity, we are led to understand that

> Civic engagement in the classroom promotes a framework of learning in which students are encouraged to understand themselves as agents or participants in their field of study and in relation to their object of study, both inside and (especially) outside the classroom. Ideally, civic engagement positions students to ask critical and meaningful questions about their own roles within their communities and social spheres of influence.[43]

Some Final Thoughts

Not much has been said yet about the academic scandal of actually taking action. The pedagogies of civic engagement, and service learning before it, requiring students to get out of the classroom and take action in the world is at the root of the controversy. It is one thing to make normative judgments; in some sense, that seems to be at the heart of the academic project. But to take action clearly violates any sense of academic neutrality, not to mention the ivory tower.

Taking action is all the more provocative in the religious studies classroom because it again evokes comparisons with, or confusion with, the object of our study—religion. We tend to think of religion as a matter of belief, and behaviors. Much of what the religious studies scholar studies is the behaviors or actions of religious people. If the civically engaged religious studies classroom is studying the social justice actions of religiously motivated people, and then calling on students to engage in acts of civic engagement themselves, then this raises the specter of "being" religious within the academic process. It is one thing for students to study normative theological analyses of social justice issues, and even to make normative judgments on these social issues. But to then "act religiously"—to become civically engaged based on the religious judgments you have made—raises the specter of "being religious" in the academy. Religiously motivated behavior can take the form of worship, but also socio-political action in the world; should the purpose of religious studies be to transform undergraduates into religiously motivated actors? While the CLEA model establishes the idea that critical thinking is fulfilled by taking action, this becomes particularly uncomfortable in a field like religious studies in which religiously motivated behavior is at the heart of what we study.

Many of the authors in this volume have provided arguments for why the subject matter and methods of religious studies make it a particularly appropriate discipline for the pedagogies of civic engagement.[44] I find these arguments convincing and compelling. I can imagine a future academy in which a broader, more religiously and cross-culturally inflected view of the self and meaning has come to predominate the academy's self-understanding of its mission, due to the successful infiltration of religious studies disciplinary sensibilities into the rest of the academy.

However, when I think of the contention between religious studies and theology—a contention that bedevils our discipline and that we cannot seem to get past, although we are all so familiar with it, tired of it, fatigued by it, and have nothing new to say about it, and about which the next generation of scholars has no solution except to ignore it and move on—then I fear that the pedagogies of civic engagement in religious studies may inflame this schism in our discipline. Not only that, but many are still fighting the battle to establish legitimate academic credentials of the study of religion on campuses. It is not yet over: There is a continuing need to educate colleagues that our field is not churchy Bible study, fluff, and contemplation of the self. If religion departments spearhead the effort toward pedagogies of civic engagement, it is all the easier for other real, rigorous departments to dismiss the pedagogies as not-really-academic work.

Normative judgments, and taking action, are particularly problematic for the religious studies classroom, for real historical reasons. Perhaps we ought to lay low and let other disciplines take the lead on this. Perhaps, when pedagogies of civic engagement have become the norm in the academy, religious studies professors can participate along with the rest of their colleagues and it will not be controversial, even within the discipline itself. And once the rest of the liberal arts are busy making normative judgments on political, social, and ethical relations, and requiring students to articulate and act on their deepest values and commitments as part of the academic project, then perhaps at that point the marginalization of theology from the academy will have been reduced. It may be that *other* disciplines adopting the pedagogies of civic engagement—pedagogies which rightfully emanate from the religion and theology curriculum—may at last accomplish the final incorporation of the study of religion (even the *religious* study of religion) into the academy.

It is counterintuitive and would take a lot of discipline to not jump out in front to lead this revolution. It is certainly ours to lead. But maybe we can lead this revolution best from behind. Maybe we can pretend to let the other disciplines bring us along.

The "ought" that emerges from critical thinking about social conditions need-n't be located with the gods or in the religious studies classroom. We have seen herein that it emerges from materialist and discursive analytic traditions in the academy as well. The "ought" should be just as much at home in political science, philosophy, economics, and so forth.

In any case, once you have made the move expressed in the CLEA model and realized that critical thinking is consummated in judgment and action, then it is no longer a religious affair—or else all of critical thinking gets folded into a religious self-development project. All clear critical thinking involves existential position taking and action. It is either the case that this is because religion permeates all our critical thinking (permeates all of society) or because of the histor-ical and cultural practice of demarcating a certain realm of human behavior and speech as religious. And if this is the case, then why would McCutcheonites be so concerned to keep their classrooms free of what is just a human-constructed categorical distinction?

Notes

1. See the arguments by Posman and Locklin in chapter 2 of this volume.
2. Posman and Locklin, 5ff.
3. See chapter 10 of this volume, by Carolyn Medine, 174.
4. See the discussion of Martha Nussbaum (*The Clash Within*, 2007) and Frank H. T. Rhodes ("Universities and the Democratic Spirit," 2006), cited in chap-ter 2 of this volume, by Posman and Locklin, 3–4, 17 (nn. 1 and 4).
5. Readers might also be interested in Fred Glennon, "Service-Learning and the Dilemma of Religious Studies: Descriptive or Normative," in *From Cloister to Commons: Concepts and Models for Service Learning in Religious Studies*, ed. Richard Devine, Joseph A. Favazza, and F. Michael McLain (Washington, DC: American Association for Higher Education, 2002), 9–24.
6. Russell T. McCutcheon, *Critics Not Caretakers: Redescribing the Public Study of Religion* (Albany, NY: State University of New York Press, 2001). See as well a more recent title, with contributions from a broad swath of allies, William E. Arnal, Willi Braun, and Russell T. McCutcheon (eds.), *Failure of Nerve in the Academic Study of Religion: Essays in Honor of Donald Wiebe* (Sheffield, UK: Equinox Publishing, 2012).
7. Russell T. McCutcheon, "What Is the Academic Study of Religion?" University of Alabama. http://rel.as.ua.edu/pdf/rel100introhandout.pdf (accessed May 19, 2014; italics in the original).
8. Stanley Fish, *Save the World On Your Own Time* (Oxford and New York: Oxford University Press, 2008).
9. "Missions & Objectives," University of Alabama. http://ua.edu/mission.html (accessed May 19, 2014).

10. Medine, this volume, 176.

11. "The Mission of the University of Georgia," University of Georgia. http://www.uga.edu/profile/mission/ (accessed May 19, 2014).

12. See chapter 9 of this volume, by Elizabeth W. Corrie, 149.

13. Corrie, this volume, 154.

14. Corrie, this volume, 155.

15. Corrie, this volume, 157.

16. See chapter 4 of this volume, by Marianne Delaporte, 63.

17. Delaporte, this volume, 64.

18. See chapter 8 of this volume, by Nicholas Rademacher, 126.

19. Rademacher, this volume, 131–32.

20. Rademacher, this volume, 126.

21. Rademacher, this volume, 127.

22. McCutcheon, "What Is the Academic Study of Religion?" (see n. 7), accessed May 19, 2014.

23. See chapter 7 of this volume, by Philip Wingeier-Rayo, 119.

24. See chapter 3 of this volume, by Melissa C. Stewart, 52.

25. Stewart, this volume, 53–54.

26. Barbara E. Walvoord, *Teaching and Learning in College Introductory Religion Courses* (Malden, MA: Wiley-Blackwell, 2007).

27. Stewart, this volume, 55–56.

28. Stewart, this volume, 55.

29. Stewart, this volume, 50. The quotation is from Forrest Clingerman and Reid B. Locklin, "'Pedagogies for Civic Engagement': Collaborations and Complications in Religious Studies." Paper presented at the 10th annual National Outreach Scholarship Conference, University of Georgia, Athens, Georgia, September 29, 2009 (UMS provided by the authors).

30. Stewart, this volume, 50.

31. Delaporte, this volume, 63.

32. See chapter 11 of this volume, by Derris and Runions, 184ff.

33. McCutcheon, "What Is the Academic Study of Religion?" (see n. 7).

34. Derris and Runions, this volume, 199.

35. See the oft-cited opening passages of Jonathan Z. Smith's *Imagining Religion* (Chicago: University of Chicago Press, 1988), xi, as well as Timothy Fitzgerald, *The Ideology of Religious Studies* (Oxford and New York: Oxford University Press, 2000) and Tomoko Masuzawa, *The Invention of World Religions: Or, How European Universalism Was Preserved in the Language of Pluralism* (Chicago: University of Chicago Press, 2005).

36. McCutcheon, "What is the Academic Study of Religion?" accessed May 19, 2014.

37. Derris and Runions, this volume, 196.

38. Chilson's assignment with the *Analects* (discussed in chapter 3 of this volume) demonstrates this degree of normativity as well.

39. Derris and Runions, this volume, 196–97.
40. See chapter 5 of this volume, by Rebekka King, 82.
41. King, this volume, 82.
42. King, this volume, 76.
43. King, this volume, 76.
44. See chapters 10, 11, and 3 of this volume, by Medine, Derris and Runions, and Stewart, respectively, as well as chapter 2, by Posman with Locklin.

Dreams of Democracy

Tina Pippin

*Revolutionary change does not come as one cataclysmic
moment (beware of such moments!) but as an endless succes-
sion of surprises, moving zigzag toward a more decent society.*

—HOWARD ZINN[1]

"CIVIC ENGAGEMENT" HAS a lot of names and incarnations; for example, service
learning, experiential learning, in-community learning, university-community
partnerships, participatory action research, grassroots movement building. Each
of these manifestations has theoretical and ideological grounding that ranges
from career externships and internships (through a career planning office) to
academic (experience, research-based learning, and theory-practice learning).
The chapters in this volume show the range of and possibilities for academic
connections for undergraduate students and faculty beyond the walls of their educational institutions.

In the first section of this book, the authors set the framework for this volume
and for any discussion of civic engagement. From the complex intellectual issues
to the diversities of social locations, to mutual accountability in society and "motivated action" for social justice—these four components of the CLEA model of
civic engagement are interwoven, while forming a critical conversation on multiple levels. These are difficult dialogues across multiple constituencies and power
bases. In their discussions of the CLEA model, Locklin and Posman raise the
necessary questions about both individual and systemic roles in civic engagement. For example, is a main role of the university to uphold the (neoliberal, capitalist) status quo? Or is the university an institution of higher questioning toward
"the beloved community," that challenges the status quo? In other words, is one
role—and responsibility—of the university to challenge injustices? I am thinking
of, for example, the case of inclusion of "undocumented" immigrant students in
my home state and the creation of Freedom University at the University of Georgia.[2] The spectrum of civic engagement is long, and as many institutions "lean
in" toward the corporate model of civic engagement as/for career development

and planning, the articles in this volume challenge us to think toward working with diverse communities to create a more just world.

I want to take further this template of the CLEA model, with special focus on action and the question of civic engagement in the classroom as transformative learning. I want to follow the line taken by Locklin and Posman from Freire and bell hooks to other critical pedagogues who provide further conversation on knowledge, experience, power, ideology, and the structural underpinnings of oppression and injustice. The lens of critical and radical (and some anarchist) pedagogies (plural) provides opportunities for further critical reflection. After a brief introduction to the continuum of civic engagement movements, I want to engage critical pedagogy theories as a way of conversing with the range of ideas in chapters in this volume. Critical pedagogy will also open up some opportunities for dialogue with the possibilities of civic engagement in religious and theological studies. And critical pedagogy also serves as the grounding for social justice and change.

I am working from a basic definition of critical pedagogy from Paulo Freire, who saw education as a space for critique, conscientization, resistance, possibility, hope, and liberation from oppression. For Freire critical pedagogy offers students and teachers a way out of the "banking method" of education and into learning and speaking the "word," while bringing their experience of the world to bear. Critical pedagogy is about paying attention to multiple forms of oppression in both the seen and the unseen operations of power in the classroom and the world. Freire's seminal book, *The Pedagogy of the Oppressed* (1970/1997),[3] is the theoretical starting point for a movement that includes Marxism and neo-Marxism, feminisms, critical race theory, postmodernism, postcolonialism, anarchism, and grassroots organizing and activism. My purpose here is to offer a response to these articles through the lens of critical pedagogies (plural) and to ask: Where are the boundaries in mainstream civic engagement thinking, and what do critical pedagogies (and the social movements they inspire) tell us about the possibilities for social transformation?

Democracy on the Continuum

Civic engagement in higher education has multiple origins. John Dewey is one of the earliest theorists, with educational theory grounded in the practice of democracy. For Dewey, "A democracy is more than a form of government; it is primarily a mode of associated living, of conjoint communicated experience."[4] The lived experience of the world and the classroom intersect. Dewey saw his students with/in their whole contexts and engagement with their worlds, working with them to practice democracy in the classroom and beyond.

Dewey's educational theory provided the background for theories of civic engagement. There is a genealogy from Dewey through social psychologist Kurt Lewin to Paulo Freire to David Kolb and many others. Variables ranging from learning styles and multiple intelligences to social justice theories and concepts of individual and systemic transformation inform civic engagement pedagogy. Kolb furthered the connection of experience to knowledge, as theory is to practice for Freire, and he raised the importance of the reflective piece as key to becoming a change agent in society.[5]

Civic engagement pedagogy has multiple roots. Almost always noted as a key source document is Boyer's 1990 article on engaged scholarship, in the Carnegie Foundation report *Scholarship Reconsidered*. Boyer summarized the scholarship of discovery, integration, shared knowledge, and the application of knowledge. Professors are to become "'reflective practitioners,' moving from theory to practice, and from practice back to theory, which in fact makes theory, then, more authentic. . . ."[6] Boyer stresses "that the work of the academy ultimately must be directed toward larger, more humane ends. . . ."[7] Boyer called for efforts to bridge the divide between "town and gown" and called scholarship to become fully accountable to society.

Another important document is the *Wingspread Declaration* of 1999 by Campus Compact, a community engagement organization founded by college presidents in 1985.[8] This Declaration calls for engaged and public scholarship both at and beyond the institution. Their operating question concerns deconstructing the individualistic and competitive nature of higher education and understanding all parties at an institution as "agents of democracy" that are connected with their communities.[9] Democracy is understood as relational, in a sort of "it takes a village" approach. Students are not empty receptacles to be filled by expert faculty; in Freirean fashion, students ". . . need to be understood as co-creators of their learning."[10] This learning, facilitated by and with faculty, consists of "real projects of impact and relevance through which students learn the skills, develop the habits and identities, and acquire the knowledge to contribute to the general welfare."[11] The participants at this 1999 conference set as their guiding question the responsibility of all constituents at an institution to work toward a democratic society: "What will it mean for our institutions, comprised of faculty, students, staff, and administration and guided by deliberations of trustees, to be filled with the democratic spirit as whole institutions?"[12]

The starting point for this project was with the institutional commitments, both internally and externally. Democracy is defined in more conservative terms; there is no oppositional politics here. The "democratic spirit" involves a needed connection of the institution with local and global communities. Trustees and administrators are supporters of this broader understanding of scholarship and engaged learning. The goal is in "making democracy come alive,"[13] but what if these newly learned skills and knowledges lead to critique of the institution—for example, its investments, environmental footprint, low-wage pay to custodial and dining hall staff, institutional racism, etc.? And what role does the community play in research and teaching?

The Kellogg Commission on the Future of State and Land-Grant Universities document, "From *Returning to Our Roots: The Engaged Institution*": Executive Summary with 'Seven-Part Test,'" began to answer this question of the role of community partners in civic engagement relationships.[14] This document holds that

> By engagement, we refer to institutions that have redesigned their teaching, research, and extension and service functions to become even more sympathetically and productively involved with their communities, however community may be defined. . . . Embedded in the engagement ideal is a commitment to sharing and reciprocity. By engagement the Commission envisions partnerships, two-way streets defined by mutual respect among the partners for what each brings to the table.[15]

The Executive Summary also addresses what students bring back to the institution from their experiences in community: "We believe an engaged university can enrich the student experience and help change the campus culture,"[16] providing research opportunities for students and faculty, but, even more, connecting the university with problem-solving and social change in their communities. They call for plural definitions of community that are situated in place/s. Relationships and mutual accountability are central to the engaged campus.[17] The focus is on mutuality and the benefits of maintaining and nurturing relationships: "Close partnerships with the surrounding community help demonstrate that higher education is about important values such as informed citizenship and a sense of responsibility.[18]" The Kellogg Commission Summary devised a "Seven-Part Test" for engaged institutions: "1. Responsiveness"; "2. Respect for partners"; "3. Academic neutrality"; "4. Accessibility"; "5. Integration"; "6. Coordination"; "7. Resource partnerships."[19] Commitment and leadership vision from administration is key, as is funding support and commitment to the "long haul." The assumption is that there are transformative possibilities for both the institution and the community.

Since the mid-1980s Campus Compact has set a standard for civic engagement in higher education, with over 1,100 colleges and universities as members. They define their mission and vision as follows:

> *Mission:* Campus Compact advances the public purpose of colleges and universities by deepening their ability to improve community life and to educate students for civic and social responsibility.

> *Vision:* Campus Compact envisions colleges and universities as vital agents and architects of a diverse democracy, committed to educating students for responsible citizenship in ways that both deepen their education and improve the quality of community life. We challenge all of higher education to make civic and community engagement an institutional priority. Students engage and reflect in academic courses and internships, learning civic skills of both research and practice.[20]

Campus Compact draws on Kolb's format for theory-practice-reflection in being a resource for faculty and students in developing courses and partnerships in community. The emphasis is on real and reflective involvement of institutions of higher education in their communities, and also on the encouragement for lifelong citizenship.

Similarly, the Kettering Colloquium produced a white paper on democratic engagement in 2009 outlining the challenges of community involvement and democracy. Their central question is:

> How can colleges and universities cultivate caring and creative democratic citizens and advance democracy in schools, universities, communities, and society? What sort of institutional commitments are needed to foster civic engagement among students and among academics in order to advance participatory democracy on campus, in the community, and the wider society?[21]

The Kettering paper moves toward a more egalitarian relationship with community partners. They emphasize that "Democratic engagement seeks the public good with the public and not merely for the public as a means to facilitating a more active and engaged democracy."[22] This statement comes close to the participatory action research movement (PAR), in which researchers work in tandem with community members to set research questions and goals. PAR works through and with the knowledge and experience of the grassroots, through a "deliberative democracy."[23] In its most ideal form PAR recognizes and deconstructs the hierarchy and divide between researcher and community. The brush against Freirean theory is evident in these organizations and white papers that call for equalizing the distance between higher educational institutions and their social and political contexts.

A more recent organization takes Campus Compact's mission and vision a bit further, with a focus on connecting undergraduate and especially graduate education (through their PAGE program, Publicly Active Graduate Education Fellows) to public scholarship and action. Imagining America: Artists and Scholars in Public Life defines its mission and vision:

> *Vision:* Publicly engaged artists, designers, scholars, and community activists working toward the democratic transformation of higher education and civic life.

Mission: Imagining America creates democratic spaces to foster and advance publicly engaged scholarship that draws on arts, humanities, and design. We catalyze change in campus practices, structures, and policies that enables artists and scholars to thrive and contribute to community action and revitalization.[24]

The consortium Imagining America calls for "publicly engaged scholarship," or PES.[25] Timothy Eatman summarizes the vision of Imagining America: ". . . a new citizenry is emerging within the academy."[26] This citizenry imagines democratic change within certain (foundation funded) boundaries. For example, the main goals of the Imagining America group are:

- "Scholarship and Creativity in the Real World"
- "Negotiating Collaborative Work"
- "Reflection in Context"
- "Communicating with Others"[27]

The linking of scholarship and work in the public sphere takes a multiplicity of skills, from research to ethnography to writing and speaking to theater to collaboration with community partners to create new spaces for learning—and social action. In engaging communities Imagining America foregrounds the arts, especially theater. This organization is pushing the civic engagement field further through their emphasis with the arts and activism and their concern with equitable university and community partner relationships.

Imagining America (IA) Associate Director Kevin Bott suggests that the organization's orientation toward social justice gives special priority to diversity and inclusion and the added element of play: "Positioning ourselves as a higher education consortium at the forefront of elevating and disseminating community strengths and knowledge points toward a critical responsibility to leverage the academy's resources to strengthen those communities. Otherwise, there will truly be 'no there.'"[28] After Bott attended the IA conference as a graduate student in 2006, he concluded "that higher education was about civic identity and existed to fulfill, in part, a democratic purpose."[29] But what if the institutions that provide the spaces for the civics lessons and experiences that lead to student enlightenment and transformative action in the world also are the spaces of oppression, upholding corporate, neoliberal models of work and multiple hierarchies of power? Bott dismantles the normative idea of the separation between knowledge and activism in higher education and shows what "publicly engaged art and scholarship" entails.[30] He stresses: "To sustain oneself through the work of effecting change, one must connect the individual acts that attempt to alter departmental and institutional stances toward engagement to the larger goals and ideals of democratic renewal, civic agency, and higher education's role in a democracy."[31] In these ways Imagining America has begun to ask the questions of the complex ethical and political relations in civic engagement activity.

Imagining America is on the edge of more radical pedagogical theories and practices. Their PAGE fellows take the vision of Imagining America even further. For example, Chris Dixon and Alexis Shotwell ask how graduate students, from an often precarious power position in the academy, begin to combine their activism and scholarship: "How might activist grad students concerned with fundamentally transforming this society make sense of the university? How might radicals involved in the university relate to it, evading its pitfalls and exploiting its openings? And most importantly, how can the space of the university be made useful for building broad-based radical left movements?"[32] They offer five suggestions:

1. "Understand the Academy as a Nexus for Organizing and Capacity-Building."
2. "Work with Undergraduates."
3. "Organize Grad Students."
4. "Question Professionalization and Individualism."
5. "Build Accountability to Movements into Research and Teaching."[33]

They call for collaborative work and movement building. They also make accountability a central aspect of activism and of teaching: "When, as academics, we think of ourselves as standing in solidarity with movements as equal participants in struggles for social transformation, our relationship to what work we do, how we share it, and for whom we're doing it might fundamentally change."[34] They want to "use the classroom as a place to teach for liberation."[35] Ideally, the activist-scholar/scholar-activist no longer has to be a split self in the classroom. In my own context at a small, southern, liberal arts college, I do not worry about the costs of activism at my college to me as a full professor, but to my department and thereby to my students. Am I limiting their opportunities (in terms of new faculty hires, more general institutional support) through my own oppositional work? The "split self" is embedded in a web of power relations that calls for constant negotiation. As Dixon and Shotwell show, the positions of students in the hierarchy have to be mapped out. They offer ways for activist graduate students to "fit in" the academy—that is, to not get kicked out of programs, to be able to write their passion in a dissertation, and to be hirable in (or outside) the academy. Imagining America broadens the usefulness of graduate education, making it more relevant for a democratic society. The logical progression is a systemic change in the structure of higher education, one in which the transformative movements are students and faculty working in curricular and extracurricular ways with their communities. This is a utopian ideal that would involve a revolution in higher education. Just imagine: university presidents, along with trustees, students, faculty, custodians, landscapers, and all other institutional stakeholders at the U.S. Social Forum, all fostering democratic spaces at their institutions and conceiving new commitments to transforming the world.

Organizing for Change

Back to reality: Imagining America and all the other groups just mentioned, and all of us who teach or work at non-profit educational groups, are embedded in the neoliberal, capitalist system. Neoliberalism is about freedom and human dignity, while holding fast to global, capitalist principles. For example, the Occupy Movement was a response to the neoliberal defense of the elite 1 percent and the political and economic policies that protected their interests against the 99 percent.[36] Civic engagement is done in this neoliberal context, even with resistance and real, transformative community partnerships and the rest. How do we loosen the corporate ties that bind us in civic engagement? Brandon Kliewer offers one critique of neoliberalism's hold on civic engagement. He examines how neoliberal ideology both informs and hampers civic engagement work for justice.[37] One aspect of this capitalist hold is the presence of foundations in funding university programs, and in defining the parameters of "citizenship" and "engagement." He gives as an example the Americorps VISTA program, funded by the Corporation for National and Community Service, with goals that limit systemic justice work.[38] Governmental and private foundations have (neoliberal) strings attached. The reality is that most of the funding for the mainstream civic engagement organizations comes from foundations; there is no pure, ethical ground.

This practice of citizenship in the world takes not only interpretation but also reflection of one's social location. Sylvia Gale, for example, uses an exercise in her classes to get students to think about their roles in the world ("Roles of Engagement: A Workshop Exercise"): "1. In the center of your blank piece of paper, write the thing that you are for. This is your central commitment. The exercise works best if you express this in the simplest, most general terms possible."[39] Next you define "the roles that you currently inhabit in relationship to this commitment," connecting the roles with the central commitment and circling the most important roles.[40] The messy connections eventually start to come together in a more coherent whole on the page, especially if colored pencils are used. Gale relates, "The newness that emerges in this kind of 'roles thinking,' however, is that the juice lies *in the intersections* themselves; the projects literally take shape in the spaces between roles. If this is so, then perhaps the highest goal of the engaged public scholar—the end state of the professional trajectory—is not the integration of roles but an ongoing and dynamic multiplicity."[41]

Another interesting example of a course in which students are civically engaged is from Marshall Ganz's Leading Change Network. In the syllabus for his course, "Organizing: People, Power & Change," Ganz explains the responsibility of class participants and thus reveals the underlying pedagogy of the course:

> This course is for students interested in learning to how to create social change through collective action. There are no prerequisites. Students with and without "real world" experience find the class equally useful. Students with a strong a commitment to the community, organization, or goals on behalf of which they are working will be most successful. Because it is a course in practice, it requires trying new things, risking failure, and stepping outside your comfort zone. As reflective practitioners, students will learn through critical reflection on their experience, feedback and coaching. If you are not prepared to step outside your comfort zone, this class is not for you.[42]

This call to "step outside your comfort zone" is fundamental in most civic engagement courses.

Another prominent example is the Clemente Course. Earl Shorris started the Clemente Course in the Humanities in 1995 after hearing the stories of imprisoned poor people. From the beginnings at Bard College, Shorris expanded the program to teach humanities to the poor and homeless in the United States and Mexico. Using university and college professors and artists and others to teach courses in philosophy, history, art history, critical thinking, and writing, Shorris saw a way for those imprisoned from poverty to find empowerment and participation in political life. Full citizenship means educated citizens. Part of the Clemente Course mission statement includes civic engagement: "participants develop crucial tools to set in motion personal and societal change, and are empowered to participate more fully in civic life." One of their goals also defines civic engagement in a particular way: "To strengthen habits of reflection and critical thinking so that students are better able to control the direction of their lives and engage effectively in action to improve their communities."[43] The rhetoric that students "are empowered" can easily slide toward traditional hierarchical models of education and goes against the philosophy of more Freirean-influenced groups such as the Highlander Center. In the Freirean model, students, with the teachers, create the spaces for mutual empowerment. Everyone brings some knowledge and experience about civic engagement that can be shared. Power (connected with knowledge) is not a commodity held only by the teacher. And it earns dividends when invested in a communal bank.

There is often institutional backlash to certain forms of engagement that might threaten the neoliberal status quo. In this volume, Marianne Delaporte mentions a report done by the California Association of Scholars for the Regents of the University of California, "A Crisis of Competence: The Corrupting Effect of Political Activism in the University of California," from April 2012.[44] This report links radical, extreme, leftist (usually named as socialist and Marxist) faculty with the decline not only of the curriculum and student learning, but with the nation itself. The report uses rhetoric such as "diluted diplomas" and "injury to democracy" as strong blaming of these leftist faculty for poor textbook choices: they provide Beverly Tatum's *Why Are All the Black Kids Sitting Together in the Cafeteria?* as an example (!)—a definite targeting of critical race scholarship. The report states that "political activism is the opposite of academic teaching and re-search."[45] The report calls immoral any involvement of the university in political activism, such as the Occupy Movement. The claim is ultimately that such political involvement drastically reduces the quality of education. So the commitments and activism of Howard Zinn, the students in the Killer Coke movement, around seventy-five campus living wage movements, the Dreamers, along with Occupy and others, are bringing the university and the country down. This report reifies the corporate ties of universities and makes transparent the aversion of the status quo toward human and civil rights. The National Association of Scholars claims political neutrality, but it is part of a wider and extremely influential, conservative political agenda. Civic engagement pedagogy raises the questions about who defines democracy, and the power relations that monitor the acts of defining.

The Challenge of Democracy

Since the dominant ideology at undergraduate institutions in the United States is neoliberalism, the civic engagement we do may be in collusion with institutional corporate ties, or in opposition to them, or, more likely, a complex combination of the two. In this context democracy has many definitions, depending on the definer. Corresponding theories of education also matter in defining democracy. Paul Carr contests simple definitions of democracy and critiques democracy as a catch-all term. Using work by Luis Armano Gandin and Michael Apple on "thin" versus "thick" democracy, Carr exposes most uses of the term "democratic education" as illusory and calls for critical pedagogical theory to find the thick spaces and practices.[46] Gandin and Apple studied an alternative Citizen School in Porto Alegre, Brazil, and they describe what a thick democracy looks like: "Challenging the elitist belief that impoverished people from poor neighborhoods or slums cannot participate because they are 'ignorant,' the Citizen School inverts this logic, placing the ones who live the problems at the center as the people in a privileged position to construct alternatives."[47] Critical pedagogy offers ways to disrupt and resist normative power relations and to connect democracy (and democratic education) to social justice.[48] For example, voting is an important part of a democratic society, but a thicker definition leads to an investigation of voting rights and other complexities of this form of democracy. Democracy is a form of politics, so Carr advises we see the political connection with educational theories and practices. Ultimately, for critical pedagogy the starting point for democratic education is with the grassroots, privileging their knowledge and experiences as the starting point for dialogue. And dialogue provides the grounding for movement building for social change. In this volume, Philip Wingeier-Rayo asks, "Is democracy reducible to discourse?" He answers that democracy has to be modeled as a pedagogical strategy in undergraduate courses, and the modeling must take place outside the classroom for students to engage in a dialogue with the world.

Dialogue and political participation are crucial. Democracy requires an engaged citizenship. Paul Kivel defines citizens more broadly as the "non-ruling class." He defines democracy as "the participation in decision-making by the people affected by those decisions."[49] Movement building for democracy is important and requires citizen resistance. Kivel outlines the key questions for resistance:

> Who am I in solidarity with? Who am I allied with? Who benefits from the work I do and the life I lead? Am I going to be content with a social, political, and economic structure that is exploitative, violent, mean spirited, undemocratic, and devastating to all life? Or am I ready to actively work to change the system? Do I just want to create the illusion of a safe and secure harbor for myself and my family, or will I reach out and join with others to work for justice and rebuild our communities and our world?[50]

The move from individual to systemic critique is clear here; one has to employ a criticism of self and of systems of oppression. Kivel calls for accountability, both individual and communal, as foundational for real social change. Anything less may be useful or personally transformative, but it does not embed justice in communities for the long haul.

We Make the Road by Walking

I want to return to Freire and to critical pedagogies as ways of learning to question the theories and practices of civic engagement. In his posthumous book, *A Pedagogy of Solidarity*, Freire asks, "How do we create the possibility to educate and to be educated?"[51] And back to the quote from Howard Zinn at the beginning of this chapter: What is our *moment*? And how to we determine it? And with whom do we await, prepare, and discover our moment? Zinn and Freire and many others remind us that our historical and political contexts are important to our situatedness in the classroom. We have to get out of our comfort zones (Ganz) to transform our teaching, and ourselves as teachers, and thus to be full participants with our students.

Broadly speaking, in his major books Freire moved from the oppressed to critical consciousness to hope to solidarity. He did so while working with a range of groups and was primarily located in institutions of higher education and the state. Still, he was always informed by the Brazilian peasants who educated him about their struggles. Literacy was a central theme for Freire, for with reading and writing came citizenship and power. Who are our cohorts on the journey? Freire reminds us, "As a consequence of thinking in favor of whom, in favor of what, in favor of what dream I am teaching, I will have to think against whom, against what, against what dream I am teaching."[52] In this way Freire tempers fatalism with hope, through collective dreaming of possibilities of freedom and justice, and democracy. This dreaming is too often in opposition with the ruling elite, the status quo, and with its indoctrination of students. Freire acknowledges the classroom is no neutral, objective zone. He clarifies that critical pedagogy is not about indoctrination to a Marxist or neo-Marxist doctrine. "Teachers should not have to hide their dreams, but they have the duty to say that there are different dreams."[53] And even further, "The teacher must be a question who embodies and becomes a testimony."[54]

Freire calls for a delineation of the operating ideologies in society, and how this is a first step to building a movement:

> My first step would be to work in something that I call the ideological map of the institution in which I am now. What do I mean by working on, or creating, or making the ideological map? It means that I need to know who I can count on, with whom I am alike, and against whom I may have to be. If I don't know the levels of power of those opposite me I cannot fight. . . . You have to be patiently impatient to do things, and if thousands of people would do that, this could transform society.[55]

Freire advocates for a critically reflective practice that is first full of questions about why the status quo remains as it is. The role of education is to create questions, especially about its own ideological commitments and practices. Freire summarizes this stance: "But at its best, education is much more than a technique, education is an understanding of the world in order to transform it."[56] And questioning is necessary for deeper understanding.

Along with questioning, it is necessary to dream big. Freire's emphasis on dreams is not impractical: dreams lead to imagining the possible. "We are surrounded by a pragmatic discourse that would have us adapt to the facts of reality. *Dreams*, and *utopia*, are called not only useless, but positively impeding.

(After all, they are an intrinsic part of any educational practice with the power to unmask the dominant lies)."[57] For those engaged in long struggles for justice in our educational institutions the journey is wearisome and there are few victories. The institution opts for survival, and the power base of economic viability, trustees, corporate support, and "best practices" all converge to ensure an institutional future. The web of relations in higher education—from the "top colleges" lists to standardized tests to grants from foundations to alumnae giving and on and on—are quite complex. More radical forms of civic engagement for social change do not hold the center (and centrist) positions. Yet there is a shared dream for human rights and social change, and those who dream it have hope.

Freire calls for the necessity of hope in the midst of the struggle of democratic education:

> Hope is an ontological need. Hopelessness is but hope that has lost its bearings, and become a distortion of that ontological need. When it becomes a program, hopelessness paralyzes us, immobilizes us. We succumb to fatalism, and then it becomes impossible to muster the strength we absolutely need for a fierce struggle that will re-create the world. I am hopeful, not out of mere stubbornness, but out of an existential, concrete imperative.[58]

There is hope, along with struggle, and along with "rage and love."[59] "One of the tasks of the progressive educator, through a serious, correct political analysis, is to unveil opportunities for hope, no matter what the obstacles may be."[60] "As a consequence, one of the things to do for the oppressed people is to work on the question of hope, to increase hope, hope in spite of it all. Because without hope, there can be no struggle."[61] The oppressor works to kill hope, so the oppressed must work to regain hope. "This happens when the oppressed are engaged at some level in a process of [political] struggle."[62]

Freire calls for educational specialists to have a particular role in teaching content, but he pushes for a wider net that includes and respects all the players in an educational institution: "What is the role, on various levels, of those at the bases—cooks, maintenance workers, security personnel, who find themselves involved in a school's educational practice? What is the role of families, social organizations, and the local community?"[63] Freire calls this reciprocal, democratic model "the knowledge of living experience."[64] This sharing of knowledges and experiences is key to choosing educational content and curriculum and to forming alliances both on and beyond campus.

So what does critical pedagogy have to say to civic engagement in the classroom? Using Freire as one spokesperson, a more holistic approach is for the pedagogy of the classroom to engage the study and practice of democracy in a way that informs movement beyond the classroom. As Melissa Stewart asks in this volume, "Is civic-*mindedness* enough or is *practice* required?" Critical pedagogy provides a bridge between experience and movement building. In the range of practicums and internships I facilitate, there is a continuum of experiences: from a 20-hour placement in a homeless shelter for women and children in a "Bible and Liberation" class (e.g., tutoring school-age children; answering phones), to a 140-hour internship at that same shelter (e.g., doing case work; forming a summer mentoring group for youth). Critical pedagogy enables us (students and teacher) to learn and analyze the context of homelessness and poverty and engage the systemic causes.

I am a strong believer that we can do civic engagement at our own institutions. In the aforementioned Bible course, the other practicum option is with our campus Living Wage Campaign, supervised by a student leader in that movement. The local begins with our classroom spaces: Our floors and walls and boards and trash and recycling and restrooms and heat and air conditioning and campus food and lawns—all are maintained by staff who make less than a living wage.[65] When students interview staff, they enter into a parallel universe to my college. After the initial "disorientation tour," they formulate their own assessments of the different dreaming of these staff (and the living wage movement and the unions) and the dreams of the administration and trustees, and begin to figure out their own dreams of social transformation.

In working to understand the difficult task of movement building, it is necessary to look to the past. The most relevant example from the past for me is the Citizenship Schools. They began in the 1950s out of the need for literacy to pass state voting tests that were required for African Americans to be able to vote. A group at a Highlander Center workshop on the United Nation's Declaration of Human Rights identified the need, and the initial action. A Charleston, South Carolina, schoolteacher, Septima Clark, along with Esau Jenkins, a bus driver on Johns Island, South Carolina, attended the workshop and made the connection from global concerns to their local situation of voting rights and literacy issues.[66] Their central questions were: "How do you treat people with respect? How do you do a program that treats people with respect?"[67] Later Bernice Robinson, Septima Clark's niece and an owner of a beauty parlor in Charleston, attended a Highlander workshop. She was inspired to start the first classes that became the Citizenship Schools. Jenkins was already using his bus as a school, teaching passengers on their trips to and from work.[68] The document Bernice Robinson used as the first reading was the Universal Declaration of Human Rights; she put it up on the wall of her shop and read it to the group. Freire comments, "Bernice used the Declaration of Human Rights as a codification . . . and when she showed the declaration to them, the *debating* started. . . . they were reading the world and not yet the words of the declaration."[69] They may not have known individual words, but the whole meaning of the document was clear.[70] In working through this document and the South Carolina voters' test, and in learning to write and read, the group reinvented themselves and found their political power.[71] The goal was a voter registration card; the group identified the primary need of political empowerment, and literacy was a skill on the way.

Critical pedagogy is instructive here. Freire's clear starting place is "trying to learn from them [the grassroots, students, etc.] how to work with them."[72] Myles Horton completes this thought: "It [Citizenship School] was a school to help people learn to analyze and give people values, and they became the organizers."[73] So what does critical pedagogy mean for civic engagement? Despite the often loose terms of hope and love and freedom and heart and solidarity, these theories open up ways to question and critique the places of students, faculty, and institutions in civic engagement work. But Seehwa Cho warns against the idealization of the teacher: "I think educators have only limited power or roles to play for social change. However, as long as we proclaim that critical pedagogy (and critical education) strives to be an agent of social change, I think it would be helpful to at least brood over what kind of society we are pursuing and imagining."[74] Thus a continuous practice of critical reflection is in order, along with openness to displacement—to discovering different spaces both in and outside the classroom for civic engagement.

Activist Dreaming

As I mentioned earlier, one track of civic engagement pedagogy engages social movements and activists.[75] The International Network of Scholar-Activists is a group that supports the World Social Forums and meets at the annual American Sociological Association meeting.[76] The U.S. Social Forum is another current-day model of a national effort to provide spaces for dialogue and movement building across marginalized groups and multiple oppressions.[77] These groups involve scholar-activists who in turn often take these movements to the classrooms and the classrooms to the movements.

As I also mentioned earlier, Imagining America has some commitments to activist movements, primarily through the work of some of their graduate fellows who are pushing these boundaries. One of the graduate student authors in *Collaborative Futures*, Chris Dixon, wrote his dissertation on the activist politics of some transformative movements. Dixon defines activism as "mobilizing people around particular issues based on morality or politics."[78] Activists are generally on the fringes of a movement, although they can also be from within oppressed communities. Dixon explains further: "Activism is thus associated with people who are relatively privileged—those who can choose to be concerned about something or not. As well, activist work frequently involves educational events. . . . It is aimed at expressing opposition to specific policies or institutions, whether through holding vigils, marching, occupying, street fighting, or some other form of action."[79] He differentiates activism from organizing, which he defines as "building the capacity of a group of people directly impacted by injustice so that they can struggle to transform their situation." Organizing involves accountability and collective action.[80] Activists are able to step in and out of movement building and hold involvement in multiple movements at once. The distinction between activism and organizing "can guide us toward more powerful, strategic, and grounded forms of political activity."[81] In this messy relationship, Dixon points out that activism can serve as a spark and organizing as grounding for action.[82] Further, he explains the transformative process of direct action organizing:

> . . . organizing [is] a collective process through which we come to encounter one another as dignified subjects and to learn new things about our world, our movements, and ourselves. This is organizing as *revelation*—a process through which all involved are transformed as we fight to transform society—and it is at the core of another politics.[83]

Movement building draws on critical pedagogy that is known as popular education. The Citizenship Schools that emerged from the Highlander Research and Education Center workshops used this term, as do Project South and other movement building groups. Dixon offers a definition of popular education as "an approach and a set of methods for helping groups of people develop critical analysis from their lived experience—linking individual understandings in a broader context—and to use that shared analysis as a basis for planning and action."[84] "Used well, then, popular education turns the facilitated process of dialogue, listening and reflection into a political weapon."[85] In the fuller range of possibilities for civic engagement, learning from and with activist groups (both on and off campus) shows alternative practices and possibilities for social change.

Conclusion: Zooming into the Future

In the field of religious studies, Jonathan Z. Smith contemplates the correlation between scholarship and civic engagement: "What ought not to be at controversy is the purpose for which we labor, that long-standing and deeply felt perception of the relationship between liberal learning and citizenship."[86] For Smith education is about learning to develop arguments and distinguishing between the range of possible interpretations. According to Smith, "In each of the central arguments between the major modes of human knowledge one is confronted with a choice as to citizenship, with a choice as to the implications and lineaments of possible worlds in which one might choose to dwell."[87] But does Smith intend that all this learning can take place in the "ivory tower" and that students need not step outside their privileged walls? Whatever his standpoint, Smith's thinking on citizenship invites an opening up of the classroom to the world. Religious and theological studies are logical places (in my mind) for these openings and dialogical practices.

I am reminded of the exercise Wingeier-Rayo (in this volume) uses in his classes to teach students perspective and point of view through storytelling with the pictures that zoom in.[88] Such an exercise engages the imagination about how stories are told and passed down to us. And stories serve as challenges to our worldview and to the status quo. This storytelling game is part of what is known as "the radical imagination," that is,

> . . . the ability to imagine the world, life and social institutions not as they are but as they might otherwise be. It is the courage and the intelligence to recognize that the world can and should be changed. . . . It's about bringing those possible futures "back" to *work* on the present, to inspire action and new forms of solidarity today. . . . Without the radical imagination, we are left only with the residual dreams of the powerful, and for the vast majority they are not experienced as dreams but as nightmares of insecurity, precarity, violence and hopelessness. Without the radical imagination, we are lost.[89]

The radical imagination provides a framework and a way of dreaming, of hoping for a just world.

Back to my classes, where first-year students are beginning to examine their stereotypes of the homeless and the poor, along with systemic racism, classism, sexism, etc. I see my students work through their stories of the homeless and of our campus's hourly staff, zooming out to the stories of the organization or movement to the stories of the people themselves. From there the zoom goes out to our educational institution and to the city and state and national governments, zooming through the history of human rights and of social movements, and on and on and back again. There are stories upon stories and movements reinvented in the retelling. What stories will emerge? Where will this dreaming lead? Civic engagement, in any and all of its many forms, is a step—sometimes a zigzag step—on the journey.

Notes

1. Howard Zinn, "The Optimism of Uncertainty," in *The Impossible Will Take a Little While: A Citizen's Guide to Hope in a Time of Fear*, ed. Paul Rogat Loeb (New York: Basic Books, 2004), 71.

2. For information on Freedom University, see http://www.freedomuniversity-georgia.com/ (accessed October 17, 2014). Their description is: "Based on the legacy of Southern Freedom Schools, we provide tuition-free education, college application and scholarship assistance, and tangible movement skills to undocumented students banned from public education in Georgia."

3. Paulo Freire, *Pedagogy of the Oppressed*, trans. Maria Ramos (New York: Continuum: 1970/1997). For a summary of the main ideas, see Peter McLaren, "Critical Pedagogy: A Look at the Major Concepts," in *The Critical Pedagogy Reader*, ed. A. Darder, M. Baltodano, and R. Torres (New York: Routledge/Falmer, 2003), 69–96; Joe Kincheloe, *Critical Pedagogy Primer* (New York: Peter Lang, 2004); and Seehwa Cho, *Critical Pedagogy and Social Change: Critical Analysis on the Language of Possibility* (New York/London: Routlege, 2013).

4. John Dewey, *Democracy and Education* (New York: The Free Press, 1944), 87.

5. See David A. Kolb, *Experiential Learning: Experience as the Source of Learning and Development* (Englewood Cliffs, NJ: Prentice-Hall, 1984). I have used the *Kolb Learning Styles Inventory (KLSI)* with my academic internship classes to provide one template for reflection on experiences; version 4 is available online: http://www.haygroup.com/leadershipandtalentondemand/ourproducts/item_details.aspx?itemid=118&type=2&t=2&gclid=CPPs873zksACFQwV7AodaxQ A3g (accessed February 1, 2015). There are recent critiques of the emphasis on the reflective piece of experiential learning. Reflection writing is at risk of being a surveillance tool; see the critique using Foucault's theories of the panopticon in David Saltiel, "Judgement, Narrative, and Discourse: A Critique of Reflective Practice," in *Beyond Reflective Practice: New Approaches to Professional Lifelong Learning*, ed. Helen Bradbury, Nick Frost, Sue Kilminster, and Miriam Bukas (New York and London: Routledge, 2010), 130–42. See also Michael Newman, "Reflection Disempowered," in *The Jossey-Bass Reader on Contemporary Issues in Adult Education*, ed. Sharan B. Merriam and André P. Grace (San Francisco, CA: Jossey-Bass, 2011), 315–20; and Alison James and Stephen D. Brookfield, *Engaging Imagination: Helping Students Become Creative and Reflective Teachers* (San Francisco, CA: Jossey-Bass, 2014).

6. Ernest L. Boyer, "The Scholarship of Engagement," in *Collaborative Futures: Critical Reflections on Publicly Active Graduate Education*, ed. Amanda Gilvin, Georgia M. Roberts, and Craig Martin (Syracuse, NY: The Graduate School Press of Syracuse University, 2012), 149–50.

7. Ibid., 150.

8. Harry Boyte and Elizabeth Hollander, *The Wingspread Declaration on Renewing the Civic Responsibilities of the American Research University*, June 1999. http://www.compact.org/wp-content/uploads/2009/04/wingspread_declaration.pdf (accessed July 10, 2014).

9. Ibid., 8–9.

10. Ibid., 8.

11. Ibid., 9.
12. Ibid., 12.
13. Ibid., 13.
14. Kellogg Commission on the Future of State and Land-Grant Universities, "From *Returning to Our Roots: The Engaged Institution*: Executive Summary with 'Seven-Part Test,'" in *Collaborative Futures: Critical Reflections on Publicly Active Graduate Education*, ed. Amanda Gilvin, Georgia M. Roberts, and Craig Martin (Syracuse, NY: The Graduate School Press of Syracuse University, 2012), 103–109.
15. Ibid., 104.
16. Ibid.
17. Ibid., 106.
18. Ibid., 107.
19. Ibid., 108–109.
20. Campus Compact, "Mission and Vision." http://www.compact.org/about/history-mission-vision/ (accessed August 5, 2014). See also the work of the American Association of Colleges and Universities (AAC&U) and their "Bringing Theory to Practice" initiative on civic engagement: http://www.aacu.org/resources/civicengagement/index.cfm (accessed August 11, 2014).
21. John Saltmarsh, Matt Hartley, and Patti Clayton, *Democratic Engagement White Paper*, New England Resource Center for Higher Education, February 2009. http://futureofengagement.files.wordpress.com/2009/02/democratic-engagement-white-paper-2_13_09.pdf (accessed August 9, 2014), 2.
22. Ibid., 9.
23. For a summary of PAR, see Jacques M. Chevalier and David J. Buckles, *Participatory Action Research: Theory and Methods for Engaged Inquiry* (London: Routledge, 2013), 31.
24. Imagining America, "Our Mission," May 2014. http://imaginingamerica.org/about/our-mission/ (accessed August 12, 2014).
25. See Timothy K. Eatman, "The Arc of the Academic Career Bends toward Publicly Engaged Scholarship," in *Collaborative Futures: Critical Reflections on Publicly Active Graduate Education*, ed. Amanda Gilvin, Georgia M. Roberts, and Craig Mart (Syracuse, NY: The Graduate School Press of Syracuse University, 2012), 25–48, particularly the discussions in "Ten Key Elements of Publicly Engaged Scholarship," 30–31, and "Pathways for Public Engagement at Five Career Stages: A Hypothetical Example," 34.
26. Ibid., 44.
27. Imagining America, "Specifying the Scholarship of Engagement: Skills for Community-Based Projects in the Arts, Humanities, and Design," in *Collaborative Futures: Critical Reflections on Publicly Active Graduate Education*, ed. Amanda Gilvin, Georgia M. Roberts, and Craig Martin (Syracuse, NY: The Graduate School Press of Syracuse University, 2012), 329–32.

28. Kevin Bott, "Forward," in *Collaborative Futures: Critical Reflections on Publicly Active Graduate Education*, ed. Amanda Gilvin, Georgia M. Roberts, and Craig Martin (Syracuse, NY: The Graduate School Press of Syracuse University, 2012), xxi.

29. Ibid., xxiv.

30. Ibid., xxiv.

31. Ibid., xxvi.

32. Chris Dixon and Alexis Shotwell, "Leveraging the Academy: Suggestions for Radical Grad Students and Radicals Considering Grad School," in *Collaborative Futures: Critical Reflections on Publicly Active Graduate Education*, ed. Amanda Gilvin, Georgia M. Roberts, and Craig Martin (Syracuse, NY: The Graduate School Press of Syracuse University, 2012), 333.

33. Ibid., 336–41.

34. Ibid., 342.

35. Ibid., 342.

36. For a summary of neoliberalism, see David Harvey, *A Brief History of Neoliberalism* (New York: Oxford University Press, 2007). The definition of neoliberalism provided by Harvey emphasizes free market capitalism and minimal state involvement: "Neoliberalism is in the first instance a theory of political economic practices that proposes that human well-being can best be advanced by liberating individual entrepreneurial freedoms and skills within an institutional framework characterized by strong private property rights, free markets, and free trade" (2).

37. Brandon W. Kliewer, "Why the Civic Engagement Movement Cannot Achieve Democratic and Justice Aims," *Michigan Journal of Community Service Learning*, Spring 2013: 72. On the concept of community, Miranda Joseph relates: "Community thus can be understood as a supplement to the circulation of state power and capital; it not only enables capital and power to flow, it also has the potential to displace those flows" (from "Community," in *Collaborative Futures: Critical Reflections on Publicly Active Graduate Education*, ed. Amanda Gilvin, Georgia M. Roberts, and Craig Martin (Syracuse, NY: The Graduate School Press of Syracuse University, 2012), 157).

38. Kliewer, "Why the Civic Engagement Movement Cannot Achieve Democratic and Justice Aims," 74–75.

39. Sylvia Gale, "Arcs, Checklists, and Charts: The Trajectory of a Public Scholar," in *Collaborative Futures: Critical Reflections on Publicly Active Graduate Education*, ed. Amanda Gilvin, Georgia M. Roberts, and Craig Martin (Syracuse, NY: The Graduate School Press of Syracuse University, 2012), 322.

40. Ibid., 322.

41. Ibid., 323.

42. Marshall Ganz, "Organizing: People, Power and Change." http://marshallganz.usmblogs.com/files/2012/08/MLD-377-Syllabus-2014.pdf (accessed August 6, 2014).

43. The website of the Clemente Course is http://clementecourse.org/mission. For the full description and history of the Clemente Course, see Earl Shorris, *Riches for the Poor: The Clemente Course in the Humanities* (New York: W. W. Norton, 2000) and Earl Shorris, *The Art of Freedom: Teaching the Humanities to the Poor* (New York: W. W. Norton, 2013).

44. California Association of Scholars. "A Crisis of Competence: The Corrupting Effect of Political Activism in the University of California" (report), National Association of Scholars, April 2012. http://www.nas.org/images/documents/A_Crisis_of_Competence.pdf (accessed August 7, 2014).

45. Ibid., 13.

46. Paul R. Carr, "The Quest for a Critical Pedagogy of Democracy," in *Critical Pedagogy in the Twenty-First Century: A New Generation of Scholars*, ed. Curry Stephenson Malott and Bradley Porfilio (Charlotte, NC: Information Age Publishing, 2011), 187–89; see the chart outlining thin and thick democracy on pages 198–99.

47. Luis Armando Gandin and Michael Apple, "Thin Versus Thick Democracy in Education: Porto Alegre and the Creation of Alternatives to Neo-Liberalism," *International Studies in Sociology of Education*, 12/2 (2002): 109.

48. Carr, "The Quest for a Critical Pedagogy of Democracy," 192–94.

49. Paul Kivel, *You Call This a Democracy?: Who Benefits, Who Pays and Who Really Decides* (New York: The Apex Press, 2004).

50. Ibid., 157–58.

51. Paulo Freire, Ana Maria Araújo Freire, and Walter de Oliveira, *Pedagogy of Solidarity* (Walnut Creek, CA: Left Coast Press, 2014), 15.

52. Ibid., 21.

53. Ibid., 23.

54. Ibid., 64.

55. Ibid., 45–46.

56. Ibid., 58.

57. Paulo Freire, *Pedagogy of Hope: Reliving Pedagogy of the Oppressed* (New York: Bloomsbury, 2014), 7.

58. Ibid., 8.

59. Ibid., 10.

60. Ibid., 9.

61. Ibid., 51.

62. Ibid., 52.

63. Ibid., 109.

64. Ibid., 110.

65. I am using calculations for living wage in the metro Atlanta area from the Economic Policy Institute Family Budget Calculator: http://www.epi.org/resources/budget/; and the MIT Living Wage Calculator: http://livingwage.mit.edu/ (accessed August 18, 2014).

66. Paulo Freire and Myles Horton, *We Make the Road by Walking: Conversations on Education and Social Change*, ed. Brenda Bell, John Gaventa, and John Peters (Philadelphia, PA: Temple University Press, 1990), 67.

67. Ibid., 69.

68. Ibid., 68.

69. Ibid., 85–86.

70. Ibid., 86.

71. Ibid., 90.

72. Ibid., 83.

73. Ibid., 123.

74. Seehwa Cho, *Critical Pedagogy and Social Change* (see n. 3), 154. Cho also warns against institutions of higher education *and* progressive educators that overuse the idea of being "change agents" in the world (Cho, 166).

75. Project South: Institute for the Elimination of Poverty and Genocide has material on movement building for workshops: e.g., *Popular Education for Movement Building, Volume II* and *The Critical Classroom*. http://www.projectsouth.org/movement-building-projects/trainings-and-tools/toolkits/ (accessed August 18, 2014). The manual on strategy is from the Midwest Academy training workshops: Kim Bobo, Jackie Kendall, and Steve Max, *Organizing for Social Change: Midwest Academy Manual for Activists*, 4th ed. (Santa Ana, CA: The Forum Press, 2010).

76. International Network of Scholar Activists. Home page. http://inosa.wikispaces.org/ (accessed July 6, 2015).

77. See, e.g., Judith Blau, Marina Karides, et al., *The World and U.S. Social Forums: A Better World Is Possible and Necessary* (Lanham, MD: Lexington Books, 2009). See also the U.S. Social Forum site: http://www.ussocialforum.net/ (accessed August 18, 2014).

78. Chris Dixon, *Another Politics: Talking across Today's Transformative Movements* (Oakland, CA: University of California Press, 2014), 160.

79. Ibid., 160.

80. Ibid.

81. Ibid., 161.

82. Ibid., 162.

83. Ibid., 169.

84. Ibid., 172.

85. Ibid.

86. Jonathan Z. Smith, *On Teaching Religion: Essays by Jonathan Z. Smith*, ed. Christopher I. Lehrich (New York: Oxford University Press, 2012), 14.

87. Ibid., 128.

88. One example to use is the inventive children's book *Zoom!* by Istvan Banyai (New York: Picture Puffins, 1998).

89. Max Hiven and Alex Khasnabish, *The Radical Imagination* (London: Zed Books, 2014), 3–4.

Bibliography

"ACE/FIPSE Project on Assessing International Learning." *American Council on Education: Leadership and Advocacy.* Accessed July 23, 2014. http://www.acenet.edu/news-room/Pages/ACEFIPSE-Project-on-Assessing-International-Learning.aspx.

Alexander, Michelle. *The New Jim Crow: Mass Incarceration in the Age of Colorblindness.* New York: The New Press, 2010.

Allison, Graham T. *Essence of Decision: Explaining the Cuban Missile Crisis.* Boston: Little, Brown and Company, 1971.

American Academy of Religion/Teagle Working Group. "The Religion Major and Liberal Education—A White Paper." *American Academy of Religion.* Accessed July 6, 2014. https://www.aarweb.org/sites/default/files/pdfs/About/Committees/AcademicRelations/Teagle_WhitePaper.pdf.

American Labor Studies Center. "Labor and Religion." *ALSC*, October 15, 2010. Accessed June 29, 2012. http://labor-studies.org/by-education-area/global-studies/labor-and-religion/.

Amerson, Roxanne. "The Impact of Service-Learning on Cultural Competence." *Nurses Education Perspectives* 31.4 (2010): 18–22.

Anderson, Jodi L., Marc R. Levis-Fitzgerald, and Robert A. Rhoads. "Democratic Learning and Global Citizenship: The Contribution of One-Unit Seminars." *The Journal of General Education* 52.2 (April 2003): 84–107.

Ansari, Shahzad, and Kamal Munir. "Letting Users into Our World: Some Organizational Implications of User-Generated Content." In *Technology and Organization: Essays in Honour of Joan Woodward*, edited by Nelson Phillips, Graham Sewell, and Dorothy Griffiths, 76–106. Bingley, UK: Emerald Group Publishing Limited, 2010.

Appadurai, Arjun. *Fear of Small Numbers: An Essay on the Geography of Anger.* Durham, N.C.: Duke University Press, 2006.

Arnal, William E., Willi Braun, and Russell T. McCutcheon, eds. *Failure of Nerve in the Academic Study of Religion: Essays in Honor of Donald Wiebe*. Sheffield, UK: Equinox Publishing, 2012.

Arnold, Roslyn. *Empathic Intelligence*. Sydney, Australia: University of New South Wales Press, 2005.

Aronowitz, Stanley, and Henry Giroux. *Postmodern Education: Politics, Culture, and Social Criticism*. Minneapolis: University of Minnesota Press, 1991.

Arum, Richard, Josipa Rosaka, and Melissa Velez. "Learning to Reason and Communicate in College: Initial Report of Findings from the CLA Longitudinal Study." *The Social Science Research Council*. Accessed January 21, 2013. http://www.ssrc.org/publications/view/C6153FC0-6654-DE11-AFAC-001CC477EC70/.

Ash, Sarah L., and Patti H. Clayton. "The Articulated Learning: An Approach to Guided Reflection and Assessment." *Innovative Higher Education* 29.2 (Winter 2004): 137–54.

Ash, Sarah L., Patti H. Clayton, and Maxine P. Atkinson. "Integrating Reflection and Assessment to Capture and Improve Student Learning." *Michigan Journal of Community Service-Learning* 11.2 (Spring 2005): 49–60.

Association of American Colleges and Universities. "Bringing Theory to Practice." Accessed August 11, 2014. http://www.aacu.org/resources/civicengagement/index.cfm.

Association of American Colleges and Universities. "Civic Engagement Value Rubric." Accessed July 23, 2014. http://www.aacu.org/value/rubrics/pdf/All_Rubrics.pdf.

Association of American Colleges and Universities. "Civic Learning: Leading Organizations." Accessed February 21, 2013. http://www.aacu.org/resources/civicengagement/organizations.cfm.

Association of American Colleges and Universities. "Liberal Education and America's Promise (LEAP): Essential Learning Outcomes." Accessed July 23, 2014. http://www.aacu.org/leap/vision.cfm.

Astin, Alexander. "Liberal Education and Democracy: The Case for Pragmatism." *Liberal Education* 83.4 (1997): 4–15.

Astin, Alexander, Helen S. Astin, and Jennifer Lindholm. *Cultivating the Spirit: How College Can Enhance Students' Inner Lives*. San Francisco: Jossey-Bass, 2010.

Astin, Alexander, and Lori J. Vogelgesang. "Understanding the Effects of Service Learning: A Study of Students and Faculty." *The Higher Education Research Institute, Graduate School of Information and Education Studies, University of California, Los Angeles*. Accessed January 21, 2013. https://www.heri.ucla.edu/PDFs/pubs/reports/UnderstandingTheEffectsOfServiceLearning_FinalReport.pdf.

Axtmann, Roland. "What's Wrong with Cosmopolitan Democracy?" In *Global Citizenship: A Critical Introduction*, edited by Nigel Dower and John Williams, 101–13. New York, NY: Routledge, 2002.

Bahr, Ann Marie B. "Interreligious Dialogue, Community Cohesion, and Global Citizenship: The Role of a Religion Program in a Rural, Land-Grant University." *Journal of Ecumenical Studies* 46.2 (Spring 2011): 242–50.

Bain, Ken. *What the Best College Teachers Do*. Cambridge, MA: Harvard University Press, 2004.

Baird, Justus. "Multifaith Education in American Theological Schools: Looking Back, Looking Ahead." *Teaching Theology and Religion* 16.4 (October 2013): 309–21.

Bandy, Joe. "What Is Service Learning or Community Engagement?" *Center for Teaching, Vanderbilt University*. Accessed January 31, 2015. http://cft.vanderbilt. edu/guides-sub-pages/teaching-through-community-engagement/.

Banyai, Istvan. *Zoom!* New York: Picture Puffins, 1998.

Barber, Benjamin R. *Consumed: How Markets Corrupt Children, Infantilize Adults, and Swallow Citizens Whole*. New York: W. W. Norton & Company, 2007.

Barbour, John D. "Grading on the Guilty-Liberal Standard." *The Chronicle Review* 53.42 (June 22, 2007): B16.

Battistoni, Richard M. *Civic Engagement across the Curriculum: A Resource Book for Service-Learning Faculty in All Disciplines*. Providence, RI: Campus Compact, 2002.

Bauman, Zygmunt. *Consuming Life*. Cambridge, UK: Polity Press, 2007.

Beaudoin, Tom. *Consuming Faith: Integrating Who We Are with What We Buy*. Lanham, MD: Sheed & Ward, 2003.

Beavis, Mary Ann. "*Fargo*: A Biblical Morality Play." *Journal of Religion and Film* 4.2 (October 2000). http://www.unomaha.edu/jrf/fargo.htm. Accessed 24 July, 2014.

Belenky, Mary Field, Blythe McVicker Clinchy, Nancy Rule Goldberger, and Jill Mattuck Tarule. *Women's Ways of Knowing: The Development of Self, Voice, and Mind*, 2nd ed. New York: Basic Books, 1997.

Belenky, Mary Field, and Ann V. Stanton. "Inequality, Development, and Connected Knowing." In *Learning as Transformation*, edited by Jack Mezirow, 71–102. San Francisco: Jossey-Bass, 2000.

Bell, Lee Anne. "Learning through Story Types about Race and Racism." In *Social Justice Education: Inviting Faculty to Transform Their Institutions*, edited by Kathleen Skubikowski, Catherine Wright, and Roman Graf, 26–41. Sterling, VA: Stylus, 2009.

Bellah, Robert N. *Religion in Human Evolution: From the Paleolithic to the Axial Age*. Cambridge, MA: Harvard University Press, 2011.

Bennett, Milton J. "Becoming Interculturally Competent." In *Toward Multiculturalism: A Reader in Multicultural Education*, edited by J. S. Wurzel, 62–77. Newton, MA: Intercultural Resource Corporation, 2004.

Berger, Ben. *Attention Deficit Democracy*. Princeton, NJ: Princeton University Press, 2011.

Berling, Judith A. *Understanding Other Religious Worlds: A Guide for Interreligious Education.* New York: Orbis Books, 2004.

Bérubé, Michael. "Professional Advocates: When Is 'Advocacy' Part of One's Vocation?" In *Advocacy in the Classroom: Problems and Possibilities,* edited by Patricia Meyer Spacks, 186–97. New York: St. Martin's Press, 1996.

Bharti Jain. "Highest-Ever Voter Turnout Recorded in 2014 Polls, Government Spending Doubled since 2009." *Times of India,* May 13, 2014. Accessed July 5, 2014. http://timesofindia.indiatimes.com/news/Highest-ever-voter-turnout-recorded-in-2014-polls-govt-spending-doubled-since-2009/articleshow/35033135.cms.

Blau, Judith, and Marina Karides. *The World and U.S. Social Forums: A Better World Is Possible and Necessary.* Lanham, MD: Lexington Books, 2009.

Bloom, Benjamin, ed. *Taxonomy of Educational Objectives: The Classification of Educational Goals: Book 1. Cognitive Domain.* White Plains, NY: Longman, 1956.

Blumenstyk, Goldie. "Manifesto for a New Culture of Learning." *The Chronicle of Higher Education,* Online Edition, May 15, 2011. Accessed June 15, 2014. http://chronicle.com/article/Understanding-the-New-Culture/127459.

Bobo, Kim. *Wage Theft in America: Why Millions of Working Americans Are Not Getting Paid—And What We Can Do about It.* New York: The New Press, 2009.

Bobo, Kim, Jackie Kendall, and Steve Max. *Organizing for Social Change: Midwest Academy Manual for Activists,* 4th edition. Santa Ana, CA: The Forum Press, 2010.

Bongiglio, Robert A. "Shorthand or Shortsightedness? The Downside of Generational Labeling." *About Campus* 13.3 (July/August 2008): 30–32.

Booth, Wayne C. "Blind Skepticism Versus a Rhetoric of Assent." *College English* 67.4 (March 2005): 378–88.

Bott, Kevin. "Forward." In *Collaborative Futures: Critical Reflections on Publicly Active Graduate Education,* edited by Amanda Gilvin, Georgia M. Roberts, and Craig Martin, xix–xxvii. Syracuse, NY: The Graduate School Press of Syracuse University, 2012.

Bouma-Prediger, Steven, and Brian J. Walsh. *Beyond Homelessness: Christian Faith in a Culture of Displacement.* Grand Rapids, MI: William B. Eerdmans, 2008.

Bowie, Fiona. "Anthropology of Religion." *Religion Compass* 2(2008): 862–74.

Bowman, Nicholas A. "Promoting Participation in a Diverse Democracy: A Meta-Analysis of College Diversity Experiences and Civic Engagement." *Review of Educational Research* 81.1 (March 2011): 29–68.

Bowman, Nicholas A. "Understanding and Addressing the Challenges of Assessing College Student Growth in Student Affairs." *Research and Practice in Assessment* 8.2 (Winter 2013): 5–14.

Bowman, Nicholas A. "Validity of College Self-Reported Gains at Diverse Institutions." *Educational Researcher* 40.1 (2011): 22–24.

Boyer, Ernest L. "The Scholarship of Engagement." In *Collaborative Futures: Critical Reflections on Publicly Active Graduate Education*, edited by Amanda Gilvin, Georgia M. Roberts, and Craig Martin, 143–53. Syracuse, NY: The Graduate School Press of Syracuse University, 2012.

Boyer, Ernest L. *Scholarship Reconsidered: Priorities of the Professoriate*. Princeton, NJ: The Carnegie Foundation for the Advancement of Teaching, 1990.

Boyte, Harry, and Elizabeth Hollander. "The Wingspread Declaration on Renewing the Civic Responsibilities of the American Research University." *Campus Compact*. Accessed July 10, 2014. http://www.compact.org/wp-content/uploads/2009/04/wingspread_declaration.pdf.

Brahm, Eric. "Globalization." *The Beyond Intractability Project, The Conflict Information Consortium, University of Colorado*. Last modified July 2005. Accessed February 27, 2013, http://www.beyondintractability.org/bi-essay/globalization.

Bringle, Robert G., Patti H. Clayton, and Julie A. Hatcher. "Research on Service Learning: An Introduction." In *Research on Service Learning: Conceptual Frameworks and Assessment: Volume 2B: Communities, Institutions, and Partnerships*, edited by Patti H. Clayton, Robert G. Bringle, and Julie A. Hatcher, IUPUI Series on Service Learning Research, 3–25. Sterling, VA: Stylus, 2012.

Bronner, Stephen Eric. *Reclaiming the Enlightenment: Toward a Politics of Radical Engagement*. New York: Columbia University Press, 2004.

Brookfield, Stephen D. "Transformative Learning as Ideology Critique." In *Learning as Transformation*, edited by Jack Mezirow, 125–48. San Francisco: Jossey-Bass, 2000.

Brookfield, Stephen D., and Stephen Preskill. *Discussion as a Way of Teaching: Tools and Techniques for Democratic Classrooms*, 2nd ed. San Francisco: Jossey-Bass, 2005.

Brown, Robbie, and Kim Severson. "Enlisting Prison Labor to Close Budget Gaps." *New York Times*, February 24, 2011. Accessed February 8, 2015. http://www.nytimes.com/2011/02/25/us/25inmates.html?_r=1&pagewanted=all.

Buber, Martin. Between Man and Man. Translated by R. F. C. Hull. London: Fontana Library, 1961.

Butin, Dan W. "Of What Use Is It? Multiple Conceptualizations of Service Learning within Education." *Teachers College Record* 105.9 (December 2003): 1674–92.

Butin, Dan W. "The Limits of Service-Learning in Higher Education." *Review of Higher Education* 29.4 (Summer 2006): 473–98.

Butin, Dan W. "Justice-Learning: Service-Learning as Justice-Oriented Education." *Equity and Excellence in Education* 40 (2007): 177–83.

Butin, Dan W. *Service-Learning in Theory and Practice: The Future of Community Engagement in Higher Education*. New York: Palgrave MacMillan, 2010.

California Association of Scholars."A Crisis of Competence: The Corrupting Effect of Political Activism in the University of California." National Association of Scholars, April 2012. Accessed August 7, 2014. http://www.nas.org/images/documents/A_Crisis_of_Competence.pdf.

Campbell, Kathryn Peltier, ed. Theme Issue on "Civic Engagement and Student Success: A Resonant Relationship." *Diversity and Democracy* 15 3 (Fall 2012).

"Campus Compact Mission and Vision Statements." *Campus Compact.* Accessed August 5, 2014. http://www.compact.org/about/history-mission-vision/.

Cannon, Katie Geneva. *Katie's Canon: Womanism and the Soul of the Black Community.* New York: Continuum, 1995.

Carr, Paul R. "The Quest for a Critical Pedagogy of Democracy." In *Critical Pedagogy in the Twenty-First Century: A New Generation of Scholars,* edited by Curry Stephenson Malott and Bradley Porfilio, 187–210. Charlotte, NC: Information Age Publishing, 2011.

Castelfranchi, Cirstiano, and Rino Falcone. "Social Trust: A Cognitive Approach." In *Trust and Deception in Virtual Societies,* edited by Cirstiano Castelfranchi and Yao-Hua Tan, 55–90. Dordrecht: Springer, 2001.

Castelli, Elizabeth A. "Women, Gender, Religion: Troubling Categories and Transforming Knowledge." In *Women, Gender, Religion: A Reader,* edited by Elizabeth Castelli with Rosamond Rodman, 3–25. New York: Palgrave Macmillan, 2001.

Center for Civic Engagement. "Mission." *Northwestern University.* http://www.engage.northwestern.edu/about/index.html.

Center for Civic Engagement. "Service Learning." *Oregon State University.* http://sli.oregonstate.edu/cce/ways-be-engaged/service-learning. Accessed January 31, 2015.

Center for Leadership and Service. "Home page." University of Georgia. Accessed February 1, 2015. http://cls.uga.edu/.

Center for Service & Learning. "Civic-Minded Graduate." *Indiana University-Purdue University Indianapolis.* Accessed July 6, 2014. http://csl.iupui.edu/teaching-research/opportunities/civic-learning/graduate.shtml.

Checkoway, Barry. "New Perspectives on Civic Engagement and Psychosocial Well-Being." *Liberal Education* 97(2011): 6–11.

Checkoway, Barry. "Renewing the Civic Mission of the American Research University." *The Journal of Higher Education* 72.2 (Mar/April 2001): 125–47.

Chevalier, Jacques M., and David J. Buckles. *Participatory Action Research: Theory and Methods for Engaged Inquiry.* London: Routledge, 2013.

Chin, Elizabeth. *Purchasing Power: Black Kids and American Consumer Culture.* Minneapolis: University of Minnesota Press, 2001.

Cho, Seehwa. *Critical Pedagogy and Social Change: Critical Analysis on the Language of Possibility.* New York/London: Routledge, 2013.

CivicAction, *Breaking Boundaries: Time to Think and Act Like a Region.* Toronto: CivicAction, 2011.

"Civic Education." *National Forum on Higher Education for the Public Good.* Accessed August 24, 2011. http://www.thenationalforum.org/Docs/PDF/Civic_Education.pdf.

Clifford, James, and George E. Marcus, eds. *Writing Culture: The Poetics and Politics of Ethnography*. Berkeley: University of California Press, 1986.

Clingerman, Forrest, and Reid B. Locklin, "'Pedagogies for Civic Engagement': Collaborations and Complications in Religious Studies." Paper presented at the 10th annual National Outreach Scholarship Conference, University of Georgia, Athens, GA, September 29, 2009.

Clough, Patricia Ticineto, and Jean Halley, eds. *The Affective Turn: Theorizing the Social*. Durham, NC: Duke University Press, 2007.

"Comcast and Netflix Reach Deal on Service." *New York Times*, New York Edition, February 24, 2014, B1.

"Community Based Learning." Notre Dame de Namur University. Accessed March 2014. www.ndnu.edu/academics/community-based-learning.

Connor, Bob. "How adequate is secularism as a basis for liberal education?" *The Teagle Foundation*. Accessed February 1, 2015. http://www.teaglefoundation.org/Resources/Additional-Resources/How-adequate-is-secularism-as-a-basis-for-libe.

Conway, James M., Elise L. Amel, and Daniel P. Gerwien. "Teaching and Learning in the Social Context: A Meta-analysis of Service-Learning's Effects on Academic, Personal, Social, and Citizenship Outcomes." *Teaching of Psychology* 36.4 (2009): 233–45.

Concepción, David W., and Juli Thorson Eflin. "Enabling Change: Transformative and Transgressive Learning in Feminist Ethics and Epistemology." *Teaching Philosophy* 32.2 (2009): 177–98.

Cooey, Paula. "The Place of Academic Theology in the Study of Religion from the Perspective of Liberal Education." In *Religious Studies, Theology, and the University: Conflicting Maps, Changing Terrain*, edited by Linell E. Cady and Delwin Brown, 172–86. Albany: State University of New York Press, 2002.

Cress, Christine M. "Student Engagement and Student Success: Leveraging Multiple Degrees of Achievement." Diversity and Democracy 15 (2012): 2–4.

Cress, Christine M., Peter J. Collier, and Vicki L. Reitenauer. *Learning through Serving: A Student Guidebook for Service-Learning across the Disciplines*. Sterling, VA: Stylus Publishing, 2005.

Culkin, John M. "A Schoolman's Guide to Marshall McLuhan." *The Saturday Review*, March 18, 1967. Accessed June 15, 2014. http://www.unz.org/Pub/SaturdayRev-1967mar18-00051.

Davies, Rick, and Jess Dart. "The 'Most Significant Change' (MSC) Technique: A Guide to Its Use (2004)." *Monitoring and Evaluation NEWS*. Accessed March 19, 2009. http://www.mande.co.uk/docs/MSCGuide.pdf.

Davis, Angelique, and Brian Mello. "Preaching to the Apathetic and Uninterested: Teaching Civic Engagement to Freshmen and Non-Majors." *Journal for Civic Commitment* 18 (2012): 1–23.

de Certeau, Michel. *The Practice of Everyday Life*. Translated by Steve F. Rendall. Berkeley, CA: University of California Press, 1988.

Delaporte, Marianne, and Hans Wiersma. "Site Visits and Civic Engagement." *Religious Studies News* October 2010. Accessed January 21, 2014. http://www.rsnonline.org/index.php?option=com_content&view=article&id=252&Itemid=333.

Delrio, Mike. "93 Million Eligible Voters Did Not Vote in 2012." *The Examiner*. Last modified November 12, 2012. Accessed February 1, 2015. http://www.examiner.com/article/93-million-eligible-voters-did-not-vote-2012.

Deming, Will. *Rethinking Religion: A Concise Introduction*. New York and Oxford: Oxford University Press, 2005.

Devine, Richard, Joseph A. Favazza, and F. Michael McLain, eds. *From Cloister to Commons: Concepts and Models for Service-Learning in Religious Studies*. Washington, DC: American Association for Higher Education, 2002.

Dewey, John. *Democracy and Education*. New York: The Free Press, 1944.

Dion, Nicholas, Rebekka King, Tyler Baker, Jingjing Liang, James McDonough, and Joshua Samuels. "Open Space Technology and the Study of Religion: A Report on an Experiment in Pedagogy." *Bulletin for the Study of Religion* 42 (2013): 28–32.

Division of Student Affairs. "Get Involved at IUPUI." *Indiana University Purdue University Indianapolis*. http://life.iupui.edu/osi/civic-engagement/.

Dixon, Chris. *Another Politics: Talking Across Today's Transformative Movements*. Oakland, CA: University of California Press, 2014.

Douglas, Mary. "Why Do People Want Goods?" In *Consumption: Critical Concepts in the Social Sciences, Volume 1*, edited by Daniel Miller, 262–71. London: Routledge, 2001.

Dower, Nigel. "Global Citizenship: Yes or No?" In *Global Citizenship: A Critical Introduction*, edited by Nigel Dower and John Williams, 30–39. New York: Routledge, 2002.

Dower, Nigel. "Global Ethics and Global Citizenship." In *Global Citizenship: A Critical Introduction*, edited by Nigel Dower and John Williams, 146–56. New York: Routledge, 2002.

Eatman, Timothy K. "The Arc of the Academic Career Bends toward Publicly Engaged Scholarship." In *Collaborative Futures: Critical Reflections on Publicly Active Graduate Education*, edited by Amanda Gilvin, Georgia M. Roberts, and Craig Martin, 25–48. Syracuse, NY: The Graduate School Press of Syracuse University, 2012.

Eberly, Don E., ed. *The Essential Civic Society Reader: The Classic Essays*. Lanham, MD: Rowman and Littlefield, 2000.

Eby, John W. "Why Service-Learning Is Bad." Villanova College website, March 1998. https://www1.villanova.edu/content/dam/villanova/artsci/servicelearning/WhyServiceLearningIsBad.pdf (accessed July 7, 2015).

Eck, Diana L. *A New Religious America: How a "Christian Country" Has Become the World's Most Religiously Diverse Nation.* New York: HarperCollins, 2001.

Eck, Diana L. "Prospects for Pluralism: Voice and Vision in the Study of Religion." *Journal of the American Academy of Religion* 75 (December, 2007): 743–76.

Eck, Diana L. "What Is Pluralism?" *The Pluralism Project, Harvard University.* Accessed July 10, 2012. http://pluralism.org/pages/pluralism/what_is_pluralism.

Ehrlich, Thomas. "Civic Education: Lessons Learned." *Political Science and Politics* 32 (1990): 245–50.

Ehrlich, Thomas. *Civic Responsibility and Higher Education.* Westport, CT: Oryx Press, 2000.

Elbow, Peter. "Bringing the Rhetoric of Assent and the Believing Game Together— And Into the Classroom." *College English* 67.4 (March 2005): 388–99.

Elbow, Peter. "The Believing Game." In *Nurturing the Peacemakers in Our Students: A Guide to Writing and Speaking Out about Issues of War and Peace,* edited by Chris Weber, 16–25. Portsmouth, NH: Heinemann, 2006.

Elbow, Peter. "The Doubting Game and the Believing Game—An Analysis of the Intellectual Enterprise." In *Writing Without Teachers,* 147–91. London, Oxford and New York: Oxford University Press, 1973.

"Empathy: College Students Don't Have As Much As They Used To." *University of Michigan News Service,* May 27, 2010. Accessed March 10, 2012. http:// ns.umich.edu/htdocs/releases/story.php?id=7724.

Ettling, Dorothy. "Ethical Demands of Transformative Learning." *New Directions for Adult and Continuing Education,* no. 109 (2006): 59–67.

Etzioni, Amatai. *Spirit of Community: The Reinvention of American Society.* New York: Touchstone Books, 1993.

Eyler, Janet. "Reflection: Linking Service and Learning—Linking Students and Communities." *Journal of Social Issues* 58.3 (2002): 517–34.

Fallis, George. *Multiversities, Ideas, and Democracy.* Toronto: University of Toronto Press, 2007.

Fallis, George. *Rethinking Higher Education: Participation, Research and Differentiation.* Montreal: McGill-Queen's University Press, 2013.

Fallis, George. "Reclaiming the Civic University." *Academic Matters* (June 2014): 3–6.

Fernhout, J. Harry. "Where Is Faith? Searching for the Core of the Cube." In *Faith Development and Fowler,* edited by Craig Dykstra and Sharon Parks, 65–89. Birmingham, AL: Religious Education Press, 1986.

Ferraiolo, Kathleen. "Is It Working?: Three Universities Take on Assessment." *Pew Partnership.* Accessed January 21, 2013. www.pew-partnership.org/pdf/new_directions/5_assessment.pdf, 101.

Finley, Ashley. "Connecting the Dots: A Methodological Approach for Assessing Students' Civic Engagement and Psychosocial Well-Being." *Liberal Education* 97 (2011): 52–56.

Finley, Ashley. "A Brief Review of the Evidence on Civic Learning in Higher Education." Association of American Colleges and Universities annual meeting, Washington, DC, January 24–28, 2012.

Fish, Stanley. *Save the World on Your Own Time*. New York: Oxford University Press, 2008.

Fitzgerald, Timothy. *The Ideology of Religious Studies*. New York: Oxford University Press, 2000.

Foucault, Michel. *The History of Sexuality: Volume 1. An Introduction*. Translated by Robert Hurley. New York: Vintage, 1990.

Foucault, Michel. *The History of Sexuality: Volume 3. The Care of the Self*. Translated by Robert Hurley. New York: Random House, 1986.

Foucault, Michel. *Society Must Be Defended: Lectures at the Collège de France, 1975–76*. Edited by Mauro Bertani and Alessandro Fontana, translated by David Macey. New York: Picador 2003.

Foucault, Michel. *The Birth of Biopolitics: Lectures at the Collège de France 1978–1979*. Translated by G. Burchell. New York: Palgrave Macmillan, 2008.

Fowler, Don D., and Donald L. Hardesty, eds. *Others Knowing Others: Perspectives on Ethnographic Careers*. Washington, DC: Smithsonian Institution Press, 1994.

Fowler, James W. *Stages of Faith: The Psychology of Human Development and the Quest for Meaning*. New York: HarperCollins, 1981.

Fox, Helen. *Their Highest Vocation: Social Justice and the Millennial Generation*. New York: Peter Lang, 2012.

Freedom University. Home page. Accessed October 17, 2014. http://www.freedomuniversitygeorgia.com/.

Freire, Paulo. "Paulo Freire—An Incredible Conversation." YouTube video, 8 mins, 14 secs. December 30, 2009. Accessed September 8, 2012. http://www.youtube.com/watch?v=aFWjnkFypFA&feature=related.

Freire, Paulo. *Pedagogy of the Oppressed*, 30th anniversary edition. New York: Continuum, 2000.

Freire, Paulo. *Pedagogy of Hope: Reliving* Pedagogy of the Oppressed. New York: Bloomsbury, 2014.

Freire, Paulo, Ana Maria Araújo Freire, and Walter de Oliveira. *Pedagogy of Solidarity*. Walnut Creek, CA: Left Coast Press, 2014.

Freire, Paulo, and Myles Horton. *We Make the Road by Walking: Conversations on Education and Social Change*. Edited by Brenda Bell, John Gaventa, and John Peters. Philadelphia, PA: Temple University Press, 1990.

Fretz, Eric. "Teaching Liberty and Practicing Deliberative Democracy in the Classroom." *Campus Compact Reader* Winter/Spring (2004): 2–3. Accessed December 16, 2008. http://www.compact.org/reader/winter04/article2-print.html.

Fuller, Robert C. *Spiritual, but Not Religious: Understanding Unchurched America*. New York: Oxford University Press, 2001.

Furco, Andrew. "Institutionalizing Service-Learning in Higher Education." *Journal of Public Affairs* 3 (2002): 209–24.

Furco, Andrew. "Service Learning: A Balanced Approach to Experiential Education." In *Introduction to Service Learning Toolkit: Readings and Resources for Faculty*, 9–13. Boston: Campus Compact, 2000.

Gabriel, Yiannis, and Tim Lang. *The Unmanageable Consumer*, 2nd ed. London: Sage Publications, 2006.

Gale, Sylvia. "Arcs, Checklists, and Charts: The Trajectory of a Public Scholar." In *Collaborative Futures: Critical Reflections on Publicly Active Graduate Education*, edited by Amanda Gilvin, Georgia M. Roberts, and Craig Martin, 315–27. Syracuse, NY: The Graduate School Press of Syracuse University, 2012.

Gambetta, Diego, ed. *Trust*. Oxford: Basil Blackwell, 1990.

Gandin, Luis Armando, and Michael Apple. "Thin Versus Thick Democracy in Education: Porto Alegre and the Creation of Alternatives to Neo-Liberalism." *International Studies in Sociology of Education*, 12.2 (2002): 99–116.

Ganz, Marshall. "Organizing People, Power and Change." Accessed August 6, 2014. http://marshallganz.usmblogs.com/files/2012/08/MLD-377-Syllabus-2014.pdf.

Ganz, Marshall. "Why Stories Matter: The Art and Craft of Social Change." *Sojourners*, March 2009. Accessed September 10, 2013. http://sojo.net/magazine/2009/03/why-stories-matter.

Garber, Marjorie B., Beatrice Hanssen, and Rebecca L. Walkowitz, eds. *The Turn to Ethics*. New York: Routledge Press, 2000.

Giles, Dwight E., Jr., and Janet Eyler. "A Service Learning Research Agenda for the Next Five Years." *New Directions for Teaching and Learning* 73 (1998): 65–72.

Gilmore, Ruth. *Golden Gulag: Prisons, Surplus, Crisis, and Opposition in Globalizing California*. Berkeley, CA: University of California Press, 2007.

Ginwright, Shawn. "Hope, Healing, and Care: Pushing the Boundaries of Civic Engagement for African American Youth." *Liberal Education* 97 (2011): 34–39.

Giroux, Henry A. "Neoliberalism, Corporate Culture, and the Promise of Higher Education: The University as a Democratic Public Sphere." *Harvard Educational Review* 72.4 (Winter 2002): 427–63.

Giroux, Henry A. *Twilight of the Social: Resurgent Publics in the Age of Disposability*. Boulder, CO: Paradigm Publishers, 2012.

Ghosh, Amitav. *In an Antique Land*. London: Granta Books, 1994.

Glennon, Fred. "Service-Learning and the Dilemma of Religious Studies: Descriptive or Normative?" In *From Cloister to Commons: Concepts and Models for Service Learning in Religious Studies*, edited by Richard Devine, Joseph A. Favazza, and F. Michael McLain, 9–24. Washington, DC: American Association for Higher Education, 2002.

Goldsmith, Jack, and Tim Wu. *Who Controls the Internet? Illusions of a Borderless World*. New York: Oxford University Press, 2006.

Gollob, Rolf, Peter Krapf, and Wiltrud Weidinger, eds. *Educating for Democracy: Background Materials on Democratic Citizenship and Human Rights Education for Teachers.* Strasbourg: Council of Europe Publishing, 2010.

Gottman, Mary. *Summary Report of the National Gathering.* Wellesley, MA: The Education as Transformation Project, 1998.

Greene, Maxine. *Releasing the Imagination: Education, the Arts, and Social Change.* San Francisco: Jossey-Bass, 1995.

Guerino, Paul, Paige M. Harrison, and William J. Sabol. "Prisoners in 2010." *Bureau of Justice Statistics,* December 15, 2011. Accessed February 8, 2015. http://www.bjs.gov/index.cfm?ty=pbdetail&iid=2230.

Gummer, Natalie. "A Profound Unknowing: The Challenge of Religion in the Liberal Education of World Citizens." *Liberal Education* 91.2 (Spring 2005): 44–49.

Hadis, Benjamin F. "Why Are They Better Students When They Come Back? Determinants of Academic Focusing Gains in the Study Abroad Experience." *Frontiers* 11 (August 2005): 57–70.

Hartman, Eric. "No Values, No Democracy: The Essential Partisanship of a Civic Engagement Movement." *Michigan Journal of Community Service* 19.2 (Spring 2013): 58–71.

Harvey, David. *A Brief History of Neoliberalism.* New York: Oxford University Press, 2007.

Hatcher, Julie A., and Robert G. Bringle. "Bridging the Gap between Service and Learning." *College Teaching* 45 (1997):153–58.

Held, David. "The Transformation of Political Community: Rethinking Democracy in the Context of Globalization." In *Global Citizenship: A Critical Introduction,* edited by Nigel Dower and John Williams, 92–99. New York: Routledge, 2002.

Hildreth, R. W. "Theorizing Citizenship and Evaluating Public Service." *PS: Political Science and Politics* 33.3 (September 2000): 627–32.

Hill, Jack A., Melanie Harris, and Hjamil A. Martínez-Vázquez. "Fighting the Elephant in the Room: Ethical Reflections on White Privilege and Other Systems of Advantage in the Teaching of Religion." *Teaching Theology and Religion* 12.1 (January 2009): 3–23.

Hinze, Bradford E. "The Tasks of Theology in the *Proyecto Social* of the University's Mission." *Horizons* 39 (2012): 282–309.

"Historyapolis Project." Accessed July 24, 2014. http://historyapolis.com.

Hiven, Max, and Alex Khasnabish. *The Radical Imagination.* London: Zed Books, 2014.

Hooks, bell. *Teaching to Transgress: Education as the Practice of Freedom.* New York and London: Routledge, 1994.

Hooks, bell. *Teaching Community: A Pedagogy of Hope.* New York and London: Routledge, 2003.

Hooks, bell. *Teaching Critical Thinking.* New York and London: Routledge, 2010.

Hornung, Maria. *Encountering Other Faiths.* Mahwah, NJ: Paulist, 2007.

Hornung, Maria. *Workbook for Encountering Other Faiths: An Introduction to the Art of Interreligious Engagement.* Philadelphia: Interfaith Center of Greater Philadelphia, 2007.

Hough, John C. "The University and the Common Good." In *Theology and the University: Essays in Honor of John Cobb Jr.*, edited by David Ray Griffin and John C. Hough, 97–124. Albany, NY: State University of New York Press, 1991.

Hovland, Kevin. *Shared Futures: Global Learning and Liberal Education.* Washington, DC: Association of American Colleges and Universities, 2006.

Howe, Neil, and William Straus. *Millennials Rising: The Next Great Generation.* New York: Vintage Books, 2000.

Hu, Winnie. "A Call for Opening up Web Access at Schools, for Learning's Sake." *New York Times*, New York edition, September 29, 2011, A12.

Hurtado, Aída. "Strategic Suspensions: Feminists of Color Theorize the Production of Knowledge." In *Knowledge, Difference, and Power: Essays Inspired by Women's Ways of Knowing*, edited by Nancy Rule Goldberger, Jill Mattuck Tarule, Blythe McVicker Clinchy, and Mary Field Belenky, 372–91. New York: BasicBooks, 1996.

Ikeda, Daisaku. "The University of the 21st Century: Cradle of World Citizens." *Schools: Studies in Education* 7.2 (Fall 2010): 246–52.

Imagining America. "Our Mission." *Imagining America.* Accessed August 12, 2014. http://imaginingamerica.org/about/our-mission/.

Imagining America. "Specifying the Scholarship of Engagement: Skills for Community-Based Projects in the Arts, Humanities, and Design." In *Collaborative Futures: Critical Reflections on Publicly Active Graduate Education*, edited by Amanda Gilvin, Georgia M. Roberts, and Craig Martin, 329–32. Syracuse, NY: The Graduate School Press of Syracuse University, 2012.

Interfaith Worker Justice. "Mission & Values." *Interfaith Worker Justice.* Accessed June 19, 2012. http://www.iwj.org/about/mission-values.

"Internet Users in North America, June 30, 2012." Accessed June 15, 2014. http://www.internetworldstats.com/stats14.htm.

Jacobsen, Douglas, and Rhonda Hustedt Jacobsen. *No Longer Invisible: Religion in University Education.* New York: Oxford University Press, 2012.

Jacoby, Barbara. "Civic Engagement in Today's Higher Education: An Overview." In *Civic Engagement in Higher Education: Concepts and Practices*, edited by Barbara Jacoby and Associates, 5–30. San Francisco: Jossey-Bass, 2009.

Jacoby, Barbara. "Facing the Unsettled Questions about Service-Learning." In *The Future of Service-Learning: New Solutions for Sustaining and Improving Practice*, edited by Jean R. Strait and Marybeth Lima, 90–105. Sterling, VA: Stylus, 2009.

James, Alison, and Stephen D. Brookfield. *Engaging Imagination: Helping Students Become Creative and Reflective Teachers.* San Francisco, CA: Jossey-Bass, 2014.

James, William C. *God's Plenty: Religious Diversity in Kingston.* Kingston and Montreal: McGill-Queen's Press, 2011.

Jaschik, Scott. "Political Engagement 101." *Inside Higher Ed.* Last modified August 30, 2007. Accessed March 3, 2013. http://www.insidehighered.com/news/2007/08/30/political.

Jones, Irwin. *Derrida and the Writing of the Body.* Burlington VT: Ashgate Publishing Group. 2010.

Kaiman, Jonathan. "Tiananmen Square Online Searches Censored by Chinese Authorities." *The Guardian,* On-line Edition, June 4, 2013. Accessed June 15, 2014. http://www.theguardian.com/world/2013/jun/04/tiananmen-square-online-search-censored.

Kant, Immanuel. "An Answer to the Question, What Is Enlightenment?" In *Practical Philosophy: The Cambridge Edition of the Works of Immanuel Kant,* edited by Mary J. Gregor, 11–22. New York: Cambridge University Press, 1996.

Keillor, Garrison. *Lake Wobegon Days.* New York: Viking, 1985.

Kellogg Commission on the Future of State and Land-Grant Universities. "From *Returning to Our Roots: The Engaged Institution;* Executive Summary with 'Seven-Part Test.'" In *Collaborative Futures: Critical Reflections on Publicly Active Graduate Education,* edited by Amanda Gilvin, Georgia M. Roberts, and Craig Martin, 103–109. Syracuse, NY: The Graduate School Press of Syracuse University, 2012.

Kiely, Richard. "Transformative International Service Learning." *Academic Exchange* 9.1 (2005): 275–81.

Kiesa, A., A. P. Orlowski, P. L. Levine, D. Both, E. H. Kirby, M. H. Lopez, et al. *Millennials Talk Politics: A Study of College Student Political Engagement.* College Park, MD: Center for Information and Research on Civic Learning and Engagement, 2007.

Kincheloe, Joe. *Critical Pedagogy Primer.* New York: Peter Lang, 2004.

King, Richard. *Orientalism and Religion: Postcolonial Theory, India and 'The Mystic East.'* New York: Routledge, 1999.

Kirlin, Mary. "The Role of Civic Skills in Fostering Civic Engagement." *Circle Working Paper* 06 (June 2003): 1–30.

Kivel, Paul. *You Call This a Democracy? Who Benefits, Who Pays and Who Really Decides.* New York: The Apex Press, 2004.

Kliewer, Brandon W. "Why the Civic Engagement Movement Cannot Achieve Democratic and Justice Aims." *Michigan Journal of Community Service Learning* 19.2 (Spring 2013): 72–79.

Kolb, David. *Experiential Learning: Experience as the Source of Learning and Development.* Englewood Cliffs, NJ: Prentice-Hall, 1984.

Korgen, Kathleen Odell, and Jonathan M. White. *The Engaged Sociologist.* Thousand Oaks, CA: Pine Forge Press, 2011.

Kuh, George D., Jillian Kinzie, John H. Schuc, et al. *Student Success in College: Creating Conditions that Matter.* San Francisco, CA: Jossey-Bass, 2005.

Lascu, D. N., and G. Zinkhan. "Consumer Conformity: Review and Applications for Marketing Theory and Practice." *Journal of Marketing Theory and Practice* 7(1999): 1–12.

Lasn, Kalle. *Culture Jam: How to Reverse America's Suicidal Consumer Binge—And Why We Must.* New York: Harper Collins [Quill], 1999.

Lauillard, Diana. *Rethinking University Teaching: A Conversational Framework for the Effective Use of Learning Technologies*, 2nd edition. London and New York: Routledge, 2004.

Laurence, Peter, and Victor H. Kazanjian, Jr. "The Education as Transformation Project." In *Transforming Campus Life*, edited by Vachel W. Miller and Merle M. Ryan, 57–72. New York: Peter Lang, 2001.

Lawry, Steven, Daniel Laurison, and Jonathan VanAntwerpen. *Liberal Education and Civic Engagement, with a New Prologue Assessing Developments in the Field Since 2006 by Steven Lawry: A Project of the Ford Foundation's Knowledge, Creativity and Freedom Program.* The Ford Foundation, May 2009. Accessed 8 September 2012. http://www.fordfoundation.org/pdfs/library/liberal_education_and_civic_engagement.pdf, 22–31.

Lawston, Jodie M. "Women and Prison: Sociologists for Women in Society (SWS) Fact Sheet." *SWS*, Spring 2012. Accessed February 8, 2015. http://www.socwomen.org/wp-content/uploads/2010/05/fact_1-2012-prison.pdf.

LeBlanc, John Randolph, and Carolyn M. Jones Medine. *Ancient and Modern Religion and Politics: Negotiating Transitive Spaces and Hybrid Identities.* New York: Palgrave Macmillan, 2012.

Dixon, Chris, and Alexis Shotwell. "Leveraging the Academy: Suggestions for Radical Grad Students and Radicals Considering Grad School." In *Collaborative Futures: Critical Reflections on Publicly Active Graduate Education*, edited by Amanda Gilvin, Georgia M. Roberts, and Craig Martin, 333–45. Syracuse, NY: The Graduate School Press of Syracuse University, 2012.

Levine, Daniel P. *The Capacity for Civic Engagement: Public and Private Worlds of the Self.* New York: Palgrave Macmillan, 2011.

Levine, Peter. "Civic Renewal in America." *Philosophy and Public Policy Quarterly* 26.1–2 (Winter/Spring 2006): 2–12.

Levitt, Peggy. "Religion as a Path to Civic Engagement." *Ethnic & Racial Studies* 31.4 (May 2008): 766–91.

Littler, Jo. *Radical Consumption: Shopping for Change in Contemporary Culture.* New York: Open University Press, 2009.

Locklin, Reid B. *Spiritual but Not Religious? An Oar Stroke Closer to the Farther Shore.* Collegeville, MN: Liturgical Press, 2005.

Locklin, Reid B. "Teaching with Complicating Views: Beyond the Survey, Behind Pro and Con." *Teaching Theology and Religion* 16.3 (July 2013): 201–220.

Locklin, Reid B., Tracy Tiemeier, and Johann M. Vento. "Teaching World Religions without Teaching 'World Religions.'" *Teaching Theology and Religion* 15(2012): 159–81.

Lopez, Mark Hugo, and Abby Kiesa. "What We Know about Civic Engagement among College Students." In *Civic Engagement in Higher Education: Concepts and Practices*, edited by Barbara Jacoby and Associates, 31–48. San Francisco: Jossey-Bass, 2009.

Love, Daniel. *Charles Moore: I Fight with My Camera*. DVD, 27 mins. 2005. Accessed July 1, 2014. https://www.youtube.com/watch?v=d0b40602LzA.

Lutterman-Aguilar, Ann, and Orval Gingerich. "Experiential Pedagogy for Study Abroad: Educating for Global Citizenship." *Frontiers* 8 (Winter 2002): 41–82.

"Magruder's American Government Homepage." *Pearson*. Accessed February 1, 2015. http://www.phschool.com/webcodes10/index.cfm?fuseaction=home.got oWebCode&wcprefix=mqk&wcsuffix=1000.

Mahdavi, Pardis. "'But We Can Always Get More!' Deportability, the State and Gendered Migration in the United Arab Emirates." *Asia Pacific Migration Journal* 20.3–4 (2011): 413–30.

"Marshall McLuhan, Man of Faith." Encounter radio program, Australian Broadcast Company. Broadcast May 19, 2012. Accessed August 15, 2013. http://www.abc.net.au/radionational/programs/encounter/marshall-mcluhan-man-of-faith/4005998.

Masuzawa, Tomoko. *The Invention of World Religions: Or, How European Universalism Was Preserved in the Language of Pluralism*. Chicago: University of Chicago Press, 2005.

McClenaghan, William A. *Macgruder's American Government*. New York: Prentice Hall, 2013.

McCutcheon, Russell T. *Critics Not Caretakers: Redescribing the Public Study of Religion*. Albany, NY: State University of New York Press, 2001.

McGowan, Thomas G. "Toward an Assessment-Based Approach to Service-Learning Course Design." In *From Cloister to Commons: Concepts and Models for Service Learning in Religious Studies*, edited by Richard Devine, Joseph A. Favazza, and F. Michael McLain, 83–91. Washington, DC: American Association for Higher Education, 2002.

McIntosh, Peggy. "White Privilege: Unpacking the Invisible Knapsack." *Independent School* 49.2 (Winter 1990): 31–35.

McLaren, Peter. "Critical Pedagogy: A Look at the Major Concepts." In *The Critical Pedagogy Reader*, edited by A. Darder, M. Baltodano, and R. Torres, 69–96. New York: Routledge/Falmer, 2003.

McLuhan, Marshall. *The Gutenberg Galaxy: The Making of Typographic Man*. Toronto: University of Toronto Press, 1962.

McLuhan, Marshall. *Understanding Media: The Extensions of Man*. New York: McGraw-Hill, 1964.

McLuhan, Marshall, Quentin Fiore, and Jerome Agel. *The Medium Is the Massage: With Marshall McLuhan*, 1968, audio recording, Accessed June 15, 2014. http://www.themediumisthemassage.com/the-record/.

Meade, Elizabeth, and Suzanne Weaver, eds. *Toolkit for Teaching in a Democratic Academy*. Allentown, PA: Cedar Crest College, 2004.

Mercadante, Linda A. *Belief without Borders: Inside the Minds of the Spiritual but Not Religious*. New York: Oxford University Press, 2014.

Mezirow, Jack. *Transformative Dimensions of Adult Learning*. San Francisco: Jossey-Bass, 1991.

Mezirow, Jack. "Learning to Think Like an Adult: Core Concepts of Transformation Theory." In *Learning as Transformation: Critical Perspectives on a Theory in Progress*, by Jack Mezirow, 3–34. San Francisco: Jossey-Bass, 2000.

Mezirow, Jack. *Learning as Transformation*. San Francisco: Jossey-Bass, 2000.

Micheletti, Michele. *Political Virtue and Shopping: Individuals, Consumerism, and Collective Action*. New York: Palgrave MacMillan, 2003.

Micheletti, Michele, Andreas Follesdal, and Dietlind Stolle, eds. *Politics, Products, and Markets: Exploring Political Consumerism Past and Present*. New Brunswick, New Jersey: Transaction Publishers, 2004.

Minnich, Elizabeth K. *Transforming Knowledge*. Philadelphia: Temple University Press, 2005.

Moglen, Helene. "Unveiling the Myth of Neutrality: Advocacy in the Feminist Classroom." In *Advocacy in the Classroom: Problems and Possibilities*, edited by Patricia Meyer Spacks, 204–12. New York: St. Martin's Press, 1996.

Morrell, Michael E. *Empathy and Democracy: Feeling, Thinking, and Deliberation*. State College: Pennsylvania State University Press, 2010.

Morrill, Richard L. "Educating for Democratic Values." *Liberal Education* 68.4 (1982): 365–76.

Morton, Keith. "Making Meaning: Reflections on Community, Service, and Learning." In *From Cloister to Commons: Concepts and Models for Service Learning in Religious Studies*, edited by Richard Devine, Joseph A. Favazza, and F. Michael McLain, 41–54. Washington, DC: American Association for Higher Education, 2002.

Moyaert, Marianne. "Biblical, Ethical and Hermeneutical Reflections on Narrative Hospitality." In *Hosting the Stranger*, edited by James Taylor, 95–108. New York: Continuum Publishing Group, 2011.

Mulcahy, Richard. "A Full Circle: Advocacy & Academic Freedom in Crisis." In *Advocacy in the Classroom: Problems and Possibilities*, edited by Patricia Meyer Spacks, 142–60. New York: St. Martin's Press, 1996.

Musil, Caryn McTighe. "Educating Students for Personal and Social Responsibility: The Civic Learning Spiral." In *Civic Engagement in Higher Education: Concepts and Practices*, edited by Barbara Jacoby and Associates, 49–68. San Francisco: Jossey-Bass, 2009.

Newman, Michael. "Reflection Disempowered." In *The Jossey-Bass Reader on Contemporary Issues in Adult Education*, edited by Sharan B. Merriam and André P. Grace, 315–20. San Francisco, CA: Jossey-Bass, 2011.

Nongbri, Brent. *Before Religion: A History of a Modern Concept*. New Haven: Yale University Press, 2013.

Nouwen, Henri J. M., Donald P. McNeill and Douglass A. Morrison. *Compassion: A Reflection on the Christian Life*. New York: Doubleday, 1996.

Nussbaum, Martha. *The Clash Within: Democracy, Religious Violence, and India's Future*. Cambridge, MA: Belknap Press of Harvard University Press, 2007.

Nussbaum, Martha. *Creating Capabilities: The Human Development Approach*. Cambridge, MA: Belknap Press, 2011.

Nussbaum, Martha. *Cultivating Humanity: A Classical Defense of Reform in Liberal Education*. Cambridge, MA: Harvard University Press, 1997.

Nussbaum, Martha. "Cultivating Humanity in Legal Education." *The University of Chicago Law Review* 70.1 (Winter 2003): 265–79.

Nussbaum, Martha. "Development Is More than Growth." *The Hindu Centre for Politics and Public Policy*, May 8, 2014. Accessed July 5, 2014. http://www.thehinducentre.com/verdict/commentary/article5985379.ece.

Nussbaum, Martha. "Education for Citizenship in an Era of Global Connection." *Studies in Philosophy & Education* 21.4/5 (July-September 2002): 289–303.

Nussbaum, Martha. "Liberal Education & Global Community." *Liberal Education* 90.1 (Winter 2004): 42–47.

Nussbaum, Martha. *Not for Profit: Why Democracy Needs the Humanities*. Princeton, NJ: Princeton University Press, 2010.

Office of Service-Learning. "International Service-Learning." University of Georgia. Accessed January 17, 2013. http://servicelearning.uga.edu/international-service-learning/.

Ondaatje, Michael. *In the Skin of a Lion*. Toronto: Knopf Doubleday, 1997.

Orsi, Robert. "Everyday Miracles: The Study of Lived Religion." In *Lived Religion in America: Toward a History of Practice*, edited by David D. Hall, 3–21. Princeton, NJ: Princeton University Press, 1997.

Ortner, Sherry B. "Resistance and the Problem of Ethnographic Refusal." *Comparative Studies in Society and History* 37(1995): 173–93.

Oxtoby, David. "Pomona College Commencement 2010." May 16, 2010. Accessed February 8, 2015. http://www.pomona.edu/events/commencement/files/2010-commencement-oxtoby.pdf.

Paffenroth, Kim. *Gospel of the Living Dead: George Romero's Visions of Hell on Earth*. Waco, TX: Baylor University Press, 2006.

Palmer, Parker. *The Courage to Teach: Exploring the Inner Landscape of a Teacher's Life*. San Francisco: Jossey-Bass, 1998.

Parks Daloz, Laurent A. "Transformative Learning for the Common Good." In *Learning as Transformation*, edited by Jack Mezirow, 103–23. San Francisco: Jossey-Bass, 2000.

Parsi, Trita. *A Single Roll of the Dice*. New Haven, CT: Yale University Press, 2013.

"Participating Institutions in the American Democracy Project for Civic Engagement." *New York Times*. Accessed February 21, 2013. http://www.nytimes.com/ref/college/collegespecial2/coll_aascu_part.html.

Perry, William G., Jr. "Cognitive and Ethical Growth: The Making of Meaning." In *The Modern American College: Responding to the New Realities of Diverse Students and a Changing Society*, by A. W. Chickering et al., 76–116. San Francisco: Jossey-Bass, 1981.

Pew Research Center. "Millennials: Confident. Connected. Open to Change: Executive Summary." Pew Research Center. Last modified February 24, 2010. http://www.pewsocialtrends.org/2010/02/24/millennials-confident-connected-open-to-change/.

Pew Research Center. "'Nones' on the Rise: One-in-Five Adults Have No Religious Affiliation." *The Pew Forum on Religion and Public Life*, October 2012. http://www.pewforum.org/Unaffiliated/nones-on-the-rise.aspx.

Pew Research Center. "U.S. Religious Knowledge Survey." *The Pew Forum on Religion and Public Life*. September 2010. http://www.pewforum.org/U-S-Religious-Knowledge-Survey.aspx. Accessed July 1, 2015.

Poppendieck, Janet. *Sweet Charity? Emergency Food and the End of Entitlement.* New York: Penguin Books, 1999.

"Popular Education for Movement Building." *Project South Institute Volume II* and *The Critical Classroom.* Accessed August 18, 2014. http://www.projectsouth.org/movement-building-projects/trainings-and-tools/toolkits/.

"Promoting Civic Engagement at the University of California; Recommendations from the Strategy Group on Civic and Academic Engagement." *Center for Studies in Higher Education.* Last modified December 2005. Accessed January 17, 2013. http://cshe.berkeley.edu/publications/docs/StrategyReport.2.06.pdf, 6.

Prothero, Stephen. *Religious Literacy: What Every American Needs to Know—And Doesn't.* New York: Harper Collins, 2008.

Putnam, Robert D. "The Civic Enigma." *American Prospect* June 2005: 33.

Putnam, Robert D. "Bowling Alone: America's Declining Social Capital." *Journal of Democracy* 6 (January 1995): 65–78.

Putnam, Robert D. *Bowling Alone: The Collapse and Revival of American Community.* New York: Simon and Schuster, 2000.

Putnam, Robert D., and David E. Campbell, with the assistance of Shaylyn Romney Garrett. *American Grace: How Religion Divides and Unites Us.* New York: Simon & Schuster, 2010.

Quart, Allisa. *Branded: The Buying and Selling of Teenagers.* Cambridge, MA: Perseus Publishing, 2003.

Rana, Junaid. *Terrifying Muslims: Race and Labor in the South Asian Diaspora.* Durham, NC: Duke University Press, 2011.

Reitenauer, Vicki L., Christine M. Cress, and Janet Bennett. "Creating Cultural Connections: Navigating Difference, Investigating Power, Unpacking Privilege." In *Learning through Serving: A Student Guidebook for Service-Learning across the Disciplines*, edited by Christine M. Cress, Peter J. Collier, and Vicki L. Reitenauer, 67–79. Sterling, VA: Stylus, 2005.

"Religious Plurality and Christian Self-Understanding." *World Council of Churches, 2006 Assembly.* February 14, 2006. Accessed March 24, 2015. http://www. oikoumene.org/en/resources/documents/assembly/porto-alegre-2006/3-preparatory-and-background-documents/religious-plurality-and-christian-self-understanding.html.

"Research University Engaged Scholarship Toolkit, Section B: Engaged Scholarship and Review, Promotion and Tenure (RPT)." *Campus Compact.* Accessed January 17, 2013. http://www.compact.org/initiatives/trucen/trucen-toolkit/trucen-section-b/.

Rhodes, Frank H. T. "Universities and the Democratic Spirit." In *Higher Education and Democratic Culture: Citizenship, Human Rights and Civic Responsibility,* edited by Josef Huber and Ira Harkavy, 39–47. Council of Europe Higher Education Series 8. Strasbourg: Council of Europe Publishing, 2007.

"Richard Dawkins—'What If You're Wrong?'" YouTube video, 1 min., 23 secs. Accessed July 23, 2014. https://www.youtube.com/watch?v=6mmskXXetcg.

Richards, Howard, "Letter to Douglass Bennett." Accessed February 21, 2013. http://howardrichards.org/peace/content/view/21/74/.

Roberts, James. *Shiny Objects: Why We Spend Money We Don't Have in Search of Happiness We Can't Buy.* New York: HarperOne, 2011.

Rocheleau, Jordy, and Bruce W. Speck. *Rights and Wrongs in the College Classroom: Ethical Issues in Postsecondary Education.* Bolton, MA: Anker, 2007.

Rosenthal, Raymond, ed. *McLuhan: Pro & Con.* New York: Funk and Wagnalls, 1968.

Rubin, Harriet. "Elaine Scarry: Using Art to Encourage Empathy." *NBCNEWS. com.* Accessed October 29, 2012. http://www.nbcnews.com/id/23397625/ns/us_news-giving/t/elaine-scarry-using-art-encourage-empathy/#. VYHQBa3bLcc.

Russell, Letty M. *Just Hospitality: God's Welcome in a World of Difference.* Louisville, KY: Westminster John Knox, 2009.

Said, Edward. *Reflections on Exile and Other Essays.* Cambridge: Harvard University Press, 2000.

Said, Edward. *Representations of the Intellectual: The 1993 Reith Lectures.* New York: Vintage Books, 1994.

Saltiel, David. "Judgement, Narrative, and Discourse: A Critique of Reflective Practice." In *Beyond Reflective Practice: New Approaches to Professional Lifelong Learning,* edited by Helen Bradbury, Nick Frost, Sue Kilminster, and Miriam Bukas, 130–42. New York and London: Routledge, 2010.

Saltmarsh, John. "The Civic Promise of Service Learning." *Liberal Education* 91.2 (2005): 50–55.

Saltmarsh, John, Matt Hartley, and Patti Clayton. "Democratic Engagement White Paper." *New England Resource Center for Higher Education.* Accessed August 9, 2014. http://futureofengagement.files.wordpress.com/2009/02/democratic-engagement-white-paper-2_13_09.pdf, 2.

Sandel, Michael J. *Public Philosophy: Essays on Morality in Politics*. Cambridge, MA: Harvard University Press, 2006.

Sander, Thomas H., and Robert D. Putnam. "Still Bowling Alone? The Post-9/11 Split." *Journal of Democracy* 21.1 (2010): 9–16.

Scarry, Elaine. "Poetry Changed the World." *Boston Review*. Accessed October 29, 2012. http://www.bostonreview.net/poetry-arts-culture/poetry-changed-world-elaine-scarry.

Schor, Juliet B. *Born to Buy: The Commercialized Child and the New Consumer Culture*. New York: Scribner, 2004.

Shor, Ira. "Educating the Educators: A Freirean Approach to the Crisis in Teacher Education." In *Freire for the Classroom: A Sourcebook for Liberatory Teaching*, edited by Ira Shor, 7–32. Portsmouth, NH: Boynton/Cook Publishers, 1987.

Shor, Ira, and Paulo Freire. *A Pedagogy for Liberation: Dialogues on Transforming Education*. South Hadley, MA: Bergin & Garvey Publishers, 1987.

Shorris, Earl. *The Art of Freedom: Teaching the Humanities to the Poor*. New York: W. W. Norton, 2013.

Shorris, Earl. *Riches for the Poor: The Clemente Course in the Humanities*. New York: W. W. Norton, 2000.

Simpson, Jeffrey, Vladas Griskevicius, and Alexander J. Rothman. "Bringing Relationships into Consumer Decision-Making." *Journal of Consumer Psychology* 22(2012): 329–31.

Skubikowski, Kathleen, Catherine Wright, and Roman Graf, eds. *Social Justice Education: Inviting Faculty to Transform Their Institutions*. Sterling, VA: Stylus, 2009.

Smart, Ninian. *Worldviews: Cross-Cultural Explorations of Human Beliefs*. New York: Pearson, 1999.

Smith, Christian, with Kari Christoffersen, Hilary Davidson, and Patricia Snell Herzog. *Lost in Transition: The Dark Side of Emerging Adulthood*. Oxford: Oxford University Press, 2011.

Smith, Jonathan Z. *Imagining Religion: From Babylon to Jonestown*. Chicago: University of Chicago Press, 1992.

Smith, Jonathan Z. "The Necessary Lie: Duplicity in the Disciplines." In *Studying Religion: An Introduction*, edited by Russell T. McCutcheon, 74–80. London: Equinox, 2007.

Smith, Jonathan Z. *On Teaching Religion: Essays by Jonathan Z. Smith*. Edited by Christopher I. Lehrich. New York: Oxford University Press, 2012.

"Social Media in the 16th Century: How Luther Went Viral." *The Economist*, December 17, 2011. Accessed June 15, 2014. http://www.economist.com/node/21541719.

Spiezo, K. Edward. "Pedagogy and Political (Dis)Engagement." *Liberal Education* 88.4 (Fall 2002): 14–19.

Spikard, James V., J. Shawn Landres, and Meredith B. McGuire, eds. *Personal Knowledge and Beyond: Reshaping the Ethnography of Religion*. New York: New York University Press, 2002.

"Spirituality in Higher Education." *Higher Education Research Institute of the University of California*, Los Angeles. Accessed February 1, 2015. http://spirituality.ucla.edu/.

Stearn, Gerald, ed. *McLuhan: Hot & Cool: A Primer for the Understanding of & A Critical Symposium with a Rebuttal by McLuhan*. New York: Dial Press, 1967.

Steinberg, Kathryn S., Julie Hatcher, and Robert G. Bringle. "Civic-Minded Graduate: A North Star." *Michigan Journal of Service-Learning* 18.1 (Fall 2011): 19–33.

Stelljes, Drew. "US Colleges and Universities Earn a Poor Grade for Civic Engagement." *Huffington Post Education*. November 10, 2014. Accessed December 5, 2014. http://www.huffingtonpost.com/drew-stelljes/us-civic-engagement_b_6127608.html.

Steves, Rick. *Travel as a Political Act*. New York: Nation Books, 2009.

Stokes, Geoffrey. "Global Citizenship." *Ethos* 12.1 (March 2004): 19–23.

"Storytelling and Social Change by Eboo Patel," *Sojourners Magazine*, February 2013, posted by the Leading Change Network at http://leadingchangenetwork.com/2013/01/31/storytelling-and-social-change-by-eboo-patel/ (accessed September 10, 2013).

Strain, Charles R. Creating the Engaged University: Service-Learning, Religious Studies, and Institutional Mission." In *From Cloister to Commons: Concepts and Models for Service Learning in Religious Studies*, edited by Richard Devine, Joseph A. Favazza, and F. Michael McLain, 25–39. Washington, DC: American Association for Higher Education, 2002.

Sutton, Richard C., and Donald L. Rubin. "The GLOSSARI Project: Initial Findings from a System-Wide Research Initiative on Study Abroad Learning Outcomes." *Frontiers* 10 (Fall 2004): 65–82.

Tarpley, Todd. "Children, the Internet, and Other New Technologies." In *Handbook of Children and Media*, edited by Dorothy Singer and Jerome Singer, 547–56. London: SAGE Publications, 2001.

Tatum, Beverly Daniel. "Talking about Race, Learning about Racism: The Application of Racial Identity Development Theory in the Classroom." *Harvard Educational Review* 62.1 (Spring 1992): 1–24.

Taylor, Paul, and Scott Keeter, eds. *Millennials: A Portrait of Generation Next, Confident. Connected. Open to Change*. Pew Research Center, 2010. http://www.pewsocialtrends.org/files/2010/10/millennials-confident-connected-open-to-change.pdf.

Thomas, Douglas, and John Seely Brown. *The New Culture of Learning: Cultivating the Imagination for a World of Constant Change*. Lexington, KY: Thomas and Brown, 2011.

Thompson, Gabriel. *Working in the Shadows: A Year of Doing the Jobs (Most) Americans Won't Do*. New York: Nation Books, 2010.

Toton, Suzanne C. *Justice Education: From Service to Solidarity*. Milwaukee, WI: Marquette University Press, 2006.

Turner, Victor. *The Ritual Process: Structure and Anti-Structure*. Ithaca, NY: Cornell University Press, 1977.

Turpin, Katherine. *Branded: Adolescents Converting from Consumer Faith*. Cleveland, OH: Pilgrim Press, 2006.

Turpin, Katherine. "Disrupting the Luxury of Despair: Justice and Peace Education in Contexts of Relative Privilege." *Teaching Theology and Religion* 11(2008): 141–52.

Ullekh, N.P. "Narendra Modi's campaigns play on fears of the Muslim minority: Martha Nussbaum." *The Economic Times*, December 15, 2013. Accessed July 5, 2014. http://articles.economictimes.indiatimes.com/2013–12-15/news/45191832_1_tagore-national-role-martha-c-nussbaum.

United States Census Bureau. "Computer and Internet Trends in America." *Measuring America*. Accessed January 7, 2014. https://www.census.gov/hhes/computer/files/2012/Computer_Use_Infographic_FINAL.pdf.

University of Alabama. "What Is the Academic Study of Religion?" Accessed May 19, 2014. rel.as.ua.edu/pdf/rel100introhandout.pdf.

Uslaner, Eric M., and Mitchell Brown. "Inequality, Trust, and Civic Engagement." *American Politics Research* 33 (November 2005): 868–94.

Van Biema, David. "God vs. Science." *TIME*, November 5, 2006. Accessed July 23, 2014. http://content.time.com/time/magazine/article/0,9171,1555132,00.html.

Venkateson, M. "Experimental Study of Consumer Behavior Conformity and Independence." *Journal of Marketing Research* 3(1966): 384–87.

Von Drehle, David. "Obama's Youth Vote Triumph," *Time*. Last modified January 4, 2008. Accessed February 21, 2013. http://www.time.com/time/politics/article/0,8599,1700525,00.html.

"Voting Age Population and Voter Participation." Accessed January 17, 2013. http://www.census.gov/compendia/statab/cats/elections/voting-age_population_and_voter_participation.html.

Walker, Rob. "Magruder's American Government," *Slate Magazine* no. 1 (2002). Last modified September 9, 2002. Accessed September 20, 2012. http://www.slate.com/articles/arts/number_1/2002/09/magruders_american_government.html.

Walvoord, Barbara E. *Teaching and Learning in College Introductory Religion Courses*. Malden, MA: Blackwell Publishing, 2008.

Walvoord, Barbara E., and Virginia Johnson Anderson. *Effective Grading: A Tool for Learning and Assessment in College*, 2nd ed. San Francisco: Jossey-Bass, 2010.

Walzer, Michael. *Politics and Passion: Toward a More Egalitarian Liberalism*. New Haven, CT: Yale University Press, 2006.

Weimer, Maryellen. *Learner-Centered Teaching: Five Key Changes to Practice*. San Francisco: Jossey-Bass, 2002.

Welch, Marshall. "Moving from Service-Learning to Civic Engagement." In *Civic Engagement in Higher Education: Concepts and Practices*, edited by Barbara Jacoby and Associates, 174–95. San Francisco: Jossey-Bass, 2009.

Welch, Marshall. "O.P.E.R.A.: A First Letter Mnemonic and Rubric for Conceptualizing and Implementing Service Learning." *Issues in Educational Research* 20 (2010): 76–82.

Welch, Marshall, and Regenia C. James. "An Investigation on the Impact of a Guided Reflection Technique in Service-Learning Courses to Prepare Special Educators." *Teacher Education and Special Education* 30 (2007): 276–85.

Westheimer, Joel, and Joseph Kahne. "What Kind of Citizen? The Politics of Educating for Democracy." *American Educational Research Journal* 41 (2004): 237–69.

Westmoreland, M. W. "Interruptions: Derrida and Hospitality." *Kritike* 2 (2008): 1–10.

"Wikipedia: SOPA Initiative." *Wikipedia*. Accessed June 15, 2014. http://en.wikipedia.org/wiki/Wikipedia:SOPA_initiative.

Wisler, Andria K. "'Of, By, and For Are Not Merely Prepositions': Teaching and Learning Conflict Resolution for a Democratic, Global Citizenry." *Intercultural Education* 20.2 (April 2009): 127–33.

White, David. *Practicing Discernment with Youth: A Transformative Youth Ministry Approach.* Cleveland, OH: Pilgrim Press, 2005.

Wiggins, Grant, and Jay McTighe. *Understanding by Design, Expanded Second Edition.* Alexandria, VA: Association for Supervision and Curriculum Development, 2005.

Wood, Wendy, and Timothy Hayes. "Social Influence on Consumer Decisions: Motives, Modes and Consequences." *Journal of Consumer Psychology* 22 (2012): 324–28.

Yearley, Lee. "New Religious Virtues and the Study of Religion." Fifteenth annual University Lecture in Religion, Arizona State University, Tempe, AZ, February 10, 1994.

Zemach-Bersin, Talya. "American Students Abroad Can't Be 'Global Citizens.'" Accessed February 8, 2015. http://www.yale.edu/yalecol/international/predeparture/pdf/GlobalCitizens.pdf.

Zemach-Bersin, Talya. "American Students Abroad Can't Be 'Global Citizens.'" *The Chronicle of Higher Education*, 54.26 (March 7, 2008): A34.

Zinn, Howard. "The Optimism of Uncertainty." In *The Impossible Will Take a Little While: A Citizen's Guide to Hope in a Time of Fear*, edited by Paul Rogat Loeb, 63–72. New York: Basic Books, 2004.

Zlotkowski, Edward, and Dilafruz Williams. "The Faculty Role in Civic Engagement." *Peer Review* 5 (2003): 9–11.

Index

AAC&U. *See* Association of American
Colleges and Universities
accountability, empathetic. *See*
empathetic accountability
action
motivated. *See* motivated action
provocative nature of, 240–41
related to civic and political
engagement, 34
active citizen, 14
activism, 259–60. *See also* motivated
action
advocacy, legitimate forms of, 211
*Advocacy in the Classroom: Problems and
Possibilities* (ed. Spacks), 209, 211
advocacy of process, xx–xxi, 206
advocacy projects, 36
affective empathy, 30
affective theory, civic engagement and,
175
Allison, Graham, 217
altruism, strategic, 172
American Council on Education, 30
American Democracy Project, 34, 169
American Grace (Putnam and
Campbell), xiv
Americorps VISTA program, 252
Analects (Confucius), 50, 234
Ancient and Modern Religion and

Politics (LeBlanc and Medine), 176
Anderson, Joni, 186
anti-environment. *See*
counterenvironment
Appadurai, Arjun, xix, 167–69, 170,
173, 177
Apple, Michael, 254
arts
civic engagement and, 250–51
providing counterenvironments, 90
Ascetic Withdrawal Project, xix, 144,
148–57, 227–28
assessment, xvi–xvii, 17, 218–21. *See
also* self-assessment
and agreement with professor's
position, 232–33
civic engagement and, 83
empathetic accountability and, 37–38
intellectual complexity and, 38, 39
motivated action and, 37–38
reflective writings and, 52–53
Association of American Colleges and
Universities, xiv, 14, 171
Association of Theological Schools, 32
Astin, Alexander, 112
AWP. *See* Ascetic Withdrawal Project

backward design, 159n15
banking model, 11, 121

CPSIA information can be obtained
at www.ICGtesting.com
Printed in the USA
BVHW03s2258131018
530080BV00002B/31/P

9 780190 692995